RESEARCH, POLICY AND PRACTICE

WORLD YEARBOOK OF EDUCATION 1985

RESEARCH, POLICY AND PRACTICE

Edited by

JOHN NISBET, JACQUETTA MEGARRY
and STANLEY NISBET

Routledge
Taylor & Francis Group

LONDON AND NEW YORK

First published in 1985 by Kogan Page

2 Park Square, Milton Park, Abingdon, Oxfordshire OX14 4RN

711 Third Avenue, New York, NY 10017

Routledge is an imprint of the Taylor & Francis Group, an informa business

First issued in paperback 2012

British Library Cataloguing in Publication Data
A CIP catalogue record for this book
is available from the British Library

Research, Policy and Practice
ISBN13: 978-0-415-39300-3 (hbk)
ISBN13: 978-0-415-50179-8 (pbk)

World Yearbook of Education

World Yearbook of Education 1985 Research, Policy and Practice

Edited by **John Nisbet** *(Guest Editor),*
Jacquetta Megarry *(Series Editor)*
and **Stanley Nisbet** *(Associate Editor)*

Kogan Page, London/Nichols Publishing
Company, New York

Previous titles in this series:

World Yearbook of Education 1980
Professional Development of Teachers
Edited by Eric Hoyle and Jacquetta Megarry
US Consultant Editor: Myron Atkin

World Yearbook of Education 1981
Education of Minorities
Edited by Jacquetta Megarry, Stanley Nisbet
and Eric Hoyle
Subject Adviser: Ken Eltis

World Yearbook of Education 1982/83
Computers and Education
Edited by Jacquetta Megarry, David R F Walker,
Stanley Nisbet and Eric Hoyle

World Yearbook of Education 1984
Women and Education
Edited by Sandra Acker, Jacquetta Megarry,
Stanley Nisbet and Eric Hoyle

First published in Great Britain in 1985 by Kogan Page Limited
120 Pentonville Road, London N1 9JN

Copyright © 1985 Kogan Page Limited and contributors
All rights reserved

British Library Cataloguing in Publication Data

World yearbook of education – 1985
   1. Education – Periodicals
   370'.5   L16

   ISBN 0-85038-907-0
   ISSN 0084-2508

First published in the USA 1985
by Nichols Publishing Company
PO Box 96, New York, NY 10024

   ISBN 0-89397-204-5

Printed in Great Britain by
The Anchor Press Ltd and bound by
William Brendon & Sons Ltd,
both of Tiptree, Essex

Contents

Part 3: Bibliography and biographical notes

List of contributors

1. Introduction

John Nisbet

Summary: The relation of research, policy and practice in education is one of interdependence and interaction. There are many ways in which research can make its contribution, and consequently the research organizations which have been established in different countries vary widely. For Part 1 of this volume contributors were asked to describe the provision for educational research and development in their countries and to identify trends. Three themes which appear across many of the reports are the recent growth in educational research, increasing central control, and new paradigms for research. The third of these is developed in Part 2, which leads us to consider the underlying question: what is the function of research in education?

How can research best contribute to policy and practice in education? The chapters which follow give a wide range of answers, and describe varying structures for funding and organizing educational research and development. There are different functions which research can perform, and different provision is needed to perform these functions. People have different expectations of research, and these are often unrealistic. Policy makers and teachers tend to look to research to provide answers to their problems; but research can perform this function only where there is consensus on values, within the framework of accepted policy, or in the context of established practice. Working out the implications of a policy, and evaluating what has been done, are examples of contributions of this kind (though neither of these is unproblematic). Researchers are more likely to see the role of research as identifying new problems, or new perspectives on problems — problem-setting rather than problem-solving (Schon, 1977) — and this is not always a welcome contribution. Researchers are reluctant to accept the limitations of conventional values, accepted policy or established practice; yet they expect their findings to be taken up by others. But implementation will happen only when the findings are seen as relevant to the issues which concern those with the responsibility of action. If it is not to be just an esoteric activity, research in education must have a context. But whose context is it to be?

If research is undertaken in the context of those who are expected to make use of the findings, the likelihood of implementation is greater. The Australian Karmel Report (1973) summarized the requirements for impact:

'The effectiveness of innovation, no matter at what level it is initiated in a school organization, is dependent on the extent to which the people concerned perceive a problem and hence realize the existence of a need, are knowledgeable about a range of alternative solutions, and feel themselves to be in a congenial climate.'

How people perceive a problem is itself influenced by research publications. Thus research shapes people's perceptions, and provides them with concepts to use in thinking about the work they do. In this way, research creates an agenda of concern:

Thus the most important influence of research is indirect, and long-term. Weiss (1977), for example, described the process as

'a gradual accumulation of research results which can lead to serious and far-reaching changes in the way people and governments address their problems.'

Taylor (1973) suggested a similar function for research:

'For the most part, the influence of research has been to *sensitize*. It has indicated the importance of certain problems and the danger of the unselfconscious use of certain procedures, without necessarily providing clear-cut calculations of advantage or a firm foundation for decision.'

Uncertainty, however, is difficult to reconcile with action and decision, and consequently policy makers and practitioners tend to impose constraints on research:

'Can national authorities sponsor the generation of uncertainty? ... Policy-makers foreclose on issues ... Social science can keep open the space.' (Husen and Kogan, 1984)

The relation of research, policy and practice is therefore one of inter-dependence and interaction. There is a range of situations in which the relations of research, policy and practice may vary widely. There is a place for policy-directed research; but there is also a place for critiques and for an ordering of concepts which may appear to be academic scholarship but are essential for the analysis of policy or practice. While researchers have agonized over the influence of research on policy and practice, there has been less concern over the growing influence of policy and practice on research. It is perhaps evidence of the impact of research — or perhaps merely the consequence of increased public funding — that the management of research is now considered to be too important to be left to the researchers. The claim of the policy makers to take control of research, allowing policy priorities to determine the choice, design, methodology and reporting, is difficult to refute when they also control funding. In its crudest form, the Rothschild (Rothschild Report, 1971) formula for publicly-supported research expressed the principle:

'The customer says what he wants; the contractor (the researcher) does it, if he can; and the customer pays.'

The consequence when politicians decide research priorities is vividly illustrated by Taylor in Chapter 3: in England and Wales currently, 52 per cent of government funding for educational research is spent on testing and examinations. Policy-directed research incurs several dangers. It may reduce the research agenda to a series of simplistic problems, dealing with short-term issues, neglecting what Bondi (1983) termed 'strategic research':

> 'that grey zone of researches that ... are not immediately of use to the customer, but lay the foundations for being able to answer questions that may be put in the future.'

Policy-directed research tends to be restricted to what is compatible with existing practice, is liable to be slow and cumbersome and too late with its results, dealing with yesterday's problems and often wrong in its anticipated priorities. Relegating the researchers to a captive or subservient role — 'all the strings are in the hands of the decision-maker' (Cronbach *et al*, 1980) — it overrides their insights and discourages initiative. But researchers must not claim a privileged part in policy decisions: their influence must be through informing and persuading those with responsibility for action. Coleman observed that 'social policy research is most often used by those without direct control over policy, who challenge the policies of those in positions of authority' (Husen and Kogan, 1984); and this is perhaps one reason for hostility to research.

Teachers and others involved in the practice of education also influence what research is done or not done. They can restrict researchers from gaining access to an adequate sample, or require that data-gathering techniques be submitted for approval in advance. Teachers often have misgivings about the contribution of research. The researcher is seen as an interloper, seeking influence without accountability, operating a 'smash and grab' procedure, out of touch with what are deemed 'relevant' issues. The dispute over who should define relevance dates back to Rousseau, who wrote in 1762:

> 'People are always telling me to make practical suggestions. You might as well tell me to suggest improvements which can be incorporated with the wrong methods at present in use.'

Pressures on researchers to take account of what is going on in their country's educational system should not be regarded as a threat to academic freedom, though they do impinge on professional standards and may require a shift of attitude. It is sound advice to keep your research perspective but also to remember the genuine concerns of others if you want to make an impact and to receive continuing support and resources. What has happened in recent years is that public funding for research is increasingly directed to applied or policy-oriented research and not to pure, conclusion-oriented research; and in the long term the effect may be to slow the pace of reform. (To be fair, it should be mentioned that the UK Rothschild report referred to above suggested that 10 per cent of public research funds should be set aside for work of the researcher's own choosing, a recommendation which has been forgotten.)

The position adopted in this chapter is a pluralist approach. To regard policy-oriented and conclusion-oriented research as in opposition to each other will only aggravate the problem. The solution does not lie in drawing up a national list of research priorities or in challenging the right of those who are not researchers to say what these priorities should be. Instead, the aim should be to bring all the partners in the research enterprise — research, policy, practice — into closer relationship, so that each may be more responsive to the requirements and perspectives of the others. As educational provision becomes more extensive, more complex and more expensive, there is an urgent need for structures to bring the partners into more effective interaction. We need research institutions which are free and strong and yet responsive. The organizations for educational research and development which have been set up in many countries in recent years differ widely in the way they have attempted to create the necessary interaction. In the belief that a comparative perspective can lead to insights beyond what is possible within a single educational system, contributors to this volume were asked to give a descriptive account of the organizations responsible for research and development, how and why they were established, why they have flourished or declined, and how their work is funded and priorities decided.

Contributors were also invited to identify issues of concern, looking ahead to future prospects and analysing the current assumptions about the nature and function of research in education. Among the themes which emerge in many of the chapters are:

1. the remarkable growth in educational research and development in the past 25 years;
2. increasing centralization and control of research; and
3. new paradigms for research, reflecting changing views on the nature of research and its contribution to policy and practice in education.

1. It is only within the past 25 years that research in education has received public funding on any substantial scale. Prior to 1960, research was mainly a spare-time amateur affair, unorganized and often ignored until its findings had percolated through into generally accepted values — an uncontrolled, slow, inefficient and (to administrators) sometimes inconvenient process. There was growing interest in exploiting the contribution of the social sciences in guiding policy, administration and practice, and in the years 1965-70 public funding of educational research and development expanded at an unprecedented rate. In Britain public expenditure on research in education multiplied ten-fold between 1964 and 1969, while in the USA expenditure doubled each year from 1964 through 1967. Never again can we expect to see such rapid growth. As Coleman points out in a paper on 'The Institutionalization of Social Policy' (Husen and Kogan, 1984):

'Social policy research is a relatively new activity in society, expanding enormously in the 1960s and 1970s from a very small base before that time. As with newly emergent phenomena generally, there has not immediately developed an institutional and normative framework within which it is carried out and used.'

The influence of policy studies on the developing pattern of educational research organizations in the USA is traced by Mitchell in Chapter 2. There is awareness of the need for analysis and evidence in policy and planning, at national and local level. In Sweden (Chapter 15), national commissions precede major legislation; in the UK, reports such as Robbins, Plowden and Warnock are accompanied by extensive national surveys; evaluation is a mandatory element in US federal funding; and local administrators everywhere arm themselves with evidence (usually selected by themselves) to meet the challenge of opposition and pressure groups. Prior to 1960, most researchers in education acted as independent agents; there then followed the establishment (or augmentation) of central agencies for research and development; and now research is an integral part of the regular administrative system in the developed countries. The role of the professional researcher in this is still uncertain. Until the 1960s, there was little money; now, it appears, there is little scope for independence.

2. The trend towards centralization and control of research in education is the second of the themes in many of the chapters. This is a natural consequence of increased central funding of research (as the title of Chapter 14 implies). The question at issue is how to secure an appropriate balance between interests, in both senses of that word: the interests of the researchers and the interests of those who commission research. 'Commission' is a relatively neutral word, but it is a commercial term, suggesting a customer-contractor relationship. An alternative term, 'negotiated research', implies a more positive role for the researchers, granting them the right to participate in decision-making and perhaps also in defining the research topic. Kogan (in Husen and Kogan, 1984) summarizes the matter by contrasting the technocratic model with a pluralistic solution:

'Those responsible for promoting policy and practice — the systems managers, the politicians, the heads of professional groups — must take decisions and elaborate policies. So at one level we might have a linear, managerial, cybernetic or technocratic model at work. But increasingly policy-makers might recognize that the research enterprise works best when it works interactively rather than in a linear fashion. In so doing, they might work best in the managerial interest when, as has become the case in government sponsored R & D for Swedish education (quoting Bjorklund) "it is the interaction between researchers and practitioners that is seen as the means whereby new studies are initiated".'

The concept of 'co-operative research' extends the consultative process more widely. The publicly-funded Scottish Education Data Archive (McPherson, 1977) which embodies this concept, seeks to open up research data to any participant who is willing to spend a few hours mastering the computerized retrieval program. But even here, the information available within the data-bank has necessarily been decided in advance. The 'action research' movement (Elliott, Chapter 18) goes beyond this, seeking to build a research attitude into the practical work of teachers by creating the necessary supportive frameworks, and recruiting teachers as researchers.

Discussion in these idealistic terms may seem unrealistic in the context of the closure of autonomous R & D institutions in England (Chapter 3) and Australia (Chapter 4) and the political and administrative pressures on research in France (Chapter 6), Latin America (Chapter 9) and the Netherlands (Chapter 10). Expectations of research often derive from a positivist belief that there are correct answers to problems, that there is a best method or a right policy which may be discovered, given adequate time and resources. The relativist prefers to look for consistency within a declared framework of assumptions; but policy makers assume that it is their prerogative to define the framework. Decisions on values are political decisions, on this view: the task of research is to deal with implementation, or perhaps to clarify the implications when values have been declared. Researchers may reject this as a limited or naive view, but it is a widely held assumption. In a recent address (Bancroft, 1984) to the Royal Society of Arts in London, the former Head of the Home Civil Service caricatured this approach by reporting a spoof notice which had once been circulated among his colleagues. (He commented: 'The intervening years have shown that it wasn't such a spoof after all.')

'The general principle approved by management is that thinking is acceptable if it is secondary to, and takes place at the same time as, some activity directly approved in the course of the planning priorities exercise. But in other circumstances it is hoped that any thinking that is found necessary will be done in staff's spare time or at weekends.

For a trial period monthly returns should be made of any inadvertent thinking that takes place during working hours, showing the approximate duration and depth. These should be submitted along with the returns of sick leave and security breaches for the period.

... In the face of more demanding programmes than ever the Department's priorities clearly require more emphasis on outputs and less on inputs: in other words more action and less reflection. Since staff resources do not permit of both it follows that the latter must be sacrificed.'

3. The third of our themes, new paradigms for research, is the most uncertain but possibly the most important. We invited a number of scholars to reappraise recent developments and to write about new developments with which their names are internationally associated; and these are presented in Part 2 of this volume. Each of these paradigms has implications for the function of research. In the end, this is what the volume is about: what is the function of research in education, how can it best contribute? It is easy to avoid the issue with a pluralist answer, that there are many

different functions. But it is important that these different functions are clearly understood. Differing perceptions of what research is and differing expectations of what it can and should do, result in frustration and disenchantment; and in the end it is research which suffers, from reduced funding and increasing central direction. A recent review from the International Development Research Centre in Ottawa (Shaeffer and Nkinyangi, 1983) argues that the contribution which research makes depends on the context within which it is done, and 'the environments for research are everywhere different'. But in a foreword to the report, Mowat observes:

> 'There is agreement that the fostering of a tradition of research — that is, of rational inquiry into social issues — should be a goal of researchers everywhere; further, that it falls to the researchers themselves to ensure that their work increasingly is perceived as a normal and useful undertaking.'

In an earlier review of this topic (Nisbet and Broadfoot, 1980), we wrote:

> 'Value issues cannot be resolved by scientific inquiry, though they may be illuminated by it ... If research is to have impact, it must become participatory, involving stakeholders in the research process. When clients or practitioners have different values from researchers, these values will operate consciously or subconsciously to deter them from commitment, and thus limit or prevent impact. Research — in education, at least — may have relied too much on the force of rationality, neglecting the pervasive influence of values. "There has been a rape of reason by rationality: we need to build an approach to science which reunites intellect and values, to restore affect to the process of inquiry. For reason is not just rational: in the way we use the word, it implies also an affective element, a judgment of value" (quoting Gideonse).'

There are different kinds of knowledge, scientific and non-scientific (see, for example, Bergendal, 1983). Perhaps the heart of the matter with which this volume is concerned is that research is conventionally limited to only one of these kinds of knowledge, and has yet to come to terms with the other.

References

Bancroft, Lord (1984) Whitehall and management: a retrospect. *Journal of the Royal Society of Arts* 132 5334: 371

Bergendal, G ed (1983) Knowledge and higher education: report from a series of colloquia held in 1981-82. Stockholm: National Board of Universities and Colleges, Almqvist and Wiksell

Bondi, H (1983) Quoted in: Research funding scrutinized. *Times Educational Supplement* 19 August 1983

Cronbach, L J et al (1980) *Toward Reform of Program Evaluation* Jossey-Bass: San Francisco

Husen, T and Kogan, M eds (1984) *Educational Research and Policy: How Do They Relate?* Pergamon Press: Oxford

Karmel Report (1973) *Schools in Australia* Australian Schools Commission. Australian Government Printing Service: Canberra

McPherson, A (1977) What is collaborative research? *Collaborative Research Newsletter* 1 1 Centre for Educational Sociology: Edinburgh University

Nisbet, J and Broadfoot, P (1980) *The Impact of Research on Policy and Practice in Education* Aberdeen University Press: Aberdeen

Rothschild Report (1971) *A Framework for Government Research and Development* HMSO: London

Schon, D (1977) In Weiss (1977)

Shaeffer, S and Nkinyangi, J A (1983) *Educational Research Environments in the Developing World* International Development Research Centre: Ottawa

Taylor, W ed (1973) *Research Perspectives in Education* Routledge and Kegan Paul: London

Weiss, C ed (1977) *Using Social Research in Public Policy Making* Heath, Lexington Books: Lexington

Part 1: Perspectives from different countries

2. Research impact on educational policy and practice in the USA

Douglas E. Mitchell

Summary: Four dimensions of the influence of educational research and evaluation over school policy and practice are reviewed in this chapter. First, the size and historical development of the research and evaluation industry in the USA are reviewed. Second, a brief survey of policy-relevant education research topics is undertaken. Third, with this background in mind, questions of research and evaluation impact on school policy and operations are examined directly. Finally, several problems related to research methodology and design that affect its impact on policy and practice are discussed.

Introduction

Over the last three decades education research and evaluation has become a major industry in the United States. It is surprisingly difficult, however, to estimate just how large the industry is. Financial support is provided by a broad spectrum of both public and private agencies. The US Department of Education (USDE), the single largest sponsor of educational research, reported expenditures of $106 million for direct support of research and development in the fiscal year 1982 (OMB, 1982). Additional millions in indirect support for research, development and evaluation are provided through USDE grants to school districts, state education agencies and universities. Substantial research funds are also provided by other federal agencies ranging from the National Science Foundation and the National Institute for Child Health and Development to the Departments of Labor and Defense. Private sources include major philanthropic foundations as well as several profit-orientated corporations. Havighurst (1982) estimates that various federal agencies supply about 70 per cent of all educational research support, with private philanthropic foundations providing another 20 per cent and the remaining 10 per cent coming from miscellaneous other sources. The latest entries into research sponsorship have included computer manufacturers who have begun to make major investments in research and development aimed at supporting the introduction of this new technology into the schools.

Research and development budgets are not only hard to locate in the highly decentralized context of US education, it is also very difficult to determine exactly what expenditures to count as support for educational R & D. Drezek *et al* (1982), for example, estimate that 0.33 per cent of all local school district budgets (roughly $425 million) goes to support programme evaluation activities. Analysis of these evaluations suggests, however, that much of this money is spent on generating political support for existing programmes rather than serious evaluation of their operations or effects (House, 1980; McLaughlin, 1975). If evaluation research is over estimated, the research work of nearly 8,000 doctoral degree candidates in education at various US colleges and universities is generally unrecognized (NCES, 1982). They undertake a substantial body of very low cost educational research each year. Except for those supported by research assistantships or training grants, their research does not show up in any research support budgets; nor does the unsponsored research work undertaken by many of their university professors.

In non-fiscal terms, the size of the educational research and evaluation industry is reflected by the fact that the federally sponsored Educational Research Information Center (ERIC) currently catalogues about 30,000 new reports and journal articles each year. This vast body of work does not include book length research reports, doctoral dissertations, or any research and development activities that are circulated privately as reports or monographs. The size of the prestigious American Educational Research Association (AERA) might also be viewed as a rough measure of the overall educational R & D effort. AERA currently claims more than 25,000 members whose occupations are closely related to either the generation or the utilization of research products. Salary and institutional support for these professionals probably exceeds $2 billion annually.

Whatever its actual size, the educational research, development and evaluation industry has come under intense scrutiny by both public policy makers and social scientists in recent years. Both enthusiastic support and deep scepticism have been widely expressed regarding the quality of recent educational research activity and its utility in the development of educational policy and practice. Economic austerity and ideological conservatism — dominant themes of US politics in the early 1980s — have encouraged a searching look at the ways in which educational research, development and evaluation activities are organized, controlled and supported. Serious questions are being asked about whether research is (or can be) properly utilized to shape educational policy and practice.

This chapter examines these issues from four perspectives. First, a brief look at the historical relationship between science and public policy formation identifies the intellectual and professional practice dimensions of the problem. Second, a review of the major topics covered in recent educational research suggests the sorts of policy and practice impact to expect. Third, questions of research impact on educational policy and practice are reviewed directly. Finally, key theoretical and methodological issues related to the problem of research utilization in education are briefly explored.

Research utilization in historical perspective

In education, as in other public policy areas, research and analysis have only recently become *formally* associated with the formulation, implementation, and evaluation of policy and practice. In the USA a major shift in the relationship between social science and public policy occurred during the 1960s. Mitchell (1981b), following Lambright (1976), relates this change to the 1968 congressional reauthorization of the National Science Foundation (NSF). That reauthorization required NSF to develop a programme of 'Research Addressed to National Needs' (RANN), shifting the criteria for governmental funding away from the pursuit of scientific knowledge for its own sake and toward research aimed at the solution of identified public problems. Ukeles (1977) identifies a similar change in the broader domain of public administration. Between 1967 and 1974, he argues, formal policy analysis moved from 'propositions to reality, from "fringe" idea to a central place in official public administration thinking'.

Fixing the exact date of this change is not too important (and depends on what one takes to be decisive in a broad reorientation that took at least a decade to complete). The important point is that the recent interest in the impact of research on policy and practice is part of a very broad reorganization of fundamental beliefs about science and about the nature and value of scientific knowledge. This reorientation toward science has both empirical and theoretical roots. The empirical roots involve changes in the *professional practice* of research and evaluation — the development of new organizations and activities aimed at bringing knowledge to bear on educational policy and practice. The theoretical roots are primarily *intellectual* and involve the development of new ideas about the relationship between science and policy.

Research and evaluation as professional practice

As a matter of professional practice the relationship between social science and public policy has a long and fascinating history. In the USA it began with an 1832 grant to the Franklin Institute to study the causes of explosions in steamboat boilers (Schilling, 1964). In addition to a report on the causes of these explosions, the researchers involved in that study produced draft legislation aimed at regulating boiler construction.

It took nearly a century, however, for the relationship between researchers and governmental policy makers to become more than a series of haphazard, tentative, and largely isolated activities. The earliest developments took place in the field of agriculture. The Morrill Act of 1862, for example, provided a major resource base for agricultural research. That resource base gradually produced a strong relationship between research and public policy in this area. The first agricultural experiment station began in 1875, a major federal aid programme was enacted in 1887 and the massive Cooperative Agricultural Extension Act was passed in 1914. Study of the difficulties encountered by Agricultural Extension agents in their efforts to get farmers to adopt new techniques (like crop rotation, hybrid seeds and mechanized cultivation) provided the basis for a theory of technological innovation that dominated early thinking about improvement of the public schools. This theory focused on social forces which foster resistance to change, but made the assumption that technical innovations will generally produce high benefits once they are adopted.

In 1929 — nearly a century after the Franklin Institute study — President Hoover established the current pattern of formal involvement by social scientists in federal policy. (See Carey, 1975, however, for a discussion of changes that took place during the later part of the 19th century.) When Hoover commissioned the Social Science Research Council to undertake a systematic study of 'Recent Social Trends', he laid the foundations for using scientific data in the analysis of public issues. This landmark study was not matched in education, however, until 1966 when James Coleman and his colleagues produced their watershed study of *Equality of Educational Opportunity* in American schools (Coleman *et al*, 1966).

The election of Franklin Roosevelt in 1932 gave a further boost to the legitimacy of scientific policy research. His widely respected 'brain trust' gave scientific policy study a really good name for the first time. Under Roosevelt, Charles E. Merriam's leadership permanently altered the role of social research in the executive branch of government. As architect of the 1939 executive reorganization plan, he stimulated the development of a social research staff in nearly every important executive office (Carey, 1975).

The current period of formalized and highly visible research utilization was stimulated by three major changes in the operation of the federal government: (1) rapid expansion in the federal courts' reliance on social science evidence in dealing with such highly controversial issues as racial bias, intelligence testing, and special education; (2) adoption of highly publicized rational planning techniques, notably the Planning Programming Budgeting System (PPBS) introduced into the Pentagon under Robert McNamara and attempted in many educational agencies in the mid-1960s; and (3) widespread use of scientific programme evaluation techniques — especially in response to federal initiatives in education and health care.

Judicial influence. In a review of social science influence on court decisions, Rossell (1980) argues that, although many of the key actors do not like to admit it, judicial decision making has been transformed in two important respects by social science evidence. First, beginning with *Sweatt v. Painter* (339 US 629) in 1950 — four years before the landmark *Brown* decisions (98 F Supp 797; 345 US 972; 347 US 483) — the courts began to rely on social science evidence to determine whether racial segregation produced significant *harm* among its victims. That is, the courts began to entertain social science evidence in establishing whether there had been a violation of the law or constitution. Second, the courts began to seek expert scientific advice on how to discharge their other major function — fashioning a *remedy* — in cases where harm has been proven (see Rist and Anson, 1977).

The use of social science to fashion judicial remedies has been broadly accepted. Using research findings to determine whether legal rights have been abridged is highly controversial, however. Some observers believe that such use reduces legal principles to probabilistic factual questions – making justice depend on the adequacy of the available science. Rossell (1980) is persuasive, however, in her argument that scientific determination of the factual basis of judicial decisions is complementary to, rather than in tension with, legal analysis.

Rational planning. The influence of research on various 'scientific' or 'rational' planning techniques used by government agencies has been widely noted (see, for example, Mann, 1975; Beckman, 1977; Nagel, 1980; Yeakey, 1983). Ukeles (1977) makes a convincing case that the (ultimately unsuccessful) effort to introduce PPBS into the federal bureaucracy during the mid-1960s was a major turning point in this process. Yeakey (1983) concurs in this judgement that rational planning processes are a major element in the development of educational policy research. While she mentions PPBS only in passing, she cites a number of other rational planning techniques as expressions of scientific policy formation.

While controversy in the judicial use of social science focuses on its legitimacy as a basis for decision making, *ineffectiveness* is the major problem in rational planning. For various reasons – many of them first noted by Charles Lindblom (1959) – public policy is only marginally influenced by research findings or rational planning processes. Occasional exceptions can be found, but these exceptions only serve to make the generally low level of scientific impact on planning more baffling.

Programme evaluation. Mandated federal programme evaluations are the third major source of expanded social science influence on educational policy and practice. Beginning with post-World War II redevelopment programmes, and expanding rapidly during the 'War on Poverty' and 'Great Society' years, federal support for mandated programme evaluations covering a broad range of health, education, and welfare policies produced the economic resources needed to support a veritable army of social scientists. These scientific programme evaluators have studied (and sometimes manipulated) a broad array of social, psychological, economic, anthropological and political variables in an effort to determine which, if any, are responsible for the success of a few programmes and the failure of many (see, for example, C.H. Weiss, 1977; Patton, 1978). These evaluations typically documented the existence of intense and often intractable problems in the use of scientific programme evaluation data to improve either policy or practice in education (see, for example, McLaughlin, 1975; House, 1980; Dreyfus, 1972). Indeed, it is typically argued that, 'the little use that has occurred has been fortuitous rather than planned' (Weitman *et al*, 1973).

Bias is another aspect of the impact issue. It is widely observed that, on those occasions when scientific evidence is utilized, science utilization tends to be biased or inappropriate to the policy decisions under consideration (Rivlin, 1971; Carlson, 1979). Policy makers are notoriously more

interested in evidence that supports their views; and scientists are frequently
charged with succumbing to policy-maker biases in gathering or analysing
their data.

The intellectual roots of educational policy research

During the same general period that the practice of scientific policy analysis
was being transformed through court deliberations, social planning techniques, and mandated programme evaluations, significant *intellectual*
developments in the interpretation and conceptualization of this process
were also taking place. Emergence of the idea that policy analysis is a
unique scientific discipline took place during a 30 year period bracketed
roughly by the 1951 publication of Lerner and Lasswell's *The Policy
Sciences* and the 1980 publication of Stuart Nagel's *Handbook of Policy
Studies*. One can find, of course, some earlier examples of a scientific
orientation toward policy. One writer traces it back to 19th century
utilitarianism in Great Britain (Klein, 1976). By some definitions it would
even be appropriate to identify Machiavelli's advice to *The Prince* in 1513
as the point of origin for scientific policy analysis (Machiavelli, 1981).

Earlier discussions lack Lasswell's vivid and self-conscious commitment
to policy analysis as a political or administrative discipline, however. They
focus largely on policies themselves, rather than on the process of policy
analysis that, in Lasswell's (1951: 3) words, 'cuts across the existing
specializations' and provides the basis for a new form of applied social
research. Lasswell recognized two dimensions within the discipline of
policy research: (1) a science *of* the policy process; and (2) the use of
science *in* the formation of particular policies. In education, a science *of*
the policy process emerged as a special field of enquiry during the 1960s
(many scholars see Eliot's 1959 essay in the American Political Science
Review as the point of origin). The field was institutionalized in the
Politics of Education Association in 1969. This professional society
formed within the AERA has a current membership of about 400 scholars
and practitioners.

Efforts at interpreting the use of science *in* educational policy formation
have been slower to develop. Initially the concepts of 'dissemination' and
'adoption' of innovative practices were borrowed from studies of agricultural development. In the 1970s, as attention became more clearly focused
on the problems of research utilization in the schools, however, it became
clear that accounting for the failure to alter dramatically school performance through research and evaluation would require much more complex
and subtle theories than those borrowed from agriculture. School performance is closely linked to constitutional rights and personal preferences, as
well as to the technological aspects of curriculum and pedagogy. Moreover,
unlike food production, the goals of education are diffuse, socially controversial, and inherently implicated in any decision to incorporate research
findings into policy or practice.

Six substantial research studies undertaken during the 1970s (Caplan,

1976; Knorr, 1975; Mitchell, 1981a; Patton, 1978; Rich, 1976; and J. Weiss, 1976) fundamentally altered our understanding of research utilization during the formation of public policies. As described more fully in the discussion of research impact on policy presented below, these studies revealed that scientific research contributes more to problem definition and to the overall orientation of policy makers to their decision-making responsibilities than to the development of particular techniques for improving specific policies.

Major topics in policy-oriented education research

It is important in assessing the impact of research on school policy and practice to distinguish between various domains of research activity. Two approaches have generally been taken to the classification of educational research. The first is to distinguish between generic *types* of research activity. A report by the United States Comptroller General (1977) divides science activities into three broad classes: gathering social statistics, conducting social research and development, and programme or policy evaluation. Wirt and Mitchell (1983) distinguish four generic types of research products, while the National Research Council (Abramson, 1978) offers a still more refined classification scheme, dividing social knowledge production and application activities into: (1) research; (2) demonstrations for policy formation; (3) programme evaluation; (4) general purpose statistics; (5) demonstrations for policy implementation; (6) development of materials; and (7) dissemination.

Whatever classification scheme is used, however, it is apparent to all knowledgeable observers that different types of social science products are utilized (if at all) in quite different ways. Social statistics, for example, are utilized in ways quite distinct from social research and evaluation products. Not only are statistics typically gathered and disseminated by distinctive agencies (without explicit research, development or evaluation mandates), they are also presented without attempting to identify either causal linkages among the various elements in the information collected or the implications of the statistics for policy problem definition or assessment.

A second, and in many ways more valuable, approach to the classification of social science research activities is to distinguish between the central issues or *topics* covered by research studies that have had a noticeable impact on education policy or practice (LaNoue, 1982). Four such basic themes can be identified in recent education research: (1) studies of racial and other educational *equity* issues; (2) patterns of school *governance*; (3) *teaching and learning* policy; and (4) the *economics of education*. As indicated in Table 1, each of these four broad topics consists of a cluster of loosely related sub-topics. Moreover, research and analysis in each topical area can be separated into those concerned with the *processes* of policy formation or implementation, and those concerned with *content* or impact of particular policies.

	Process analysis	Content research
Equity research topics		
1. Race (segregation/ desegregation)	How decisions to desegregate are made	What effects racial isolation has on children
2. Wealth (aid/ finance)	Resource generation/ allocation	Categorical programme effects
3. Location (rural/ urban/suburban)	Rural/urban tension management	Effects of programme differentiation
4. Language/ethnicity (bi-lingual/multi-cultural policy)	Mobilization and response to interest groups	How soon should English language be taught
5. Handicap (special education)	Political origin of court cases, PL 94-142, etc	Impact of main-streaming, IEPs, test bias etc
6. Gender	Politics of EEOC, Title IX, ERA and affirmative action	Impact of sex discrim-ination on job opportunities and organization processes
School governance topics		
1. Authority to act (federal, state, intermediate, district, site)	Distribution of powers and responsibilities	Effects of power or level on educational process/outcome
2. Representation/ participation (lay/ professional; client/ citizen interests)	Who gets access to decisions and how they are made	What difference it makes for educational processes or outcomes
3. Centralization/ decentralization	Community control, vouchers, advisory committees	Implementation of innovations, mandate compliance
4. Collective	Teacher power, citizen input, impasse resolution	Organizational and teacher work role effects
5. Innovation and reform	Resource control, planning, adoption, implementation	Effect of plan-variations in programme
6. Public/private (parochial/religious schools)	Politics of aid and accreditation	Quality of private vs. public education
Teaching and learning		
1. Curriculum	Politics of curriculum decisions	Programme effects on various students
2. Testing	Adoption, publication mandates	Construction, bias, interpretation
3. Personnel training and certification	Who trains, what criteria for certification	What effect does train-ing or certification have on performance

	Process analysis	Content research
4. Instructional processes	Who decides what processes to use	What difference does it make
5. Teacher work roles	Definitions, incentives	Organization and learning effects
6. School effectiveness	Improvement strategies and incentives	Factors: learning time, leadership, climate
Economics of education		
1. Manpower forecasting	Responsibility for statistics	Job opportunity and training needs
2. Human capital	Who gets access to advanced training	What are the marginal returns
3. Education production functions	What are the values or goals to be produced	What factors are responsible for results

Table 1. *Major education policy research topics*

Equity policy is examined in a very large body of research. However, no single work has matched the impact of the report by Coleman *et al* (1966) on *Equality of Educational Opportunity.* Race was the early focus of this research, with the nature and effects of decision making related to desegregation of the public schools providing the major themes of most studies. During the mid-1960s wealth replaced race as the key concept in many equity studies (see especially Wise, 1967). There were many reasons for this shift. Among the most important were: (1) documentation of large inter-district fiscal resource disparities; (2) growing realization that physical desegregation was not possible for many minority children (hence equity would have to be reconceptualized as equal resources rather than integrated school attendance); and (3) recognition that school achievement problems are more highly correlated with family and community socio-economic status than with race.

Equity policy analysis has also been concerned with problems related to student location. The inequitable effects of school and district attendance boundaries are easily linked to fiscal inequities, but they have other effects as well. Traditional tensions between rural and urban social values have been carried over into policy issues dealing with school size, creation of regional centres for vocational or special education, and the use of vouchers to permit families to choose between alternative schools (see Coons and Sugarman, 1978).

During the late 1960s and early 1970s equity policy broadened to include a number of neglected and oppressed population groups. Language and ethnic minority groups (especially Hispanics) were recognized as victims of biased treatment. Substantial attention was focused on sex discrimination in staffing as well as in programme implementation by the passage of Title IX of the Education Amendments of 1972. Most recently, children with physical, emotional, and/or learning handicaps were given special recognition in the passage of PL 94-142 (the Education for All Handicapped law) in 1975.

In contrast with the relatively recent emergence of equity as a major policy topic, *school governance* problems are as old as public education itself. The distribution of decision-making authority among federal, state, intermediate unit, school district, and school site policy makers has been an ongoing problem for both analysts and reformers. The ebb and flow of policy influence between the state and federal levels has been studied by a number of prominent scholars (Wirt and Kirst, 1982; Scribner, 1977; Leiberman and McLaughlin, 1982). Several have pronounced the demise of the local school district as an agency of educational governance (though the evidence on this point is far from convincing – see Iannaccone and Lutz, 1970; Lutz and Iannaccone, 1978).

Tensions among the several agencies responsible for governing public schools have received considerable attention. Mechanisms of *representation and participation* in policy formation have been broadly studied (elections, referenda, advisory councils, influence networks, state education agencies, legislative decision making, etc – see, for example, Mann, 1976). And the effects of centralization (or decentralization) of decision-making authority have been explored in studies of administrative decentralization, client or family choice, state and federal mandates for change, court orders, etc. At present, representation/participation analysis has led to contradictory conclusions – ranging from declarations of autocratic control over school policy by professional educators and community elites to a fairly vigorous declaration of the vitality of representative elections. Analyses of the centralization/decentralization problem have identified a fundamental dilemma in governance. Decentralized control leads to the neglect of minority interests – but centralization produces serious alienation and resistance among school personnel and local leaders, leading to reduced effectiveness of both policy mandates and general school operations. (On the latter point see Berman and McLaughlin, 1975-1978.)

Three aspects of governance policy are prominent in recent research: (1) collective bargaining for teachers and other school personnel; (2) innovation and reform in school programmes; and (3) relationships between public and private or parochial schools. The budgetary and fiscal effects of collective bargaining have received the lion's share of interest, but its impact on the reallocation of authority within the schools is emerging as a major factor in work role definitions and the delivery of educational services (see Mitchell *et al*, 1981). Studies of educational innovation and change by the RAND Corporation remain a watershed in the examination of this crucial governance problem (Berman and McLaughlin, 1975-1978). School reform strategists now recognize that providing proper compliance incentives – not just mandates for appropriate action – are crucial for successful influence over school system operations. The relationship of public and private schools has been dramatically altered by both the equity movement (which stimulated 'white flight' and the formation of new private schools), and recent programme improvement efforts (which have drawn attention to differences in the organizational characteristics and educational outcomes found in private schools — see Coleman *et al*, 1982; Heyns, 1981).

Teaching and learning processes were among the earliest topics of educational research and analysis. Only recently, however, have they been recognized as matters of explicit policy (Schulman and Sykes, 1983). This recognition has led to policy-focused studies of how authority over school curricula is distributed and how specific curriculum content decisions are made (Van Geel, 1976; Boyd, 1979). Student assessment and testing has probably received the most sophisticated scientific attention. Yet it remains a highly controversial area of policy research and action (Lynch, 1979).

Training and certification of school personnel has received major attention from state level policy makers in recent years, but that attention is not well supported by research on alternative training strategies. Instructional processes are better researched, but the policy implications of that research have been unclear. This is changing rapidly, however, as lesson structures, classroom control processes, classroom climates, and the factors affecting teacher thinking and planning processes become clearer.

Two 'hot' topics in recent teaching and learning policy are the *effectiveness* of individual teachers and school site organizations. Exploration of the work role orientations and activities of effective teachers has been undertaken by a large group of research scholars. While a number of the characteristics of effective teaching can now be confidently identified, it is not clear how policy best supports the development of these attributes. School effectiveness research has become very important in the last five years (compare Averch *et al*, 1974, with Madaus *et al*, 1980). As a matter of scientific research it is plagued with controversy, yet school improvement has become the most important topic of debate among state and federal policy makers (Note at end).

Public interest in the *economics of education* has focused on three broad areas: (1) manpower forecasting (and its attendant contributions to vocational or career education — see Doeringer and Piore, 1971; Harbison and Myers, 1964); (2) human capital formation (see Johns *et al*, 1983) and its critical appraisal by students of the political economy of education (see Bowles and Gintis, 1976; Shapiro, 1980); and (3) efforts to develop education production functions capable of describing how particular resources contribute to schooling outcomes (Brown and Saks, 1981).

Knowledge impact on policy and practice

Having reviewed the historical evolution of knowledge utilization in the formation of educational policy and practice and distinguished between the major themes of recent research and evaluation activities, it is now appropriate to examine directly the question of research impact on school policy formation and implementation. Three aspects of policy making are crucial in accounting for the utilization of research and evaluation findings: (a) the existence of *competing definitions of policy* and policy making; (b) the unique character of the policy decision-making *work flow*, and (c) the distinction between social and intellectual aspects of knowledge utilization.

Competing definitions of policy

The sharply divergent and largely incompatible definitions of policy used by various scholars make it difficult to know what is meant by the 'impact' of social research and evaluation on policy formulation or implementation. Recent attempts to define the term policy range from broad and simple statements like 'what governments do and say' (Dubnick and Bardis, 1983) to complex lists of characteristics requiring several pages to explain (see, for example, Mann, 1975). Most definitions fall into one of four generic types, however, reflecting four alternative views of the role of government in coping with fundamental human problems. As suggested in Table 2, approaches to the definition of policy differ along two basic dimensions. First (as indicated by column headings in the table) policy definitions differ in their assumptions about governmental involvement in social conflict and cooperation. Some approaches assume that governments are primarily cooperative *social service agencies* (helping to achieve social goals that would be impossible to reach through private actions alone), while others see governments as pre-eminently *conflict management mechanisms* (mediating and controlling social conflicts that would otherwise be overly destructive). Second (as indicated by the row labels in the table) policy definitions differ with regard to whether governmental actions are thought to support the achievement of social purposes *directly*, or only to fulfil social purposes *indirectly* by stimulating or restraining the actions of private citizens. The intersection of these two sets of assumptions about the role of government produces the four generic conceptions of governmental action and hence the four different definitions of policy shown in Table 2. For a discussion of the underlying social science paradigms (structuralist, functionalist, exchange and interactionist) see Mitchell, 1982.

   Structuralist conceptions of policy focus attention on the formal structural units responsible for making decisions, and emphasize the reduction of conflict through *direct regulation* of social institutions and private citizens. A typical structuralist definition of policy is, 'what governments do, why they do it, and what difference it makes' (Dye, 1972). In this view, the use of governmental policy to regulate is seen as a reflection of how *power* is (or should be) distributed in society. Whether viewed from the perspective of the 'liberal' structuralists who framed the American constitution or from a more 'radical' or Marxist perspective, structural theories share a commitment to the view that public policies can produce a proper distribution of political power that will lead to the elimination of social conflict, or at least to its just resolution. Hence, structural theories give prominence to *equity* as a primary social value, seeing destructive conflict as the result of an inequitable distribution of power.

	Theories of government as conflict management	Theories of government as service delivery
	Structuralism	*Functionalism*
Theories of direct public control	Regulate social institutions, control power, support equity	Set course of collective action, control purposes support quality
(definition of policy)	('What governments do' – Dye, 1972)	('proposed course of action ... to reach a goal' – Freidrick, 1963)
	Exchange theory	*Interactionism*
Theories of indirect public support for private action	Influence over private actions, control contracts, support liberty	Encouragement of private expression, control problem definition, support competence
(definition of policy)	('Regulation of private activity' through subsidy regulation or manipulation – Ripley, 1966)	('Conscious attempt ... to find constructive responses to problems – NAE, 1969)

Table 2. *How four theories of governmental action approach the definition of policy*

Policy, therefore, is considered primarily as a vehicle for allocating power to individuals or groups with a legitimate right to exercise it (and conversely, limiting the power of those whose interests are less legitimate). For theorists utilizing this conceptual approach, science impact on policy would be expected to result from the documentation of social inequities – but they would not expect research to have much effect on the struggle for political power or the resolution of basic social conflicts.

Functionalist policy definitions, by contrast, emphasize cooperative development of direct services to pursue specific public purposes or goals. A typical functional definition of policy is offered by Freidrick:

'a proposed course of action of a person, group, or government within a given environment ... to reach a goal or realize an objective or a purpose.' (Freidrick, 1963)

The ability of government to set policy is seen as dependent upon its ability to define and articulate public purposes. Hence, functionalists focus attention on generating *government programmes* rather than regulating private actions or social institutions. They see government as 'doing something' about the 'general welfare', rather than merely protecting the rights of various individuals or groups. Hence functionalist policy analysis gives prominence to *quality* as a central public value. Whether conceived of as a 'liberal' concern with the quality of life available to all citizens, or a 'conservative' concern with the quality of performance of public programmes and agencies, functionalism tends to prefer quality performance over egalitarian access. Specific policies are, therefore, more often criticized as inadequate solutions to public problems than as the institutionalization of inequality.

From the perspective of this theory, science utilization is expected to play a prominent role in policy formation and programme evaluation. This model of government emphasizes rationality and values the discovery of 'right' answers for social needs. The emergence of rational planning activities within government springs, no doubt, from widespread belief in this approach. The disappointing failure of these rational planning techniques to guide public policy choices reflects its limitations as an explanation of governmental action.

Exchange theories conceptualize policy as a vehicle for indirect influence over conflict by controlling the conditions for citizens' *private choices*. By controlling the right to enter into contractual relationships and by enforcing contracts once they are made, exchange policies seek to channel individual and group behaviour toward public purposes. A typical exchange view of policy is presented in Ripley's (1966) work. He identifies policy with the 'regulation of private activity' through governmental 'subsidies', 'regulations' and/or 'manipulation'. Theorists who rely on the exchange model of governmental action tend to focus attention on *liberty* as the pre-eminent social value. They believe, with Thomas Jefferson, that the 'government that governs best governs least'.

From the perspective of this theory, science impact would be reflected in the development of laws and other regulations based on documentation of their ability to improve productivity without interfering with personal liberty. Unfortunately, in education as in other policy areas, studies of productivity have been conducted with little concern for personal choice or liberty. Research on merit pay plans for teachers and educational voucher systems for families, while clearly not in the mainstream of educational research, are exceptions to this generalization.

Interactionist theories conceptualize policy as indirect encouragement of *cooperative action* by private citizens. Interactionists recognize the importance of ideological and symbolic leadership by governmental policy makers. They tend to assume that policy has its effects by controlling how individuals and groups *define the problems* which they face. The National Academy of Education offers a typically interactionist definition of policy as:

> 'the conscious attempt of officials, legislators, and interested publics to find constructive responses to the needs and pathologies which they observe in their surrounding culture.' (National Academy of Education, 1969)

This definition asserts that policy is 'conscious', and that it is concerned with 'constructive' responses to problems. The result is expected to be voluntary cooperation among citizens.

Interactionism tends to identify *competence* as the pre-eminent social value. Where functionalists emphasize the *organization* of governmental services, interaction theorists tend to be indifferent to the question of whether public or private agencies should deliver needed services. They concentrate instead on the importance of competent and enthusiastic performance by individuals as the basis for successful pursuit of public goals.

Viewed from the interactionist perspective, science impact is higher today than it has ever been. Recent research on school and teacher effectiveness is widely interpreted to mean that high performance depends upon the use of indirect policies that build group cohesiveness and shared value systems within the schools. Research studies exploring strategies of staff development and administrative leadership to achieve these ends have been widely read and are being incorporated into many educational policies.

The policy-making work flow

Despite their substantial differences, the four models of governmental action discussed above share at least one common feature. They all recognize that policy making takes time, and that policy decisions pass through several distinct *stages* between their initial identification and their ultimate implementation and evaluation. The movement of decisions through these several stages defines the educational policy-making *work flow*. The highly political and generally public character of legislative policy formation has made it relatively easy for policy analysts to distinguish between (1) initial articulation of policy interests or demands (a process which leads to the drafting of legislative bills) and (2) later stages involving deliberation, modification and aggregation of support for various proposals (handled by legislative policy committees), (3) priority setting and allocation of resources to particular policies (handled by the fiscal committees), and (4) follow-up oversight of policy implementation (typically handled through legislative staff studies of interim committee hearings). See Mitchell (1981a), Florio *et al* (1979), or Wirt and Mitchell (1983) for a fuller discussion of this decision-making work flow.

Similar staging occurs within administrative agencies responsible for adapting and implementing education policies at the state, local and school site levels.

Studies of science utilization by policy makers clearly indicate that scientific research and evaluation data serve very different functions at each of the various stages in this work flow. At the earliest stages, science serves to define problems and turn desires into concrete proposals for action. The role of research and evaluation data in this process has only recently been clearly identified. It is not yet fully understood (see Mitchell,

1981a; Wirt and Mitchell, 1983). During later stages science utilization is more obvious, but it is also more controversial. During the sifting, amending and support aggregation process of stage two, science is used to assess policy proposals — and it can play a powerful role in killing proposals that would otherwise have substantial political support. For this reason, science utilization becomes increasingly politicized as decisions move toward the stage at which resources must be committed to their implementation.

Social and intellectual functions of knowledge use

A third aspect of science influence over policy (treated in some detail in Mitchell, 1981a) concerns the difference between the intellectual and social consequences of introducing research and evaluation findings into the policy work flow. Since effective research provides meaningful descriptions of policy-relevant social phenomena it can be used as the basis for a powerful 'universe of discourse' (Robinson, 1947) for those who accept its tenets and findings. This universe of discourse helps diverse individuals and interest groups to establish a basis for collaboration and thus contributes to group solidarity and the formation of political coalitions in support of particular policy options. These social processes are vital to the development of effective influence over policy formation. Moreover, political opponents who do not understand or cannot critically appraise the research data being used to support a particular policy proposal are significantly disadvantaged in any effort to get their views adopted as official policy.

In sum, then, the impact of research and evaluation findings on policy adoption depends upon the policy model or 'paradigm' (Kuhn, 1962) used to conceptualize governmental action and the stage within the policy-making work flow at which they are introduced. The impact of science findings is both social and intellectual. Intellectually, science provides problem definition, proposal evaluation and assessment of the probability that policies are (or would be) effective in producing specific outcomes at an acceptable cost. Socially, science plays an equally important — and often unrecognized — role in mobilizing (or demoralizing) political support for various policy proposals.

The impact of science on the improvement of practice

While recent research on knowledge utilization has framed a reasonably clear picture of how policy is influenced by research and evaluation findings, the relationship of science to practice is less well understood. Throughout the 1960s and early 1970s intensive research aimed at the improvement of educational practice was found to produce only marginal results. In fact, by 1974, researchers at the RAND Corporation had concluded that, despite massive federal efforts at improving school performance, there were no known ways to ensure that schools would perform their assigned responsibilities with consistent effectiveness.

Almost immediately, however, a major breakthrough in understanding occurred. A series of research studies on the adoption of educational innovations (also conducted by the RAND Corporation, see Berman and McLaughlin, 1975-1978) highlighted the importance of involving the educators who are affected by any change in planning for its implementation and adapting it to their own unique local circumstances. At the same time a series of studies which have come to be known as 'effective schools' research began to uncover regularities in the characteristics of high performing school organizations (see Brookover and Lecotte, 1977; Edmonds, 1979; Purkey and Smith, 1982).

In combination with recent work on high performing private corporations, these studies support what might be called a 'cultural' theory of school effectiveness (see, for example, Deal and Kennedy, 1982; Peters and Waterman, 1981; Ouchi, 1981). The central theme of this cultural theory is that effective organizations are knitted together by shared social values and norms among the members – not by bureaucratic rules or technical constraints arising from resource inputs or formal organizational structures.

Perhaps the most troublesome aspect of the impact of research on practice is the tendency for educators to over-react to the latest research findings – pursuing 'quick fix' fads based on research findings that are taken out of context and generalized far beyond their data. When, for example, the presidential Commission on Excellence issued its report in 1983 asserting that a 'rising tide of mediocrity' threatens the nation's schools, thousands of educators immediately attempted to install dozens of new programmes and practices – ranging from stringent student tests for high school graduation and merit pay plans for teachers to longer school days and massive new course requirements. Most of these new programmes were rationalized as being *the* solutions prescribed by recent research findings. It is not difficult to predict, however, that many of these new initiatives will produce disappointingly little change in the schools where they are often used as shibboleths to secure political support rather than comprehensive plans aimed at reproducing the actual conditions of the research they supposedly embody.

Methodological issues in policy research

Any consideration of scientific impact on educational policy and practice would not be complete without giving serious attention to questions of research methodology. A number of scholars have concerned themselves with the relationship between research methods and the influence of research on policy and practice. The literature dealing with these issues tends to adopt one of two perspectives. The first explores issues associated with turning inherently value laden, time constrained, intensely practical policy issues into scientific research problems. This approach assumes that social research disciplines are fairly well developed and have an identifiable set of performance standards, capable (at least in principle) of producing specific, unequivocal, and universal conclusions about social behaviour. Analysts adopting this perspective tend to follow Lasswell (1951) — seeking to identify points of intersection between policy making and research. This line of enquiry has done much to illuminate problems of scientific knowledge *utilization* (see Mitchell, 1981b, for a review).

A second methodological perspective assumes that social research is an inherently polyphonic enterprise with several essentially different methods for data collection, analysis, and interpretation. Scholars adopting this approach are primarily concerned with delineating the policy-relevant characteristics of various research methods and evaluating how each can enhance or detract from the decision-making process. This strand of literature has identified several key problems associated with the application of scientific methods to policy problems.

Two problems trouble both groups of methodologists. The first is *bias*. Both scientists and policy makers have been known to allow personal, political or cultural biases to influence their judgement. In extreme cases, scientists fake their data or intentionally obfuscate its interpretation (see Carlson, 1979). Policy makers usually just ignore unwanted research and adopt non-scientific decision processes when they do not like the available research evidence. Sometimes, however, they devote substantial attention to controlling research priorities or shopping among available studies to find ones that fit their prejudices in order to minimize the likelihood that unwanted policy decisions will be reached (see Coleman, 1976, on early resistance to studies of 'white flight' from integrated schools).

In addition to outright bias, the problem of *personalized scientific authority* — the tendency for policy makers to use scien*tists* rather than scien*ce* in shaping policy — is also widely discussed (Rossell, 1980). This personalization of authority is most often lamented strongly by scholars concerned with refining scientific policy research methods. These scholars tend to feel that personal involvement detracts from the true authority of science — authority derived from the rigorous use of specialized methods for establishing valid and reliable knowledge. The personalization of authority is sometimes defended, however, as the best way to bring abstract scientific findings into the complex, subtle, and value laden processes of political decision making (see Dworkin, 1977; Bailey *et al*, 1962).

Methodological distortion of policy problems

Policy problems are often distorted when they are subjected to scientific analysis. Scientists tend to study what they know how to study — not necessarily what policy makers would like them to study. They also tend to *reconceptualize* policy problems to fit the conceptual paradigm with which they approach the explanation of social processes and thus fail to examine the problems identified by policy makers. Moreover, on a very practical level, scientific concern with validity and reliability of data frequently leads to a preference for variables with established metrics rather than those which may be interesting but hard to measure (Carlson, 1979; Hall and Loucks, 1982).

A more sweeping criticism is made by those who charge social scientists with 'abstract empiricism' — the tendency to oversimplify problems to accommodate reified research methods (see Burrell and Morgan, 1979). These critics charge that researchers tend to seek explanations only within *existing* variations in society and neglect to account for why many possible actions never occur.

Social science findings are also distorted because the research is limited in *scope* (Carlson, 1979). Data collection and analysis are expensive and time consuming as well as intellectually demanding tasks. Social research is, therefore, inevitably time- and circumstance-bound. Research projects conducted in a particular time and place can miss entirely the causal variables needed for general explanations. For practical economic reasons, research studies tend not to be either *comparative* or *longitudinal* in character (see Wirt, 1980). Most researchers study a single social programme or policy problem. Moreover, even when a research problem is broadly conceived, scientists can measure only a small number of variables over a limited number of cases. It is not surprising, therefore, that research findings easily become divergent and contradictory, providing limited and uncertain guidance to policy makers.

Recent work has concentrated on two strategies for overcoming the distortions generated by these methodological limitations. One — pioneered by Glass (1976, 1978) — is 'meta-analysis'. Meta-analysis seeks greater reliability in research through statistical examination of trends in the findings reported from a large number of comparable studies. A second strategy has been the pursuit of more comprehensive and general theories, such as the paradigms discussed earlier in this article.

Methodological problems affecting utilization

Several problems limit the utility of science in policy formation. Foremost among them is the fact that science is only one decision-making resource for policy makers (Mitchell, 1981a; Wirt and Mitchell, 1983). Political leaders held decision making responsibilities long before there were any social sciences — and they still have a broad array of non-scientific ways of identifying and selecting policy options. To be usable, therefore, social research must be cost effective — it must be worth more in enhanced decision-making capacity than it costs to find and interpret.

This need for science to be a cost efficient resource leads policy makers to be critical of scientists for equivocation and lack of explicit direction. It has also led to the realization that scientists and policy makers tend to operate in 'two cultures' with different time frames and different levels of need for certainty in their conclusions (Snow, 1959).

Conclusion

This chapter has explored the impact of educational research and evaluation findings on educational policy and practice in the United States. The review has been organized around four fundamental aspects of this problem. First, the size and historical development of the educational research and evaluation industry — at least those aspects of the industry with the greatest relevance to changes in school policy and practice — were reviewed. Second, a brief survey of the major topics treated by policy oriented educational researchers was offered. Third, several critical dimensions of science impact on policy and practice were examined directly. Finally, methodological issues affecting the impact of research and evaluation on education were examined.

Note

The most important recent policy studies include: National Commission on Excellence, *A Nation at Risk;* Education Commission of the States, *Action for Excellence;* College Entrance Examination Board, *Academic Preparation for College;* The Twentieth Century Fund, *Making the Grade;* The Carnegie Corporation, *Education and Economic Progress;* National Association of Secondary School Principals and the National Association of Independent Schools, *A Celebration of Teaching: High Schools in the 1980s;* The Carnegie Foundation, *High School: A Report on American Secondary Education;* Institute for Development of Educational Activities (IDEA), *A Study of Schooling in the United States;* and The National Science Foundation, *Educating Americans for the 21st Century.*

References

Abramson, M A (1978) *The Funding of Social Knowledge Production and Application: A Survey of Federal Agencies* National Academy of Sciences: Washington, D C

Averch, H A, Carrol, S J, Donaldson, T S, Kiesling, H J and Pincus, J (1974) *How Effective is Schooling? A Critical Synthesis and Review of Research Findings* Educational Technology Publications: Englewood Cliffs, NJ

Bailey, S K, Frost, R T, Marsh, P E and Wood, R C (1962) *Schoolmen and Politics* Syracuse University Press: Syracuse, New York

Beckman, N ed (1977) Policy analysis in government: alternatives to 'muddling through' *Public Administration Review* 27 221-264

Berliner, D C ed (1980) *Review of Research in Education,* Vol 8, American Educational Research Association: Washington, D C

Berliner, D C ed (1981) *Review of Research in Education,* Vol 9, American Educational Research Association: Washington, D C

Berman, P and McLaughlin, M W (1975-1978) *Federal Programs Supporting Educational Change* Vol IV *The Findings in Review* Rand Corporation: Santa Monica, CA

Bowles, S and Gintis, H (1976) *Schooling in Capitalist America: Educational Reform and the Contradictions of Economic Life* Basic Books: New York

Boyd, W L (1979) Changing politics of curriculum policy making for American schools *Review of Educational Research* **48** 577-628

Brookover, W B and Lecotte, L W (1977) *Changes in School Characteristics Co-incident with Changes in Student Achievement* Michigan State University, College of Urban Development: East Lansing, MI

Burrell, G and Morgan, G (1979) *Sociological Paradigms and Organisational Analysis* Heinemann Educational Books: London

Caplan, N (1976) Factors associated with knowledge use among federal executives *Policy Studies Journal* **4** 229-234

Caplan, N, Morrison, A and Stambauch, R J (1975) *The Use of Social Science Knowledge in Policy Decisions at the National Level* University of Michigan Press: Ann Arbor, MI

Carey, J T (1975) *Sociology and Public Affairs* Sage Publications: Beverly Hills, CA

Carlson, K (1979) Ways in which research methodology distorts policy issues *The Urban Review* **11** 1-16

Coleman, J S (1976) Policy decisions, social science information and education *Sociology of Education* **49** 304-312

Coleman, J S, Campbell, E Q, Hobson, C J, McPartland, J, Wood, A M, Weinfield, F D and York, R L (1966) *Equality of Educational Opportunity* Government Printing Office: Washington, D C

Coleman, J S, Hoffer, T and Kilgore, S (1982) *High School Achievement: Public, Catholic and Private Schools Compared* Basic Books: New York

Coons, J E and Sugarman, S D (1978) *Education by Choice: The Case for Family Control* University of California Press: Berkeley, CA

Deal, T E and Kennedy, A A (1982) *Corporate Cultures: The Rites and Rituals of Corporate Life* Addison-Wesley: Reading, MA

Doeringer, P and Piore, M (1971) *Internal Labor Markets and Manpower Training* D C Heath: Lexington, MA

Dreyfus, D (1972) Limitations of policy research in congressional decision making *Policy Studies Journal* **1**

Drezek, S, Monkowski, P G and Higgins, P S (1982) Current versus perceived-ideal procedures for determining educational program-evaluation budgets: a survey of school evaluators *Educational Evaluation and Policy Analysis* **4** 97-108

Dror, Y (1967) Policy analyst: a new professional role in government *Public Administration Review* **13** 197-203

Dubnick, M J and Bardis, B A (1983) *Thinking about Public Policy, a Problem-solving Approach* Wiley: New York

Dworkin, R (1977) Social sciences and constitutional rights — the consequences of uncertainty *in* Rist, R C and Anson, R J (1977)

Dye, T R (1972) *Understanding Public Policy* Prentice Hall: Englewood Cliffs, NJ

Edmonds, R R (1979) Effective schools for the urban poor *Educational Leadership* **37** 17-23

Florio, D H, Behrmann, M M and Goltz, D L (1979) What do policy makers think of educational research and evaluation? Or do they? *Educational Evaluation and Policy Analysis* **1** 61-87

Freidrick, C J (1963) *Man and His Government; An Empirical Theory of Politics* McGraw Hill: New York

Galpin, R and Wright, C eds (1964) *Scientists and National Policy Making* Columbia University Press: New York

Glass, G V (1976) Primary, secondary, and meta-analysis of research *Educational Researcher* **5** 5-8

Glass, G V (1978) Integrating findings: the meta-analysis of research *Review of Research in Education* **5** American Educational Research Association: Washington, D C

Gordon, E W ed (1983) *Review of Research in Education*, Vol 10, American Educational Research Association: Washington, D C

Hall, G E and Loucks, S F (1982) Bridging the gap: policy research rooted in practice *in* Lieberman and McLaughlin 1982

Harbison, F and Myers, C (1964) *Education, Manpower, and Economic Growth* McGraw Hill: New York

Havighurst, R J (1982) Philanthropic foundations *in* Mitzel 1982

Heyns, B L (1981) Policy implications of the public private school debates *Harvard Education Review* 5 519-525

House, E R (1980) *Evaluating with Validity* Sage Publications: Beverly Hills, CA

Iannaccone, L and Lutz, F W (1970) *Politics, Power, and Policy: The Governing of Local School Districts* Charles E Merrill: Columbus, OH

Johns, R L, Morphet, E L and Alexander, K (1983) *The Economics and Financing of Education* (fourth ed), Prentice Hall: Englewood Cliffs, NJ

Klein, R (1976) The rise and decline of policy analysis: the strange case of health policymaking in Britain *Policy Analysis* 2 458-475

Knorr, K D (1975) The nature of scientific consensus and the case of the social sciences *in* Knorr, Strasser and Zilian (1975)

Knorr, K D, Strasser, H and Zilian, H G *eds* (1975) *Determinants and Control of Scientific Development* Reidel: Dordrecht, Holland

Kuhn, T (1962) *The Structure of Scientific Revolutions* University of Chicago Press: Chicago, IL

LaNoue, G R (1982) Political science *in* Mitzel (1982)

Lambright, W H (1976) *Governing Science and Technology* Oxford University Press: New York

Lasswell, H D (1951) Introduction *in* Lerner and Lasswell (1951)

Lerner, D and Lasswell, H D *eds* (1951) *The Policy Sciences* Stanford University Press: Stanford, CA

Lieberman, A and McLaughlin, M W *eds* (1982) *Policy Making in Education,* Eighty-first Yearbook of the National Society for the Study of Education, Part I, University of Chicago Press: Chicago, IL

Lindblom, C E (1959) The science of 'muddling through' *Public Administration Review* 19 79-88

Lutz, F W and Iannaccone, L (1978) *Public Participation in Local School Districts* D C Heath: Lexington, MA

Lynch, P (1979) Public policy and competency testing *Education and Urban Society* 12 65-80

Machiavelli, N (1981) *The Prince and Other Political Writings* (translated by B Penman) Dent: London

McLaughlin, M (1975) *Evaluation and Reform: Elementary and Secondary Education Act of 1965, Title I* Ballinger: Cambridge, MA

Madaus, G F, Airasian, P W, and Kellaghan, T (1980) *School Effectiveness: A Reassessment of the Evidence* McGraw Hill: New York

Mann, D (1975) *Policy Decision Making in Education* Teachers College Press: New York

Mann, D (1976) *The Politics of Administrative Representation* D C Heath: Lexington, MA

Mitchell, D E (1981a) *Shaping Legislative Decisions: Education Policy and the Social Sciences* D C Heath: Lexington, MA

Mitchell, D E (1981b) Social science utilization in state legislatures *in* Berliner (1981)

Mitchell, D E (1982) Governing schools *in* Mitzel (1982)

Mitchell, D E, Kerchner, C T, Erck, W and Pryor, G (1981) The impact of collective bargaining on school management and governance *The American Journal of Education* 89 147-188

Mitzel, E *ed* (1982) *Encyclopedia of Educational Research* The Free Press: New York

Nagel, S *ed* (1980) *Handbook of Policy Studies* D C Heath: Lexington, MA

National Academy of Education (1969) *Policy Making for American Public Schools* National Academy of Education: New York

National Center for Educational Statistics (NCES) (1982) *Digest of Educational Statistics* Government Printing Office: Washington, D C

Office of Management and Budget (OMB) (1982) *Budget of the United States Government, Fiscal Year 1983* Government Printing Office: Washington, D C

Ouchi, W (1981) *Theory Z How American Business Can Meet the Japanese Challenge* Addison-Wesley: Reading, MA

Patton, M Q (1978) *Utilization Focused Evaluation* Sage Publications: Beverly Hills, CA

Peters, T J and Waterman, R H Jr (1981) *In Search Of Excellence: Lessons from America's Best-Run Companies* Harper and Row: New York

Purkey, S C and Smith, M S (1982) *Effective Schools – A Review* Wisconsin Center for Education Research, University of Wisconsin: Madison, WI

Rich, R F (1976) Uses of social science information by federal bureaucrats: knowledge for action vs knowledge for understanding. A paper presented at the annual meeting of the Midwest Political Science Association, Chicago, Illinois, April, 1976.

Ripley, R B ed (1966) *Public Policies and their Politics* New W W Norton: New York

Rist, R C and Anson, R J eds (1977) *Education, Social Science, and the Judicial Process* Teachers College Press: New York

Rivlin, A (1971) *Systematic Thinking for Social Action* Brookings Institution: Washington, D C

Robinson, D S (1947) *The Principles of Reasoning* (third ed.) Appleton-Century-Crofts: New York

Rossell, C H (1980) Social science research in equity cases: a critical review *in* Berliner (1980)

Schilling, W R (1964) Scientists, foreign policy, and power *in* Galpin and Wright (1964)

Schulman, L and Sykes, G eds (1983) *Handbook of Teaching and Policy* Longman: New York

Scribner, J ed (1977) *The Politics of Education* The Seventy-sixth Yearbook of the National Society for the Study of Education, Part II, University of Chicago Press: Chicago

Snow, C P (1959) *The Two Cultures and a Second Look: Expanded Version of the Two Cultures and the Scientific Revolution* Cambridge University Press: London

Ukeles, J B (1977) Policy analysis: myth or reality? *Public Administration Review* 23 221-228

United States Comptroller General (1977) *Social Research and Development of Limited Use to National Policy Makers* General Accounting Office: Washington, D C

Weiss, C H ed (1977) *Using Social Research in Policy Making* D C Heath: Lexington, MA

Weiss, J (1976) Using social science for social policy *Policy Studies Journal* 4 234-238

Weitman, D R, Horst, P, Taber, G M and Whaley, J S (1973) Design of an evaluation system for NIMH *Contract Report 962-7* The Urban Institute: Washington, D C

Wirt, F M (1980) Comparing educational policies: theory, units of analysis, and research strategies *Comparative Education Review* 24 174-191

Wirt, F M and Kirst, M (1982) *Schools in Conflict* McCutchan: Berkeley, CA

Wirt, F M and Mitchell, D E (1983) Social science and educational reform: the political uses of social research *Educational Administration Quarterly* 18 1-16

Wise, A (1967) *Rich Schools, Poor Schools* University of Chicago Press: Chicago

Yeakey, C C (1983) Emerging policy research in education research and decision-making *in* Gordon (1983)

3. The organization and funding of educational research in England and Wales

William Taylor

Summary: Educational research in England and Wales is characterized by pluralism of funding, diversity of organization and the absence of 'system'. The educational research efforts of the Social Science Research Council, the Department of Education and Science, the Schools Council, the National Foundation for Educational Research and a number of independent foundations are reviewed, with particular reference to recent developments. There has been a marked tendency for the recent policies of funding bodies to favour 'policy-oriented' rather than 'curiosity-oriented' work, and some diminution of responsive-mode funding. There is less 'free money' available for research, and the 'floor of support' for university-based work has been weakened by financial restraints in higher education. A substantial volume of resources is still devoted to various forms of educational research, however, and most of the bodies engaged in such work ten years ago are still active, albeit with reduced resources and, in some cases, less participative and representative forms of governance.

Overview

The organization and funding of educational research in England and Wales is not the responsibility of any single official or private agency, it has not developed on a planned basis, and it is characterized by plurality, diversity and informal contacts rather than by anything that could sensibly be called a 'system'. Although the overall scale of expenditure is modest in relation to, for example, the total national education budget, it is still considerable in absolute terms, probably amounting to an order of magnitude of some £25 to £30 million annually. The largest part of this sum is accounted for by the percentage of university academic staff time devoted to research. Government funds are distributed among universities by the University Grants Committee on the understanding that all university teachers have a responsibility to engage in research. The departmental allocation of resources within each university is a matter for its Council, Senate and Finance Committee. There is no national formula. In accordance with history, formal and informal judgements of quality and need, and university politics, some departments do better than others. It is claimed that the University Grants Committee bases its allocations on the assumption that 30 per cent of staff time overall will be devoted to research.

Some sources put the figure higher. Some universities apply a 'research factor' in their internal allocations, whereby those departments successful in obtaining external support from foundations and from the research councils are 'rewarded' by larger allocations of resources. In 1982-83 the salaries of academic and academic-related staff in university departments, schools and institutes of education in England and Wales amounted to £21,977,000. Taking the 30 per cent estimate of research time, this suggests that some £7 million of this total is attributable to educational research.

Not all universities with departments or schools of education are involved in educational research to an equal extent. University Grants Committee figures on expenditure from educational research grants and contracts by the 33 universities concerned show that London University alone spent 39.4 per cent of the total. No other single university spent more than 7 per cent, and in 13 cases the share of the total was less than 1 per cent. University Grants Committee funds are intended to provide what is called the 'research floor'. Insofar as resources other than academic staff time are needed for the projects and programmes that stand upon this 'floor', these must usually be sought from the government-funded research councils (Science and Engineering, Agriculture and Food, Natural Environment, Medical, and Economic and Social), from government departments, from international agencies, or from independent trusts and charitable foundations. There is no research council for education. Research in this field is within the remit of the Economic and Social Research Council (until 1 January 1984 known as the Social Science Research Council). A limited volume of funds for studies that fall within the category of educational research also comes from some of the other councils. The Department of Education and Science currently spends approaching £10 million per annum on directly funded educational research of a policy-oriented character, a substantial proportion of this sum being used to support projects and programmes in universities and polytechnics. Degree-level and post-graduate courses and research opportunities are also offered by the polytechnics and many of the colleges and institutes of higher education that, together with the universities, contribute to higher education provision in England and Wales. Polytechnics and colleges do not receive explicit 'research floor' funding. Means are often found for a modest proportion of the resources made available through the local education authorities that fund them to be used to support research. Government departments and the research councils make grants and award contracts to polytechnic and college staff. The total volume of educational research undertaken in the non-university sector of higher education is, however, still small.

The major centre of research activity outside the universities is the National Foundation for Educational Research (NFER), established in 1944 and now located in its own premises some 20 miles from London. The Foundation has a total staff of around 120, and an annual budget of £1.8 million, derived from local education authority subventions and from contracts awarded by the Department of Education and Science (DES), by trusts and by other bodies.

Not everything that could reasonably be regarded as educational research is based at university, polytechnic and college departments of education or at the NFER. There are staff in departments of sociology and psychology, in various medical and child care specialities, in the research sections of local education authorities, employed by major charities, in government departments other than education and science, in further education colleges and schools, in the media and in private companies, all of whom in various ways engage in aspects of educational research, publish in the papers and journals of the trade and participate in professional conferences and gatherings.

Education is not a single discipline. Within the ranks of those who hold posts in the subject in departments and institutes there are men and women whose initial training might have been in one of the subjects of the school curriculum, or in any of the social sciences, or in philosophy or history. Most of them specialize in an aspect of educational study or research that draws upon their undergraduate and graduate training and experience. To an extent unusual in most other academic specialisms, some have switched disciplinary orientations at quite an advanced stage in their careers — from teaching physics to the study of educational adminis-tration, for example, or from music to psychology or sociology. In the larger schools and institutes of education the multi-disciplinary basis of educational studies is recognized through explicit departmental or sub-departmental organization.

In their 1981 study, Dooley et al found that 51 per cent of practising educational researchers were employed in universities, 13 per cent in polytechnics, 21 per cent in colleges of higher education (which for the most part had developed and diversified from former single-purpose colleges of education), 2 per cent were in research institutes, 6 per cent in primary or secondary schools and only 4 per cent elsewhere. A 'surprisingly high' proportion of educational researchers in universities, polytechnics and colleges were found to work other than in departments of education.

Lines of communication tend to be among specialists in particular aspects of educational research rather than within institutions. There is a Universities' Council for the Education of Teachers (UCET) which has a standing committee concerned with research, and a corresponding Poly-technic Council. Research issues are more prominent, however, in the work of bodies such as the British Educational Research Association (BERA), the Philosophy of Education Society, the education sections of the British Psychological Society and the British Sociological Association, the British Educational Management and Administration Society, the History of Education Society, and the many other voluntary, subscription-based organizations active on the educational scene (usually with British in their title and embracing the educational system of Scotland as well as that of England and Wales).

Outlets for the publication of research findings are numerous. There are at least 20 journals in which papers and reports regularly appear. The

British Education Index provides a comprehensive listing of publications in the field, and the NFER is responsible for producing (with financial assistance from the DES) a Register of Current Research. Such sources are increasingly supplemented by European and international data bases in education and the social sciences. There remains scope for considerable improvement in the availability of information on current research, especially in respect of the taxonomies used and the degree of discrimination applied to deciding what can be classified as 'research' and what is merely the statement or restatement of opinion.

Research and practice

Before looking at the work of some of the agencies involved in funding educational research, it may be useful to say something about its impact on educational practice.

In relation to total expenditure on education, and to the scale of research activities in fields such as science and engineering, medicine and agriculture, educational research in England and Wales is of modest dimensions. Except when controversy breaks out over politically salient findings on such matters as achievement scores or examination performances, moral education or discipline, its public and professional profile is low. When educational research is noticed, it tends to get a bad press on grounds of irrelevance or jargon or imprecision or lack of agreement among its experts.

The number of those involved full time in any aspect of educational research is quite small. Most of the work is done by junior researchers on short-term contracts, and by university teachers in time left over from teaching and other responsibilities. Yet the impact of research on what goes on in classrooms and lecture halls, and on what is said in debating chambers and committee rooms, cannot be measured in terms of how much is spent or how rare are the instances we can identify when research findings were critical for a particular decision or choice of action.

I have argued elsewhere (Taylor, 1973) that one of the chief functions of research in the social sciences in general, and in education in particular, is to make us aware of the existence and the dimensions of problems, to reveal their interconnections, to rule out some of the more obvious 'solutions', to add to and refine the concepts we employ to describe and to evaluate phenomena, to indicate which aspects are foreground and which background — in other words to sensitize us to what might otherwise be ignored, misunderstood or acted upon in blind faith.

Seen thus, it is not difficult to illustrate the existence of connections between research and policy. Examples include work on social class and educational opportunity and how we think about the organization of secondary education: awareness of the limited impact that initial teacher training has on the development of teacher professionalism, and the consequent stimulation of interest in strengthening in-service training

(INSET); the implications of studies of individual and group learning for the development of school-based and school-focused modes of INSET; investigations of the relations between class size and learning outcomes which pointed up the high opportunity cost involved in bringing about marginal improvements in staff-student ratios, and recognition of the fact that pupils' occupational orientations are formed well in advance of their exposure to formal counselling and guidance efforts.

In all these and a host of other areas, awareness — through reading, attendance at lectures and seminars, participation in conferences, the writing and discussion of administrative papers and interaction with peers — of a cumulation of research findings in a particular direction influences our agenda of concerns, the way in which we conceptualize problems and our choice of priorities for action. Sometimes such research creates awareness of what otherwise might be ignored. Sometimes it reinforces and helps to legitimate a line of thought and of action that reflects a particular set of educational values or objectives. Sometimes it throws doubt on the wisdom of going further down a particular path — the process that Wirt (1982:17) has referred to in the broader context of social science research as 'removing the unsupportable from discussion of public life'.

Such sensitizing is not, however, the whole story. Since the study of education draws upon many different disciplines and specialisms, few have knowledge of more than a small part of its total domain. It follows that outside our own narrow field, we are often incapable of judging the extent to which a particular finding has been crucial for other specialists, or has opened up fruitful lines of enquiry or action and closed others, or has 'settled' an issue in a way that, for a time at least, seems conclusive for fellow-researchers and for practitioners.

It is impossible here to review the work of all the agencies that help to sustain educational research efforts in England and Wales. Something does need to be said, however, about the main sources of such research support, with particular reference to the former Social Science Research Council (now the Economic and Social Research Council), the Department of Education and Science, the Schools Council for Curriculum and Examinations and the independent foundations. Whilst the National Foundation for Educational Research is a recipient rather than a provider of research funds, the importance of its work justifies consideration in a separate section.

The Social Science Research Council

As educational provision expanded in scale and scope from the end of the 1950s, it became more obvious how little systematic knowledge existed about what went on in classrooms, schools and administrative offices. The Crowther Report of 1959 (Central Advisory Council for Education) commented that 'In view of the very large sums of money that are spent on education every year, the expenditure on educational research can only be described as pitiable'. The heads of the departments and institutes of education of universities in England and Wales quoted this passage in a memorandum of May 1963 advocating the establishment of a self-standing Educational Research Council, and drew attention to a statement made in the House of Commons in 1962 to the effect that 'the Department of Scientific and Industrial Research spends more on research into glue than is spent on research in education'.

At the time few disagreed about the importance of educational research and the need for more of it. There was less agreement about how it might best be organized. Following the publication of the Crowther Report, a working party set up by the Ministry of Education had recommended that direct Ministry funding for projects and programmes be stepped up. Given this provision (albeit on a modest scale at first) there were those who thought that the more fundamental kinds of research on education would benefit from being pursued in close relation to other work in the social sciences, rather than under the sponsorship of a separate research council. The committee on the future of research in the social sciences set up by the Government under the chairmanship of Lord Heyworth considered the question and was in favour of educational research being one of the responsibilities of the Social Science Research Council, which they recommended be established forthwith.

The new Council began work in 1966. It set up an Educational Research Board (ERB) alongside 11 other specialist committees responsible for subjects within the social sciences. The Board continued in existence until 1982, when the Council's Committee structure was reorganized and the Board's functions were taken over by the new Education and Human Development Committee.

During the 16 years of its existence the ERB disbursed only modest sums in support of research projects and programmes in relation to the total resources available for educational research. I calculated in 1972 that its then share of this total was of the order of 8 per cent (Taylor, 1973). Nor has education ever attracted a large share of the studentships allocated by the Council in support of research training. In 1980-81 only 3.4 per cent of the 1,500 awards made were in this field, although it can be assumed that some of those in other subjects were for research relevant to educational issues. Yet the influence of the SSRC on educational research has been far greater than these percentages might suggest. There are several reasons why this should be so.

Especially in its early years, the Council was seen as the source of support for fundamental rather than applied research, the latter being the special province of the Department of Education and Science that had taken over the role of the former Ministry of Education in the early 1960s. This perceived division of labour lent prestige to work funded by the Council, further enhanced by the rigorous process of peer appraisal to which proposals for support were known to be subjected. The highest success rate of grant applications recorded in a single year for the whole range of subjects within the remit of the SSRC was 44 per cent in 1974-75. In 1976-77 the success rate fell as low as 22 per cent. Such rates were a function of funds available as well as a judgement on the quality of applications received, but the quality aspect was prominent in professional perceptions of the Council's work. To obtain grant funding from the SSRC conferred a mark of peer approval which did not apply in quite the same way in the case of support obtained from some other funding bodies.

The studentships which the Council allocated each year to departments and institutes of education were also regarded as indications of institutional standing. Individual applicants for such studentships had to name the departments in which their award would be held. The choices made, and the ERB's decisions about which departments were the most suitable locations for particular kinds of work to be pursued, were carefully scrutinized by university teachers of education.

Other factors which gave the Council greater influence on educational research than the scale of its activities might suggest were the support it provided for influential programmes such as the pre-school research carried out by a number of individuals and teams in universities; its establishment of designated research units with longer-term support – only one of which, however, was in educational research (the Thomas Coram Research Unit at the University of London Institute of Education) – and the initiatives that it undertook in such matters as accountability in education under the auspices of its Research Initiatives Board (RIB).

The setting-up of the RIB in 1974 was an innovation in relation to the way in which the Council had hitherto gone about funding research activity. In the words of its Annual Report for that year (p.10), the Council had 'no systematic way of handling those topics where it wished to promote research activity, and proposals were generally dealt with by *ad hoc* machinery – not always satisfactorily'. Proposals falling within the remit of the new Board would be those coming from some source other than the would-be researcher. The Council was at pains to point out that the introduction of these procedures did not '... in itself necessarily imply an increase in initiatives as opposed to research supported by the responsive mode.'

The problem to which the setting up of the RIB was a response was by no means unfamiliar to members of the Council's Educational Research Board. As early as 1968-69 they had begun to identify certain research priority areas, such as teacher education, pre-school provision and the education of minorities, in which they wished to stimulate applications for support. As Ward (1973:54) commented, the ERB had adopted 'a rather uneasy stance' on the question of a passive versus a directive role in research support:

'On the one hand they are not happy about an active directive role, but on the other hand they seem to be able and willing to determine priority areas and persuade researchers to work in them.'

In reporting the establishment of the RIB, the Council stressed its belief that 'most worthwhile ideas for research in social sciences have originated with the researchers themselves' (Annual Report, 1974-75:12) but argued that 'some potentially important fields of research fail to attract sufficient interest'. It was when this happened that initiatives might need to be taken by the Council.

By the next year, 'national needs' were beginning to receive greater emphasis. While the responsive funding of research remained 'a cornerstone of SSRC policy' it was not to receive a significantly larger share of the Council's budget (Annual Report 1975-76:8). The Report went on to state:

> 'One assumption underlying the decision to undertake initiatives is that the social sciences have an important contribution to make towards the solution of social problems and that the SSRC has an important role to play in giving some direction to the processes involved.' (Ibid:18)

The new Board had agreed that priority should go to supporting work useful 'for the formation of economic and social policy', and that special attention should be given to the research infrastructure and to multi-disciplinary studies. By the following year the Council could claim that the research initiatives mode of funding 'is now coming to be better understood and appreciated ...', and that the Council had been extending the system into areas 'which bear closely upon the critical problems of the national life'.

These emphases reflected political, professional and public concerns about the state of the economy, the social consequences of high rates of inflation, and the 'value' of the investment made in education — particular-ly in higher education — since the mid-1960s. The ideals and hopes with which the setting up of the SSRC had been associated were under attack. There was criticism about the allegedly small proportion of SSRC-supported students who obtained their degrees during the currency of their awards. The rapid growth in the social sciences that had been one of the most striking characteristics of university and polytechnic expansion in the late 1960s and early 1970s was slowing. Money was getting short. As recently as 1974-75 the Council had been able to state in its Annual Report:

> 'With many professional activities it is well recognised that labour has to be treated as a capital input rather than a current input. We plan to have so many doctors and so many school teachers, rather than to spend so many millions a year on their salaries ...'

But by the end of the decade cash limits were the rule, even in these pro-fessional fields. Between 1978 and 1981 the resources available to the SSRC were reduced in real terms by some 20 per cent. It became clear that the multiplicity of committees, panels and *ad hoc* groups set up over the years to deal with the Council's remits in research support and training were creating a heavy administrative burden and weakening channels of communication. The activities of the Research Initiatives Board alone had led to the creation of some 25 separate panels. Some rationalization was called for, and the Council responded by creating a new and simpler structure with only two Boards (for research and post-graduate training respectively), six standing committees (for social affairs, education and human development, industry and employment, economic affairs, environment and planning, and government and law) and a small number of Council sub-committees. It was planned that the two Boards would in due course disappear as their functions were assumed by the Council and the Committees. The new structure was to come into operation by May 1982. But before this could happen, the Secretary of State ordered an external enquiry into the work of the Council, to be undertaken by Lord Rothschild, whose report of the organization and management of government research and development (1971, Cmnd 4814) had established the 'customer-contractor' principle in research funding. It has been suggested (Flather, 1982) that the Government had at first wished simply to abolish the Council, but had been dissuaded from 'a quick kill' by some of their senior civil servants and junior ministers.

Lord Rothschild's report on the Social Science Research Council (1982, Cmnd 8554) was published in May 1982. Contrary to the expectations of those who had feared the worst, the report recommended that the Government 'should not dismember or liquidate the SSRC' (para 1.10). Certain deficiencies were identified that should be rectified, but the Government was advised not to further reduce the Council's budget in real terms, and to avoid further external enquiries for a period of at least three years. In a statement that particularly attracted attention, Lord Rothschild averred that the abolition of the SSRC 'would not only be an act of intellectual vandalism ...; it would also have damaging consequences for the whole country — and ones from which it would take a long time to recover' (para 11.19).

The SSRC was 'greatly encouraged' by the outcome of the Rothschild enquiry. The Secretary of State accepted the recommendations, but was unable to guarantee the Council's budget for three years, and a further small reduction was subsequently imposed. But survival was assured.

The new committee structure was introduced immediately after the completion of the Rothschild Report. The education community was by no means happy about the disappearance of the Educational Research Board. During the 16 years of its existence it had become a familiar and generally respected feature of the educational research scene. Service upon it was no sinecure. The Chairmanship, in particular, imposed heavy demands on the time and attention of its part-time occupants, who had at the same time to go on running their own university departments. The system by means of which research applications were processed, refereed, evaluated and judged required members to devote considerable time to pre-meeting preparation and, in the case of requests for programme support, to site visits. All this strengthened the ERB's status as a guardian of standards, and the ability of a department to attract SSRC grants and studentships was regarded as a significant mark of its professional and academic standing.

Anxieties about the new arrangements had less to do with fears about any relaxation of standards than with the ability of educational research as such to hold its own among the broader range of subject matter for which the new multi-disciplinary Education and Human Development Committee would be responsible. The new committee issued a discussion paper on its priorities for research, and made clear that

'... by proposing research along particular lines, the Committee has no wish to discourage good proposals of all kinds made through the normal research grant scheme. Many lines of research attract proposals without the Committee's promptings. Innovative research proposals in particular can arise which no Committee is likely to invent. There are areas, however, in which a Committee may perceive that − for one reason or another − insufficient work is being done.'

The main headings of the list of topics offered were information technology, knowledge structures, social influences on child development, teacher education, special educational needs, regional varieties of British English, children in care and the 16 to 19 age group.

Although the acceptance by the Government of the main Rothschild recommendations meant that the future of the SSRC was assured, the continuation of its name was not. In October 1982 the Secretary of State asked the Council to consider 'whether its name might not more accurately reflect the range of studies and methods embraced by its work'. After considerable internal debate, it was finally resolved that the word 'Science' should be dropped, and on 1 January 1984 the SSRC became the ESRC − the Economic and Social Research Council. Although the cuts of recent years have much reduced the Council's ability to finance projects and programmes and to fund studentships and other forms of research training, it is likely to continue to exercise a significant influence on the scope and direction of research in education, and on the training of research practitioners.

The Department of Education and Science

The Education Act of 1944 (which still provides the legislative basis for a great deal of current educational practice) included provisions that enabled the Ministry of Education to fund educational research. But up to the beginning of the 1960s these were used only to provide grant-in-aid for the work of the National Foundation for Educational Research (NFER).

The working party set up by the Ministry in response to the Crowther Report of 1959 and criticisms made in Parliament of the knowledge base of educational policy and practice recommended that direct initiatives be taken to fund research. At first, the sums involved were modest. In 1962-63 grants totalled only some £20,000. Within the next few years, however, a rapid expansion took place in the number of projects sponsored by the Ministry (which became the Department of Education and Science in 1964). By 1972, the Department was able to issue a list of some 264

projects on which work had been completed. The distribution of these
between topics is of interest in relation to subsequent developments.
Seventeen categories were used, corresponding fairly closely to the
'Branches' of the Department's own internal organization. These are
shown below, with the number of projects on which payment of grant had
been completed by 1972.

A.	Schools Organization	19
B.	Schools Curriculum	6
C.	Schools Examinations	7
D.	Projects commissioned for the Central Advisory Councils for Education (England and Wales)	15
E.	Projects commissioned for the Schools Council for Curriculum and Examinations	34
F.	Special Education	15
G.	Further Education	23
H.	Teacher Training and Supply	14
I.	Higher Education	5
J.	General	19
K.	Sociology in Education	14
L.	Educational Technology	42
M.	Modern Languages	19
N.	Educational Planning, Economics and Finance	11
O.	Architects and Building Projects	11
P.	Science	10

During the 1960s the Department financed a wide range of research, much
of it in the responsive mode, ie on the basis of proposals submitted by
researchers themselves. By the end of the decade the Department was
moving from a policy of 'passive patronage' to one of 'active commissioning'. In the words of the then Secretary of State for Education, Mrs
Margaret Thatcher:

> 'By the late 1960s it was becoming clear that a policy of general
> support for research on the basis of patronage could not be relied
> upon to produce results of practical value to the Department in its
> own concerns — successful as it might be in its broad purposes of
> promoting the growth of activity and adding to the sum of human
> knowledge about Education.' (Speech to the Annual Conference of
> the NFER, December 1970)

This new policy-oriented approach was recognized as imposing constraints
on officials and research workers alike. The former could no longer merely
satisfy themselves as to the soundness in research terms of a particular
proposal and then leave the researcher to get on with the work. Instead,
they would need 'to expose [their] problems, and their own thoughts
about them, to people whose background and approach will — if they do
their job properly — lead to awkward questions. It requires them to take
an active interest, perhaps even an active part, in the work as it develops.'

For the research worker, some limitations on freedom to define the problem in his own terms, and acceptance of the perspectives and constraints of the policy maker offered the compensation of 'the expectation that his work will contribute to the formation of national policy'.

The views expressed by Mrs Thatcher in this statement reflected the active role in educational research that by 1970 was being taken by the Social Science Research Council and by the Schools Council. These bodies could be expected to take on research and development activities of a kind the Department had previously financed but which would not now sit easily with the policy of active commissioning of policy-relevant studies. The statement also reflected a certain scepticism on the part of politicians and officials about the value of much of the work supported over the preceding years. Such scepticism tended to be more strongly felt by Conservative administrations than by Labour, who claimed a greater commitment to knowledge-based social engineering, rather than dependence upon the operation of markets.

As the institutional structures committed to educational research grew in size and complexity and economic constraints began to influence resource allocations, so opportunities grew for doubts to be expressed about the 'usefulness' of a proportion of the research being undertaken by universities and research organizations. Attempts to relate such work more directly to policy concerns, and to involve officials more closely in its execution, would enable a greater measure of 'quality control' to be exercised than in the case of 'free research' financed in the responsive mode.

The Department continued to be an important source of funds for educational research throughout the 1970s. A statement about the objectives of its directly funded research programme was made in reply to a 1977-78 Council of Europe enquiry:

'The two main objectives of this department's involvement in educational research are:
a. to improve the quality of educational processes and their outcomes, especially in those areas where there is greatest public concern, and where there are the greatest opportunities for improvement through government action.
b. to assist the formulation of national policies and enlarge the foundations of knowledge on which these are based; and to monitor and evaluate the implementation of such policies.'

The so-called 'Great Debate' on education of 1977-78 had identified the performance of schools as one such area of public concern, and a substantial proportion of the Department's research budget was soon taken up with performance assessment. By the beginning of 1984 over 42 per cent of DES research spending was on aspects of pupil performance. The total departmental commitment to research amounted to nearly £10 million, spread over nine policy fields. The percentage spent on each of these is shown overleaf, calculated from the Department's List 1, 'Current

Educational Research Projects Supported by the DES'.

DES Educational Research Support Across Nine Policy Fields (Percentage of total current programme expenditure, calculated from DES List 1, 1984)	%	% sub-total
1. Nursery, pre-school and transition to infant school		0.79
2. Pupil performance		
a. The assessment of performance unit	42.37	
b. The effectiveness of schools	6.69	
c. General	2.81	
		51.87
3. Children with special needs		
a. Gifted children	0.99	
b. Ethnic minorities	3.08	
c. General	5.07	
		9.14
4. Transition from school to work		18.49
5. Curriculum		
a. Mathematics	3.15	
b. General	2.38	
		5.53
6. Teacher training		1.42
7. Management in education		
a. Staffing	5.64	
b. General	2.33	
		7.97
8. Further and higher education		
a. Further education	2.56	
b. Higher education	1.82	
c. Adult education	0.25	
		4.63
9. General		0.02
Total		100.00

Examination of the projects funded under each of these headings shows that the intentions of the Department to devote its resources to policy-oriented research have been largely fulfilled. It is rather more doubtful if the effect has been to create a new relationship between officials and researchers whereby the former participate more actively in the research process and the efforts of the latter can more clearly be seen to influence policy making. Some officials are more interested in research than others. Even within the overall commitment to policy-oriented research, there are inevitably differences in the extent to which research findings can be 'used' in the processes of policy-making and implementation. Although the emphasis is now on 'commissioned' work — sometimes offered on the basis of tenders submitted by universities and research organizations in response to published specifications — there is still a place for funding in the responsive mode. The Department is 'prepared to consider proposals submitted by research institutions from outside the Department, provided they satisfy [its] criteria or can, if necessary, be modified to meet the current research needs of the Department' (List 1, 1983:1).

The DES has directly funded educational research for more than 20 years. During that time many hundreds of projects and programmes have been supported. Some of the resulting reports have, at least for a time, exercised an important influence on thinking and action in their respective specialist fields. Some have been the subject of controversy. Others have been given little attention, even by those directly involved in work to which the project claimed to relate. Ministers and officials have not always shown public enthusiasm for their research programme. A statement by one Permanent Secretary to the effect that 'the great thing about research is that a part of it is rubbish and another part (I will not be specific about the proportions) leads nowhere and is really indifferent' has been quoted as typical of the Department's attitude. Yet just as it is difficult to generalize about the overall impact of a research programme as varied and diverse as that of the Department, so it is unjustified to take one or two individual public statements as adequate indications of what all Ministers and officials believe to be the value and impact of educational research.

Despite all the doubts and vicissitudes to which the research programme has been subject, the lack of publicly expressed conviction about its usefulness, and the apparent inability of the Department to make up its mind about the best way to manage its own research effort (first organizing it centrally in its planning group, then devolving responsibility to individual policy branches), the fact remains that the Department has gone on funding work in universities, polytechnics and specialist research organizations for over two decades. To spend £10 million per annum on research may not be much in relation to the total education budget. It certainly does not satisfy many of those who are acutely conscious of continuing deficiencies in the knowledge base of educational practice. The distribution of funds within the research budget, with nearly half going to various aspects of the assessment of performance, fails to please those with other priorities. Nonetheless, fears that governments would cease direct funding of educational research altogether, and of the possibility of political interference, have not been realized. The Department is active in directly supporting valuable policy-oriented work, and seems likely to remain so.

The Schools Council for Curriculum and Examinations

Systematic efforts to reform the school curriculum did not begin with the

efforts of the Nuffield Foundation and other independent bodies in the
early 1960s, important as these were in paving the way for the setting up
of the Schools Council for Curriculum and Examinations and the spate of
curriculum development and research that went on under its auspices over
the next 15 years. There have always been curriculum reformers who wish
to convert teachers to their views. Some have set up schools which
embody their ideas. The curriculum development movement that developed
in the United States and in this country in the late 1950s and early 1960s
was different.

1. It made explicit the association between the updating of syllabuses
   and teaching methods in the schools and such broader objectives as
   the improvement of national economic performance, the promotion
   of social justice and the creation of a more responsible democracy.
2. It had no specific commitment to a particular educational method or
   set of curriculum principles; its emphasis was on ways in which
   curriculum change would be brought about and on the relations
   between research, innovation, experiment, evaluation and implementation.
3. It required active teacher involvement in the process of development,
   through participation in the governance of curriculum agencies, the
   appraisal of new materials, school-based experiment and trial, and
   subsequent evaluation.
4. It enjoyed strong official support. Government money was used to
   establish suitable agencies and to back their endeavours to reform
   the work of primary and secondary schools.
5. It was thought important that the bodies concerned should be free
   from day-to-day government interference, and accountable to the
   teachers whose efforts they existed to encourage and to redirect.

All these considerations featured in the decision to set up the Schools
Council for Curriculum and Examinations in 1964. The Ministry of
Education was conscious of post-Sputnik emphases in the United States on
improved teaching and learning in science and mathematics, as well as in
other subjects, and of the efforts that independent foundations such as
Nuffield were beginning to make in this country. International organizations were also showing an interest. Official UK delegates began to feel
that it was not enough to 'incant the doctrine that in Britain the teacher
was a law unto himself' (Gosden, 1983:76).
    The initial step of setting up a Curriculum Study Group within the
Ministry soon ran into trouble. Teachers' organizations feared an increase
in centralized control in an area in which teachers claimed a large measure
of autonomy — although there had been a long period from the closing
decades of the 19th century to the immediately pre-World War II years
when the then Board of Education had laid down syllabuses and issued
'Handbooks of Suggestions for Teachers'.
    After a period of consultation in which the Ministry was at pains to
show that central control of the curriculum was neither desired nor

contemplated, the Schools Council came into being in October 1964. Given its representative character, with local education authorities, teachers, universities, commerce and industry all given places on its Council and steering committees, its structure was inevitably complicated.

The new Council inherited a substantial volume of curriculum work already under way, and soon began to add projects and programmes of its own. Within five years it was responsible for some 93 separate projects covering most aspects of the school curriculum, and was already speaking of the need for 'consolidation' and the extension of existing projects by means of dissemination years.

The distinction between curriculum development and curriculum research within the Council's spread of activities was never clear-cut. In the words of its report for 1970-71 (p. 19):

> 'On the one hand, development work must take account of existing research knowledge in its planning stage; the evaluation of curriculum development work is essentially a research exercise; and terminal evaluation demands the rigour and technical know-how of the researcher. Equally any research proposal submitted to the Council is likely to be approved only when a pay-off in terms of immediate value to teachers in classrooms can be anticipated, which means in effect that all Council research projects are intended to promote curriculum development.'

On this basis, the Council judged that about a quarter of its projects were part of its research programme, 'in that the emphasis is on investigation, survey, testing and examinations rather than on the production of class-room teaching materials'. It was also suggested that large-scale research programmes such as the Council had funded during its first few years of operation were less likely to find favour in future. It was anticipated that 'fundamental research' would be supported by bodies such as the SSRC. The Schools Council would also need to devote its limited resources to other priorities, such as examinations.

Despite these caveats, for some time the Council continued to be an important source of research funds in education. A high proportion of its research and development projects were located in university schools, departments and institutes of education. In 1972 I calculated that it provided about a fifth of all the funds available in support of educational research, including those derived from University Grants Committee block grants to universities (Taylor 1973:16).

In reviewing the first ten years of its life the Council again emphasized that it had been no part of its role 'to determine the curriculum which any school might use; rather, the Council's aim has been to make available a wide range of materials and suggestions which schools might adopt or adapt as they felt to be desirable' (Annual Report, 1974-75:11). Although some changes had been made to the constitution of the Council, it was still 'a free association of equal partners representing all the principal education interests, but with a teacher majority ...' (Ibid: 10).

The range and catholicity of the Council's research activities can be seen from the titles of the research studies published in the single year 1975-76. These were:

Authority and Organization in the Secondary School
The Aims of Primary Education: a study of teachers' opinions
A Science Teaching Observation Schedule
Science 5-13: a Formative Evaluation
The Development of Writing Abilities (11 to 18)
The Reliability of Examinations at 16+
O Level examined: the Effect of Question Choice
Parents and Teachers
Curriculum Evaluation Today: Trends and Implications.

The year 1976 saw the initiation of what came to be called the 'Great Debate' in Education. The Labour Government then in power had become conscious of the way in which the Conservative opposition was exploiting apparent public dissatisfaction with the performance of the nation's schools. The then Prime Minister asked for a report from senior officials at the Department of Education and Science. Although never published, parts of this report, popularly known as the 'Yellow Book', subsequently appeared in the press. It was clear that officials shared some of the politicians' anxieties about the quality of schooling. A speech by the Prime Minister at Ruskin College, Oxford, which reflected certain of the 'Yellow Book's' concerns, sparked off a public debate in the course of which the work of many established institutions came in for comment and criticism.

The Schools Council was not excluded from this process: paragraphs 50 and 51 and Appendix Five of the 'Yellow Book' referred specifically to the Council. They stated:

'The Schools Council has performed moderately in commissioning development work in particular curricula areas; it has had little success in tackling examination problems ...; and it has scarcely begun to tackle the problems of the curriculum as a whole. Despite some good quality staff work, the overall performance of the Schools Council has in fact, both on curriculum and on examination, been generally mediocre. Because of this and because the influence of the teachers unions has led to an increasingly political flavour − in the worst sense of that word − in its deliberations, the general reputation of the Schools Council has suffered a considerable decline over the last few years.' (quoted in Tomlinson, 1981:8).

The then Chairman of the Council persuaded the Secretary of State that an internal, rather than external, review was the best way of dealing with the criticisms reflected in the 'Yellow Book'. The Governing Body agreed in January 1977 that an internal review of the Council's role, constitution and structure should be undertaken, and during 1978 a number of changes were made. Prominent among these were constitutional amendments which, it has been argued, served to strengthen the hand of the Department of Education in the Council's affairs, and to diminish the power of the teachers' professional organizations. In parallel, the Council decided to introduce a new pattern of funding research and development activities. In the words of its Chairman:

> 'In future, the Council will adopt a programme of work which has been agreed as necessary by the constituent parts of the education service and those it serves — teachers, the Department of Education and Science, local education authorities and representatives of parents, employers and the public. It will not, therefore, be reacting to relatively unconnected and sporadic proposals from the world of research and curriculum development; instead it will have a coherent programme made up of themes which have been identified as needing work done on them.' (Schools Council Report 1978-79, Chairman's Preface: 5).

Following its reconstitution, the Council declared a moratorium on new work and, after an extensive round of consultations, announced five new three-year programmes. These were concerned respectively with purpose and planning in schools, helping individual teachers to become more effective, developing the curriculum for a changing world, individual pupils and improving the examination system.

But this was not enough to assuage the criticisms expressed in the 'Yellow Book' to the effect that the Council's work was only 'mediocre' and that teacher control meant in practice domination by teacher trade unions which had increasingly politicized the Council's proceedings. As part of a general review of 'quangos', the DES initiated an external review.

As in the case of Lord Rothschild's later review of the Social Science Research Council, the outcome of the Review was rather more favourable to the Council than some had feared. It was recommended that the Council should continue as a representative body and with its existing functions. The Council's Chairman greeted the report as a 'clear affirmation' of the importance of the Council and the need for its continuing existence.

In the event, the Secretary of State did not feel able to accept the Review's recommendations, and decided the Council should be closed down in its existing form and be replaced by two smaller bodies, one for examinations and the other for curriculum, each consisting of members who, after appropriate consultation, would be appointed by the Secretary of State himself.

At the time of writing these new bodies were only just beginning work. It remains to be seen what resources they have at their disposal for support of research and development activities, but in January 1984 it was announced that the Secondary Examinations Council would be undertaking a 'multi-million pound research and development programme' linked to the Secretary of State's call for higher standards in schools and the introduction of criterion referenced tests (Wood, 1984).

It is too early to assess the overall impact of the Schools Council's work

on the curriculum of primary and secondary schools during the 19 years of
its existence from 1964 to 1983. Studies that it undertook on the take-up
and impact of its development activities were not particularly encouraging.
In the words of the Council's Secretary in the Report for 1978-79 (p. 9)
one study had shown 'that the Council needs to find more effective ways
of stimulating change, since much of the Council's work has evidently
made little impact on the intended audience'. In relation to developments
in educational research, Council-sponsored activities did a good deal to
emphasize the need for attention to be given to dissemination; revealed
weaknesses in the 'rational curriculum planning' model of educational
change; stimulated study of the social and educational organization of
classrooms; provided opportunities for significant numbers of teachers to
spend a period attached to university education departments; developed
innovative methods for the monitoring of examinations, and made
available a very large quantity of teaching materials and ideas in nearly
every aspect of the primary and secondary curriculum. For nearly 20 years
the Schools Council was an important element on the educational research
scene in England and Wales. Its successor body, the School Curriculum
Development Committee, which met for the first time in February 1984,
has assumed responsibility for a number of major projects initiated by the
Schools Council, including a major review of science teaching in the
secondary school, the teaching of economics to 14- to 16-year-olds and of
geography to the 16 to 19 age group, the industrial project, guidelines for
review and internal development in schools, the mother-tongue project and
dealing with disruptive pupils. These studies will require an expenditure of
about £600,000 a year. It can be expected that the Curriculum committee
will itself initiate new work. The disappearance of the Schools Council as a
representative body does not mean that curriculum research in England or
Wales will cease or become less important, but it may indicate the wish of
central government to exercise more influence on the direction of such
research and development work.

The independent foundations

Educational researchers in England and Wales looking for project support
are not limited to the agencies funded from public funds such as the DES
and the SSRC. They are also able to apply to one of the many independent
foundations and trusts that make grants for work in this field. Such bodies
include well-known names such as Nuffield, Leverhulme, Gulbenkian,
Wolfson, Ford, Rowntree and Van Leer, a variety of specialized charities
that commission or sponsor work relevant to their own particular concerns,
and many smaller, lesser-known trusts that from time to time are willing to
find money for a deserving educational cause.
    Some of the independent trusts have more-or-less explicit policies as to
the kinds of work they are willing to support. For example, the Leverhulme
Foundation, which backed a major review of higher education in Britain

between 1981 and 1983, has indicated that it is particularly interested in research projects in education that have to do with 'the improvement of training for industry and the better use of human resources in general'. During one recent year support was provided for work on educational policy and British manufacturing industry; the careers and training of science and engineering graduates; the educational needs of technicians employed by small firms; the development of teaching materials on statistics for 16- to 19-year-olds; the evaluation of teaching strategies in political education; children's understanding of spatial terms in musical and mathematical contexts, and the educational progress of mature students. In the quinquennium 1976-80 the Trust spent more than £1 million on some 65 different research projects in education.

Another body currently active in educational research is the Gulbenkian Foundation, which particularly supports work in the Arts and with an 'action' component. Recent studies backed by Gulbenkian include major reviews of music and dance education, the teaching of the Arts in schools and in higher education, and the treatment of gifted children in schools.

Examination of the list of projects being undertaken by the staff of one of the larger university schools or departments of education would show a very broad spread of support, including the major public bodies and a number of specialist and independent sources. Generally speaking, staff are free to look for backing for their work from any likely source. There is no official or university requirement that public funding bodies be approached or informed about a particular initiative. Lack of formal coordination between the various sources of funding for research may produce some superficial loss in 'efficiency', in that consideration of a less than adequate proposal can take up the time of more than one agency, but it greatly reduces the possibility that some 'spurious orthodoxy' will inhibit the funding of an unusual but promising idea. The lack of a coordinated system of educational research funding in England and Wales, and the multiplicity of relatively small bodies involved may look untidy, but such pluralism also has great advantages.

The National Foundation for Educational Research

The NFER began life with the aid of a grant from the Carnegie Corporation of New York and in association with the University of London Institute of Education. Sir Fred Clarke, Director of the Institute from 1943 to 1948 had been involved in the pre-war International Examinations Enquiry, and the origins of the NFER are attributed to the Committee which oversaw the English and Welsh contribution to that enquiry. The Foundation was formally constituted in 1945. From the beginning it was constituted as a body representative of a wide range of educational interests – the local education authorities that maintain schools and employ teachers, the universities and the teachers' associations.

Nearly four decades later, the Foundation retains its representative character. It also retains, despite considerable diversification and a greatly increased scale of activity, its original commitment to the improvement of all aspects of guidance, testing, assessment, and examination.

In a policy statement issued in 1953, the NFER stated its intention to 'concentrate on problems of educational guidance in a wide sense of that term' (Yates, 1972:8) and to develop a programme 'designed to assist teachers to discover abilities and aptitudes, to demonstrate the most suitable methods and materials of learning, and to indicate the standards of achievement which can reasonably be expected.' This commitment has been maintained. At the time this statement was issued, the NFER published 36 tests. Thirty years later, the 'Educational Guidance and Assessment Catalogue' runs to 70 large pages and lists some 230 separate tests and instruments, some generally available, others restricted to registered users.

In 1950-51 the NFER had a total income of the order of £14,000. In 1983, operating income from sponsored research, from membership subscriptions – mainly local education authorities – and from other sources totalled over £1,700,000. A very large proportion – over 90 per cent – of sponsored research income is from the Government. The Department of Education and Science and the Welsh Office provide £1,123,000 and a large part of the remainder also comes from official bodies, including the Department of Education for Northern Ireland, the Department of Employment, the Department of Health and Social Security, and the British Library.

The DES/Welsh Office support for NFER in 1983 provided for 24 separate projects in the form of grants and contracts, varying in amount from more than a quarter of a million pounds (Monitoring Performance in Language) to as little as £2,315 (Evaluation of the Oxfordshire Language Unit). The larger contracts show a strong emphasis on the monitoring of performance, reflecting the concern that the DES has in recent years shown for greater instructional effectiveness. That this concern is still high on the educational agenda was shown in the speech delivered in January 1984 to the North of England Education Conference by the Secretary of State for Education, Sir Keith Joseph. The work of the DES-based Assessment of Performance Unit, which performs rather similar functions in England and Wales to the National Assessment of Educational Progress (NAEP) in the United States, is heavily dependent on the development and evaluation studies undertaken by the NFER. The monitoring teams for mathematics, English and foreign languages are all part of the Foundation.

By no means all the Foundation's current work is concerned with testing and assessment. Among the projects on which grant was paid in 1983 was a critical review of research on the education of ethnic minority children, the exchange of management information on educational policy and practice, careers officer management by pupil appraisal systems, evaluation of the training of hearing therapists, and the production of a register of current educational research. This last is a particular responsibility of the Foundation, and the Register provides the only source of information about the full range of work going on in universities, polytechnics, colleges, local authority research units, government departments and other specialized agencies. The Foundation is also active in the dissemination of research results.

As the sources of funding, the range of work and the number of specialist university- and polytechnic-based units grew during the 1960s, and the differentiation implied by systematic testing became unfashionable, there were those who thought that the NFER would lose the position in educational research that it had occupied since 1945. No such loss has occurred. The Foundation's commitment to and expertise in many aspects of educational testing and guidance has stood it in good stead at a time when the improvement of standards and of pupil performance has been high on the policy agenda. Although the Foundation's work is by no means confined to these areas, it has not attempted to develop the broader and more theoretical interests that some university-based observers would have liked to see. As befits an organization backed by local education authorities and teachers' organizations, the Foundation has retained an essentially practical orientation, emphasizing service and responsiveness to policy needs rather than theoretical innovativeness. With a professional and support staff some 130 strong, the NFER is Britain's largest single-purpose unit conducting research into education, and given its recent success in competing for DES research contracts, seems likely to retain this position. The functions that it performs are in many other systems the responsibility of units within Ministries of Education. The constitution and basis of governance of the NFER reflects the importance that is attached in England and Wales to the concept of a partnership in educational provision between government, the local authorities, the teachers' organizations and the universities and other higher education institutions. Although it is often argued that this partnership is rhetorical rather than real, and that central government has been assuming a more and more dominant role, the fact remains that local authorities continue to maintain schools and to employ the teachers that staff them, and that institutions of higher education enjoy substantial freedom from direct government control. Although the current scale of the NFER's activities is dependent on continuing success in attracting research contracts from government and elsewhere, its constitutional independence as a company limited by guarantee is of no little importance in relation to the partnership concept.

Centralism, control and the future

Increased centralism in education implies a movement of power and authority away from individual teachers, heads and local authorities towards national bodies. Such imagery may give a false impression of what has been happening in the last ten years in England and Wales. It suggests that decisions formerly taken at institutional or local level are now taken nationally. The reality may be that the absence of central decision making reflected not local autonomy but the ability to rely upon an implicit consensus about what needed to be done and how it might be tackled. It could reasonably be assumed that teachers and heads and local authority administrators had been socialized within a framework of agreed common values which made external control unnecessary.

This assumption has been weakened on two main fronts. First, by the effects of rapid social and technological change, which has undermined traditional structures of authority and compliance, has vastly increased the scale of educational activity, and has created complex structures of management and control. Second, by greater likelihood of action based on the pursuit of single-interest economic advantage. Given the necessity that governments feel of containing public expenditure in order to control inflation, the likelihood of central initiatives is much increased. This is not so much a shift of power from local and institutional to national levels, as the intervention of the state in areas of national life hitherto ordered by an implicit consensus. As might be expected, the rhetoric of this process includes frequent references to 'national needs', the importance of 'coherent policies' and the value of participation, all of which testify to the loss of value consensus to which the central initiative is a response.

Rapid change and single-interest politics also create an atmosphere of anxiety and uncertainty, a fear of control being lost and worries about the consequences of disorder. Economic difficulties put a premium on wealth-creating activities and on the value of science and technology. These influences come together in attempts to render educational processes in terms of technique rather than art, in the importance attached to efficiency and value for money, even in the attractions of the computer as a symbol of greater certainty and control. In such an atmosphere, organizations and activities which cannot readily establish a legitimate production function, which possess structures of governance inherited from the days of rapid economic and educational growth, and which are identified with values inconsistent with contemporary social goals are inevitably at risk.

Conclusion

I have argued (Taylor, 1973) that if educational research is to prosper it requires an appropriate institutional framework, adequate resources of money and manpower, and a sympathetic political and professional climate. Few of those currently active in the field would maintain these conditions are well met at the present time. With the demise of the Schools Council and the virtual withdrawal from the educational research scene of some of the independent agencies active in the past, there are now fewer sources of outside support available. The universities have suffered major cuts in staffing and resources, and there have as yet been few 'new blood' posts allocated to education to replace those left unfilled or lost as a result of resignation and full-term and premature retirement. Since there is a tendency for younger lecturers to be more active in research than their seniors, changes in the age-structure of education staff in universities and polytechnics will to some extent diminish overall research capacity in this (as in other) fields. There are still few opportunities to make a career in educational research, although lack of employment possibilities elsewhere ensures no shortage of well-qualified applicants even for short-term appointments. With growing emphasis on all kinds of in-service training for serving teachers, there has been an increase in the numbers registering for and obtaining higher degrees, although most of this growth has been in taught courses at Master's level rather than for research awards. There are current anxieties about the emphasis that research councils (including the ESRC) are putting upon the training element in research programmes for higher degrees. Until now the measure of success has been the final product, in the shape of a completed thesis, the subsequent publications that derive from it and the impact of the work on ideas and practice in the specialism concerned, rather than the production of better qualified research workers. Such an approach has been justified in part by the absence of opportunities for those who obtain research degrees to continue with active research careers. There is some official interest in rethinking the traditional research-based PhD in a way that, as in the United States, makes greater provision for taught course elements and systematic training in research methodology. This could make for difficulties in the case of subjects like education where a high proportion of research students are part-time.

Universities and other higher education institutions active in educational research have expressed some anxiety about the effect on their work of the time commitment implied by new requirements for more detailed accreditation of the initial teacher education programmes with which many staff are involved. The length of the one-year post-graduate certificate in education course in university and polytechnic departments of education is to be increased to 36 weeks. University staff maintain that this will cut the time available for personal and team research and for research supervision.

There are anxieties about the weakening of the 'research floor' that has come about as a result of cuts in university resources since 1981. Such anxieties are not restricted to education. A series of reports from the Advisory Board for the Research Councils (ABRC), from the Royal Society and from other bodies has underlined the potential consequences for research of a reduction in resources. Even if project and programme money continues to be available, the capacity of universities to operate within the dual system of research support (UGC-provided 'research floor' plus project funds) will have been weakened.

The fact that research council grants do not include an element for 'overheads' is an important consideration in assessing the effect of resource constraints on the floor of support.

There is also concern about greater centralized control. To a much greater extent than in the past, funding bodies have felt the obligation to develop explicit support policies and to state their priorities. There is less 'free money' (Taylor, 1981) available than in the past. Insofar as this helps to focus research interest on issues of pressing public concern, and to legitimate expenditure that might otherwise be vulnerable, it contributes to the maintenance of support for and the impact of educational research. There is always the risk, however, that current themes and immediate problems may divert attention from more fundamental questions, on which research is more difficult to justify in terms of early pay-off. It is tempting for researchers whose real interest is in such fundamental questions to present their requests for funds in a form that promises more by way of early outcome than it is in practice possible to deliver. The inadequacies of the resulting reports do nothing to strengthen the claims of educational research for a larger share of resources.

Research in education, as in other scientific, social and applied fields, is virtually open-ended in its capacity to absorb funds — provided that an adequate number of trained research workers are available. There are thousands of topics on which it would be good to have better information based upon careful observation, close documentary study, rigorous conceptual analysis and systematic experiment. The amount that governments and private agencies are willing to spend on such research turns on calculations of benefit based upon political and professional opinion about the possibility of research yielding well-founded information and judgements about the uses to which such knowledge can be put, and about the likelihood of its being successfully used to achieve desirable ends. Given the contested nature of many educational values, research support is more easily obtained for projects that promise some tangible outcome, such as the validation of a particular teaching technique, or the development and standardization of a useful test, or the measurement of the relative success that different teachers and schools have in achieving their objectives, than for studies of broader and less easily defined problems. This should cause no surprise. It is part of the responsibility of the bodies concerned, however, to ensure that an appropriate balance exists between various kinds of educational research, loosely categorized as policy-oriented, strategic, basic and fundamental, and that a sufficient proportion of available funds is spent in the responsive mode to ensure that new and promising, if unorthodox, proposals — and people — receive consideration and support. If research is merely the handmaiden of current policies, then its potential as a source of knowledge that can be employed for the improvement of educational practice is likely to remain unfulfilled.

References

Central Advisory Council for Education (1959) *Sixteen to Nineteen* (Crowther Report) HMSO: London
Cohen, L, Thomas, J and Manion, L eds (1982) *Educational Research and Development in Britain 1970-1980* NFER-Nelson: Windsor
Dooley, P A, Graham, N C and Whitfield, R C *et al* (1981) *Survey of Educational Researchers in Britain* Aston Educational Enquiry, Occasional Paper No 4: The University of Aston: Birmingham

Flather, P (1982) Conspiracies and counterplots *Times Higher Educational Supplement* 22 January

Gosden, P (1983) *The Educational System since 1944* Martin Robertson: Oxford

Mitzel, H E ed (1982) *Encyclopaedia of Educational Research* Fifth Edition: [Four Volumes] The Free Press: New York

Oldham, G ed (1982) *The Future of Research* Leverhulme Programme of Study into the Future of Higher Education, Monograph 4. Society for Research into Higher Education: Guildford

Rothschild, Lord (1971) *The Organisation and Management of Government Research and Development* (Cmnd 4814) HMSO: London

Rothschild, Lord (1982) *An Enquiry into the Social Science Research Council* (Cmnd 8554) HMSO: London

Schools Council (1980) *Annual Report for 1978/79*

Social Science Research Council (1975) *Annual Report for 1974/75*

Social Science Research Council (1976) *Annual Report for 1975/76*

Suppes, P ed (1978) *Impact of Research on Education: some case studies* National Academy of Education: Washington DC

Taylor, W ed (1973) *Research Perspectives in Education* Routledge and Kegan Paul: London

Taylor, W (1981) Education research and development in the UK *International Review of Education* 27 179-196

Tomlinson, J R G (1981) *The Schools Council: a Chairman's Salute and Envoi* Schools Council: London

Ward, V (1973) *Resources for Educational Research and Development* NFER Publishing Co: Windsor

Wirt, F (1982) Nec-conservatism and national school policy *Educational Evaluation and Policy Analysis* Nov/Dec 6

Wood, N (1984) Exams Council answers Sir Keith's call *Times Educational Supplement* 13 January

Yates, F (1972) *The First Twenty-five Years: A Review of The NFER* The Foundation: Slough

4. Research and development in Australia since the 1960s

Peter W. Musgrave

Summary: Because of the applied nature of much educational research its funding must be closely linked to the political circumstances of any country and to the ideology of the party in power. In Australia, a federal system, this has meant considerable reliance upon the Commonwealth government. Between the early 1970s and 1983 the government changed four times, with major consequent swings in the nature, organization and extent of funding for educational research. In 1973 the conservative coalition, just beginning to fund such research, was replaced by a Labor government which, at least initially, poured money into education. Between 1975 and 1983 the conservatives cut back severely on all educational expenditure, but savagely on that for research. Since early 1983 Labor, despite an ideological commitment to education, has been unable, except marginally, due to economic circumstances, to increase research funding. Such overseas influences as new methods of research have been mediated through the ideology of the governing party and because of the anti-centralist commitment of the conservatives, so long in power, control of the Australian education research effort has for the most part remained vestigial.

Introduction

In the Education Research Act (1970), by which what was later to be called the Education Research and Development Committee was established, research was defined as 'systematic investigation in a particular field' (§ 3). Educational research has at least two special characteristics: it relates to a field that is applied in nature and it is inextricably intertwined with politics. Hence, it is inevitably influenced by the political structure — in Australia a federal system, by changes in the parties elected to power and by shifts in the ideologies that govern them. Such influence has been very clear in Australia in the years since 1970 during which changes have occurred four times in the ruling party at the Commonwealth level. This chapter will sketch the major ways in which those changes affected educational research and its organization in Australia.

Prior to 1970 the Liberal/Country Party (conservative) coalition had been in power in Canberra since 1949, though there had on occasion been Labor governments in office in individual States. The Australian federal contribution had traditionally been interpreted in such a way that education was on the States', not the Commonwealth's, agenda, though there was the possibility that the Commonwealth could grant some funds to States for such specific purposes as aid to students. This loop-hole was rarely, and then pragmatically, used and certainly not to assist research until 1965 when the Australian Research Grants Committee (ARGC) was established. (See Dunn, 1965, for an account of educational research in Australia in the mid-1960s.) There was even then still some support for the formerly strongly held view, especially in industry, that in general the results of research should be brought into Australia from centres of excellence overseas rather than that research should be generated within this country. There was, however, a growing pressure upon the conservative coalition, increasingly from the Labor opposition, to do more for education at the national level and to do so within a coherent, theoretically based policy, grounded in national enquiries that enabled rational planning.

At the end of 1972 the Labor party were returned to office with Mr E.G. Whitlam as Prime Minister and with a mandate to establish a Schools Commission to oversee a programme of assistance to education, based on the needs of schools and students. During the years 1972-75 the two Whitlam governments pursued a Fabian policy of basing major legislation and much administration upon largely policy-oriented enquiry. Particularly in the field of education their initiatives led to the creation of institutions, such as the Curriculum Development Centre in 1973, which carried out and encouraged curricular research and development. Furthermore, these governments injected a huge increase of funds into the schools and tertiary institutions. The economic problems which were largely responsible for the subsequent change of government can in great part be traced to this rapid rise in welfare expenditure and even prior to its dismissal in November, 1975 Labor had already begun to tighten its budgetary belt.

The Fraser conservative governments in office from 1975 till early 1983 claimed to be monetarist in economic policy and their Liberalism was based in the view that wherever possible States' rights should be respected, but particularly was this the case in the field of education, a field traditionally reserved to the States. These two ideological factors, both working against the previous large-scale Commonwealth aid to education, were strengthened by the conservative belief that much of the current high level of youth unemployment was attributable to the inefficiencies of the educational system. Furthermore, the recent (1983) return to power of Labor under Hawke has occurred under such difficult economic circumstances that, whatever their ideological sympathy for education, their financial room for manoeuvre is too small to increase aid to education greatly. However, since research in all fields, including education, is seen as vital for economic rebirth and also is comparatively cheap, it is in this field that some relief to contemporary educational stringency may come.

Developments in educational research

Conservative beginnings: to 1972

Despite the establishing of the ARGC in 1965 there was no central policy
or even focus for educational research in Australia, certainly until 1970
when the Australian Advisory Committee for Research and Development
in Education (AACRDE) was founded by the Coalition Government.
Research was uncontrolled, scattered and very largely undertaken in three
categories of institution: State education departments, the universities and
the Australian Council for Educational Research (ACER).

State education departments In each State there was some administrative
mechanism servicing the education department with information on recent
educational research, undertaking small practically-oriented projects in
areas of perceived need and developing new school curricula. Arrangements
differed by State; thus, in Victoria there were both a curriculum and
research branch and a psychology and guidance branch, but in Western
Australia there was one research and planning and special duties branch.
Each State undertook the research and development seen as necessary by
its departmental officers and politicians. There was no overall policy of
any nature whatsoever until the late 1960s when the Australian Education
Council (AEC), the regular meeting of State Ministers and Directors-
General of Education, began to support projects for curricular development
in the field of science that involved more than one State; initially three
States supported the Junior Science Education Project, but from 1969 to
1974 all States financed the Australian Science Education Project for
school years 7 to 10.

An investigation was undertaken by ACER in 1972 on research into
education in Australia. This revealed that about 320 professional staff
were employed in the Commonwealth Department of Education and the
State education departments on research and related activities, 120 on
curricular activities and 15 to 20 on guidance/psychological work. This
number had doubled since 1968. The two most common categories of
work done related to general surveys and measurement, especially in relation to selection and prediction of success (Radford, 1973: 23-9). In the
last field the work of the various examination boards in each State,
variously the responsibility of the education department and/or the
university sector, was also important. The great majority of this research
did not gain wide publication, merely being circulated in mimeographed
form within the relevant State education department.

The universities Until 1974 the States retained primary responsibility
for funding the universities, though considerable funds were available on a
matching basis from the Commonwealth. The universities had, almost
since their beginnings in the 1850s, been seen as utilitarian educational
institutions. Thus, faculties or departments of education were defined
primarily as sources of professionally trained teachers, though their staff
did do some research. The 1972 investigation found that 'research and
related activities ... represented about 30 per cent of their working profes-

sional time' (ibid:55). A small flow of funds came from ARGC and some from local charitable foundations. Students working for research degrees did provide one way of building up a basis of research findings about Australian education, though a very large proportion of such students worked on the history of education rather than on, for example, school processes or the problems of learning. In 1970 there were three doctorates and 53 masters' degrees in education awarded by Australian universities, though 85 and 748 candidates respectively were enrolled for these degrees. What has to be emphasized is that, unlike research in the natural sciences, the great majority of all this higher degree work was undertaken not by full-time students, but by teachers working part-time in their off duty hours.

The ACER The ACER was founded in 1930 with considerable financial assistance from the US Carnegie Foundation, but by the post-war era a pattern of funding, based on grants from the States and the Common-wealth, had been established (Connell, 1980). Its activities were, therefore, somewhat constrained by its view of its paymasters' needs and by the utilitarian perspective, taken by politicians and their constituents, of education in Australia. By the 1960s the then Director saw 'four main areas of research and service activity': test development; the undertaking of surveys, studies of organization, curricula and methods; the maintenance of information about Australian education; and the provision of advisory, testing and counselling services (Radford, 1973: 104).

The ACER was concerned about the lack of communication between educational researchers in Australia and particularly about the diffusion of research findings to those who could use them. It published monographs, held the business, though not editorial, responsibility for the *Australian Journal of Education,* and itself published the *Quarterly Review of Education* (after 1973 the *Australian Education Review*). ACER served as a link to the overseas educational research community, especially in taking a major part in such international projects as the International Association for the Evaluation of Educational Achievement, and its Director played a big role in founding in 1971 the Australian Association for Research in Education, which has since become an important channel for the diffusion of research within the Australian professional educational community.

By 1972, therefore, educational research was showing some signs of breaking out of its chrysalis. Recently-founded institutions were to serve it well when funds became more readily available. The sense of educational urgency brought to Canberra by Labor might lead to larger projects, more quickly completed and in areas other than measurement and psychology — the ACER investigation showed just over 40 per cent of Australian research work to be in such areas in 1972 (Radford, 1973: 112).

The Labor years: 1972-75

The huge increase in funds for education that marked the first two years of Labor government was channelled both through existing administrative structures and also through new semi-autonomous government commissions, set up according to a well established Australian tradition for specific purposes.

The Schools Commission In line with Labor's election mandate, the Schools Commission was established in practical though not statutory terms within weeks of the new government taking office. Its purpose was to recommend coherent policies based on need and grounded in research, either existing or sponsored to answer some specific problem. The Schools Commission did allocate funds to research by its own officers and by those working in, for example, universities to examine the issues related to its stated priorities. Therefore, work was initiated on sexism in schools, on community participation in school governance, and on education for adolescents. The main function of the Schools Commission, however, was to allocate funds to schools and, therefore, much effort went into the establishing of sound and appropriate indices of educational need.

The Curriculum Development Centre (CDC) The Labor government also established a Commonwealth centre to develop curricula, to examine curricular issues, and to diffuse related information. The CDC's officers themselves did relevant work, but much was generated by the establishing of working parties which, for example, published papers on core curriculum and on consumer education, and by the contracting to individual research workers or to State departments the development of particular curricula. In the first category was the creation of materials to teach aspects of health and human relationships and in the second the development of eight large sets of materials for use in social education. The extensive involvement in such work of teachers and/or the officers of State education departments was one index of the Labor Government's deeply-held belief in as wide as possible a participation by community workers in educational decisions.

The Education Research and Development Committee (ERDC) The AACRDE was renamed as the ERDC on 1 January 1976. The AACRDE had been founded as a result of pressure triggered off by the 1967 Fink Memorial Lecture, given at Melbourne University by Sir Hugh Ennor, then First Secretary of the Commonwealth Department of Education. A meeting followed in 1968 at ACER as a result of which information about the state of educational research in Australia was gathered so that a submission could be put to the government. This was done and a deputation of the ACER and AEC met the Minister late in 1969. At the time 'a little more than $2.0 million per annum' appeared to be spent in support of educational research (ACER Reports, 1967-1968: 97-98; 1968-1969: 14-16). On 16 April 1979, Mr Bowen, the Minister for Education, told the House of Representatives of the creation of the AACRDE which was to advise on the disbursement of a grant for educational research, initially of $0.25 million, during the financial year 1970-71. The terms of reference of the AACRDE were innovatory in that unlike ARGC the Committee could propose projects for itself as well as allocate funds to submitted projects and, furthermore, it could grant funds towards training research workers, since there was a concern that Australia lacked a strong supply of trained researchers in education (Proceedings House of Representatives, 1970, Vol. 66: 1216-18).

The immense increase in funds available for educational research can be seen by the rise in the annual grants made by the AACRDE shown in Table 1. What has to be remembered is that these funds were only one part, though the major, of the total available for this purpose, since the Schools Commission, the CDC, and such coordinating bodies as the Commission of Advanced Education were also funding educational research. In addition, policy-oriented research into education was initiated on a large scale by, for example, the Poverty Commission and the House of Representatives Committee on Special Learning Disabilities. In the first case a Poverty Commissioner for Education was appointed whose office sponsored the largest single-focused programme of educational research to date carried out in Australia (*Australian Government Commission of Enquiry into Poverty*, 1976) and in the second the government requested the AACRDE to commission through the ACER the project on standards of literacy and numeracy that has become the Australian base for any similar future studies (Burke and Keeves, 1977).

	Requests		Granted	
	Numbers	*Total Amounts* *($million)*	*Numbers*	*Total Amounts* *($million)*
1973	162	2.53	43	0.30
1976	202	3.93	81	0.82
1978	246	4.70	88	0.95
1980	207	5.34	98	0.80

Table 1 *AACRDE/ERDC funding: 1973-80 (selected years)*
Source: Reports of AACRDE/ERDC

Initially the AACRDE had a part-time Chairman, Professor P.H. Partridge of the Australian National University, but in 1973 Cabinet approved the appointment of a full-time Chairman. Administrative difficulties delayed this appointment until 1975. After an interim period in 1974-75 Mr S.S. Dunn, formerly Dean of Education, Monash University, was appointed as the first, and ultimately the only, full-time Chairman, and remained in office until 1981.

The ERDC came to occupy a very central place in Australian research in education. Firstly, as already noted, it granted funds, where previously any finance for research in education had been very scarce. These funds were channelled not only to the recipients seen as traditional, that is to the universities, but also to the State education departments and the colleges of advanced education, including teachers' colleges. An examination of the annual reports shows a wide range of projects was funded, although, not

surprisingly in view of the nature of the existing supply of educational
research workers in Australia, the conclusion must be that those in the
traditional field of psychological and measurement research were the main
recipients. However, some sociological research was funded and a scattering
of projects based on case study of ethnographic methods is apparent.
Secondly, the ERDC did establish priority areas for research: multi-cultural
education; the impact of social and demographic factors; recurrent education; and 'what is happening in the classroom' (ERDC Report, 1976-77: 7).
Small advisory committees were established to pursue these priorities.
Thirdly, dissemination was seen as important and a sub-committee was
established in 1976. A series of monographs, as far as possible using simple
English, was published, based on projects funded by the ERDC; seminars
and workshops were financed; and attempts were made to use the membership of planning and steering committees for projects as a means of
disseminating research findings (ERDC Reports 1975-76: 10; 1978-79: 6).
Fourthly, the ERDC coordinated the research activities of the Department
of Education and of the CDC (ERDC Report 1975-76: 5 and 7). Lastly,
much attention was given to the training of research workers. This had for
some time been seen as a need, but assumed greater importance when
many overseas assessors' reports on applications to the AACRDE for funds
'forced ... the conclusion that generally speaking the standards of design
of educational research projects in this country leave room for considerable
improvement' (AACRDE Report 1972-73: 15). Grants were given to maintain workers whilst undertaking training at universities, or making visits to
overseas centres; seminars organized by the professional body, AARE,
were funded; and the interviewing procedures used to vet applications
were consciously used as training sessions.

The universities Though some of the research grants made by the ERDC
went to colleges of advanced education (CAEs), the greater proportion
went to the universities. In the years between 1972 and 1980 the universities received between 53.6 (1975) and 65.8 (1977) per cent of the funds
granted; for CAEs the percentages were 17.7 (1973) and 26.8 (1975);
most of the remaining funds went to State education departments. These
grants financed a research output that was greater and often of a more
substantial nature than previously, since larger samples and the use of
research assistants became possible.

At the same time there was a big rise in the numbers of students undertaking research degrees in education. In 1971 six doctorates and 59
masters' degrees in education were conferred, whilst 97 and 951 students
respectively were enrolled for the two levels of degrees. By 1980 the
figures were: 42 doctorates and 415 masters conferred; 389 and 3,224
students respectively were enrolled. A still small, but larger than in 1971,
proportion was now working full time, though the level of the grants
awarded by the Commonwealth to maintain those undertaking research
for higher degrees was unattractive to experienced teachers, often already
married with a growing family.

In addition to their expanded role in undertaking research and supervising higher degree students the universities functioned as the major guardians of the educational research effort. It was their staff in the main who served on the ERDC, advised governments and others on projects, and acted as referees on the proposals made to the ERDC, and as editors of and referees for the educational journals. University lecturers wrote the texts for students that demonstrated what was now known, what was speculated and where research was needed. Yet, even though a large number of practising teachers were students, the link between the educational research force, whether in universities or at ACER, and the classrooms was still weak. Despite such attempts as the establishing, as early as 1929, of State institutions for educational research, formally linked to ACER and represented on its governing council, this weakness has remained (Connell, 1980: passim).

Backtracking with the conservatives: 1975-83

During their last year in office the Labor government had already begun to decrease the scale of their educational funding. The conservatives cut deeper. Amongst other outlays, research funds were affected; the 1977-78 budget reduced the ERDC funds by 20.5 per cent at a time of fairly rapid inflation. Yet considerable contract funds were still available for specific purposes allied to such policy initiatives as increasing the effort put into technical education, a sector much favoured by the conservatives at a time of economic stringency.

'The Razor Gang' The Liberal-Country Party coalition under Fraser set up a Review of Commonwealth Functions, soon christened 'the razor gang', in an endeavour to economize and to rationalize government activities. The ideology behind its recommendations, which were very largely accepted, was shown by the Prime Minister in introducing its recommendations to the House of Representatives on 30 April 1981. In relation to education he said:

> 'Consistent with a reduced role for the Commonwealth in activities which are the proper preserve of the States, the Curriculum Development Centre will be abolished unless the States are prepared to meet 50 per cent of the operating costs. Special support for educational research and the ERDC will be terminated. This will allow the States to determine their priorities in these areas.' (Proceedings House of Representatives, 1981, Vol. 122: 1835)

Furthermore, 'In-house and contracted research activities of the Department of Education [will] be scaled down' (ibid: 1843). Three months later the Minister, Mr Wal Fife, told the House that 'some funds for educational research will be available under coordinated arrangements across the educational portfolio' (ibid: 3114). The exact nature of these arrangements is still (1983) unclear and, as might have been expected, particularly at a time of economic difficulty, the States do not appear to have taken up the ground vacated by the Commonwealth.

The ERDC was closed down officially on 5 June 1981, though its programmes were not all ended until March, 1983 (Report of ERDC, 1980-81 and 1981-82: 1). It was not closed down because it was not doing its job well. Indeed, in a written answer to a question from Senator Button, the then Minister, Senator Carrick, told the Senate on 10 June 1981, that

> 'ERDC performed its functions in an entirely adequate manner. As a result of its work, both Commonwealth and State authorities have a sound base on which to plan future research programmes.' (Proceedings Senate, 1981, Vol. 90: 3012-3)

The possibility of plans has been put in the place of actual research, research training and diffusion, initiated by an innovative and relatively inexpensive body.

The tertiary sector The educational effort of the tertiary institutions was also cut savagely, especially in the teacher training sector of the CAEs where forced amalgamation in each State created instability in staffing and teaching which left little time or emotional energy to give to research. The universities lost numbers in their initial training courses, but paradoxically suffered no immediate fall in enrolments for higher degrees whether by course work or by research. This seemed to be due to a feeling amongst teachers in both State and independent sectors that in the hard times now upon them promotion would come more readily to those who were more highly qualified. Thus enrolments for doctorates rose from 380 in 1980 to 415 in 1981 and for masters' degrees from 2880 to 3224.

Funds that had come from the ERDC, the CDC or the Schools Commission were not replaced by grants for the ARGC, but university departments did receive a substantial proportion of the funds available for contract research. Such projects were usually associated with policy-oriented problems and sometimes apparently with attempts to justify increased status. Some university lecturers were averse to having a large proportion of departmental research activities tied to applied work which implied some loss of freedom, certainly in the choice of problem, in the university research effort. Furthermore, much, though not all, of this contract research was based on questionnaire type methods, overtly atheoretical and therefore inimical to the qualitative research methods associated with the reborn and increasingly popular hermeneutical tradition.

ACER The ACER celebrated its golden jubilee in 1980 and its recently appointed Director told an international seminar held in Melbourne to mark this occasion of plans for future research, linking his approach closely to contemporary social change. He therefore saw as important foci certain critical issues: poverty, unemployment, the rising average age of secondary students and transition programmes from school to work. In addition, he laid emphasis on the impact of technology, especially computers, upon educational research and practice (Keeves, 1981: 241-50).

The formidable and very real reputation, national and international, of the ACER has been built upon 50 years of largely statistical research, increasingly of a sophisticated nature. The ACER was, therefore, in an admirable position to gain from the greater availability of funds for contract research. It was accustomed to policy-oriented requests from the States and Commonwealth. Its recent series of major studies on literacy and numeracy fit this interpretation well. The ACER has also continued to put much effort into dissemination and has begun jointly with the New Zealand Association for Educational Research to issue regularly a moderately priced journal, *Set: Research Information for Teachers,* that contains reports, specially written for teachers, of local educational research projects with implications for the schools.

Conclusion

During the early 1970s there was a world-wide demand for greater expenditure on education and on research into its nature and problems. Political ideologies, influencing both sides of party politics, supported decentralization and what some see as less stringent methods of research. These tendencies were felt in Australia, but were mediated by a federal political system, control of which changed four times within the period 1972 to 1983.

Control of the Australian educational research effort had been vestigial until 1970 when the AACRDE was founded, but any control of the direction of educational research that it and its successor, the ERDC, was beginning to exercise disappeared when it was destroyed in 1981. The only control now, as before 1970, comes from the power and nature of the prevailing political ideology and at the moment that ideology ruling the Labor government at present in office is not far removed in educational matters from that of its conservative predecessor, though its possible support for developmental and applied research is shown by its resuscitation of the CDC as a purely funding agency in the Budget for 1983-84.

This control is strengthened by the fact that an increased proportion of the funds available for educational research takes the form of contracts for policy-oriented work based on problems defined as such by those currently in power. This situation supports existing political and educational positions and favours instant answers reached by traditional quantitative research methods so brilliantly employed by the ACER throughout its long history as a research institute, rather than the use of the qualitative methods favoured by many in the universities and by some radically-oriented teachers. Some of the most fruitful research in the humanities and the social sciences has always depended upon hard thinking rather than large scale funding. It is clearly to such research, unfunded, uncontrolled and maybe qualitative in nature, and, perhaps, emanating from the universities that Australians must at present look if they want radical change in areas not defined by governments as educational problems.

References

Australian Government Commission of Inquiry into Poverty (1976) *Poverty and Education in Australia,* 5th Report AGPS: Canberra

Burke, S F and Keeves, J P eds (1977) *Literacy and Numeracy in Australian Schools, Vols. I, II and III* AGPS: Canberra

Burke, S F and Keeves, J P eds *Literacy and Numeracy in Australian Schools, Vols. I, II and III* AGPS: Canberra

Connell, W F (1980) *The Australian Council for Educational Research, 1930-80* ACER: Hawthorn (Victoria)

Dunn, S S (1965) Educational research in the light of Australian experience *in* M Young *ed Innovation and Research in Education* Routledge and Kegan Paul: London, pp 157-74

Keeves, J P (1981) Societal change and its implications for educational research in Australia *in* P Karmel *ed Education, Change and Society* ACER: Hawthorn (Victoria) pp 239-53

Radford, W C (1973) *Research into Education in Australia* AACRDE Report No. 1 AGPS: Canberra

Acknowledgement

I have been helped in writing this paper by my colleagues Professors P J Fensham and R J W Selleck and by my former colleague Mr S S Dunn, full-time Chairman of the Educational Research and Development Council, 1975-81.

5. Educational research in Canada

Edward A. Holdaway

Summary: Canadian educational researchers have made substantial contributions to knowledge and improvement of practice, but their work could and should be more effective. In Canada, educational research is mainly funded by provincial governments. Such research, as well as that funded by the larger local school boards, is usually closely related to policy issues. Concerns about low levels of financial support for researcher-generated studies led to detailed examinations of Canadian educational research in the early 1980s.

Most educational research is conducted by university staff and graduate students. The relatively low level of support of education proposals by the federal Social Sciences and Humanities Research Council has mainly resulted from small numbers of applications, procedures of the council, and difficulties in dealing with proposals which are closely related to practical matters such as curriculum development.

Partly because the control of education is vested in Canada's ten provinces and two territories, federal initiatives in educational research are minimal. Several national associations fund, conduct, sponsor or promote educational research.

A trend away from traditional research designs is becoming obvious in Canada as more emphasis is placed upon ethnographic and case study methods in particular. Some other trends and concerns involve Canadianization of educational research, the formation of research institutes, computer applications, the relationship between research and policy/practice, teacher-research linkages, communication and publication.

Introduction

The education of Canada's 25 million people is the constitutional responsibility of the governments of each of the ten provinces and two territories. Provincial governments do not operate regular schools, as this responsibility is delegated to local boards of education in jurisdictions referred to as school districts, school divisions or counties. Federal government involvement is generally restricted to international representation, education of native peoples, operation of agencies which fund research, operation of Department of Defence schools, and indirect financial support for post-secondary education. The right of each province to control the operation of formal education within its borders is firmly protected, with some provincial officials even occasionally proposing that this control extends to educational research.

Funds for educational research are provided mainly by the federal government (especially by the Social Sciences and Humanities Research Council of Canada, and in-house or contracted research sponsored by government departments), provincial governments (through in-house or contracted research), the larger school districts, educational organizations, and some foundations. Because the largest volume of educational research in Canada is conducted by university staff and graduate students, the financial base of educational research expenses includes salaries paid from government grants to universities.

During 1981 the Canadian educational research scene was examined through three state-of-the-art reviews funded by the federal Social Sciences and Humanities Research Council of Canada (SSHRC) and conducted by the Canadian Society for the Study of Education (Andrews and Rogers, 1982), the Canadian Society for the Study of Higher Education (Sheffield, 1982) and the Canadian Association of Deans of Education (Stapleton *et al*, 1982). The activity was prompted by the perception that the SSHRC has not supported educational research as well as it has other disciplines, despite the levels of expenditure and the extensive role of education in society. In the view of Wisenthal (1982:1), who summarized the reviews, this apparent indifference resulted from the sensitivity of federal bodies to provincial control over education, and 'more specifically from the lack of tradition in scholarly, theoretical and empirical research within the education community itself'. He also concluded that educational research in Canada is considerably less developed than it should and could be.

These concerns should not obscure the productive aspects or the fact that not all educational research requires considerable funding. Canadian educational researchers have made substantial contributions in many areas. In educational psychology, Canadian researchers have been very active in the areas of learning, special education, pre-school activities, measurement, evaluation and counselling. Similarly, researchers in educational administration in Canada have been recognized internationally for their work in leader behaviour, organizational climate, decision making, organizational behaviour and job satisfaction. Other notable Canadian research areas include sociology, history, philosophy and vocational education.

This chapter describes the development of the present educational research structures in Canada and current issues in conducting educational research. Its content draws heavily upon information and opinions expressed by authors listed in the References and Acknowledgements. Because the same information and opinions have been presented elsewhere by a variety of authors, it has been deemed unnecessary to identify in this text the source of every statement.

History

For nearly 100 years the recommendation has been voiced in Canada that a national educational research body be established: such national bodies were established twice for short periods until the provinces lost interest (Sheffield 1982:56). This situation has been described by Stewart (1974: 17): 'Research, interprovincially, has had its pioneers and explorers but their efforts did not lead to any permanent establishments in the barren lands of non-federal, non-provincial territories.'

In the late 1930s, the Canadian Education Association (CEA), aided by the Canadian Teachers' Federation, was primarily responsible for establishing the Canadian Council for Educational Research (CCER). The Carnegie Corporation of New York provided some financial support for CCER. However, CCER was terminated in 1945. Research directors were appointed by the Canadian Teachers' Federation in 1953, and by both CEA and the Association of Universities and Colleges of Canada in 1958. Following such increased interest, the Canadian Council for Research in Education (CCRE) was formed about 1961 to identify research needs, help bridge the research-implementation gap, coordinate research projects in identified priority areas, and disseminate research findings. CCRE performed valuable work, including the preparation of the *Canadian Education Index*. Most of its funds came from provincial governments, but these were not sufficient to allow CCRE to conduct research. In view of its financial and organizational limitations, CCRE took the initiative in 1967 to establish the Canadian Educational Researchers' Association (CERA). In 1972 CCRE played a major part in the formation of the Canadian Society for the Study of Education (CSSE), which is now Canada's foremost scholarly educational association. CCRE ceased to exist in late 1972, and many of its functions and responsibilities were transferred to the CEA.

At that time, the following national organizations served the interest of educational scholars — the Canadian Association of Deans of Education, the Canadian Association of Foundations of Education, the Canadian Association of Professors of Education, the Canadian Educational Researchers' Association, the Comparative and International Education Society of Canada, and the Canadian Society for the Study of Higher Education. Some dissatisfaction with the situation in the early 1970s was generated by the lack of integration of efforts of these associations, insufficient representation of education at national level, secretarial and financial difficulties, few national educational publications, and the strong US attraction in the absence of equivalent Canadian activities. CSSE was formed as an umbrella organization to serve the needs of the member associations listed above and to help overcome these dissatisfactions and difficulties. The Canadian Society for the Study of Higher Education decided not to join CSSE. During 1972-74 the Canadian Associations for Curriculum Studies, for the Study of Educational Administration, and for Educational Psychology were formed as member associations of CSSE. The Canadian Association of Professors of Education became the Canadian Association for Teacher Education in 1978. CSSE now has about 1500 members and has a permanent office in Ottawa; it publishes the *Canadian Journal of Education* and a *Yearbook* and has been successful in representing education nationally.

Ryan and Butler (1982:247) attribute the relative recency of Canadian educational research mainly to the slow emergence of doctoral degree programmes. In 1900, only the University of Toronto offered advanced degrees in education: its PhD degree was authorized in 1897. It was joined by the Universities of Alberta and Ottawa in the 1920s and by five others in the 1940s. Throughout most of this century, the Universities of Toronto and Alberta have dominated the educational research scene in Canada: several other universities are now also major participants. The Ontario Institute for Studies in Education (OISE) was founded by the Ontario Legislature in 1965. OISE is a unique institution in that it provides graduate studies in education, as an affiliate of the University of Toronto, while having a responsibility to conduct research of interest to the Ontario Ministry of Education, to disseminate research findings, and to assist in the implementation of these findings. Most faculties of education in Canadian universities offer both undergraduate and graduate programmes.

The history of federal government funding of educational research is far more brief. The Canada Council, which operated largely independently of the federal government, first included education as an eligible discipline about 1971. In 1978, its research-support function was assumed by SSHRC, which has less independence. The other major actors in the Canadian educational research scene, namely federal government departments, provincial government departments and the larger local school boards, started to become active about 1960. Some promising organizations which were deeply committed to educational research, such as the Alberta Human Resources Research Council and the Atlantic Institute of Education, have been terminated by provincial governments.

Description

National departments/agencies/associations/federations

The Canadian federal government departments and agencies involved with either conducting or funding educational research include Statistics Canada, the Department of National Health and Welfare, the National Research Council, and the Department of Indian and Northern Affairs. Statistics Canada provides data for many research projects conducted by other government departments, associations and individuals, and has undertaken some detailed research on aspects of post-secondary education and employment.

The Council of Ministers of Education, Canada, is a coordinating body consisting of representatives of *provincial* departments/ministries of education. It has no research staff, but it does commission some research projects or arrange that research be undertaken by committees. For example, the Council worked with the Federal-Provincial Task Force on Student Assistance which reported in 1981, and is represented on the Canadian Committee on Financing University Research.

Some educational research is conducted or supported by national bodies such as the Canadian Education Association, the Canadian Teachers' Federation, the Canadian School Trustees' Association, and the Association of Universities and Colleges of Canada. National associations of researchers/scholars, such as the Canadian Societies for the Study of Education and Higher Education, support educational research activities through conferences, publications, research inventories and lobbying. Both the Economic Council of Canada and the Science Council of Canada have undertaken some research on education, particularly in the post-secondary field. The Science Council (1983) has also undertaken a comprehensive study of elementary and secondary school science, which included analyses of provincial policies and text books, and a survey of science teachers. The International Development Research Centre, an autonomous public corporation established by the Parliament of Canada in 1970, stimulates and supports educational and other research which can benefit developing countries. Grants are generally made to an established local institution for specific projects, for example, research on literacy, school-to-work transition, and self-learning programmes.

Social Science and Humanities Research Council of Canada

SSHRC is the main source of funds for researcher-generated social science studies in Canada. SSHRC provides funds for Research Grants, Leave Fellowships, Postdoctoral Fellowships, Doctoral Fellowships and Special MA Scholarships. All education awards are classified by SSHRC as 'Education', 'Educational Administration', or 'Educational Psychology', but in this chapter they are all referred to collectively as 'Education'.

The SSHRC Research Grants category includes Standard Research Grants (up to $100,000 in one year and up to $250,000 over three years) and Major Research Grants (over these amounts); in addition, the SSHRC General Research Programme provides block funding for universities ($1,574,750 in 1981-82) to allow requests of up to $2,500 to be administered by each university. Strategic Grants are also made to support (1) thematic research projects in the following areas which are perceived by SSHRC to be of national importance — population ageing, the family and the socialization of children, the human context of science and technology, women and work, and managing the organization in Canada, and (2) special area programmes in the development of management research, Canadian studies research tools, and small universities. SSHRC also provides funds for publications, conferences, operations of learned societies, and international scholarly cooperation. The number of awards and the amounts allocated in 1981-82 for some programmes are shown in Table 1.

SSHRC (1983:4-5) makes the following statements on the eligibility of research proposals:

1. SSHRC 'supports research focused on the study of individual human beings and human society and culture whether the work is under-

taken within a traditional discipline or as an interdisciplinary venture'.
2. SSHRC 'recognizes that education research falls clearly within its
   domain insofar as it is aimed at the advancement of knowledge'. It
   will consider both theoretical and applied proposals as long as they
   are of high quality and the results will have broad significance for
   educational research. Such proposals can include both professional
   development and the preparation of materials for teaching purposes.

Programme	Education		Total	
	Number	*Amount in thousands of dollars ($CAN)*	*Number*	*Amount in thousands of dollars ($CAN)*
Standard Research Grants[a]	29	691	645	10,931
Major Research Grants[b]	1	197	25	5,328
Fellowships/Scholarships	136	1,181	1,779	17,138

a   These were called Research Grants prior to 1982-83.
b   These were called Negotiated Grants prior to 1982-83, and included
    major editorial projects.

Table 1 *Funds awarded by SSHRC in 1981-82: proportion going
to education*
Source: SSHRC, *1981-82 Annual Report*

Proposals are ranked according to merit by committees of specialists after
receiving peer reviews. The criteria used by the committees and assessors
are scholarly significance, appropriateness and clarity of the theoretical
approach, soundness of research plans, competence and experience of the
applicant, social relevance or practical importance (where applicable), and
appropriateness of budget estimates. Standard Research Grants have
certain conditions attached; especially notable are those related to (1) an
ethics review and adherence to detailed ethical guidelines for research
proposals involving human subjects, and (2) the depositing of data collected in survey research in a recognized data-bank.

Provincial ministries/departments/agencies

Since about 1970, most provincial ministries/departments have had
research divisions which conduct educational research projects and/or
contract with individuals or groups to conduct projects. The emphasis is
normally upon studies which have a potential impact upon policy. At one
extreme, six provincial government departments and agencies in British
Columbia undertake, commission or support research in post-secondary
education: at the other extreme, the government of New Brunswick does
not undertake educational research but vests control and funding of educational research within the jurisdiction of its universities. In the Province of

Québec, a general research fund (Formation de chercheurs et action concertée – FCAC) provided about $3 million per annum for educational researchers in 1982-83 out of a total of approximately $17.5 million (Cliche, 1982). University staff receiving an FCAC grant are expected to involve graduate students in their research projects.

In Alberta, the Planning and Research Branch of the Department of Education (1981) has as its major objective 'the establishment and integration of policy analyses and developmental research'. Its Planning and Analysis Section 'identifies existing and future problems and generates policy alternatives', whereas its Research and Evaluation Section co-ordinates research and disseminates results (Eddy, 1982). The Planning and Research Branch conducts some studies although most are contracted. Its 1983 priority areas included exceptional children, the evaluation of pupils, schools and programmes, and the use of technology in education. Two recent projects were the development of models for school finance and teacher supply and demand. A 1982 project compared the relative effectiveness of teaching a Grade 12 mechanics course by traditional methods, by regular correspondence methods, and by Telidon, Canada's videotex system (Montgomerie, 1982).

Ontario probably has the most developed overall educational research 'system' of any Canadian province. Many of its operations are similar to those described above for Alberta, but it differs in two important aspects. First, the Ministry of Education provides $2 million per annum to OISE to fund applied research projects in areas of mutual interest to the Ministry and OISE, with OISE deciding which particular projects are to be undertaken. Second, the Ministry of Education's Information Centre manages ONTERIS, the Ontario Education Resources Information System, which is a computerized, current, comprehensive, on-line, bibliographic data base.

Some independent research institutes also exist, with the Educational Research Institute of British Columbia probably the best known. It is an independent, cooperative agency which receives provincial funds and whose board members include representatives from many educational organizations.

School district research

Most of the larger school districts in Canada employ educational researchers. This practice became common about 1970 and grew to a plateau about 1975, but the current climate of financial restraint is adversely affecting the volume of school district research.

Such research clearly focuses upon applied matters relevant to the particular school district (Wright, 1982). At the Toronto Board of Education (TBE), most studies are requested by board trustees, although some are suggested by central office employees, principals, counsellors and teachers. Small grants are sometimes awarded to in-school educators. These TBE studies deal with most aspects of education, for example, curriculum, programmes, teaching materials, testing, administration, special education, alternative schools, and drop-outs. The TBE Research Department also produces research syntheses, prepares literature reviews, analyses information from retrieval systems, and maintains liaison with external agencies interested in educational research. This TBE approach is similar to that employed by other large school districts. An unusual project is the extensive annual survey conducted by the Edmonton Public School District in Alberta of the attitudes of students, parents, staff and the community towards education generally and district operations specifically.

Scope and sources of support

In 1981 the Canadian Association of Deans of Education conducted a questionnaire survey of educational research being carried out by members of faculties of education. They ascertained that 723 projects costing $12,516,262 (excluding faculty salaries) were underway in 1981-82 (Stapleton *et al*, 1982: 16-18). The percentage distributions of numbers of projects and dollar support are shown in Table 2. The Deans concluded that (1) SSHRC funds comparatively little of the total educational research effort in Canada, (2) because the $12.5 million figure includes both research and development, the expenditure on basic educational research is much less, and (3) $12.5 million is a very small percentage of the total annual expenditure of about $20 billion on education in Canada (Wisenthal, 1982:3).

Source of Funding	% of Projects	% of Funding
Provincial departments/ ministries of education	39.1	31.7
Other provincial sources	5.8	16.2
SSHRC	8.0	5.5
Other federal sources	7.6	19.6
University internal sources	14.9	1.2
School boards	2.6	1.1
Private industry	1.7	5.8
Other	20.2	19.6

Table 2 *Percentages of educational research projects and funding for projects classified by source of funding*
Source: Stapleton *et al*, 1982: 16-18

Issues and challenges

Many of the issues and challenges facing educational researchers in Canada are similar to those being experienced in other Western countries. Some relate closely to the performing of educational research, while others relate more to linkages between educational researchers and their clientele and funding sources.

Research activity

The current low level of Canadian educational research activity seriously affects the contribution that educational research could make to solving Canada's national educational problems. The deans of education (Stapleton *et al*, 1982:6) stated that they want 'to see an increase in the amount of high quality educational research that is conducted in this country' and 'to increase the collective capacity of our faculties to conduct such research'. Andrews and Rogers (1982:13) noted that 'in most faculties of education, the active researchers constitute a small minority of the total faculty'. This concern about research volume is not restricted to the school level of Kindergarten to 12th grade. Sheffield (1982:Preface) has made this assessment:

> 'the history of the [post-secondary] enterprise is inadequately docu-
> mented, goals are only dimly perceived, the characteristics of effective
> teaching are poorly understood, little is known about the outcomes
> of PSE, the formulation of public policy in the field requires constant
> analysis and re-analysis, and the problems of financing and manage-
> ment ... persist in forms old and new.'

Stapleton *et al* (1982:18-19) listed several barriers to competition for SSHRC funding — a teachers' college tradition, the recent development of faculties of education, the pre-eminence of teaching over research, the scarcity of rewards for productive researchers, and the lack of suitable faculty infrastructures. They also recommended that traditional educational research methodology should be complemented by other approaches which deserve consideration in SSHRC competitions. These include ethnographic, inductive and descriptive studies, as well as those which involve paradigm shifts resulting from better conceptualization and more variety in data-gathering techniques. Canadian educational researchers are now extensively using this wide variety of techniques, but this is not evident in either SSHRC-funded projects or the articles published in the *Alberta Journal of Educational Research* from 1955 to 1979 (Hersom, 1980:270). Increasing use of ethnographic/qualitative procedures has resulted partly from the shift from psychological to sociological/philosophical emphases. Greenfield has been at the forefront in advocating that traditional empirical methodology be replaced by a phenomenological approach. For example, he has advocated that we should 'place greater emphasis upon the specific as opposed to the general as a starting-point for inquiry' and that we take seriously the basic question 'What is the relation between the unique event and the context in which it exists?' (Greenfield, 1979:33).

Simultaneously, several other developments and concerns are obvious. As these are familiar to researchers in other countries, they will not be discussed in depth. The increasing processing power of computers is being used to manage large data files more readily and to use procedures more appropriate for analysing educational data than the Fisher/agricultural models. The requirements of special education and the emphasis upon accountability have contributed to the preparation of testing materials such as those in the Ontario Assessment Instrument Pool. Attention is also being paid to the balance in emphasis on the basic-applied research continuum, to the perceived overuse of cross-sectional research at the expense of both longitudinal studies and studies which consider the future, to the need for more multi-disciplinary research in some areas, and to the desirability of more programmatic research which may or may not involve research teams.

Further, educational research in Canada has been heavily influenced by US practices for reasons related to geographical proximity, the graduate training in the US of many Canadian university staff members, the volume of US research, and important US conferences such as that of the AERA. Tomkins *et al* (1981:4) concluded that 'there are few distinctively Canadian research efforts in curriculum although there are many excellent studies now being done within the Canadian context'. The *CSSE Review* included this relevant recommendation: 'That SSHRC encourage the Canadianization of imported research by funding replications and extensions of research originally done elsewhere and Canadian modifications and field trials of educational programmes, practices and materials developed elsewhere' (Andrews and Rogers, 1982:20). Crozier *et al* (1976:186), in their OECD report on Canadian education, also noted the US influence and perceived a 'need to take a national view of Canadian education research, information and dissemination problems'. A related matter involves the frequent advocacy of the establishment of university research institutes. This recommendation was included in the *CSSE Review:* 'That SSHRC establish research institutes at selected university locations for the various sub-fields of education to foster collaborative research and development efforts' (Andrews and Rogers, 1982:23). Sheffield (1982:40) has made a similar statement:

> 'My present view is that Canada would benefit from the establishment of a relatively independent national agency for policy-oriented research on the whole spectrum of post-school education. But even if the ideal facility were created, it alone could not be what is needed.'

The applications of computers to various aspects of education are gaining a great deal of attention. To increase awareness of work done elsewhere in Canada, an on-line index, similar to Ontario's ONTERIS, is urgently needed to provide immediate access to Canadian research documents and published articles. The major obstacle to this proportionately inexpensive development lies in the difficulties associated with creating national agencies in a federation. With regard to instruction, a considerable amount of research into computer-assisted learning (CAL) has been conducted in various Canadian centres. For example, The University of Alberta began R & D work in CAL in 1967. In 1970, the National Research Council (NRC) initiated a cooperative R & D CAL program: this national-level involvement was deemed to be necessary at that time because of high costs to local centres and the paucity of operational applications (Brahan, 1983:1). NRC was mainly concerned with development of CAL technology, while participating external organizations concentrated upon applications and delivery.

External matters

The first major external matter described in this section involves the concerns of the Canadian educational research community about SSHRC. Low submission rates and low success rates have led to education being underfunded by SSHRC since 1978. For example, the success rate for educational research proposals in 1981-82 was 48 per cent as compared with 68 per cent for all other disciplines. Educational scholars have also been less successful in obtaining SSHRC Leave Fellowships. This relative lack of success troubles those educational researchers who consider that the standing of a discipline is directly related to the financial support that it receives for researcher-generated studies. The main factors leading to underfunding of education were identified in the three state-of-the-art reviews as follows:

1. 'The perception exists that SSHRC, its officials, and the assessors it chooses are so wedded to classical and experimental research designs that a proposal which deviates from those is unacceptable' (Stapleton *et al*, 1981:22);
2. SSHRC has not funded proposals emphasizing educational applications and development, especially in the curriculum areas;
3. confusion has occurred as to which federal agency funds which sort of proposals, especially in the area of psychology;
4. a bias appears to exist against educational research;
5. the length of time taken to reach a decision is discouraging, especially in comparison with US practices and even more so with practices used in funding contract research;
6. uninformed assessors are used by SSHRC too frequently; and
7. the SSHRC expenditure control systems are too rigid.

After conducting a survey of Canadian social scientists, Adair and Davidson (1981) concluded that the current SSHRC requirements were too complex and contrary to research methods, often requiring that much of the proposed research project be already completed. Therefore not all of the explanatory factors listed above are unique to education. Wisenthal (1982: 7), after examining the minutes of SSHRC meetings, found 'little reference to the specific needs of the education community', and no evidence that education proposals require special processing; but he reported a generally unstated attitude that great caution should be used in establishing the eligibility of educational research proposals on account of provincial jurisdiction. Wisenthal (1982:6) also considered that education as a discipline deserves more consideration from SSHRC: he saw modern educational research as having firm theoretical bases in a variety of social sciences, and pointed out that 'the study of education ... has attracted the interest of a growing number of academics from faculties other than education'. To ascertain the actual situation, Wisenthal analysed 230 educational research proposals submitted to SSHRC from 1975 to 1980. He estimated that only 2 per cent of the 3,196 education faculty members in Canada had received SSHRC research grants in that period as compared with 21 per cent of all 18,404 eligible social science and humanities faculty members. Successful educational research proposals tended to rank higher in quality than those in other disciplines, causing Wisenthal to ponder whether they needed to be better in order to obtain approval.

The lack of SSHRC support for curriculum proposals and the negative effect of this action upon curriculum researchers across Canada has been deplored by Tomkins *et al* (1981:98-99): they recognized the provincial sensitivities, but believed 'that the SSHRC can initiate national research and development programmes which will buffer foreign influences on our schools and still meet with approval by ardent localists'. However, some curriculum research projects have not been rigorous, have been of a practical nature with local interest, and lacked generalizability.

Consideration of the concerns described above led to the following recommendations, among others, in the *CSSE Report* (Andrews and Rogers, 1982):

1. that SSHRC assign equal priority to high-quality research regardless of its theoretical orientation;
2. that SSHRC establish priority areas for educational research of national interest;
3. that SSHRC assessors be prominent Canadian educational researchers;
4. that generalizable curriculum development and evaluation studies be fully eligible for SSHRC fundings; and
5. that adjudication practices be redesigned to produce the shortest possible turnaround time.

The second major external matter is the research-policy/practice relationship. Canadian social science researchers are being asked increasingly to identify the impact that their activities have had upon both policy and practice. Rogers (1982) has provided the following examples of how educational research has influenced practice in Canada: (1) the recognition that US tests and norms for intelligence testing led to development of Canadian equivalents; (2) special programmes for the handicapped have been developed from research which sprang from legislation requiring school boards to provide universal special education. Ryan and Butler (1982:258) have stated that 'Funding agents, both private and governmental, increasingly will demand evidence that research can and will be translated into practice.' This trend is fortunate because researchers have had to consider applications and implications more closely. It is unfortunate because it creates the impression that basic research and knowledge creation are to be de-emphasized and more applied research encouraged. However, administrators and researchers need to recognize that the influence of the findings of educational research upon policy is usually *indirect*, through means such as identifying problems, conceptualizing issues and influencing the climate of opinion. Reasons why research has had little apparent, direct impact in Canada and elsewhere include the organizational and intellectual isolation of researchers from decision makers, conflicting conclusions reached from similar studies, and the difficulties incurred in recommending action based upon research findings. Policy is determined mainly by the social, cultural and economic forces existing in a particular political jurisdiction, but occasionally an individual research project does directly influence policy. For example, evaluation studies of behaviourally disturbed children in one school district led to an increase in the number of school centres offering programmes for these children. A research officer provided this assessment:

> 'I can cite many cases in my own board where policy initiatives leaned, in part, on research findings (eg, implementing an "early" French Immersion) or where practice was altered due to, among other things, research findings (eg, in revamping our standardized testing practices). Research findings alone might have provoked little attention. But where there is some awareness of a need to attend to some matter, some perception of need to act (or not to act), then research findings tend to be catalytic.'

Some OISE staff members feel that their work has strongly influenced policies and practices related to curriculum and student evaluation in Ontario, and that evaluation research has had more impact than have other types of research. But an OISE Task Force (Gage *et al*, 1981:3) drew this conclusion: 'Even with a wealth of resources and time, an attempt to assess the Institute's impact in the classroom could easily have been futile, given the difficulties of disentangling the subtle influences of research-based practices from many other factors.' At the post-secondary level, Ahamad (cited in Sheffield, 1982:51) concluded that reports of Canadian commissions on education varied in their degree of influence for reasons related to timing, commission membership, and the presentation and marketing of the report rather than the quality of the investigation. Sheffield (1982:51) observed that even though recommendations of provincial enquiries are not always accepted, they do make use of existing research results and generate more research projects. He also considers that 'National commissions are unlikely — unless there are great advances in federal-provincial cooperation.'

Gilliss (1979) has addressed the relationship between teachers and educational research in considerable depth. She states that two main types of barrier impede teachers from consulting research literature when seeking solutions to their classroom problems. The first type of barrier hinders access to relevant research findings and researchers. The second type of barrier is labelled by Gilliss 'intellectual' − insufficient understanding of research, inadequate background in educational research in preparation programmes for teachers, lack of time to peruse findings, and the superior attitudes of researchers towards teachers. To overcome some of these barriers Gilliss suggests certain approaches including giving teachers the chance to become true collaborators in research activities and preparing more state-of-the-art reviews especially for teachers. These approaches have been supported by Deiseach (1979), who as the CEA Research Officer for several years worked closely with researchers in school districts.

Further, more publications about Canadian educational research in progress and research findings are required. The communication among researchers themselves, as well as among researchers, administrators and politicians, leaves much to be desired. Within a university, research conducted by individual departments in a faculty of education is commonly unknown to other departments. Tomkins *et al* (1981:88) consider that many practice-related reports which now lie hidden in files could, with little additional effort, be publishable in academic journals. The *CSSE Report* recommended that SSHRC increase its support for an improved communications infrastructure.

Concluding comments

Educational research in Canada is funded, conducted and promoted by a wide variety of national and provincial organizations. Provincial governments provide the greatest amount of financial support, mainly for contract research: the federal support for essentially basic research is comparatively small. Various reports have concluded that Canadian educational research is underfunded, underdeveloped, parochial, concentrates upon applied aspects, and lacks major impact. National initiatives are minimal because provincial control over education inhibits such action. The attitudes of SSHRC towards educational research together with its low levels of financial support, cause concern.

However, grounds for optimism exist. Some excellent work is being performed in Canada by individual researchers, and some institutions rank quite highly on the world scene. As a result of the reviews conducted in the early 1980s, SSHRC has approved the proposal that education be added to the list of thematic areas receiving special research support, pending availability of funds. Larger numbers of faculty members appear to be getting involved in educational research in response partly to the reduction in emphasis upon traditional methodology and perhaps partly to the recent attention paid to the field of education. Such improvements may lead to research programmes of varying type and scale relevant to national concerns and interests, which education in Canada sorely needs. These could involve areas such as computer applications, curriculum evaluation, the school-work transition, and effectiveness of schooling. It is to be hoped that provincial politicians and their officials will not attempt to place inappropriate fences around educational research conducted within their borders, but rather will do all that they can to encourage development of such necessary nation-wide programmes.

References

Adair, J G and Davidson, R (1981) *Research Activity of Social Scientists* Report to the Social Science Federation of Canada: Ottawa
Alberta Department of Education (1981) *Seventy-Sixth Annual Report, 1980-81* Edmonton
Andrews, J H M and Rogers, W T eds (1982) *Canadian Research in Education: A State of the Art Review* Social Sciences and Humanities Research Council of Canada: Ottawa
Brahan, J W (1983) *CAL Technology — Decade Past, Decade Present* Paper presented at Fourth Canadian Symposium on Instructional Technology, Winnipeg
Cliche, Y (1982) *Rapport annuel, 1981-82* Fonds FCAC pour l'aide et le soutien à la recherche: Québec
Crozier, M, Eide, J, Hamm-Brücher, H, Noah, H and Vanbergen, P (1976) *Reviews of National Policies for Education: Canada* Organization for Economic Co-operation and Development: Paris
Deiseach, D (1979) *Educational Research in Canada: the Sum of the Parts is Greater than the Whole* Paper presented at Canadian Society for Studies in Education Conference, Saskatoon
Eddy, W P (1982) *Annual Research Highlights* Alberta Department of Education: Edmonton
Farquhar, R H and Housego, I E eds (1980) *Canadian and Comparative Educational Administration* Education-Extension, University of British Columbia: Vancouver
Gage, N L, Husén, T and Singleton, J W (1980) *Report of the Task Force on the Impact of the Research, Development and Field Activities of The Ontario Institute for Studies in Education: Summary and Conclusions* Ontario Institute for Studies in Education: Toronto
Gilliss, G C (1979) *Increasing Teacher Knowledge and Appreciation of Research* Paper presented at Canadian Education Association conference on Research and the Classroom Teacher, Winnipeg
Greenfield, T B (1979) *Research in Educational Administration in the United States and Canada: an Overview and Critique* Paper presented to British Educational Administration Society, Birmingham
Hersom, N (1980) Twenty-five years of research in education: 1955 to 1979 *Alberta Journal of Educational Research* 26 262-75
Holdaway, E A (1976) The organization of educational research: some European issues relevant to Canada *Canadian Journal of Education* 1 5-17
Holdaway, E A (1980) Educational administration in Canada: concerns, research and preparation programs *in* Farquhar and Housego (1980)
Holdaway, E A and Friesen, D (1980) *Canadian Society for the Study of Education: Development and Challenges* Department of Educational Administration, University of Alberta: Edmonton
Hunka, S (1978) *Prospectives in Educational Research* Opening Address to Canadian Educational Research Association: London, Ontario
International Development Research Centre (1983) *Review of IDRC Activities 1982:* Ottawa
Montgomerie, T C (1982) *Telidon Distance Education Field Trial* Alberta Department of Education: Edmonton
Rogers, W T (1982) *Research in Canadian Education: Contributions to Canadian Society* Unpublished paper, University of British Columbia: Vancouver
Ryan, D W (1983) *Sponsored Research in OISE: a Report to the OISE Board of*

Governors Ontario Institute for Studies in Education: Toronto

Ryan, D W and Butler, L F (1982) Effectiveness of teaching: the Canadian experience *Studies in Educational Evaluation* 7 247-62

Science Council of Canada (1983) *Annual Report, 1982-83:* Ottawa

Sheffield, E (1979) *Policy-oriented Research on National Issues in Higher Education* Discussion paper for the colloquium on data needs for higher education in the eighties, Statistics Canada: Ottawa

Sheffield, E ed (1982) *Research on Postsecondary Education in Canada* Social Sciences and Humanities Research Council of Canada: Ottawa

Social Sciences and Humanities Research Council of Canada (1982) *1981-82 Annual Report:* Ottawa

Social Sciences and Humanities Research Council of Canada (1983) *Research Grants: Guide to Applicants:* Ottawa

Stapleton, J J, Allard, M, MacIver, D A, MacPherson, E D and Williams, T R (1982) *Education Research in Canada: Aims, Problems and Possibilities* Social Sciences and Humanities Research Council of Canada: Ottawa

Stewart, F (1974) *Once More unto the Breach* Report of the Executive Director of the Canadian Education Association for 1973-74: Toronto

Tomkins, G, Connelly, F M and Bernier, J-J (1981) *State of the Art Review of Research in Curriculum and Instruction* Submission to the State of the Art Review of Educational Research for the Canadian Society for the Study of Education

Wisenthal, M (1982) *Education Research: Future Expectations and Past Performance* Social Sciences and Humanities Research Council of Canada: Ottawa

Wright, E N (1982) *Role and Function of Research Units in Boards of Education in Ontario* Paper presented to Association of Educational Research Officers of Ontario, Toronto

Acknowledgements

The information and opinions provided by the following people specifically for preparation of this chapter are gratefully acknowledged: B D Anderson, J H M Andrews, R Ayotte, C H Bélanger, J J Bergen, R E Blair, J W Brahan, B Burnham, R H Farquhar, H K Fisher, D Friesen, G Gilliss, J Girard, T B Greenfield, A Henderson-Nichol, N L Hersom, B M Hildebrand, I E Housego, J S Hrabi, S Hunka, B Levin, P J H Malmberg, S McDowell, H Mosychuk, C Roebothan, W T Rogers, D W Ryan, B J Shapiro, D Sibbett, M W Wahlstrom, T R Williams and E N Wright.

6. The present state of educational research in France

Louis Legrand

Summary: Educational research has undergone a development of some importance over the last 20 years. Whereas before 1968 it was principally devoted to
enquiries in the fields of educational psychology and academic and professional guidance, it has subsequently developed in two new dimensions: the
sociology of education, with the emphasis placed on the obstacles in the way
of the democratization of teaching, and curriculum innovation. In this latter
area research has been principally in the hands of teachers organized into
educational movements but lacking sufficient concern for evaluation and the
conditions of implementation. The period since 1975 is notable mainly for the
research done into evaluation of the functioning of the educational system
along with the development of empirical studies.
    The impact of educational research on the decision makers remains a
matter of speculation. The great reforms were inspired by economic and sociological studies but they were not accompanied by specific research, except in
the last period when the authorities instituted the system of evaluative feedback which was mentioned above. As for curriculum innovations, they have
remained qualitative without enough care being taken over precise observation
of the conditions of implementation. This situation can be explained by the
very centralized character of the French educational system and the existence
of a large inspectorate. Moreover, the very strongly academic nature of the
professional training of schoolteachers, who are for the most part quite
unaware of psychology and sociology, does not enable them to understand
empirical research.

A recent survey, undertaken under the auspices of the Council of Europe
by the Centre National de la Recherche Scientifique (CNRS) and the
Institut National de la Recherche Pédagogique (INRP) provides an up-to-
date overview of this question (INRP-CNRS, 1980-82). A report submitted
to the minister for research and technology has also provided interesting
details in this area (Carraz, 1983).

According to the survey, there are at present in France 87 research
centres in which some 900 researchers are working on approximately 500
research projects. These overall figures, however, conceal a very great
diversity. The size and importance of these 87 centres varies enormously.
Only 33 can be considered as being engaged in full-time research and, of
these, only eight employ more than 20 researchers. The other centres
consist of departments within universities in which the researchers are

teachers whose primary commitment is to students and who conduct research at the same time.

The type of research undertaken is itself very varied. Only six organizations are engaged on more than 20 financed research projects. Most of the other projects are in fact theses in the course of preparation, and are consequently individual undertakings of narrower scope than group projects.

The main centres specifically devoted to research are:

- l'Institut National de Recherche Pédagogique (108 researchers)
- le Laboratoire de Psychologie Différencielle (21 researchers)
- l'Ecole Normale Supérieure de Saint-Cloud avec le Centre de Recherche et d'Etude pour la Diffusion du Français (28 researchers)
- le Centre de Sociologie de l'Education et de la Culture (35 researchers)
- l'Institut de Recherche sur l'Economie de l'Education (8 researchers)
- le Centre d'Etudes et de Recherches sur les Qualifications (87 researchers)
- le Centre de Formation et de Recherche de l'Education Surveillée (18 researchers)
- le Service des Etudes Informatiques et Statistiques du Ministère de l'Education Nationale (12 researchers)

It is virtually impossible to get a sufficiently precise idea of the sums devoted to research because of the scale of university research which is not generally financed separately from teaching activities. It is interesting to note, however, that three principal sources of finance correspond to three distinct types of research. First, there are the resources emanating from the Ministère de l'Education Nationale, which mainly cover the research undertaken by the Institut Pédagogique National, whose primary field of interest is applied research into the curriculum in association with the 'Ecoles Normales' and with teaching establishments. Second, there is the Centre National de la Recherche Scientifique which finances allied laboratories, sited within universities and devoted to pure scientific, sociological, psychological, linguistic and economic research (21 associated centres). Third, there is the funding for universities which is devoted primarily to financing advanced students whose work is theoretical rather than commissioned. It is appropriate to underline the fact that this finance comes exclusively from government sources.

The relative importance of different thematic groupings of this work should be underlined. From 500 research projects included in the survey, the following figures emerge:

- 94 involve description and evaluation of the education system
- 23 are on the philosophy and the history of education
- 91 on the psychology of education
- 37 on the sociology of education
- 41 on the economics of education
- 76 on teaching methods
- 35 on education technology

- 10 on adult education
- 22 on socio-cultural handicaps

Applied research projects outnumber other activities; the main reason for this is the numerical and financial importance of the Institut National de Recherche Pédagogique, with 108 researchers and 61 projects in progress in 1982.

Historical background

The current situation, described above, is in fact a very new one in the French context. The survey quoted above noted: 'Of the 71 organizations which replied to this question, 12 were established before 1960, 13 were created between 1960 and 1969, and 46 were established after 1969. From 1965 onwards the setting up of these organizations has accelerated: 16 organizations were created prior to 1965, and 55 were created subsequently' (INRP-CNRS, 1980-82). The fact that educational research in France is of recent date is particularly characteristic if one compares it with the long history of such research in the Anglo-Saxon context. This situation can partly be understood in historical terms but also, probably, in terms of the structure of the French education system — a factor to which we shall devote more detailed attention in the concluding sections of this chapter.

From an historical point of view, four separate periods can be distinguished:

1. From 1930 to 1950 research on education in France developed on three main fronts: First, research into the problems of educational and professional guidance, with the foundation in 1928 of the Institut National d'Orientation Professionelle by Professor Henri Piéron and his successor, Maurice Reuchlin. The first work on the statistical analysis of test results in France also dates from that period (Reuchlin, 1954; Piéron, 1963). Second, the research carried out in the field of educational psychology by Henri Wallon and René Zazzo. This work deals essentially with pupils experiencing educational difficulties and stimulated a large number of studies published in the review *Enfance* (1952-53). Third, university-based research into experimental education by René Husson and Gaston Mialaret, co-founders of the Association Internationale de Pédagogie Experimentale de Langue Française along with the Swiss researchers, Robert Dottrens and Samuel Roller, and the Belgians, Raymond Buyse and Fernand Hotyat (Mialaret, 1954). Experimental education remained for a long time a restricted area, and was the exclusive preserve of a small number of committed researchers. Educational and professional guidance and educational psychology had, on the other hand, a marked influence on the evolution of ideas and institutions. Henri Wallon was, along with Paul Langevin, co-signatory of the famous plan which bears their names and which inspired all the

reforms in the French education system between 1945 and 1975.

2. From 1950 to 1968, university-based research into education developed
   in three directions: First, the economics of education, with the studies
   of Jaccard (1957) and Fourastié (1963) which demonstrated the
   economic necessity of mass education. In addition, research was done
   into the sociology of education by Bourdieu and Passeron (1964) and
   Beaudelot and Establet (1971). Their focus of interest was the critical
   examination of the failure of the education system as a sociological fact
   and the denunciation of the segregated pattern of the schooling and
   the conservative role played by the 'dominant ideology'. For over 30
   years this research has fuelled political discussions about schools and
   has had a more or less overt influence on the various reforms stemming
   from the Langevin-Wallon plan. Second, research has been carried out
   into the application of linguistics to the teaching of French as a foreign
   language with contributions from two main centres: the Centre de
   Recherche et d'Etude pour la Diffusion du Français (CREDIF) and the
   Bureau d'Etude de Langue et Civilisation (BELC). And finally – less
   well-known in the field of educational science but having a considerable
   theoretical importance – research into instructional psychology carried
   out at the University of Paris V and under the aegis of the Ecole des
   Hautes Etudes en Sciences Sociales by teams working along Piagetian
   lines in liaison with the Centre d'Epistemologie Génétique of Geneva
   (Gréco, 1963; Oléron, 1963; Bresson, 1965).

3. During these two periods (leaving out of account the structural changes
   in the educational system brought about by the creation of the middle
   school and the political debates which accompanied them) these research
   projects did not have very significant repercussions in terms of the day-
   to-day practice in French classrooms. The situation was totally different
   between 1968 and 1975. This period witnessed a proliferation of
   research initiatives in the field of teaching method and the foundation
   of most centres of educational research; the considerable development
   of the INRP (Majault, 1981) also dates from then. Similarly notable is
   the establishment of departments of education in universities which
   accompanied the official recognition of these developments, prompted
   by Maurice Debesse and Gaston Mialaret. The spate of innovations
   began in mathematics, and in the transformation of syllabus content
   under the inspiration of university teams working together under the
   name of BOURBAKI. Then came the turn of applied linguistics with
   the transfer into the teaching of French of the discoveries of generative
   and distributional linguistics. Finally there came the transformation of
   science education and education in social sciences. These innovations
   were essentially due to the efforts of teams of practitioners working in
   tandem with university researchers outside the professional hierarchy
   and using the administrative umbrella of the INRP. This general trend
   encountered considerable resistance, particularly from the inspectorate,
   and provoked acrimonious polemics with political repercussions. We are

at present witnessing a heated revaluation of these innovations, with a more or less general desire to turn back the clock. This desire is all the stronger because the innovations were accompanied by a profound parallel transformation in the education system, brought about by the pressures of urbanization, industialization and the breaking up of traditional family structures, plus the emergence of a new youth mentality which found its most forceful expression in the disruption of 1968 (Legrand, 1977; Geminard, 1977; Cros, 1981).

4. From 1975 there began a 'digestion' of previous findings along with a politically based revaluation of educational science, which the conservative political element sees as being of Marxist inspiration. Innovation has yielded to a preoccupation with evaluation. This explains the development of centres devoted to the evaluation of the educational system, with the transformation of the Statistical Studies Service of the Ministry into a Centre for Evaluative Research, and the downgrading of the Institut Pedagogique, which is no longer allowed to undertake large-scale work but has to restrict itself almost exclusively to small-scale projects of evaluation and observation. The advent of a left-wing government in 1981 has slightly eased the situation, but financial constraints remain along with a fairly general scepticism regarding innovation. The state of play in 1980 and 1982, on the basis of which this chapter was written, is probably only a temporary situation. It is impossible to predict the future lines along which educational research in France will develop.

The role of educational research in the French context

The late development of research in education in France shows sufficiently well that such studies are not integrated in an organic and permanent way into the functioning of the educational system. Granted, there have been great changes, like the 1959 reform, for example, which raised the school leaving age to 16, and the creation of comprehensive middle schools catering for the 11- to 16-year-old age group. Similarly, the contents of official syllabuses have changed a great deal over the last 20 years. But these changes owe little to rational, empirical studies. An accurate appraisal of these changes should take into account both recent history and the levels at which research can be influential.

The most obvious impact of educational research in France is the dominance that sociological research has come to hold in the constantly renewed political discussions and polemics centring on the school. The researches of Bourdieu and Beaudelot have fuelled the debates about democratization and the related question of parental choice in the past, and continue to do so. The causes of school failure and the possible remedies that can be applied to this are constantly incorporated in the context of sociological, psychosociological and psycholinguistic studies. Curricular innovations have also provided material for polemics in the fields of mathematics, of applied linguistics and of the social sciences.

It is against this background, and as an extension and accompaniment to these discussions, that educational research has been able to exercise a decisive influence over the political decisions which have left their mark on the French education system over the last 30 years (Capelle, 1974; Legrand, 1977). And in this case too, it has been sociological research and research into the economics of education that have underpinned the great reform of 1959 which ushered in the single system of education for children from 6 to 16 years. But it has basically been a matter of assimilating the results of theoretical research, often of foreign origin, and not the results of empirical experiments carried out in France. Decisions have been and still are taken on the basis of work done by commissions on which researchers sit in a consultative capacity. It is very seldom that decisions are taken on the basis of experiments. It is, for the most part, a question of rapid qualitative trials supervised by the inspectorate. It was not until 1975 with the reforms of René Haby that there emerged a concern for the scientific evaluation of the effects of educational reforms and the formation of a study group in the Statistical Study Service of the Ministry of Education. Even then, it must be borne in mind that the impact of such evaluation has been practically nil as far as subsequent decisions were concerned. The advent of a Socialist government has had no marked effect on these time-honoured practices. Decisions are still taken on the basis of the work of national Commissions, and the researchers consulted often see the advice they have given interpreted and transformed out of all recognition. In this area, opinion rules, and choices are made regardless of advice. It is political choices, along with economic imperatives, that carry the day.

It is important to point out that, on the question of structures, experiment has always been considered the prerogative of the authorities and has never been allowed except within narrowly defined limits. The idea of putting to the test a system which is off-course in terms of prevailing political tendencies has always been considered inadmissible. Moreover, quantified findings have traditionally been considered unimportant except insofar as they relate to rises in the birth-rate and the awarding of diplomas, knowledge in these areas having always been thought essential for economic planning. Since 1975, there has been a perceptible renewal of interest in empirical studies within the limits outlined above.

On the question of the subject matter of instruction we have already drawn attention to the importance which educational innovation has assumed in France since 1965: new mathematics, applied linguistics and reconstituted social sciences are very much to the fore in educational writing and have prompted a whole range of tests in numerous schools and teacher training colleges. But, once again, the process is far from being a rational one. In the first place, these innovations are still qualitative without any concern for objective evaluation. They are nothing like what the Anglo-Saxons call curriculum studies, but are much closer to educational movements, or even to the fashions which arise spontaneously from the grass roots — and often in open or latent conflict with the educational hierarchy. In the last analysis it is pressure groups (teachers of mathematics, teachers of French, and so on) who collude to force the central authorities to set up study groups which will produce new official texts even before there has been time for the results to be evaluated. This has given rise to consequences which were predictable but which were taken into account only at a very late stage, with a general tide of opinion, along with a new and irrational distrust of changes which are nonetheless necessary. The breakthrough of innovation and the related development of centres for educational research were in any case the result of the shock which the central authorities received in 1968. There was a certain loosening of the structure of the governmental machine, which went on for several years and which allowed some headroom for initiatives which had until then been held in check. This serves to explain the often 'missionary' nature of the innovators and the accumulated distrust they have generated among their political masters. The same explanation holds true for the questioning attitude towards educational innovation by conservative authorities since 1975 and the shift from action research towards evaluation, which these same authorities saw as an elegant way of stemming the tides of innovation.

How then, in our conclusion, can we explain this very ambiguous nature of educational research in France?

It is clear that the highly centralized nature of the State and of the educational system, along with the importance of the numerous and highly organized groups of inspectors, makes it unnecessary for those responsible for education to use any more elaborate techniques of coercion and control. This tendency is consolidated by the fact that the training of schoolteachers remains by tradition almost exclusively academic. Instructional psychology and sociology are not taught to teachers in training. Only primary school teachers in Ecoles Normales follow a course which includes a social science component. Again, it should be noted that for over 40 years the teachers in the Ecoles Normales were recruited directly from the traditional secondary sector, without specialized training in teaching method.

The teaching profession is therefore not ready to listen to what empirical researchers have to say. For them, research means personal innovation and pedagogical movements. Only the technocrats who take decisions are, by virtue of their economic background, sensitized to more advanced types of research and evaluation. Herein lies the reason for the use which has been and will continue to be made of macroscopic research in the formulation of structural decisions. This is a source of permanent misunderstanding between the Ministry and the technocrats who work for it on the one hand and the practitioners on the other. Structural decisions which emanate from on high and the modifications to content and method which accompany them appear suspect and manipulatory. Reforms are always something inflicted on the profession, and even those which come from the grass roots immediately become suspect to the teaching profession from the moment they are taken up by the directorate and officially adopted in ministerial circulars. This goes to explain the constant pendulum-swings in the trade union positions, advocating reforms which run counter to the prevailing political climate, and then resisting them as soon as the authorities adopt them. There is no way out of such a situation except by genuine decentralization and by the devolution of local responsibilities to schools themselves for the development of syllabuses and for the self-evaluation of their performance. But the precise implication of this is that the central authority must accept the need to relinquish its prerogatives, and the teaching unions must give up the power which they derive from centralization. Despite the present political position, it is far from certain that this new situation can come about in a country marked by centuries of Jacobin centralization and humanist culture with a literary bias (Legrand, 1983).

References

Beaudelot, C and Establet, R (1971) *L'école capitaliste en France* Masperio: Paris
Bourdieu, P and Passeron, J C (1964) *Les héritiers* Les éditions de Minuit: Paris
Bresson, F (1965) Langage et communication *in* Fraisse et Piaget *ed Traité de Psychologie* T. VIII. PUF: Paris
Capelle, J (1974) *Education et politique* PUF: Paris
Carraz, R (1984) *Recherche en éducation et socialisation de l'enfant* Rapport au Ministère de la Recherche et de la Technologie, la Documentation Francaise: Paris
Cros, L (1981) *Quelle école, pour quel avenir?* Casterman: Paris
Enfance, no. spécial 5 (1952-3): *La psychologie scolaire* PUF: Paris
Fourastié, J (1963) *Le grand espoir du vingtième siècle* Gallimard: Paris
Géminard, L (1977) *L'enseignement éclaté* Casterman, Paris
Gréco, P (1963) Apprentissage et structures intellectuelles *in* Fraisse et Piaget *ed Traité de psychologie* T. VIII. PUF: Paris
Institut National de Recherche Pedagogique et Centre National de la Recherche Scientifique (1980-2) *Repertoire des organismes francais de recherche en sciences de l'éducation*, INRP-CNRS: Paris
Jaccard, P (1957) *Politique de l'emploi et de l'éducation* Payot: Paris
Legrand, L (1977) *Pour une politique démocratique de l'éducation* PUF: Paris
Legrand, L (1983) *Pour un collège démocratique* Rapport au Ministère de l'Education Nationale, La Documentation Francaise: Paris
Majault, J (1981) *Comptes, mécomptes, descomptes* Casterman: Paris
Mialaret, G (1954) *Nouvelle pédagogie scientifique* PUF: Paris
Oléron, P (1963) Les activités intellectuelles *in* Fraisse et Piaget *ed Traité de psychologie* T. VIII. PUF: Paris
Piéron, H (1963) *Examens et docimologie* PUF: Paris
Reuchlin, M (1971) *L'orientation scolaire et professionnelle* PUF: Paris

7. Educational research in the Federal Republic of Germany

Wolfgang Mitter

Summary: The paper begins with an attempt to clarify the term 'educational research' in the historical context of the Federal Republic of Germany during the 1960s and attempts to relate it to the contemporary debate on fundamental and methodological issues of social science theory characterized by a confrontation between the adherents of traditional 'pedagogics', analytical-empirical research and the 'critical theory' of the Frankfurt School (with its impact on 'action research'). There then follows an analysis of the events and factors whose appraisal is thought to be necessary for understanding the development of the interrelation between policy makers and educationists in the 'reform period' of the early 1970s.

The focal section is devoted to the institutionalization of educational research whereby special attention is paid to the duality of 'independent' (universities, non-governmental institutions) and 'dependent' (state institutes) research centres. The paper concludes with a stocktaking of the present situation and an outlook into the 1980s, dealing with topical issues of organization and funding, discussing questions concerning the impact of educational research on policy and practice and offering insight into recent trends in the area of research methodology which point to a 'new' empiricism, amalgamating quantifying and qualifying methods.

Retrospect

The start in the 1960s

The term 'educational research' (Bildungsforschung) has a comparatively short history in the Federal Republic of Germany. Its application can be traced back to the early 1960s which mark a turning point in the history of educational policy in that country. Those were the years when the needs of the educational system, until then regarded as rather an issue of secondary importance, became relevant in discussions both among the general public and in the bodies responsible for schools and other educational institutions.

The year 1963 may be considered as a visible proof of the turning point. The following events of that year bear witness:

(a) Federal Chancellor Ludwig Erhard, on succeeding Konrad Adenauer to the chancellorship, declared that the educational issue was equal in significance to the social issue of the 19th century.

(b) The Standing Conference of Laender Ministers of Education pub-
     lished a document which for the first time contained the long-term
     requirements of schooling and study and an estimate of the finan-
     cial requirements needed for the implementation of the respective
     plans and proposals.
(c) Eugen Lemberg published the book *The Educational System as a
     Subject of Research* with a number of articles by prominent
     domestic and foreign educationists, including his own prospective
     contribution: 'From educational science to educational research:
     the educational system as a social institution' (Lemberg, 1963a: 21
     et sq).
(d) The Max-Planck-Institute for Educational Research was founded
     (in West Berlin) as the second supraregional institute of that kind.
     (The first institute — the German Institute for International
     Educational Research — had been set up at Frankfurt am Main in
     1952.)

In their intention to further the expansion of the educational system,
policy makers found themselves in serious difficulties, insofar as reliable
data and instruments necessary for efficient planning were not readily
available. Therefore 'educational planning' (Bildungsplanung) was put on
the agenda of educational policies which entailed the establishment of
planning divisions in the Ministries of Education and the commissioning of
experts to carry out trend studies. However, those external initiatives
would not have had such far-reaching effects within a few years had they
not coincided with internal reconsiderations in the academic disciplines
constituting the new research area.

First, until then education and upbringing had been the monopolized
domain of the disciplines of 'pedagogics' (Pädagogik) and psychology,
more or less separated in teaching and research. The new approach opened
the door to other disciplines: sociology and economics, followed by
political science, administration and management, jurisprudence etc. The
collaboration among those disciplines underlined the demand for multi-
disciplinarity.

Second, objectives and contents of educational studies were questioned.
Traditional pedagogics had been focused on the history of educational
ideas on the one hand and individual educational situations and actions on
the other, thereby greatly benefiting from the rich heritage which had
been laid down in the 19th century and remarkably extended in the
'reform movement' (Reform-pädagogik) during the first decades of the
20th century. However, the new research area has concentrated on the
investigation of the educational system as a social institution. As far as its
objectives are concerned, there has been an articulate turn from the former
(though never uncontested) focus on epistemological issues to a direct
commitment to the improvement of the educational system. To whatever
extent practice-orientation had been included in traditional pedagogics (to
be exemplified by Herbart's concept of the 'educating school') it has
become a constituent part of 'educational research'.

Third, the 'realistic turn in pedagogical research', as announced by Heinrich Roth, also in 1963, signalled the entry of 'explaining' (as distinct from 'understanding'), in the form of analytical-empirical methods, into the new research area (Roth, 1963: 109 *et sq*). Following the patterns developed in practice in the United States within the guide-lines of behaviourism and learning theory, quantifying procedures, measures and instruments took possession of existing and newly established university institutes and were accepted as the exclusive methodological approach in the new institutes outside the universities.

Summarizing this retrospect to this point one can certainly discover striking parallels to trends in other Western countries, due to a great extent to the fact that the formation and development of educational research was considerably stimulated by young educationists and sociologists who had studied and worked at some time in the United States. On the other hand the 'Federal German case' is characterized by the inclusion of the methodological schools' (Methodenstreit) which affected the foundations of social science theory. In that discussion the 'positivists' — as the adherents of 'classical' empirical methods — had to fight on two fronts:

(a) against the philosophy-bound 'pedagogics' and the 'hermeneutic method' which had been derived from the humanities and had been recognized as the predominating method applied in that discipline;

(b) against the effects of the 'critical theory' (Frankfurt School) of the just-established 'educational science' (Erziehungswissenschaft) which had superseded the traditional 'pedagogics'. This 'critical method', while dedicated to social criticism as far as its theoretical foundation is concerned, has to some extent merged 'hermeneutic' and 'empirical' methods. Besides, its adherents emphasized the integration between research and practice and have therefore shown considerable commitment in the area of 'action research'.

The whole outline presented here would be unbalanced unless the German pioneers of the 'realistic turn in pedagogical research' were mentioned. One has to think of the various forms of practice-oriented educational research (Tatsachenforschung), which were presented in the first decades of this century under the catchwords 'experimental pedagogy' (Experimentelle Pädagogik), 'descriptive pedagogy' (Deskriptive Pädagogik) etc.

The 'reform period' of the early 1970s

With educational theory oriented to the three reconsiderations mentioned above, educational research made a remarkable contribution to the 'reform period' of the early 1970s. Policy makers and school administrators showed considerable concern for educational research, which met with widespread approval and a readiness for cooperation among the community of educationists (this term now being related to the multidisciplinary structure). In retrospect from today's situation the picture seems to differ a great deal from the expectations now shared by policy makers as well as researchers. In the meantime critics have emphasized the two following points:

(a) Many educationists overestimated their chances of influencing innovations and, at the same time, underestimated the strength of the traditional attitudes of the groups concerned (parents, teachers, officials etc) and the long-term persistence of human feelings in general. Therefore a good part of their innovative efforts suffered from lack of thorough empirical enquiry (in spite of the proclaimed 'realistic turn'!) or their data were devalued by predictive statements which were not confirmed by the data base.

(b) The policy-making agencies did not take a serious interest in the educational research for which the researchers themselves were responsible and which was not directly supervised. They regarded educational research only as a means to legitimate their actions and intentions. This point, of course, cannot be confined to the period described and will be taken up again later.

This form of reproducing the criticism highlights its dominant feature. Less extreme in their appraisal have been various statements marked by moderate arguments and refinements of opinion. Bearing this spectrum in mind, one can nevertheless draw the conclusion that retrospective criticism has really hit the weakest points in the relation between educational policy and educational research in the 'reform period'. At least one can argue that the following effects of that apparent tension have since become evident:

(a) in the successful strategy pursued by the Laender governments to establish research institutes directly attached to them;

(b) in a widespread disappointment among 'independent educationists' (working at universities and non-governmental research institutes) at being excluded from immediately influencing educational policy and practice.

While considering these effects one has, however, to add that researchers working in governmental institutes often do not abstain from striving for a certain 'autonomy' in determining themes and methods and that, on the other hand, governments have not totally stopped hiring university professors for commissioned projects for which special expertise is needed.

The institutionalization of educational research

Educational research carried out in university institutes and the non-governmental supraregional institutes at Frankfurt and West Berlin has been focused on basic investigations. This statement is not thought to be contradictory to the fact that they have often indulged in practice-oriented enquiries and commissioned projects based on contracts with ministries and other governmental agencies. This was particularly true of the Max-Planck-Institute for Educational Research in the early 1970s when it cooperated closely with the German Educational Council (Deutscher Bildungsrat). This advisory body to the Federal Government and to the Laender governments published a large number of substantial reports and recommendations utilizing the outcomes of empirical enquiries; the widest attention and response was gained by the 'Structure Plan' (Deutscher Bildungsrat, 1970), because this document (for the first time in the educational history of the Federal Republic of Germany) covered the educational system as a whole.

Nonetheless there has been a growing shift in the institutionalization of educational research, as far as the practice-oriented and applied type ('development') is concerned, from commissioning 'external' experts (in universities and non-governmental institutes) to establishing educational research institutes under the direct supervision of Laender Ministries of Education. The initiatives of the Laender in this area resulted in the foundation of the following institutes:

- 1965 West Berlin: 'Pedagogic Centre' (Pädagogisches Zentrum), reorganized in 1974;
- 1966 Bavaria (Bayern): beginning of the establishment of the 'Centre for Educational Research' (Zentrum für Bildungsforschung) at Munich, consisting of four (since 1983: three) 'State Institutes' attached to the Bavarian Ministry of Education;
- 1970 Baden-Wuerttemberg: 'Institute for Educational Planning and School Development' (Institut für Bildungsplanung und Schulentwicklung) at Stuttgart, reorganized and renamed 'State Authority for Education and Instruction' (Landesstelle für Bildung und Unterricht) in 1976;
- 1971 Schleswig-Holstein: 'State Institute for School Practice and Theory' (Landesinstitut für Praxis und Theorie der Schule);
- 1974 Rhineland-Palatinate (Rheinland-Pfalz): 'Working Office for Curriculum Development and Coordination' (Arbeitsstelle für Lehrplanentwicklung und -koordination) at Bad Kreuznach;
- 1975 Hessen: 'Hessian Institute for Educational Planning and School Development' (Hessisches Institut für Bildungsplanung und Schulentwicklung) at Wiesbaden;
- 1978 Northrhine-Westphalia (Nordrhein-Westfalen): 'Institute for Curriculum Development and In-service Training' (Institut für Curriculumentwicklung, Lehrerfortbildung und -weiterbildung) at Neuss, integrating special working groups which had been active since 1973; reorganized and renamed 'State Institute for School and In-service Training (Landesinstitut für Schule und Weiterbildung) and removed to Soest in 1983;
- 1979 Lower Saxony (Niedersachsen): 'State Institute for In-service Training of Teachers' (Staatsinstitut für Lehrerfortund -weiterbildung) at Hildesheim which also devotes part of its activities to educational research.

Only the smallest Laender (Bremen, Hamburg, Saarland) have neither institutes of their own nor have started any initiatives in that direction.

The Laender institutes have not engaged in fundamental research. Instead they have focused their activities on the evaluation of pilot experiments which have been going on at the various levels of the educational system (from preschool to higher education and teacher training). Until the beginning of the 1980s the overall responsibility for the initiation and evaluation of the pilot experiments lay with the Federal-Laender Commission for Educational Planning and the Promotion of Research (Bund-Laender-Kommission für Bildungsplanung und Forschungsförderung) on the basis of the Comprehensive Education Plan (Bildungsgesamtplan) in 1973; however, the Federal Government and the Laender governments could not agree on the reassessment it was subject to in 1981. The Federal-Laender Commission consists of eleven representatives of the Federal Government and one representative of each Land government. The representatives of the Federal Government hold eleven votes, which are cast jointly whereas the representatives of the Laender governments each hold one vote. The Commission takes its decisions on the basis of a three-quarters majority of its members' votes. Therefore neither the Federal Government nor the Laender governments (as a group) can realize their intentions against opposition from the other side. As for educational research including enquiries within state schools the Laender are, nevertheless, in a better position, insofar as they are free to initiate projects outside the section coordinated by the Federal-Laender Commission. The Federal Government is dependent on the consent of all Laender (within the section coordinated by the Federal-Laender Commission), or of the individual Land in a special case which is usually formalized by bilateral agreement. This inequality of competency corresponds to the power structure in the Federal Republic of Germany, allocating the 'cultural sovereignty' (Kulturhoheit) to the Laender.

The Federal Government only supervises non-school vocational training and further training. Within this area of responsibility the 'Federal Institute of Vocational Training' (Bundesinstitut für Berufsbildung) was established in 1970 and has been reorganized three times since then. Its function within the Federal Government's educational policy is to promote and further develop vocational training by way of research. Such research is particularly concerned with scientific observation, investigation and evaluation of the conditions and demands of training. It also includes the scrutiny of contents and objectives and their adaptation to technical, economic and social developments.

Completing the presentation of the practice-oriented section of educational research, two supraregional institutes which are non-governmental but strongly affiliated to governmental authorities and commissions deserve mention: the 'Institute for the Pedagogy of Natural Sciences' (Institut für die Pädagogik der Naturwissenschaften) attached to the University of Kiel and the 'German Youth Institute' (Deutsches Jugendinstitut) at Munich.

The funding of educational research is generally determined by the status of the respective institutions. While the governmental institutes are directly and totally financed out of the state budgets, there is no uniformity with regard to the university and the independent non-governmental institutes, insofar as their basic finances are provided by the Laender (in the case of the universities) or in the form of joint funding schemes shared by the Federal and Laender authorities. Besides, the institutions belonging to the latter group are dependent on supplementary funding by sponsoring agencies, such as the German Research Council (Deutsche Forschungsgemeinschaft) and the Volkswagen Foundation.

Stocktaking and outlook

As in other industrialized countries, the oil crisis of 1973, followed by the first economic recession, entailed the end of the 'reform period'. The second recession, starting at the end of the 1970s and extending into the 1980s, has reinforced this development and given way to a predominating pressure for what conservatives in Western Germany have called the 'change of the trend' (Tendenzwende), as opposed to the preceding 'reform period'. However, this macroscopic picture needs to be differentiated, insofar as it does not throw light on the multifarious innovations taking place at the grass roots, ie in class-rooms, places of non-formal education etc.

It would be too simplistic to claim that the external factors caused by the economic recessions with their budgetary consequences have been solely responsible for the 'change of the trend'. There is certainly some justification for the view already mentioned that the euphoric expectations which had been raised by many statements and declarations could not have been fulfilled even in a stage of economic prosperity. One must consider not only the issue of finance in this context, but also the neglect in orientating the attitudes of affected people and groups to the new goals. This is why both the curtailment of school and research budgets and the feeling of disappointment at the non-fulfilment of hopes have coincided and consequently doubled the effect of disenchantment. Educational research has been considerably affected by the disillusioned atmosphere characterizing educational policies after the 'reform period'. Judging from the quota of expenditure on educational research in the public budgets, the cuts have not been too bad so far, although one must admit that 'stabilized' quotas conceal the factual rise of expenditure (on staff, writing and printing materials, mailing etc). The budgetary issue, however, only reveals one side of the coin, because it does not regard the qualitative change that has taken place since the middle of the 1970s in the distribution of the means available for research projects. The expansion of the section occupied by the governmental institutes distinctly illustrates the current trend, for the shift from (comparatively) 'independent' to 'dependent' research has been connected with the change in the primary function of educational research. In the 'reform period' it was (or was said to be) directly assigned to the goal of 'consultation'. The advance of the governmental institutes has signalled a growing demand for purely developmental projects, ie support of the implementation of structural and, above all, curricular changes based on preceding political or administrative decisions.

One should not overlook the advantages of this shift towards the predominance of implementation-oriented research in terms of short-term efficiency. In this context one has to take into additional account that ministerial divisions for educational research have intensified and improved their own expertise. However, the critics have based their contrasting arguments on the inability of the comparatively rigid and inflexible structure of governmental institutes to cope with middle- and long-term tasks, apart from their avoidance of conclusion-oriented research. It seems that such criticism has not left the addressees (in ministries etc) untouched; for example, there were three successful seminars, which CERI organized together with the Federal-Laender Commission, the Austrian Ministry of Education and Art and the (Swiss) Conference of Cantonal Directors of Education, about issues in evaluating pilot experiments in the school systems (BLK, 1979, 1981).

At these three conferences the participants — ministerial officials and educationists — agreed on the desirability of a diversified organization of educational research which should be allocated according to the various purposes which determine the interrelation between research and policy on education:

    (a) university institutes and 'independent' (non-governmental supraregional institutes to be primarily devoted to fundamental (conclusion-oriented) research and decision-oriented applied research;

    (b) governmental ('state') institutes to focus their activities on implementation-oriented applied research and development.

Until now it has remained an open question whether these proposals will be put into practice. The prospects for such a 'division of labour' are, among other things, dependent on how the non-governmental agencies mentioned above will be able to go on sponsoring university and 'independent' institutes.

As regards the 'security' of working conditions the governmental type of research institution is, at least up to the present, privileged with regard to financing. However, there is another kind of restraint. From their beginnings, governmental institutes have been subject to the current educational policies of their 'masters', ie the respective Laender governments. In the 1970s there were two cases where researchers working in state institutes came into conflict with their ministers because of incongruities between the outcome of certain enquiries and official educational policies. In both cases, namely in West Berlin (1974) and Baden-Wuerttemberg (1976) the governments 'solved' the controversies by revising the status of their institutes, which in the event meant de-grading them.

Has educational research had any recognized impact on educational policy during the past 25 years? An unequivocal answer to this question cannot be given as regards narrow-range enquiries in the area of testing achievements and abilities in certain school subjects (eg reading comprehension, mathematics, foreign languages). Certain impacts are relatively easy to identify, since the evaluation of curricular pilot projects has motivated governmental agencies to revise parts of the syllabuses concerned. Impacts of wider-range enquiries are much less discernible. However, there is reason to assume that pilot projects in this category have also influenced educational policies. This may be demonstrated by the evaluation programmes of the Federal-Laender Commission. In particular, this is true of innovations in class-room differentiation (mixed ability grouping, individualization, setting models of different kinds, etc), although one must take into account unavoidable reductions in reliability due to the isolation of variables. Finally, it is the interrelation between a 'dependent' status of researchers (working in governmental institutes or on commissioned projects) and the determination of themes to be dealt with which has to be borne in mind. To give the topical example of 'multiculturalism' in West German schools, recent enquiries have been focused on 'integrated' or 'segregated' classes, with both producing 'positive' outcomes and thus supporting the dissimilar policies of the commissioning Laender. In this context the proposed strategy towards a 'division of labour' in favour of a stronger promotion of 'independent research' should be seen as a plea for a corrective, apart from the desirability of competitiveness as such.

Besides the issues of organization, finance and impact, methodological considerations remain on the agenda. Referring to the 'conflict of methodological schools' in the late 1960s there has been a significant trend towards a reconciliation and even amalgamation of the three methodological approaches. This trend may lead to an 'integrative pluralism' (Roth, 1976: 152) to be centred upon a 'new' empiricism characterized by the enrichment of the former exclusively dominating quantifying methods with qualitative activities. In this new approach participatory observations, portfolio techniques, open interviews and 'ethnographic' evaluations play an essential role. However, clarification is still needed as regards the empirical reliability of the qualitative methods (Garz and Kraimer, 1983).

Summing up this overview, educational research in the Federal Republic of Germany will have to continue its route in a period which is not characterized any longer by 'big reforms' in the education system. On the other hand this overview would give an incomplete and one-sided impression unless it persuaded the reader to pay attention to facts and trends which justify prediction in a spirit of moderate optimism, based mainly on local initiatives both in research institutions and in schools.

References

Aurin, K (1969-70) The role of empirical research in educational planning and policy-making *Western European Education* 1 74-92
Bund-Länder-Kommission für Bildungsplanung und Forschungsförderung (1979) *Evaluation schulischer Neuerungen* CERI-Seminar Dillingen 1977 Klett-Cotta: Stuttgart

Bund-Länder-Kommission für Bildungsplanung und Forschungsförderung (1981) *Dimensionen und Grenzen der Evaluation schulischer Neuerungen.* CERI-Seminar Neusiedl am See 1979 Klett-Cotta: Stuttgart

Deutscher Bildungsrat (1970) *Strukturplan für das Bildungswesen* Bundesdruckerei: Bonn

Deutscher Bildungsrat (1974) *Aspekte für die Planung der Bildungsforschung* Bundesdruckerei: Bonn

Di Iorio, F ed (1983) *Innovazione educativa e riforma dell'insegnamento primario* Centro Europeo dell'Educazione: Frascati, Italy

Führ, Ch (1979) *Education and Teaching in the Federal Republic of Germany* Carl Hanser Verlag: München/Wien

Garz, D and Kraimer, K eds (1983) *Brauchen wir andere Forschungsmethoden? Beiträge zur Diskussion interpretativer Verfahren* Scriptor: Frankfurt am Main

Ingenkamp, K ed (1980) *Forschung und Lehre sind frei ...* Beltz Verlag: Weinheim/Basel

Klafki, W (1976a) Erziehungswissenschaft als kritisch-konstruktive Theorie: Hermeneutik, Empirie, Ideologiekritik *in* Klafki (1976b)

Klafki, W (1976b) *Aspekte kritisch-konstruktiver Erziehungswissenschaft* Beltz Verlag: Weinheim/Basel

Lemberg, E (1963a) Von der Erziehungswissenschaft zur Bildungsforschung: Das Bildungswesen als gesellschaftliche Institution *in* Lemberg (1963b)

Lemberg, E (1963b) *Das Bildungswesen als Gegenstand der Forschung* Quelle und Meyer: Heidelberg

Malmquist, E in cooperation with Grundin, H (1975) *Educational Research in Europe Today and Tomorrow* CWK Gleerup: Lund, Sweden

Mitter, W and Weishaupt, H ed (1977) *Ansätze zur Analyse der wissenschaftlichen Begleitung bildungspolitischer Innovationen* Beltz Verlag: Weinheim/Basel

Mitter, W and Weishaupt, H ed (1979) *Strategien und Organisationsformen der Begleitforschung* Beltz Verlag: Weinheim/Basel

Mitter, W (1983) Le recenti ricerche sulla scuola primaria nella Repubblica Federale Tedesca *in* Di Iorio (1983)

Roth, H (1963) Die realistische Wendung in der pädagogischen Forschung *Die deutsche Schule* 55 109-19

Roth, L ed (1976) *Handlexikon zur Erziehungswissenschaft* Ehrenwirth Verlag: München

Roth, L ed (1978) *Methoden erziehungswissenschaftlicher Forschung* Verlag W. Kohlhammer: Stuttgart

Terhart, E (1982) Interpretative approaches in educational research *Cambridge Journal of Education* 12 141-60

8. Educational research in India: a review

H. S. Srivastava

Summary: The review starts with the emergent demand on educational research to enable education to catch up with progress in other fields, leading to statements on what educational research ought to do in this direction. The main agencies supporting and sponsoring research in India are described. Reviews of educational research in India are then discussed, classifying studies into 20 categories and briefly evaluating work in each of these areas. The main shortcomings of educational research studies in India are enumerated and encouraging trends are identified. The review concludes with an assessment of the future of educational research.

Introduction

Educational research is both a challenge and a hope. Though the environmental situation in different parts of the globe has undergone a phenomenal change, education somehow has not shown a corresponding rate of growth and advancement. The first task of educational research, therefore, is to help education grow faster, to catch up with progress in social, economic, political, industrial, technological and scientific fields. But we should accept that it is difficult for educational innovations alone to change the social order. We should therefore restrain our ambitions in this regard and aim at a realistic target.

Though several aims of educational research can be identified, three stand out as most prominent from the functional point of view: (a) the results of educational research should influence policy making at the governmental level; (b) educational research should potentially help the teacher in improving instructional procedures and practices; and (c) educational research should help in improving the level of achievement of individual students and the standard of education in general. Thus educational research ought to contribute towards

- changing education rather than studying the changes in education,
- making education a self-renewing and self-generating process by incorporating research as a built-in component of educational administration,
- encouraging interaction of education with other fields through

mutual give-and-take, and
- helping bridge the gap between educational theory and educational practice.

As yet, educational research has fallen far short of realizing these goals.

Agencies supporting, sponsoring and conducting research in education

There are a number of agencies, organizations and institutions engaged in educational research in India. These can be broadly divided into two categories: those that deal with research in education exclusively; and those which promote research in a number of fields, of which education is one.

Agencies dealing with research in education exclusively

The National Council of Educational Research and Training (NCERT), New Delhi was established in 1961 by merging a number of existing specialized institutions which the government of India had set up with a view to providing academic support for improving the quality of school education in India. The Council is an autonomous organization and functions as an academic adviser to the Ministry of Education and Culture, which draws upon the expertise of the NCERT in formulating and implementing its policies and programmes in school education. The Council is fully financed by the government of India.

The Council undertakes the following programmes and activities towards realizing its objectives:

- conducts, aids, promotes and coordinates research in all branches of school education;
- organizes pre-service and in-service training mainly at an advanced level;
- organizes extension services for institutions, organizations and agencies engaged in educational reconstruction;
- develops and experiments with improved educational techniques, practices and innovations;
- collects, compiles, processes and disseminates educational information;
- assists the states and state-level institutions, organizations and agencies in developing and implementing programmes for the qualitative improvement of school education;
- collaborates with international organizations like UNESCO, UNICEF, etc and with national level educational institutions of other countries;
- extends facilities for training and study to educational personnel from other countries; and
- serves as the academic secretariat of the National Council of Teacher Education.

Research and support for research are important activities of the NCERT. In addition to the Departments/Units of the National Institute of Education (NIE) at Delhi and the Regional Colleges of Education (RCEs) at Ajmer, Bhopal, Bhubaneshwar and Mysore which undertake research, the NCERT supports educational research by providing financial assistance to outside organizations. Most of the research undertaken or supported by the NCERT is in identified areas of priority.

The NCERT set up the Educational Research and Innovations Committee (ERIC) in 1974, as a special mechanism for supporting research. This Committee includes eminent researchers in education and allied disciplines from universities and research institutes and representatives from the State Institutes of Education and State Councils of Educational Research and Training, together with all the Professors and Heads of Departments/Units of NIE and the RCEs. The main functions of the ERIC are:

- to support research and innovative projects in education and allied sciences;
- to provide fellowships for undertaking research in education;
- to award publication grants for PhD theses, monographs, etc; and
- to disseminate research findings from time to time and to organize research conferences.

The research proposals that NCERT receives from its departments/units are first evaluated by a Screening Committee. Evaluation of the proposals is generally made on the criteria of value, adequacy of design, etc. The research studies are both basic and applied and their findings are constantly fed into the various programmes of the Council for the qualitative improvement of school education. The research proposals received from other institutions and requests for publication grants are evaluated by eminent experts in different fields of specialization. At the doctoral level research on educational problems is supported through fellowships; and as part of the faculty improvement programme, members of academic staff are also offered study leave and grants for research pursuits.

The National Institute of Education Planning and Administration, New Delhi (NIEPA) is an autonomous institution, established in 1970 and originally known as the National Staff College for Educational Planners and Administrators, assuming its present name in 1979. The objectives of the Institute are:

- to undertake research in educational planning and administration;
- to provide training and consultancy services in this field;
- to arrange for the orientation of senior educational administrators from the Centre and the States; and
- to collaborate with other Asian countries.

The research activities of the Institute are aimed at diagnosing inadequacies in current educational planning and administration and suggesting remedial action. While theoretical under-pinning is a necessary aspect, being steadily strengthened, the emphasis is on applied research.

The Directorate of Adult Education, New Delhi was established in 1971 by separating the Department of Adult Education from the NCERT, and it now functions directly under the Union Ministry of Education and Culture. The Directorate does not itself undertake research but sponsors and supports individual and institutional research in the area of adult education. The main focus is on themes which are likely to yield findings potentially capable of improving the ongoing programmes of adult education. Some of the main areas of adult education in which research projects are funded by the Directorate are planning and management, the motivation of clients, instructional materials and media, monitoring and evaluation, and the education of workers.

The Central Hindi Institute, established in 1961 basically for training Hindi Teachers, has now expanded its functions to include research and development on themes related to Hindi Language. Through The Central Institute of Indian Languages, Mysore, the government provides facilities for the study of languages other than the mother tongue. The study of tribal languages is one of its important functions. The Institute develops improved teaching methods, prepares teaching materials and trains second language teachers at its Regional Languages Centres, and also conducts research necessary for this purpose. The Central Institute of English and Foreign Languages, Hyderabad, which was granted university status in 1973, trains teachers of English and foreign languages. In addition to the development of methodology and production of teaching materials for the use of Indian teachers of these languages, the Institute undertakes research through its own staff and research scholars.

There are many schemes for the propagation of Sanskrit and other classical languages like Arabic and Persian. The Rashtriya Sanskrit Sansthan (The National Sanskrit Directorate) promotes the study of Sanskrit, and a bureau, Taraqui-e-Urdu, has been set up for the promotion of Urdu. While development is the main function of these institutions, they also undertake and sponsor research projects in their specific fields.

Institutions such as the State Institutes of Education or State Councils of Educational Research and Training are in fact the state level counterparts of the National Council of Educational Research and Training and perform similar functions including research. They have a number of specialized departments manned by experts in fields such as curriculum, evaluation, teaching-aids, guidance and so on. The State Boards of Secondary Education, responsible mainly for conducting public examinations at the secondary and higher secondary levels, also undertake a wide variety of functional studies and investigations of problems of assessment.

The Centre for Advanced Studies in Education (CASE) MS University, Baroda is a specialized centre funded by the UGC (see below). Since its establishment in 1963 it has supported and sponsored research in education by giving grants and fellowships in addition to the projects conducted by its own faculty.

Institutions including education as one of the several areas of research

The University Grants Commission (UGC), established in 1965 by Act of Parliament, coordinates and determines standards in the universities. Towards this end, it offers various types of grants to different universities for maintenance and development. All universities, institutions of university status and colleges function under the umbrella of the UGC. Many of these have departments of education and allied disciplines like psychology, which pursue research in the area of education and receive grants to support fellowships and other expenditure for the purpose. Besides studies by individuals for pursuing work at PhD, MPhil and MEd levels, many of the university departments and teachers' colleges also undertake departmental research projects in education with the financial support of the UGC. The UGC has also opened Centres for Advanced Research in different disciplines: one catering for education functions at the MS University of Baroda as mentioned above.

The Association of Indian Universities acquired legal status in 1973 but had functions from 1925 under its old name as the Inter University Board. Of late, the Association has taken up two areas for in-depth research, examination reform and the economics of education.

The Indian Institute of Advanced Studies, Simla, set up in 1965, is a centre for advanced research in humanities, social sciences and natural sciences. It is a community of scholars engaged in exploring new frontiers of knowledge aimed at making major conceptual developments and at offering inter-disciplinary perspectives on questions of contemporary relevance.

The Indian Council of Social Science Research (ICSSR) New Delhi, an autonomous organization, was established by the Government of India in 1969 with the primary objective of promoting research in the Social Sciences. The work of the Council extends over different disciplines, and education is included among these. The principal instruments employed by the ICSSR to meet its objectives are research grants, fellowships, training programmes, documentation services, data archives, publications, seminars and the development of an infra-structure to improve the capacity for research through established regional centres and by grants to selected research institutions. In making grants ICSSR covers those institutions which do not come within the purview of the University Grants Commission.

The Indian Council of Historical Research, New Delhi, set up in 1972, enunciates and implements a national policy of historical research and encourages scientific writing of history. It operates research projects, offers fellowships, publishes theses and monographs and translates source materials and important history books. The Indian Council of Philosophical Research, Lucknow, was set up by the Central Government in 1981 to promote studies and research in philosophical themes. The Tata Institute of Social Sciences, Bombay, and the Institute of Social and Economic Change, Bangalore are other institutes which support and sponsor research on aspects of education.

Reviews of educational research in India

Research in the field of education in India was a rare phenomenon until the 1960s. It has picked up only in the last two or two-and-a-half decades. Valuable research efforts have since been invested both through individual initiatives and also by educational research agencies in India.

Reviews of educational research in India have been very few. The subject was touched upon probably for the first time as a part of the review of education in Indian universities undertaken by the UGC in the early 1960s. Then in 1966 and 1968 the National Council of Educational Research and Training, New Delhi, brought out two publications entitled 'Educational Investigations in Indian Universities'. The first of these covered studies and investigations undertaken at the PhD level and the second one dealt with those at the MEd level. Both these publications covered the period 1939-1966. Then in 1968, the NCERT also brought out the Third Indian Yearbook of Education which was devoted to educational research.

A parallel venture was the publication of a Directory of Behavioural Science Research in India brought out by the Behavioural Science Centre, Delhi, in 1966, covering studies between 1925 and 1965 (Pareek and Kumar, 1966). Subsequent to this, in 1970, the Tata Institute of Social Sciences, Bombay, published a review of the Sociology of Education (Chitnis, 1970). The Indian Council of Social Science Research has also since 1971 taken up the publication of research abstracts in different subject areas of the social sciences and the social science aspects of other disciplines, including education. In 1977, the Acharan Sahkar Delhi also brought out a Directory of Indian Behavioural Science Research (Pareek and Sood, 1977).

The first comprehensive review in the field of education was done by Buch (1974), who edited the Survey of Educational Research in India from the Centre for Advanced Studies in Education in Baroda, covering studies up to 1972. Five years later, Buch (1979) brought out the Second Survey of Educational Research covering the period from 1973 to 1978. These two reviews of educational research classified studies and investigations into 20 sub-divisions. While the affinity of the themes is supposed to be the basic principle linking the studies in these 20 clusters, the divisions are not mutually exclusive and one can always find overlaps. The accompanying table lists these groups along with the number of studies in each group in the two surveys of educational research. The first of these gives 729 classified studies undertaken up to 1972 and the second gives 751 classified studies plus 31 included in the appendix, all undertaken up to 1978. Within the space available, it is not possible to give a detailed analysis of these studies. However, a very brief critical analysis can be attempted, highlighting prominent features and noting shortcomings of studies in the identified areas.

Concentrating on the philosophers and ideologies of social reformers, religious leaders, literary stalwarts and political thinkers, studies in the

Areas of educational research	First survey of educational research (studies up to 1972)	Second survey of educational research (studies 1973-1978)	Total
1. Philosophy of education	28	14	42
2. History of education	42	48	90
3. Sociology of education	56	100	156
4. Personality, learning and motivation	60	19	79
5. Guidance and counselling	42	40	82
6. Tests and measurement	82	70	152
7. Curriculum, methods and textbooks	69	71	140
8. Programmed learning	19		19
9. Correlates of achievement	44	48	92
10. Educational evaluation and examinations	101	41	142
11. Teaching and teacher education	21	28	49
12. Teacher education	46	68	114
13. Educational administration	53	86	139
14. Economics of education	14	19	33
15. Social and adult education	21		21
16. Educational surveys	31		31
17. Comparative education		11	11
18. Educational technology		22	22
19. Higher education		46	46
20. Non-formal education		20	20
Appendices		31	31
Total	729	782	1511

philosophy of education have been mostly historical or descriptive, mainly based on library information. Being often replications of already accomplished work, they have remained short of making any concrete contribution to the field. It does not really seem justifiable to categorize these as studies in philosophy because they use only secondary or tertiary sources of information and also because the rigour of philosophical criticism is conspicuous by its absence in their treatment. Studies in the area of history of education are mostly related to renaissance movements, institutions, ideologies or the work of pioneers. Often they have presented bare facts without interpretation or attempts to establish links with other fields. Studies invariably display a lack of familiarity with researches or contemporary work in India and abroad.

Sociology of education is one of the areas where problems have been studied mostly at the micro level. A majority of these relate to the differential characteristics or background of students and teachers — interests, attitudes, achievement levels or proficiency levels, values, aspirations in respect of differences in sex, socio-economic status, religious beliefs, environmental settings, etc. These studies have, by and large, been conducted on random samples and interviews, and case studies and questionnaires have been the common tools of investigations.

The problems of teachers and students and their interactions with various environmental factors constitute the main themes of studies in the area of personality, learning and motivation. These studies have mostly used non-parametric statistics and have depended on survey methods which put a serious constraint on the scope of the correlational investigation that is their essence. In the areas of guidance and counselling in both educational and vocational sectors, studies are mostly descriptive, correlational and predictive. They have concentrated on the needs, aspirations, preferences, aptitudes and problems of mostly the average high school and college students. Thus studies on other age-groups and on bright and dull students have remained a gap to be filled.

Construction of tests, inventories and rating scales on personality, intelligence, creativity, attitudes, aptitudes and their correlates has been the main focus of work in the field of tests and measurement. While the earlier effort concentrated on general aspects of personality, the later studies addressed themselves to specific attributes as well. In the area of curriculum, methods and textbooks studies have been segmented, relating to different subjects of the curriculum and not to the curriculum as a whole. Furthermore, while curriculum development has been studied by several, the transactional nature of the curriculum has not attracted due attention and the competencies related to the curriculum have escaped the attention of researchers almost completely. Studies on curriculum change also are insignificant in number.

As a comparatively new field of education, programmed learning studies have also been few. Most of them relate to comparisons between the traditional and the programmed approach to individual differences in learning and the outcomes of this approach, its potential in different curriculum areas, and the different forms of learning materials for both instructional and remedial work.

Socio-economic conditions, personality traits and other factors influencing pupil competencies have been studied as correlates of achievement. These studies are extensive and psychometric, not intensive and experimental, and being isolated and often repetitive, they have not been able to make any significant contribution to educational theory and practice. An area which has evoked the interest of the largest number of researchers is educational evaluation and examinations. Studies in this field are descriptive, correlational, regressional, experimental, analytic and factorial, and deal with achievement tests, diagnostic tests, prediction tests and admission tests. These researches are functional rather than fundamental, and in spite of enjoying the highest tally among research studies, gaps can still be found, like studies related to mastery learning, criterion-referenced testing and the relationship between testing and learning.

Studies of teaching and teacher education have concentrated mainly on characteristics of effective teaching, and the attitudes, behaviours, scholastic and non-scholastic attributes, adjustment, age/maturity and sex differences have been studied. These, by and large, are correlational studies, surveys, inferential investigations and predictive researches most of which are descriptive. Questionnaires, interviews, check-lists, rating scales and tests have been the common tools of investigation with Flanders' Interaction Analysis and Category System being the favourite. Teacher education and its administration (theory and practice) has evoked a number of studies from teachers' colleges, university departments of education, State institutes of education and the National Council of Educational Research and Training. Comparative and historical studies and those related to the efficiency, values and traits of teachers constitute the main pattern of investigations. Not only are the methodologies and the tools used traditional but the defined territorial application of these studies seriously limits their scope.

Research on educational administration covers a wide spectrum of subjects like educational planning and financing, educational problems and reform ventures, educational supervision and organizational climate, educational agencies and infra-structure, educational acts and regulations, educational policies and their implementation and so on. These investigations basically conceive of educational administration as an outcome of the cumulative influences of various elements and do provide insights into other disciplines. In the 1960s comparative and historical studies were mainly undertaken in this field. The 1970s witnessed a major shift towards studies on human relations in administration with due cognisance of the social, psychological and economic needs and aspirations of the functionaries. In the field of economics of education the main areas of research are financing of education, expenditure on educational development, education and productivity, costs of education etc. These are mainly cost-benefit or cost-effectiveness studies related to a specific situation, and longitudinal studies are rarely to be found. Many are historical and descriptive researches based on existing documents or occasionally on questionnaires. Studies on relationships between education and development and education and employment do not seem to have attracted attention from researchers as yet.

Research in social and adult education has also been mainly descriptive, historical or diagnostic, with very few experimental studies. Even the latter have used a layman's commonsense approach rather than venturing into the realm of sophistication. Attitudes, interests, competencies and motivation of learners have been the common themes exploited, with interviews, questionnaires or the study of documents as the main source of data.

Educational surveys have so far been attempted in 1957-59, 1965-67, 1973-74, 1978-79; surveys of teacher education were conducted in 1963 and 1969, and a survey of physical education in 1967. These surveys present statistical compilations of data on factors related to education and have been extensively used as the basis of many a policy decision, from the level of the Planning Commission to that of district level administration.

Research in comparative education includes comparisons of school education and teacher education and studies of the influence of one system of education on another; but comparative studies worth the name have yet to be undertaken. Studies in educational technology have been few, mainly after 1972 and most consisting of small experiments on the impact of programmes. Studies in higher education are also few, mostly on topics like the growth and structure of higher educations, its administration and financing, methodologies and technology of instruction, and the implementation and evaluation of reform. A common theme is the need to make higher education an instrument of social and economic reconstruction and of the technological regeneration of society. Higher education and employment is an evident gap in this area which deserves priority.

Formally organized non-formal education is, of course, a new concept associated with the establishment of non-formal education centres for elementary and adult education. The content and methodology of the modular courses offered by these centres constitute the main themes of research in this area. Learner motivation has been studied, as also has community participation in such ventures. The field being new, there is need to conduct studies on the immediate outcomes and long range impact of the programme.

Strengths and weaknesses of research in education in India

The study of the abstracts of these 1,511 research investigations constitutes the basis of deductions about the shortcomings and strength of educational research in India. The following are some of the main shortcomings:

1. the dependence of some studies on only library information and the use of secondary and tertiary sources of information;
2. presentation of basic facts without attempts at interpretation, as in research on the history of education;
3. lack of familiarity of some investigators with researches or contemporary work in India or abroad;
4. frequent use of conventional tools of data collection which often put serious constraints on the scope of research, as in studies in the area of personality, learning and motivation;
5. micro-level studies without any macro-level treatment or vice versa;
6. emphasis on psychometric rather than experimental approaches;
7. broad generalizations from studies with small samples;
8. isolated, *ad hoc* studies as in the area of programmed learning;
9. lack of attempts to establish relationships with other fields.

In spite of these shortcomings, there are emerging trends and directions that are positive indicators of the strengths that research is steadily gaining in India. Systematic longitudinal research projects are gradually replacing the former *ad hoc* sporadic research ventures. Individually conducted research is yielding place to institutional or team research projects, and this in turn has diverted the attention of the researchers from studies focusing on specific situations to extensive field studies and intensive case studies as well.

Traditionally there were areas which invited only micro-level studies while others were considered to be fertile ground for macro-level investigations. Now both macro- and micro-level approaches are being adopted in studies wherever possible. Traditional concentration on problems within the classroom is rapidly giving way to studies beyond its four walls. Thus investigations which used to be based on academic themes are now taking cognisance of the social, economic, cultural, political and other related problems and their interaction with educational processes. The classical approach of selecting research themes related to specific disciplines is also now being replaced by inter-disciplinary research based on real, rather than hypothetical, problems. An analytical interpolative approach is preferred to a composite methodology.

The growing enthusiasm of researchers for experimental research as compared to earlier descriptive or historical research is also an encouraging development. This has also, in turn, led to greater sophistication in the collection of data, its statistical analysis and its interpretation.

Last but not the least is the growing use of research findings for policy decisions.

The future of educational research

The need for periodically reviewing the progress of research in the context of established national and educational policies cannot be understated. As part of this, some *research on research* could be recommended to find out the quantum of research which has gone into operational use. Funds for research will have to be protected because with every budget cut, social services are the first hit and among them education is the worst sufferer. Within the field of education too, the axe tends to fall on research because of pressing demands for developmental work.

It is not possible for all research to be conducted through established agencies, at governmental or private level. More outside institutions and individuals with competence to execute this function should be identified and the work given to them with guaranteed financial support. While this has started happening in some places, the idea has yet to pick up.

This review is not meant to be a theoretical discussion on educational research, but a practical assessment of its problems and prospects. Educational research will have to be judged on its potential for resolving the crisis that grips our educational scene. It is time that research in education should take its proper place and assume its responsibilities so that educational gulfs are bridged, imbalances are corrected and our goals realized.

References

Buch, M B *ed* (1974) *A Survey of Research in Education (Up to 1972)* Centre for
    Advanced Studies in Education, M.S.: University of Baroda: Baroda
Buch, M B *ed* (1979) *Second Survey of Research in Education (1972-1978)* Society
    for Educational Research and Development: Baroda
Chitnis, S (1970) *Sociology of Education in India — A Review* Tata Institute of
    Social Sciences: Bombay
National Council of Educational Research and Training (1966) *Educational Investiga-
    tions (PhD) in Indian Universities (1939-66)* NCERT: New Delhi
National Council of Educational Research and Training (1968a) *Educational Inves-
    tigations (MEd) in Indian Universities (1939-66)* NCERT: New Delhi
National Council of Educational Research and Training (1968b) *Third Indian Year-
    book of Education (Educational Research)* NCERT: New Delhi
Pareek, U and Kumar, V K (1966) *Behavioural Science Research in India (1925-65)
    — A Directory* Behavioural Science Centre: Delhi
Pareek, U and Sood, S (1977) *Directory of Indian Behavioural Science Research*
    Acharan Sahkar: Delhi

9. Educational research in Latin America

Ernesto Schiefelbein

Summary: Research centres, professional journals and researchers in Latin America in the early 1980s have multiplied tenfold since 1970. Around 150 research reports are produced each year and the main problem now is diffusion and use of what is produced, and also how to continue operating at this level given economic and sometimes political constraints. There is a growing interest in using the products of research, but access to the available research is still difficult. It is not easy to break the monopoly of knowledge and to offer access to such knowledge to the more needy marginal groups of society. There are many examples of impact of available research, mainly in terms of the state school system. But recently there is an increasing amount of research aimed at overcoming unjust prevailing socio-economic regimes or improving forms of government condemned as abusive. Among the tendencies vaguely felt, but gaining momentum in the region, are participatory (action) research, evaluative research of current programmes, comparative education studies and state-of-the-art reviews that systematize available knowledge and relate it to assumptions in those areas where no objective knowledge is available.

Overview

Several events seem to have shaped the type of research and institutions which have been responsible for educational research in Latin America. For example, in the late 1950s the interest in 'educational planning' forced authorities to spend time and effort in gathering suitable information to describe accurately the state of the educational system. UNESCO co-operated in those activities, training people in planning techniques, including relevant ways of collecting information and tabulating performance indicators.

The contribution of economists started in the early 1960s with studies of manpower requirements that followed the Mediterranean Project model launched in the 1950s by OECD. The Organization of American States (OAS) provided technical assistance (with support from OECD) and reports were prepared for most of the countries in the region. Rate of return studies were prepared later on in several cases.

Meanwhile, universities pursued their usual studies in curriculum development, experiments in pilot schools (trying out alternative pedagogical ideas), validation of tests of intelligence and achievement, and historical analysis of educational ideas. In the mid 1950s joint efforts by educators and sociologists were undertaken in many countries.

The Alliance for Progress launched by the Kennedy administration in the early 1960s encouraged the preparation of educational plans. Most of the available educational research studies were used in those exercises. Many gaps were identified and planners started to ask for more research.

In 1970 the Ford Foundation convened a meeting of educational researchers and decision makers in Buenos Aires (Argentina). The agenda aimed to identify the main research gaps in order to channel funds into those areas. However, Latin American participants argued the need to support the development of a number of research centres in their countries which would be able to detect these gaps. Later the Ford Foundation accepted their demands, gave grants to several centres and some 10 to 20 people were trained at the doctoral level in good American and European universities. A parallel proposal to fund the exchange of research results through an abstracting system was rejected on the grounds that little research of high quality was being produced in the region at that time.

The Centro de Investigacion y Desarrollo de la Educacion (CIDE) started the abstracting system with its own resources in a very modest way. In 1977 the International Development Research Centre (IDRC) in Canada provided a grant to establish a regional exchange centre (REDUC). By 1980 REDUC encompassed eight participating associated centres in Argentina, Brazil, Bolivia, Chile, Colombia, Mexico, Paraguay, Uruguay and Venezuela and a bi-annual abstract journal (RAE) was being published. With different sources of funding, 11 professional journals with a regional circulation were launched in five countries in the 1970s and are still appearing regularly, while only seven remain from older times.

By the end of the 1970s it was clear that the volume of research was much larger than in the previous decade. Around 100 to 150 research papers of good quality were produced annually at that time in Latin America. From four centres operating in the 1960s with less than 20 full-time investigators, the numbers had increased tenfold. Nine directors of educational research centres met for the first time in 1973 in Oaxtepec (Mexico), and since then six meetings have followed. Joint studies, on-the-job training and the specialized journals were some of the results of such meetings. However, the main result from all this development was that Latin American specialists no longer needed to communicate among themselves exclusively through American or European journals, or to be introduced to each other through a non-Latin American scholar. These direct relationships should make a significant impact on the flow of information all over the region.

In 1980 the time was ripe for an evaluation of these developments. The Seminario 80 was convened in Isla Negra (Chile) in April 1980. Some 20 participants represented that number of research institutions, mostly private, covering ten countries of the region. In addition, six organizations providing bilateral, regional or international assistance were represented by nine observers. 'Caught between criticisms of the quantitative, empirical, experimental approach to educational research and the reservations moderately expressed by a few participants against a mainly sociologically oriented approach, the seminar found it difficult to develop a balanced approach to (educational) research. It succeeded certainly in stressing the importance of action research and of emerging research patterns derived from Freire's concept of adult education' (Carelli, 1983). With communication among researchers identified as a prime concern, the group endorsed further development of the educational information network (REDUC). The United States Agency for International Development (USAID) provided funds to work with seven centres in identifying, abstracting and publishing relevant research reports and studies. The main results are described in the following section.

Research structure

In Latin America 'research' has been used for a long time in a very restrictive sense. For many educators 'research' used to be identical with 'replicable research on relations between relevant variables' aiming at the expansion of general knowledge about education. It is only recently that 'accurate description', 'design of educational materials' and 'data gathered for preparing projects' or 'data gathered in the process of monitoring' have also been considered research. The expansion of the concept is closely paralleled by the expansion from the type of research carried out in the universities to the research carried out in the Ministries of Education and private centres.

For a long time funding of research was done indirectly in the form of the free time of professors in universities (or Normal Schools) and as expenses of the statistical offices in the Ministries of Education. During the early 1960s processing of educational statistics and preparation of reports were carried out by the Planning Offices of the Ministries of Education. During the late 1960s representatives of the Ministries of Education agreed to devote money for experiment and research that was matched two-to-one by the USA. The so-called Maracay Agreement allowed the launching of many experimental projects, more ambitious research projects and the establishment of Research Agencies (Comisiones Nacionales de Investigacion en Ciencia y Tecnologie, CONICYT) in several countries. Although education has been allocated small amounts of money by the research agencies, the fact that they are considered at the same level as medicine or engineering has represented an important advance in the status of educational research.

Table 1 shows the proportional changes over time in the different sources of research reports used in the planning processes of two countries, Chile and Costa Rica. While the total number of reports produced by schools of education has increased in both countries, their proportional contribution does not show significant changes between the first and last stages of each planning cycle.

Stages of the planning cycle	Schools of education	Other university institutions	Ministry of Education	Other institutions	Total
		Source			
					%
Chile					
1960-64 (Pre-planning)	48% (25)	19% (10)	27% (14)	6% (3)	100 (52)
1965-70 (Planning)	25% (26)	15% (16)	44% (47)	16% (17)	100 (106)
1971-80 (Operation)	45% (67)	17% (25)	9% (13)	29% (43)	100 (148)
Total	39% (118)	17% (51)	24% (74)	20% (63)	100 (306)
Costa Rica					
1964-74 (Pre-planning)	13% (11)	35% (31)	34% (30)	18% (16)	100 (88)
May 74-Apr 78 (Planning)	27% (23)	41% (35)	21% (18)	11% (10)	100 (86)
May 78-Apr 82 (Planning)	13% (24)	22% (40)	52% (95)	13% (25)	100 (184)
Total	16% (58)	30% (106)	40% (143)	14% (51)	100 (358)

Table 1 *Use of research reports in educational planning in Chile and Costa Rica*
Sources: Investigaciones para el planeamiento de la educacion: el caso de Chile (1960-1980). CINTERPLAN-OEA, Santiago, 1981; Investigaciones para el planeamiento de la educacion: el caso de Costa Rica (1964-1982). CINTERPLAN-OEA, Santiago, 1984.

The research activity of the Ministries of Education changes substantially over time. The maximum in both countries occurs in planning periods, except that in Costa Rica the first of the two planning periods has a relatively low level of Ministry involvement in research. 'Other university institutions' and 'other institutions' (mainly private centres) have increased their absolute number of research reports over time, but their combined share in the total research production increases in the case of Chile and decreases in the case of Costa Rica. It must be mentioned that most of the private centres are funded by foreign agencies.

The AID and IDRC grants to REDUC are creating new linkages in each country and across the countries. Table 2 shows that eight Latin American countries held their first educational research meetings in the early 1980s. Those meetings were attended by researchers, decision makers, university professors and, in a few countries, by students preparing for a teaching career.

Countries	National meetings of researchers and practitioners			
	Number of meetings	Date of first meeting	Date of last meeting	Number of participants (last meeting)
Argentina	–	–	–	–
Bolivia	1	1980	–	33
Costa Rica	2	1981	1983	60
Colombia	1	1980	–	120
Chile	7	1969	1983	400
Ecuador	1	1981	1984[a]	35
Mexico	2	1979	1981	800[b]
Nicaragua	–	–	–	–
Panama	2	1981	1982	35
Paraguay	1	1981	1984[a]	46
Peru	2	1981	1983	50
Rep. Dominicana	1	1981	1984[a]	105
Venezuela	4	–	1982	54

Countries	Bibliographies and abstracts published			
	Bibliographies of research reports and papers (number of entries)	Bibliographies of press reports and articles (number of entries)	Abstracts of research reports and key documents	Micro-fiches
Argentina	2000	–	50	–
Bolivia	561	600	120	–
Costa Rica	1100	490	410	–
Colombia	–	–	30	–
Chile	6984	2500	900[c]	924
Ecuador	432	1000	190	–
Mexico	–	–	–	–
Nicaragua	–	–	–	–
Panama	250	400	120	–
Paraguay	355	2400	181	–
Peru	4400	–	90	90
Rep. Dominicana	806	1823	125	–
Venezuela	–	–	125	–

[a] Provisional date

[b] In addition, some 1700 students attended

[c] CIDE Santiago also published some 2000 abstracts of Latin American countries not included in the table or prior to the operation of the national centres.

Table 2 *National research meetings and publication of bibliographies and abstracts, by countries in Latin America*
Source: E. Schiefelbein (1983) Oferta y demanda de servicios, productos y subproductos de la informacion sobre educacion en America Latina, *Documentos de Trabajo 17*, Centro de Investigacion y Desarrollo de la Educacion (CIDE): Santiago.

In addition, for the first time in history in each of the countries there are centres where bibliographies, abstracts and microfiches from all Latin America may be consulted. Bibliographies are classified under 37 headings (following a context, inputs, process and results schema), while the 5,800 abstracts are classified according to the UNESCO Thesaurus for education. All exchanges among centres are carried out directly. Although each centre is proudly independent, they all recognize the advantages to their own users of cooperating within the REDUC network. In addition, strong cooperative links have been established between REDUC and the UNESCO regional office in Santiago (OREALC), the UNESCO regional office concerning higher education in Caracas (CRESALC) and the International Educational Reporting Service (IERS) operated by the International Bureau of Education (IBE) in Geneva.

A trend towards centralized control?

The situation of research in the two countries described in Table 1 seems to be representative of the whole region. On that assumption, since both the university centres (including Normal Schools) and the private centres are autonomous, therefore, half or more of the research studies are carried out beyond any centralized control.

However, there are several trends and activities that, in practice, may affect how priorities are decided. For example, most of the large surveys (including the Census of Population) are sponsored by the government and in some cases their use requires previous approval by authorities. Computers and large data-banks (as in Mexico and Venezuela) are owned by the government although the new waves of microcomputers may reduce the problems of access to large-scale processing. Several countries are now interested in mounting Management Information Systems (for example, Costa Rica, Chile, Mexico, Peru and Panama) and they will eventually store relevant information for further research. Research funds tend to encourage specific goals for research (to increase efficiency) and to provide money for those willing to meet those goals. Research contracted with consultants is also expanding: the effects of this go beyond the specific projects contracted, because consultants avoid topics of research which relate to aspects of the prevailing socio-economic pattern considered unjust and abusive. Finally, some military regimes (as in Argentina, Brazil, Chile or Uruguay) have directly controlled universities and in these cases the government has influenced the choice of university research topics, objectives, focus and methodology.

On the other hand, as suggested in Table 2, there are some countervailing forces that encourage free circulation of information and establish mechanisms for encouraging the wider use of the network products. There are multiple sources of support for an increasing attention to 'action research' carried out by individual teachers in the classroom (although the task is too ambitious), and there are many oral communication channels for the exchange of information. Finally, there is a steady increase in the networks related to education and in their sponsoring organizations (Schiefelbein, 1978).

The large absolute number of reports may in itself be a defence against detrimental centralization. It is not possible to control so many different approaches to educational research, but growing attention to information as a powerful means to achieve goals (or to arouse criticism) will keep bureaucrats and politicians (or military powers) trying to influence the selection of research topics and methods. In Brazil alone, US$4.3 millions were spent in 1978-79 in 229 educational research projects, but the results seemed to be rather meagre (Castro and Bordignon, 1980).

The demand for additional research in education

The increase in the number of centres, professional journals and researchers, and the interest in more information appropriate to decision making, as mentioned above, are two indications of the demand for educational research. During the past regime the Mexican Minister of Education hired a leading educator to brief him weekly on key results of actual educational research. Costa Rica obtained support from the World Bank to hire consultants to design a Management Information System (though economic recession postponed the implementation). Administrators are now better trained and many of them know how to read research reports and are willing to do so. All this evidence suggests increased demand.

Table 3 presents the answers from a sample of individuals receiving materials from IDRC, the Research Review and Advisory Group (RRAG), the World Bank and other institutions. There was a relatively high response rate from the Latin American participants, especially from those interested in 'development and policy' and those interested in 'research'.

The same high level of interest was evident at the July 1982 meeting of the Ministers of Education held in Saint Lucia. Eleven countries (from a total of 35) mentioned their need for technical assistance in 'research, evaluation, experimentation and information'.

Access to available research results

In spite of the large demand for specific research results potential clients seldom find what they are looking for. Lack of efficient libraries and documentation centres limit access to relevant information to a small elite.

Table 4 shows the limited amount of information about 'financing of education' readily available in Latin America. The new REDUC network, at the end of its third year of operation, is able to provide access to roughly one third of the relevant materials, but access to the other two thirds would require help from large foreign libraries or the United Nations or OAS libraries operating in regional centres or headquarters.

	Teaching	Research	Develop- ment and policy	Survey responses	RRAG members	Response rate
Developing countries:						
Latin America	2	22	17 ⎱	49	258	19%
Caribbean	4	–	– ⎰			
Africa and Asia	6	18	6	44	366	12%
Developed countries						
USA	6	5	11 ⎱	32	98	33%
Canada	4	4	2 ⎰			
Europe and Australia	5	7	4	16	110	15%

Table 3 *Areas of review reported 'most useful' among materials from*
IDRC, RRAG, World Bank: 1982 Survey of RRAG members
(IDRC: International Development Research Centre, Canada;
RRAG: Research Review and Advisory Group)
Source: N. McGinn and E. Schiefelbein (1983) *Experiences in the promotion of*
educational research in the Third World: RRAG and state-of-the-art reviews,
International Development Research Centre, mimeo (Tables 1 and 10).

Only a few reports circulate widely, and only 2 per cent of the reports
were available in four or more of the ten libraries included in the search.

The situation described for the topic 'financing of education' seems
representative of education in general. This type of information led the
participants in 'Seminario 80' to identify diffusion of information as the
main bottleneck of educational research in Latin America. Diffusion
includes not only a wider distribution of available materials, but also the
preparation of state-of-the-art papers which summarize the massive
amount of information in each topic and suggest possible explanations of
the contradiction sometimes apparent among available results. Each day it
is more difficult to read all available materials and even more difficult to
digest the evidence into a manageable form.

The impact of research and implicit models of its function

One example of influential research is the evidence gathered during the
early 1960s on enrolments. Descriptive reports of enrolments, in the
context of 'human capital' theories, were a factor in the impressive expansion of basic education in Latin America.

However, it is difficult to obtain information on the impact of specific
pieces of research, since reports leading to decision making are usually

confidential and are not generally available. In the case of Chile (Schiefelbein, 1981) the following examples were identified, and probably these are valid also in other countries. Thus, in Chile, available research helped to resist pressures from teachers for a reduction of class size to the magic number of 30; policies to reduce repetition in first and second grades of elementary education have been influenced by research; the supply of textbooks has been improved extensively and free of charge; and reports on 'unfair' distribution of higher education subsidies have led to amendment of the fee system at university level.

Library or centre searched	Number of reports located	Reports in one centre only	Available in other centres				
			2	3	4	5	7
Hamburg	36	27	3	2	3	1	—
Bonn	8	2	—	1	2	2	1
ERIC	8	3	1	1	—	2	1
Toronto	36	19	9	2	3	2	1
Ottawa	11	7	2	1	—	—	1
IIEP Paris	28	13	10	2	2	—	1
UNESCO Paris	28	16	9	2	—	1	—
Santiago[a]	100	89	7	1	1	1	1
REDUC	104	87	11	3	1	1	1
Theses	6	—	6	—	—	—	—
Totals[b]		263	58	15	12	10	7
Entries	303	263	29	5	3	2	1

[a] In Santiago, all United Nations regional centres: Economic Commission for Latin America, UNESCO, ILO and UNICEF.
[b] The numbers in the Totals row exceeds the numbers in the Entries row below it because of multiple availability in other centres.

Table 4 *Availability of research reports on the finance of education in Latin America, by documentation centres (December 1982)*
Source: E. Schiefelbein (1983) *Educational Financing in Developing Countries*, International Development Research Centre IDRC-IS38e, Ottawa.

Ministries of Education are now commissioning specific pieces of research. Although the experience of Brazil described above (p. 131) was disappointing, a study on quality problems of the curriculum in Costa Rica was more successful; and a report on the transfer of public schools in Chile to the counties (municipalidades) induced the authorities to discontinue the transfer policy. In El Salvador the evaluation of the educational television system by a team of participants in the 1973 World Bank seminar on educational projects persuaded the Ministry of that country to include the initial elementary grades in the system.

Many such specific examples of the impact of research reports can be quoted. But other dimensions of the impact of research are more subtle. As a result of research, decision makers tend to take more dimensions of the problems into consideration: problems are examined from a more complex set of perspectives and interrelationships. Teachers also can be helped to identify some of the problems which they face and to find specific pieces of research which may help them to solve those problems (Toro, 1983). Political opposition groups have built up their own research centres (usually on a small scale) to allow them to move away from rhetoric towards specific facts that are considered unjust or abusive. The growth of research has thus made the discussion of public educational issues more of a debate with facts and arguments, replications and rejoinders, rather than a series of assertions or monologues by different groups.

At a more general level, the 'oral tradition' that pervaded the pedagogical ideas in Latin America is being transformed into a 'written tradition' with the help of research activity. There is still a long way to go, but each advance adds to the total effect. Some researchers have contributed to this process by acting in the role of 'broker' between scholars and decision makers (Myers, 1981).

In summary, research results may have a different 'value' for each social group and there is no way to reach consensus on their absolute value. It is important that each group should have access to the available knowledge and be able to retrieve from libraries or experts the information likely to be of value for that specific group.

New styles of research

The interest of political opposition in research has been linked with criticisms that educational research is subordinated to the exclusive needs of the state school system. There is increasing interest in research patterns derived from Freire's concept of adult education and in participatory research. Those who adopt these new styles of research are interested mainly in non-formal education and in action research, designed to combine research with action to confer benefit on the people affected by the experiments. These groups are usually outspoken (unless they work in countries with highly repressive governments). In spite of many attempts, however, few rigorous research studies have been produced so far.

The Ministries of Education are concerned mainly with non-generalizable evaluations of educational projects or materials, or with the description of issues in the operation of the educational system that may eventually lead to changes in educational policies. Efforts are being made to define key indicators in the analysis of how the system operates and to collect appropriate data on a continuous basis in order to systematize information on the management process itself, or to introduce evaluation procedures in new projects. It is too early yet to reach a judgement on the effectiveness of these innovations.

Though neither of these approaches aims to produce generalizations, eventually both may contribute to general knowledge through comparative studies or some type of meta-analysis. This may also prove to be the outcome of attempts to train teachers to adopt an action research approach, and to identify research findings which they can put to good use, as mentioned above (Toro, 1983).

Comparative studies will probably be encouraged by the availability of research reports resulting from the operation of REDUC and by the increasing demand for state-of-the-art reviews on specific topics with material from developed nations and from Latin American countries.

A final point to mention is the increasing number of attempts to produce diagnostic reports on aspects of the educational system of a country on the basis of a mixture of research results and assumptions in fields of study where no objective data are available. We must make a precise distinction between knowledge and guesswork, but it is often worthwhile to attempt a reconstruction of the 'scenery' from the limited knowledge at hand. If this is not attempted, there is a danger that decision makers may not make the effort to take account of the evidence that has been gathered, even though it is incomplete.

One would hope that some researchers may build on available knowledge as an accumulation process (assuming a continuing linear development), while others will use the limited research findings to identify contradictions which may lead to a new synthesis. To argue about the meaning of the available knowledge is better than to ignore it.

References

Brahm, L and Gutierrez, G (1983) REDUC, an educational documentation network serving development in Latin America *UNESCO Journal of Information Science, Librarianship and Archives Administration* 5 89-94

Carelli, D (1983) Review of Seminario 80 *International Review of Education* 29 101-2

Castro, C and Bordignon, G (1980) Da pesquisa a toamada de decisao: existem caminhos privilegiados? *in* Schiefelbein and Garcia Huidobro (1980)

Centro de Investigacion y Desarrollo de la Educacion (CIDE) (1983) *Indices de Resumenes Analiticos sobre Educacion* 1 1-281

Myers, R (1981) *Connecting Worlds: a Survey of Developments in Educational Research in Latin America* IDRC-TS35: Toronto

Schiefelbein, E (1978) Educational research networks in Latin America *International Review of Education* 24 483-500

Schiefelbein, E (1981) Research, policy and practice: the case of Chile *International Review of Education* 27 153-62

Schiefelbein, E (1983) *The Role of Educational Research in the Conception and Implementation of Educational Policies: the Latin American experience* IIEP-UNESCO: Paris

Schiefelbein, E and Garcia Huidobro, J (1980) *La investigacion educacional en America Latina, situacion y perspectivas* CIDE-REDUC: Santiago

Toro, B (1983) *Diffusion and Use of the 'Resumenes Analiticos en Educacion (RAE)' and Increasing 'REDUC Network' Capacity* OISE: Toronto (mimeo)

10. The Netherlands: educational research at a crossroads

Chris van Seventer

Summary: In The Netherlands, educational research is under attack because of a political shift in priorities. Research policy development has reached stalemate. In the recent past, the policy for the improvement of educational research was constructed on two supporting strategies. One strategy was intended to bring the stakeholders together in the national agency's (SVO) council and to place them in charge of a nation-wide programming process. This resulted in a legal statute defining the rules and confirming SVO in a broker position. The other main strategic line emphasized the 'institutionalization' of the research work. This was partly necessary to compensate for shortcomings in the traditional university patterns, but it was also intended to improve standards, to guarantee the accumulation of knowledge and experience, and to organize activities in accordance with a customer-contractor principle. The political uncertainty described above, and other policy dilemmas, stem from a mistaken understanding of the relationship between research, practice and policy in education. The 'enlightenment' theory is not sufficiently taken into consideration. Evaluation research is at present under particularly heavy pressure. In this area what is required are macro-organizational measures, professional standards and the development of new models. In Dutch society the burden of education is growing heavier. This also results in an unstable situation in the area of research. Yet at the same time it also clarifies the challenge of future educational research.

Introduction

I should like to begin by making two general points in connection with this chapter.

1. The system which I describe here is in a very unstable state. At present it is under criticism from its sponsors. In fact the position of the educational sciences is altogether rather unstable. The relationship between education and society at large is suffering from lack of clarity. These three phenomena are, up to a point, interdependent. This uneasy situation clarifies the title of this essay. It is difficult to give a clear appraisal of the situation in educational research as we find it at the beginning of 1984. Circumstances may soon alter the validity of my remarks.
2. I am not an expert with practical experience in the field of research.

My role is that of a general manager in charge of the organized part of his country's research into aspects of education. So I am something of a bureaucrat, a politician and an entrepreneur all rolled into one. As for schools, I believe they play a vital part in determining the quality of life enjoyed by an individual. And I do not see why research could not be used to improve education just as it has improved agriculture, or Philips' electrical products. But I bear in mind some words from one of America's learned journals: 'There may be a certain utility in acknowledging how little we in fact know about schools, how much we may be living in the first days of educational research' (Daedalus, Summer 1981).

In a small country like The Netherlands, academic work of any sort depends greatly on international cooperation. It would be a mistake to think otherwise. However, active international relations are not the most obvious feature of our national effort in the educational sciences. On the other hand, in a more passive way, our social sciences are greatly indebted to foreign literature from countries with different cultural patterns. A recent policy statement by the Dutch government on the development of the behavioural and the social sciences (November 1983) called us a triple-stream country. Many influences can be recognized from German, French and Anglo-Saxon sources. Since the Second World War, however, the flow of knowledge from the social sciences in the United States of America has been the most marked. The picture may be slightly different if we consider only educational research, but this is the general impression.

We can categorize broadly and say something about these three influences. In France the social sciences followed the path beaten out by the humanities. Their development has been concentrated in institutions outside the universities. The social sciences in the Federal Republic of Germany stem from ancient philosophical-theoretical traditions. Empirical social science research in Germany is still rather young. Here too, several institutes for this type of research have been established outside the universities, by the Max Planck Company as well as by the National Science Foundation. In the United Kingdom, on the other hand, we see a long tradition of empirical approaches. The main stream seems to be within university life, and support from bodies like the Social Science Research Council is relatively minor. I think the recent Rothschild episode in the UK which was symbolized by the customer-contractor principle, is particularly interesting. Finally, from the United States comes an overwhelming wave of empirically based methodologies and research literature. It can be assumed that educational research in The Netherlands is influenced by developments in all these countries.

History

In The Netherlands, nationally organized empirical research in the field of educational studies began in the second half of the 1960s. At present the main contributions to our educational research come from such disciplines as instructional psychology and educational sociology. Some universities experiment with a course in education which is based on the previous pedagogically oriented training. Recently, a university training curriculum has begun to offer a course in educational technology; this may lead to new directions in the field.

Before the mid 1960s, educational enquiry meant almost the same as asking pedagogical questions. The emphasis lay on philosophical and theological debate, not the gathering of empirical data. Values and beliefs were held to be more important than empirical knowledge. The history of Dutch culture determined an emphasis on religious attitudes, which was intermixed with educational ideas. It was a rare exception when educational enquiry used the discoveries made in disciplines like psychology or sociology, not to mention linguistics, the political sciences, or law.

Interdisciplinarity is a prerequisite for educational research as an academic discipline. In The Netherlands interdisciplinarity was not born within the university, but fostered by an act of government. The Dutch government needed education-policy oriented information; it was aware of developments in this area in the United States of America. So in 1965 it set up a National Foundation for Educational Research (SVO, Stichting Voor Onderzoek van het Onderwijs). This foundation was to organize investigations into the state and the intricacies of education as a social system. The history of this endeavour is closely interrelated with, and complicated by, problems of management and organization. So in the following section I shall give a brief summary of an historical rise and fall and rise again. The abilities and disabilities of our system in adopting scientific ways and means will be illustrated in the second part, when I take the example of evaluation research in education as a critical point in our development.

The mainstream of Dutch studies in education today is influenced by two insights: the understanding gained from cognitive psychology, that man is an information processor; and the sociological realization that we should never stop asking the question: what makes a school a better institution? The greatest challenge would be to merge programmes from these two branches into a real cross-fertilization. For an optimistic, and perhaps rather gullible manager like the present author, the international landscape does offer some, as yet hazy, hope. A general theory of learning and teaching might be born one day. Education might greet its own J.M. Keynes from the ranks of the international research community.

Educational psychologists have realized that human learning and development are so closely related that neither is explicable without the other. I see possibilities of an alliance between, for example, the late Piaget and Herbert Simon. This process could be enriched in The Netherlands by the inheritance from the pedagogical tradition with its phenomenological-hermeneutic attributes. However, as far as those attributes are concerned there remains the problem of distinguishing between sustained evidence, ideological bias and individual preferences.

The improvement of educational opportunity and the quality of school and classroom management remain major areas of research, especially psychological, sociological and organizational. In The Netherlands there are only three university chairs in the area of Sociology of Education and School Organization. This shows a certain imbalance, with the dominance of a psychological approach towards the huge problems which confront educational policy and educational practice. An alliance between psychology and sociology is required here.

Organization

The Foundation for Educational Research (SVO) is responsible as a national agency for much of the educational research carried out in The Netherlands. The agency does not carry out its own research. It acts as an intermediary — a broker — between customers and contractors. It works for policy makers such as the State Department of Education. Other clients are found among school boards and teachers' professional organizations. The contractors come from universities, but most of them are institutes specialized in educational research. The foundation is legally obliged to spend 80 per cent of the net annual budget on commissioned research for the above-mentioned customers. Half of that money is used for ministry research. The other 20 per cent is used to encourage proposals from the research community. Two thirds of the seats on the foundation's council are occupied by representatives from the educational unions. The other members are research workers. The council's main task is to produce a nation-wide matrix of research projects, oriented to a certain level of education (eg the reform of primary education or the transition from school to work) or to equally important problem-oriented designs (like motivation issues in the classroom).

The pioneering phase of SVO lasted from its inauguration in the 1960s until about 1975. Then a two-year transition stage followed. The lack of organization of the educational sciences as a special branch of the social sciences in the universities had become apparent. To fill this need, some financial support was allocated to building up an infrastructure of specializing research institutes, affiliated to universities but autonomous. It was desirable to see some financial and scientific returns, and partly because of this it became customary to ask mainly these special institutes for research proposals. Policy plans were also made to shift the pattern from separate projects to larger-scale, cohesive programmes. But this began too late. Public criticism of the lack of impact was steadily growing; the climate was no longer that of the 1960s. Furthermore, during this period, for the first time financial support failed to expand. There is a final explanation — last but not least — of why this was a period of transition. The minister became a customer wanting to give detailed specification of research needs. As for the agency's budget, the minister wanted to have a finger in this pie.

Beginning in 1977, there came a period of consolidation. The policy of creating the educational research's own infrastructure was strengthened. After exhaustive negotiations, which continued until 1982, this led to a series of long-term contracts between the agency and the universities, offering guarantees to a reduced number of research institutes. At the same time, the policy of building a national system around SVO led to the setting up of five standing workshops. They were to develop long-term research programmes around themes such as instructional psychology, motivation in the classroom, curriculum development, social inequality in schools and educational innovation. This policy aimed at an accumulation of information, experience and skills. But first, public belief in educational research had to be restored. One very serious problem which we now encountered was in connection with our sponsoring minister. What precisely was his role? We felt that he was intruding more and more into the realm of independent research, and that this course was mistaken. A tendency had developed to produce short-sighted results. Work carried out often lacked a wide significance. In 1981 a new legal constitution was drawn up for SVO and its national system, which was meant to put an end to these difficulties. It was also meant to establish an equilibrium between different audiences, the minister as a customer among them. The picture of an independent brokers' agency, as described in the first paragraph of this section, emerged.

However, the system which developed was vulnerable in three ways. In the first place, there is a critical financial limit built into the system. If SVO's financial means, approximately 95 per cent of which come from the government, are reduced below this critical limit, the cybernetics of the system will be disturbed. For then there would be no acceptable balance between current expenditure on the infrastructure and the money spent on research. As a consequence, the system could come under attack from the taxpayer's point of view, and rightly so. A second weak point stems from the customer-contractor principle. If the intermediary agency cannot sufficiently fulfil its role as a broker and as a maintainer of quality, the customer becomes too much a master and the researcher too much a slave. This involves the risk that much educational research becomes little more than lackeying to vested interests. Thirdly, there is the possibility of splinter groups forming, with consequent loss of central power. The system has the quintessential prerequisite that all functions – programming, financing, negotiating and quality judgement – are coordinated by one organizational body. If this central organization disintegrates, research loses public confidence.

In 1983 the State Secretary responsible for SVO presented it with the following announcement: it was probable that in the fiscal year 1984 there would be a budget cut of one third. This threat created a crisis. At the time of writing (January 1984), the outcome was still uncertain. But it was because of this that at the very beginning of this chapter I warned about the unstable situation. The official reason given by the State Secretary in his announcement was derived from the general economic cutbacks current in government policy. However, his argument is far from convincing: it has emerged that several million guilders are still available, and are as yet unallocated, in the general national budget for research and development. It sounds more as if this policy shift reflects a change in attitudes: as if educational research has lost the support of the national policy makers.

Policy under pressure

The present setback in the organization of educational research in The Netherlands is a new manifestation of a paradox which has been there right from the beginning of more empirically based scientific enquiries. On the one hand the minister stimulated this research enterprise, because he wanted systematic answers to his questions. On the other hand he and his civil servants appear to feel threatened by research activities which are truly independent. Because of this political attitude, some intriguing questions arose. SVO decided to invite experts from many countries to a symposium in May 1981. The proceedings were published in September 1982 as *Social Science Research and Public Policy-Making; a Reappraisal* (Kallen *et al* eds 1982). In March 1983 SVO issued several publications showing the results of an overall assessment of a series of research projects, previously initiated by the minister in the framework of large-scale innovation in education. One of the conclusions was that most of this research fell down into a chasm between education and research on the one hand and politics on the other hand (Scheerens, 1983).

In educational research in The Netherlands the tension between policy for knowledge and knowledge for policy frequently lapses into a vulgar power struggle. One cause of this tension lies in the different time schedules involved. A politician wants to use research results, but has the simultaneous desire to survive the next elections. A teacher may cooperate in a piece of research; after a while, however, he wants some practical information from the report. Generally, the taxpayer wants to know if pupils learn more and better than before the investment in research was made. But except in development projects which produce useful instruments for guiding school practice, really detailed answers are only part of a long-term process of 'enlightenment' (Weiss, 1982).

The difference between, on the one hand, the political and bureaucratic culture and, on the other hand, the attitudes and assumptions of academia, causes further tension (Caplan, 1982). Furthermore, we should be aware of a spirit of rivalry between politicians, civil servants and social scientists. All of them, in a way, are employed to deal with considerations of common good, and to show concrete results to the nation. But the academic in a free society is protected by academic freedom. Politicians and bureaucrats may find that position alarming, and express a need for other checks and balances. This may be very apparent in an applied field of the social sciences, like educational research. The most important item at stake in research policy is the protection of the freedom to criticize.

However, there is the never-distant dilemma arising from two simultaneous urgent needs: getting the timing right and serving your customer (Dockrell, 1982). An autonomous research agency, in spite of this dilemma, has to resist pressure to place relevance above quality. It should be constantly repeated that research design and reports are worthless unless they conform to a certain standard. The idea of special paradigms for tailor-made social science research may be seductive. But in the end it means the surrender to expediency, defined as those research outcomes which sound agreeable and comfortable for the customer.

I think that for several reasons educational research is confronted more with this type of dilemma than some other branches of the social sciences. Education as a system is loaded with personal values. That does not create the best intellectual climate for rational analysis. The teaching profession generally is seen as an art, not as a science. Perhaps rightly so, but this should not prevent the systematic use of empirical data in in-service training programmes. This kind of a support structure for education, however, is strikingly underdeveloped in The Netherlands. The existing support structure is not oriented to in-service training of teachers themselves, but to offering special assistance from change agents outside the school. Further-more, a teacher does not have the material incentives to use research data such as those available, for example, to a farmer. Thirdly, educational research itself is still very young as an empirical discipline and has only a small body of knowledge. We are also still waiting for a strong research community, nationally and internationally. The average research worker in our field also tends to behave as an individual artist, and hesitates to use the tools of an industrial enterprise or to see the importance of com-municating with colleagues and with other disciplines. To counter this, our foundation's research policy stressed 'institutionalization'. Finally, the educational sciences have to deal with methodological problems in the selection of relevant variables against a background of systems of education which are highly sensitive to changes in society at large.

The case of evaluation research

Experiences in evaluation research illuminate these problems very clearly. The Netherlands can be considered as a developing (or under-developed) country in this context. There is a striking difference between it and, for instance, the United States. My earlier observation, that empirical methods have to compete with almost theological approaches in questions of educa-tion and pedagogics is a partial explanation of this difference. A cognate reason stems from the method of running official experiments in our educational system.

All recent large-scale and nation-wide innovatory programmes in education can be seen as pursuing a policy of reform shaped more than ever before by government initiatives. This clashes with the professional autonomy of the teachers, the legally recognized relative autonomy of school boards and the partly petrified and denominationally 'segregated' Dutch school system itself. These programmes were launched in a period when public opinion was permeated by an ideology of bottom-top democracy. The aims and objectives of the programmes, including the introduction of an experiment with comprehensive education for the lower age group of secondary schools, can only be described in very global, vague and neutral terms.

Nevertheless, at the minister's request, millions of guilders were spent on a series of research projects which were intended to evaluate the innovatory programmes. SVO's assessment of the results provided a far from rose-coloured picture. Key people gave an overwhelmingly negative judgement of the relevance to policy of most of this research. The experts consulted were extremely critical both of its significance and of the quality of research techniques applied. In the area of research management, responsibilities were not clearly defined nor were they clearly distributed over the authorities concerned. This caused serious problems. There were difficulties in cooperation between schools and researchers. These two groups frequently came into conflict over the methods, techniques, and instruments employed. This in turn led to a loss of response and a lowering of standards. Some essential research instruments were even abandoned, or administered under less than strictly controlled conditions.

Furthermore, it should be noted in passing that in the case of comprehensive schools the goals of evaluation had never been made clear. The initiating political debates did not answer the question of whether the experiment was supposed to show *if* middle schools were to be introduced or merely to establish *how* the idea might be realized in practice.

Under such circumstances research may well be seen as a pawn between different interest groups. The professionalization of evaluation research is needed as a protection against this. As a basic regulating principle we can take the standards of utility, feasibility, propriety and accuracy as formulated by a joint committee in the United States (Stufflebeam, *et al*, 1981). Evaluation models which seek to express conflicting interests about the purpose of evaluation are also needed. An example is the 'betting model' (Hofstee, 1982). In this model, different audiences and special interest groups who are at loggerheads are urged to bet on their predictions of the outcome of new programmes *before* evaluation research is conducted. This prevents them from manipulating and neutralizing research results afterwards. In this way, the comparison which lies at the basis of any evaluation affects hypotheses or predictions, instead of experimental and/or control conditions. The evaluation is between parties, not between realities. We are going to try this approach in some cases of curriculum evaluation. However, we do not think this will be sufficient. What we need chiefly are managerial-organizational conditions at a macro-level, for the improvement of evaluation practice in the pedagogical area. It is a prerequisite to have an autonomous and independently-acting research body with a strong steering capacity.

Incidentally, it was only a few months after the publication of SVO's retrospective assessment of Dutch innovation-oriented educational research that the State Secretary issued the crippling budget message which I mentioned above.

Education's burden

The tasks of any system of organized schooling vary, in their number and importance, with differences in (the appreciation of) social development. Today, in a country like The Netherlands, with an open economy, the accumulation of tasks is becoming a burden. In this process the pressure on educational research also grows heavier.

Schools, and education generally, face some crucial problems. Elsewhere in society, groups like the family, clubs and associations, and employment unions, are all contributing less pedagogically and having less impact on people's lives. School then is asked to function as a 'total institution' (Etzioni, 1982). Furthermore, it is increasingly difficult for the school to act as a change agent in society. The school is also confronted with higher demands for numeracy and literacy; schools must learn to live with computers, and must provide prophylactics for television mania. In a period of economic slump (as now) public financing of education runs into difficulties. A further contributor to contemporary instability is the demographic trend. And now vast numbers of school leavers are gazing into an empty space between education and the labour market.

Education policy at the political level was previously concerned with structures of the traditional system. But today — and tomorrow — the school must be dealt with as a multipurpose agency; the central issues in the policy debate may be assumed to spring from the content of curricula. I also expect a revival of philosophies of recurrent education; these could forge a link between education and society at large, and make a contribution towards solving the enormous problems of unemployment. Finally, public attention might be redirected from general education towards vocational education. In this process education might once more be seen as a major national resource which could make a significant contribution to the national economy.

The challenge posed by educational research is clear. An invigorating research agenda could be proposed. The burden of education can be shouldered. A corporate strategy can be designed, with bold and daring goals. But all the time the lessons of the past should be remembered.

References

Caplan, N (1981) Social research and public policy at the national level *in* Kallen *et al* (1982)

Dockrell, W B (1981) The contribution of national surveys of achievement to policy formation *in* Kallen *et al* (1982)

Etzioni, A (1982) *in American Education* (November and December volumes, US Department of Education)

Hofstee, W K B (1982) Evaluatie: een methodologische analyse *Tijdschrift voor Onderwijsresearch* 5

Kallen, D B P, Kosse G B, Wagenaar H C *et al* eds (1982) *Social Science Research and Public Policy-Making: a Reappraisal* SVO-NFER Nelson: Windsor

Scheerens, J (1983) *Het sectoronderzoek: onderwijsonderzoek in de marge van beleid en wetenschap?* SVO-Flevodruk: Harlingen

Stufflebeam, D L ed (1981) *Standards for Evaluations of Educational Programs and Materials* (Joint committee on standards for educational evaluation) Holt Rinehart Winston: New York

Weiss, C H (1981) Policy research in the context of diffuse decision-making *in* Kallen *et al* (1982)

Acknowledgements

This chapter was prepared with the technical assistance of Drs Gerard B Kosse, SVO staff officer; style amendments were made by Ms E W Shaffer.

11. Educational research in New Zealand

Raymond S. Adams

Summary: Education research is undertaken in universities, the State Department of Education, the New Zealand Council for Educational Research (a semi-autonomous national organization), and various voluntary and some commercial organizations. There are some 50 full-time educational researchers and numerous part-timers in the country.

A relatively modest first 40 years has been followed since the 1960s by increased activity in all sectors, with greater financial and public support following. Research undertaken tends to be concerned with matters related to learning, teaching and evaluation. Controversial issues of national moment whether political, economic, philosophical or ideological are seldom confronted. Funding comes mostly from the government, either directly or indirectly, a matter not without significance for the autonomy and independence of researchers and the development of critical analyses of prevailing conditions.

A recent OECD review of New Zealand education, in commenting on research, concluded that examples of five types of institutional structures could be observed (OECD, 1983). The structures, taken from a report of an international symposium (UNESCO, 1980), were:

1. university-based centres, departments, units and faculties;
2. national educational research centres;
3. autonomous, private educational research institutions;
4. research divisions or units in government ministries;
5. local research centres, units or schools.

After commenting on aspects of educational research, the Review ended on something of a 'sweet and sour' note. On the one hand, it commended 'the overall picture of education research ... in relation to the size of the system', but on the other it criticized the system for its lack of institutional links with the general field of social enquiry and the lack of institutional mechanisms for achieving national coordination and setting priorities.

There are few grounds for quarrelling with the OECD account or its conclusions. Accordingly this present chapter will first use the UNESCO categories as a basis for its own more detailed description of educational research and second, in looking at the issues confronting educational research, attempt to explain, in this Orwellian year, why circumstances are as they are.

Background

University-based centres, departments, units and faculties

New Zealand first sanctified the study of education at university level in 1922, by giving it formal recognition and departmental status within the Faculty of Arts. In this way was established a division of labour that has persisted, with only slight modification, ever since. The State (teachers') Training Colleges were left to produce (and, *de facto,* license) teachers, and the universities were left to produce educational intellectuals. Predictably, debates over the practice-theory dichotomy flared up regularly thereafter. In truth the students at both institutions were often the same, so that teachers who were 'trained' at the colleges and 'educated' at the universities received rather a fulsome diet of education.

Initially, this separation of university and state had its effects on educational research as it struggled to gain support and recognition. Most university research was incestuous, undertaken to meet the thesis or diploma requirements of students. Much of it was small scale, egocentric and, because of allegiances to foundational disciplines, notably psychology and philosophy, somewhat arcane, at least from the schooling system's point of view. Thus, little of it served to make New Zealand aware that research might be useful. One significant outcome, however, was the establishment of what sociologist Nash has referred to with exasperation as the 'psychological hegemony' (Nash, 1981) that continues to have a pervasive influence on New Zealand education.

Relatively recently, four of the six universities have, in collaboration with their local teachers' colleges, instituted B Ed and M Ed degrees. As well, the university departments have forsaken, to a considerable extent, their previous self-appointed and somewhat self-righteous roles as critics of the education system. Concurrently, their researchers have come to be consulted, sponsored and used more and more by the State Department of Education.

In the 1960s, after some 40 years of meagre support and negligible recognition, university educational research began to prosper. Three factors contributed in particular. First, research benefited from the burgeoning optimism and affluence of the 1960s and 1970s. Second, New Zealand academics discovered North America. Forsaking Britain, they began taking sabbatical leave at American universities where research was booming. Third, the old convention of solo research so characteristic of earlier years began to be replaced by team-based research.

All this found particular expression in New Zealand in a burst of interest in classroom research – not in the Flanders tradition but certainly influenced by his timely visit in 1957. As well, the new contacts made with specific North American universities began to produce 'connections' – Canterbury with Illinois (Nuthall and Lawrence, 1965; Nuthall, 1973), Auckland with Toronto (Glynn, 1971), Otago/Massey with Missouri (Adams and Biddle, 1970).

In the period since 1970 three aspects of university-based research became particularly noteworthy — the emergence of (1) substantive research that has either gained international recognition in its own right or bids fair to do so, (2) reappraisals of local historical events and their effects on educational evolution, and (3) a preoccupation with evaluation studies. Comments on each follow.

Substantive research. Longest established and best known is the work by Professor Marie Clay, on young children's reading difficulties (Clay, 1979). Her initial explanatory studies have led into diagnostic and remedial programmes that, under the title 'Reading Recovery', are being put into practice throughout the country. At the University of Waikato, Professors Osborne and Freyberg (Osborne, 1982) and their associates have been engaged for some years in the study of pupils' interpretations (or more aptly misinterpretations) of science concepts, the logics behind their interpretations, and the educational implications of them. Kirkland and his collaborators (Kirkland *et al*, 1983) at Massey are undertaking intensive studies of infant crying, its effects on mothers, and techniques for the alleviation of stress in violence-prone parents.

Historical reappraisal. Influenced to varying extents by revisionism, several scholars are re-assessing earlier historical interpretations provided by the then establishment orthodoxy. Viewing events somewhat more critically, they have discerned exercises of power and influence which earlier interpretations had self-righteously ignored. McKenzie at Otago and Shuker, Openshaw and Snook at Massey are representative of the trend.

Evaluation. Coincidental with the government's determination that all new policy development must be evaluated together with provision of funds to make it possible, university education departments have found themselves venturing into evaluation projects of one sort or another. The range is considerable. For example, in the last five years, one university alone (Massey) has evaluated *inter alia:* an indigenous educational microcomputer; a new architectural design for a secondary school; a novel rural education programme; curriculum packages on smoking and alcohol education; the impact of new information technologies on a university and secondary school; and a scheme for the direct funding of community groups in 'problem' localities.

In brief summary, university research, after 40 years of modest and largely ineffectual effort, has in the last 20 years come of age. Impetus has been gained from better financial provisions, the development of research teams, international contacts and public recognition at national and international level.

National educational research centres

In a sense, the country's one national educational research centre, the New Zealand Council for Educational Research (NZCER), might also fit under category 3 in that it is, to some extent, private and autonomous.

Established in 1934 by a seeding grant from the Carnegie Corporation of New York, it started modestly enough with a director and three others and the hope that with its value once recognized, New Zealand would take full responsibility for its continuation. By 1984, NZCER was a QANGO (quasi-autonomous non-government organization) with a staff of 17 professional researchers and 22 ancillaries, an annual government grant of approximately $800,000 and an operating budget of about $1,250,000.

It is true to say that NZCER carried the main burden of educational research in the early years, partly because the national Department of Education was quiescent and the universities were preoccupied and partly because of the excellent foundational work of Dr C.E. Beeby, its first director.

As research has developed in New Zealand, NZCER's place in it has remained secure, although its role appears to be undergoing change. In its early years, NZCER was available to contribute to the formation of national policy. For example, Parkyn's meticulous study of entrance to the university (Parkyn, 1967) played a substantial part in the development of the current accreditation-based system.

In the last two decades, NZCER's role has become defined and confined by the organizational structure it evolved in an attempt to coordinate its work and attract government support. Thus, it has come to concentrate to some extent on (1) test development, (2) early childhood, (3) Maori education, and (4) vocational and adult learning. Nonetheless, the range of activity undertaken is considerable, leading to publications on matters as diverse as: educational planning in Indonesia (Beeby, 1979); *Oceanic Languages and Formal Education in the Pacific* (Benton, 1981); politics of education (Clark, 1981); museum education services (Hall, 1981); parents helping in pre-schools (McDonald, 1981); *SWOT: Study WithOut Tears* (Jackson *et al*, 1982), etc.

Once NZCER served to encourage and support research work done by academics in universities. In recent years this role has diminished as university departments have grown and opportunities for research have improved. The staff at NZCER now find themselves increasingly called upon to provide advice and assistance for individuals, schools and organizations wishing to undertake investigations of their own. Policy-related research has receded in the process.

NZCER has continued to play a part on the international scene. For example, it undertook some budgetary and administrative responsibility for the IEA study of mathematics, it is one of the participating organizations in APEID (Asian Programme for Educational Innovation for Development), it has an affiliated institute in Fiji, acts as agent for the East-West Centre of Hawaii and has, of course, links with other research agencies throughout the world.

On the verge of its 50th anniversary, NZCER can look back with satisfaction on a distinguished history and forward with confidence to an interesting future. It is currently examining its divisional structure in the light of contemporary research needs. It is also considering whether the local research institutes, which have only a nominal connection with the parent body, might play a more prominent part in the affairs of NZCER and the membership of the governing board.

Autonomous private educational research institutions

There currently exists no private organization that is exclusively devoted to educational research, although several commercial and non-commercial organizations do undertake some. The Heylen Research Centre has from time to time included education-related questions in its national surveys. Link Associates are also available for social research of one kind or another and have on occasion been commissioned by the government to provide 'second opinions' on educational matters. As well, associations such as the Society for Research on Women, and the New Zealand Educational Administration Society do undertake educational research.

Under this heading must also fit, though slightly uncomfortably, a relatively young organization that has the potential to affect quite considerably the nature, scope and style of educational research. The New Zealand Association for Research in Education was born in 1979 and attracted over 100 to its first annual meeting. It now has a membership of 300, mostly from university departments of education, teacher's colleges and NZCER but also with a sprinkling of departmental officers, teachers, students and others from the general field of social science. The Association provides a forum for discussion on research, has already produced a *State of the Art* publication (NZARE, 1980) and is contemplating sponsoring research of its own. It is tending to think of itself as the mouthpiece for educational research — a role that not too many would deny it.

Research divisions or units in government ministries

Unlike planning, which tends to be diffused throughout the various sectors of the national Department of Education, there is a designated research and statistics division. It has an operational staff of 22 and is concerned primarily with the annual production of a comprehensive array of statistics. It also undertakes some relevant departmental research in its own right but, more significantly in the general research scheme of things, enters into contracts with universities, teachers' colleges and other agencies and individuals for designated pieces of research. Once there used to be considerable scope for researchers to specify their own interests and gain government support. For example, the Clay Reading Studies and the Osborne and Freyberg Science Learning Project were both funded (and quite handsomely) following researcher initiatives. Some sponsorship of this kind survives but increasingly the department has come to indicate its own areas of interest, calling for specific studies for specific purposes.

The department's annual research report for 1982-83 listed: (1) some 35 current contract projects; (2) 13 divisional projects of its own; (3) 162 publications in their Research Acquisitions and (4) 24 publications in the Research Report series. The topics covered were characteristically diverse, ranging from 'absenteeism' through child management, environmental education, Japanese, distance education and management training to tests of intelligence, attitudes, achievement and fitness.

Because the education system is quite strongly centralized, the education department's own operation is multi-faceted and extensive. Within its many divisions specific research is undertaken from time to time. Noteworthy here is the work of the curriculum development division. With 22 staff devoted to the production of materials and resources for schools, a considerable amount of time is spent in field testing, trialling and evaluating.

In summary then, the department maintains the national educational statistics and sponsors research contracts either in the general interest or specific to government obligations. As well, divisions other than the designated research division undertake research for their own purposes.

Local educational research centres, clinics or schools

Economies of scale and traditional habits of mind pre-dispose New Zealanders to think nationally rather than locally on most public issues. Education is no exception and the thought that a local district might take responsibility for educational provision is as alien to conventional thinking as is blaming anybody other than the government for educational deficiencies.

In such a climate, the development of local educational research centres has simply not occurred. The nearest to them, however, is to be found in the six teachers' colleges. Each undertakes some educational research, occasionally of a general nature but, more characteristically, for domestic consumption or relating to the training programmes of students.

If local educational research effort is to develop, either it will do so through the teachers' colleges or through the local educational research institutes affiliated to a revitalized NZCER.

Comment

It can be said that more educational research is being undertaken now and by more people and in more diverse ways that at any other time in the country's history. The State of the Art monograph produced by the New Zealand Association for Research in Education lists a comprehensive array of studies which, though peppered with complaints from reviewers that not enough is being done, indicates a considerable amount of activity. The 15 chapter topics were: early childhood education, child development, education of Maori children, special education, guidance and counselling, sociology of education, women and education, history of education, measurement and testing, classroom studies, behaviour analysis, reading, science education, mathematics education and continuing education. Three hundred and sixty-four authors were cited in the publication — on average about two or three times apiece.

Funding for research has become much more available in recent years.

The education department normally has approximately $250,000 for disbursement. NZCER has for its own purposes more than $1 million also ($982,900 in 1981), although, because policy favours equipment, little is given to labour-intensive educational research (nothing in 1981). Researchers in education may also gain funding from other sources, such as the Mental Health Foundation, Medical Research Council, Alcohol Liquor Advisory Council, National Heart Foundation and, occasionally, from commercial interests.

Even so, circumstances are not idyllic and grounds for concern remain on a number of counts. These are the focus of the next section.

Issues

This final section will start where the OECD Review left off. The Review (1) stressed the importance of research and its relevance for decision making and policy development; (2) suggested the desirability of co-ordinating the research effort better; and (3) drew attention to certain omissions, notably of the application of research in economics and philosophy to major contemporary educational issues. Elsewhere the Review indicated what it thought those issues were, viz. the family as a basic social institution, ethical and cultural diversity, public/private responsibility, economic restructuring, technological change, employment, and public expenditure.

At the surface level, the OECD analysis is reasonable and over the next decade interest in the nominated issues will wax and wane as political and academic enthusiasms fluctuate. However, at a deeper level there remain a number of fundamental issues which may be endemic wherever there exists a powerful state system and researchers who, though ostensibly autonomous and academically free, are nonetheless dependent on it. Discussion follows.

The current emergence of educational research as a potentially useful and even significant activity comes at a time that is not altogether opportune. Once education itself was held in high political and social regard as the means for societal and personal advancement. As economic conditions have worsened, with overseas indebtedness reaching new and dramatically high levels and unemployment rising from virtually nothing in 1977 to 130,000 (6 per cent of the work-force) in 1984, education is no longer seen as so salient or potent. The drives at the national level for economic development and at the personal level for job security have caused education to be regarded as instrumental – on the one hand to national economic ends and on the other to personal vocational survival. Oddly, education is often found wanting for failing to produce solutions to both problems although neither were of its making.

In such a climate where political sensitivity is transcendent and social and financial egalitarianism declines, the gap between rich and poor grows, political positions become more polarized, ideologies more entrenched and radical right and radical left increasingly talk past each other.

The dilemma for educational researchers, though an old one, has become more pertinent — what ends shall educational research serve and for whom and, given the source of funds, by what means?

Economies in research effort and cost would be achieved if research activities were better coordinated and if mechanisms existed for establishing priorities effectively but, predictably, there would be some cost. As a society, New Zealand has been relatively cohesive but the education fraternity is not. Primary, secondary, pre-school and university levels are all somewhat isolated from each other and are not particularly sympathetic to each others' concerns. The education department is also seen as an institution somewhat apart — despite its pervasive influence and a number of marriages of convenience made for specific purposes. A common educational good is rarely acknowledged by all and, more rarely, promoted. Education 'causes' tend to be interest-group specific.

Within the disunited profession, the idea that educational researchers might be the catalysts for coordination is more appealing than it is realistic. Research as an activity cannot readily demonstrate its value and is not considered to have high priority. It could be readily sacrificed by economizing politicians or by the fraternity itself once advantage in doing so became apparent. Thus vulnerable, researchers, even if newly united, would be dependent on the political and economic power of their patrons. If schisms develop between government and educational agencies (and ill-will is not unknown), researchers might well provide a convenient scapegoat.

The inference to be drawn from this interpretation is that in the present writer's view, academic freedom and institutional autonomy are not so well respected that researchers who might seek shelter thereunder to advance politically unacceptable positions would either be effective or be likely to receive support.

Reality, then, may determine that the research environment stays pretty much as it is. But even if it continues in the uncoordinated and relatively haphazard way that has been characteristic of the past, there are other aspects of it that cause concern.

Critical self-appraisal has not yet become an acceptable tradition in education — partly because psychology, not noticeably self-critical, has been dominant (Nash, 1981) and partly because the necessary self-confidence is lacking. Positivism is more readily accepted than would be the case in Britain or wherever epistemological debate is active.

Accordingly, what is defined as research tends to be in the positivist tradition, quantitative, technocratic and reportedly 'value free'. Indeed, most of this chapter reflects a tacit acceptance of such a definition. However, debate over the philosophical and methodological implications of such a position is starting. If, predictably, positivism begins to lose way, how the consumers of educational research will react to 'softer, contextually sympathetic' methodologies is itself unpredictable. What the effect will be on evaluation studies sought and promoted by the government is difficult to gauge. Already in some studies the incompatability between the interests

of the evaluated and the interests of those paying for the evaluation have
posed delicate political and ethical problems.

Whether researchers will consequentially retreat into 'safe' studies is an
open question. That, however, is not alien to New Zealand's history.
Rarely have researchers grasped educational nettles. The one or two
studies that have raised public furore have been undertaken not by New
Zealanders but Americans — on Maori youth (Ausubel, 1961) and corporal
punishment (Mercurio, 1972). There have been few contemporary studies
of power and influence at the policy level and even fewer at the school
level. For example, the mechanisms that serve to ensure which part of the
secondary school population will constitute the mandatory 50 per cent of
failures in each of the subjects in the public School Certificate Examination remain unexamined and the means by which Maoris and Polynesians
become disproportionately over-represented among the failures of the
schooling system are equally avoided.

Self-conscious, critical self-appraisal establishing what and how the
system operates are matters discussed in only the most general of terms.
Such issues will only come under scrutiny when researchers act in defiance
of established interests or when the establishment itself considers such
knowledge to be valuable.

In the prevailing circumstances there has developed an uneasy relationship between the research community and the educational establishment
which must and presumably should honour its obligations to the prevailing
political authority. The growth and development of educational research
undoubtedly owes much to the personal efforts of the Director General of
Education, Mr W. Renwick and his belief in its intrinsic value. But in a
small community where even official relationships tend to carry personal
overtones, and where the political implications of actions are increasingly
apparent, pressure to conform to common, established or influential
positions is strong. Furthermore, there is no recognized set of values or
operating principles that make 'maverick' positions acceptable. What seems
to be needed is a clearer recognition of the different purposes and uses of
the different kinds of educational research and commentary. Clearly, the
establishment should carry out the policies of the democratically elected
government and to that end might reasonably commission research helpful
to its ends. At the same time, a vital and responsible education system
needs and should support its critics. That both forms of research are useful
and desirable needs more overt recognition than is currently the case.

References

Adams, R S and Biddle, B J (1970) *Realities of Teaching* Holt, Rinehart and Winston:
    New York
Ausubel, D P (1961) *Maori Youth* Price Millburn: Wellington
Beeby, C E (1979) *Assessment of Indonesian Education: A Guide in Planning*
    NZCER: Wellington
Benton, R (1981) *The Flight of the Amokura: Oceanic Languages and Formal*

Education in the Pacific Educational Research Series, No. 63, NZCER: Wellington

Clark, M ed (1981) *The Politics of Education in New Zealand* Studies in Education, No. 29, NZCER: Wellington

Clay, M M (1979) *Reading: The Pattern of Complex Behaviour* Heinemann: Auckland

Glynn, E H (1971) University of Toronto, Classroom Applications of Self-determined Reinforcement *in* Olson (1971)

Hall, C (1981) *Grandma's Attic or Aladdin's Cave: Museum Education Services for Children* Studies in Education, No. 30, NZCER: Wellington

Jackson, P, Reid, N A and Croft, A C (1982) *SWOT: Study WithOut Tears* NZCER: Wellington

Kirkland, J, Deane, F and Brennan, M (1983) About CrySOS: A clinic for people with crying babies *Family Relations* 32 (4)

McDonald, G (1981) *Working and Learning: A Participatory Project on Parent-Helping in the New Zealand Playcentre* Studies in Education, No. 32, NZCER: Wellington

Mercurio, J A (1972) *Caning, Educational Rite and Tradition* Syracuse University: Syracuse, NY

Nash, R (1981) Ideology and the ideological effects of educational practice *Delta* 29 November 1981

New Zealand Association for Research in Education (1980) *Research in Education in New Zealand: The State of the Art* NZARE/Delta: Palmerston North

Nuthall, G A (1973) Contemporary models of teaching, Chapter 2 *in* Travers *ed* (1973)

Nuthall, G A and Lawrence, P J (1965) *Thinking in Classrooms* NZCER: Wellington

OECD (1983) *Reviews of National Policies for Education: New Zealand* OECD/CERI: Paris

Olson, R D ed (1971) *Selected Readings for Educational Psychology* McCutcheon Publishing: Berkeley, Ca

Osborne, R J (1982) *Learning Science: A Generative Process* Graduate School of Education, UCLA

Parkyn, G W (1967) *Success and Failure at the University* Vol. 1, 1959, Vol. 2, 1967 NZCER: Wellington

Travers, R M W ed (1973) *Second Handbook of Research in Teaching* Rand McNally: Chicago

UNESCO *International Colloquium: Research and Practice in Education* held in Bucharest (Romania) in November 1980

12. Educational research in Poland after the Second World War

Czeslaw Kupisiewicz

Summary: The chapter reviews the topics, organization, financing, assumptions and results of educational research studies in Poland in the years 1945-83 by universities and research centres.

Institutionalized education needs constant updating in aims, method, content, organization and resources. When this is done on the basis of well planned, systematic educational research, the outcomes as a rule are better than when this basis is lacking. This conclusion applies equally to the micro-domain of classroom teaching and to the macro-scale organization of the whole educational system and the socio-economic and cultural conditions which affect its functioning.

The aims and problems of educational research need to be considered in the context of contemporary realities. Two dimensions of reality are identified. The national dimension includes, for example, the particular economic difficulties which affect the state of education and how people perceive its value. The international dimension influences, for example, people's awareness of and feelings about community, and indirectly their attitudes to education. Because of these realities this chapter stresses that the right to exist is secured not just by slogans such as 'learning to be', but also by less optimistic slogans such as 'learn or perish'.

In Poland, during the years after the end of the second world war, a notable development of various forms of education occurred. As a result not only was illiteracy eliminated — that sad heritage of the 20 years between the wars and the long-lasting occupation by Hitler's forces — but also the first stage of secondary education became compulsory and the second stage (leading to the Certificate of Maturity) was universally available. The system of higher education was also extended. At present, in consequence of this development, almost 60 per cent of each age group in Poland now receive at least 11 years of education, gaining qualifications to work in various practical occupations, and over 40 per cent receive the Certificate of Maturity in a lyceum or in a technicum, which confers the right of entry to higher education. On average, about 18 per cent of each age group take advantage of this right. In addition, many persons in Poland take part in various extra-mural courses of popular education, in centres for learning foreign languages, for example, and also take advantage of educational programmes by radio and television.

All this required, and continues to require, a considerable organizational effort and substantial expenditure from education authorities, not always proportional to the needs and educational aspirations of the Polish community. This unprecedented development of various forms of education, within schools and beyond, had to be established on a solid basis of educational research. At all levels of education, from kindergarten to institutions of higher education, there was a transition from an elite provision to mass education, and consequently it was necessary to institute reforms of aims and content, as well as of organization and method. This chapter describes the educational enquiries in Poland during the period 1945-83 which were among the more important elements in these reforms. In particular, the chapter reviews research institutions, their finance and organization and the application of research to educational practice.

Institutions of educational research and their finance

In Poland, firstly, educational research has been, and still is, the responsibility of certain departments in universities and higher schools of pedagogy. Members of these departments combine research in the main disciplines of education with their teaching of students and staff development for junior members of the teaching staff. Outstanding in this field of research are the universities of Warsaw, Poznan and Cracow, and, among higher schools of pedagogy, the school in Cracow where especially important studies have been conducted in educational technology, together with computer-assisted instruction. The administration of universities and higher schools of pedagogy is the responsibility of the Ministry of Science, Higher Education and Technology.

In addition to these centres, educational research is also conducted by institutes under the direction of the Ministry of Education. The oldest of these was the Institute of Pedagogy, founded in 1950. In 1972, it was transformed into the Institute of Pedagogic Research, whose aim was to conduct enquiries into the principles and modernization of the pre-university level of education and also the organization of primary and secondary education. In 1972 also, a number of new institutes were created:

- an institute of enquiries concerning youth, with a remit to analyse the conditions, processes and results of education, as well as the participation of youth in socio-economic and cultural changes in the country;
- an institute of teacher education, to work out the content, form and method of the initial training and continuing development of teachers, and to guide the activities of the Teachers' Radio-Television University (NURT);
- an institute of vocational education, to initiate and conduct enquiries into the social economical and pedagogical problems of vocational schools, and the relation of this type of school to national economics and culture, and to prepare plans and programmes for vocational

schools;
— an institute for school syllabuses, whose activities cover research and development of content and method in the area of general education. This institute also produces plans and syllabuses for elementary ('basic') schools and for secondary schools of general education. In Poland, the 'basic' schools follow a standard curriculum throughout their eight forms, attended by children from age 7 to 15. The secondary schools of general education have four forms, attended by teenagers from age 15 or 16 to 19 or 20, of whom a substantial majority will subsequently apply for admission to higher education.

The research needs of the Ministry of Science, Higher Education and Technology are met by the Institute of Scientific Policy, Technological Progress and Higher Education, established in 1973. The task of this Institute is to investigate the efficiency of scientific research, the link between science and economics and technology, planning and forecasting the growth of higher education, and also generally the education of students and future research workers and the improvement of educational provision and methods in higher schools.

Since 1972 in Poland there has also been research into what are called the 'nodal problems'. These generally are interdisciplinary researches of considerable importance to the national economy and culture. For example, among the 'nodal problems' in the domains of economic, social and cultural life, one finds the topic, 'The development of education in contemporary society'. In tackling this theme, representatives of various disciplines participate — educationists, doctors, psychologists, those who deal with information, sociologists, economists and so on. They investigate problems such as: the health of children and young people in Poland; the development trends in secondary education in the industrialized countries of the world; the development of science and technology and the curriculum in schools of general and vocational education; global problems of mankind and education; an outline of the idea of education for the future; the education of teachers in an epoch of changing civilization; failure in school, its causes and remedies; and so on. Administrative personnel for research into these nodal problems are supplied by the Ministry of Education. However, control of the research is in the hands of a Commission attached to the Polish Academy of Sciences. It is this Commission which evaluates the results and makes proposals for financing the research.

The body which coordinates the investigations described in the previous paragraph is the Committee of Pedagogical Disciplines of the Polish Academy of Sciences. This is a national council consisting of outstanding representatives of educational studies, but it does not have at its disposal the necessary administrative structure which would allow it to manage the coordination of research effectively. Consequently the results of coordination by the Committee, for the present at least, have not been entirely successful.

In addition to the establishments mentioned above, research in education in Poland is also carried on in educational institutes attached to medical schools, higher agricultural colleges, polytechnics, physical education colleges, higher schools of economics and so on. The researches however are mainly studies of methods, organized to meet the specific needs of the various institutions.

To conclude, the promotion of educational research and popular dissemination of its findings is the particular role of the Polish Pedagogical Association which was founded in 1981. This is a national organization affiliated to the Polish Academy of Sciences, to which educationists from many universities and government institutes belong. All these institutes and organizations are financed by the State. The total number of personnel employed amounts to about 1,500 persons, including over 40 professors of educational disciplines.

The organization of educational research and its problems

The legal-organizational basis for educational research conducted by the various establishments described in the previous section takes the form of research programmes, some lasting many years (usually three or five) and some for one year only. These programmes are based on decisions by State authorities — for example, the decision of July 1981 concerning the universal provision of education up to the Certificate of Maturity in secondary schools. Alternatively, they may be based on resolutions of the Polish Academy of Sciences — particularly, on the Resolution of the Second Congress on Polish Education in June 1973. Another source for research is the recommendations of the Committee of Experts on the reform of the educational system, as in the May 1973 'Report concerning Education in Poland'. The Committee of Experts was a national organization, comprising pre-eminent representatives of educational theory and practice. This body, on the instructions of the educational authorities in the early 1970s, carried out a thorough analysis of the educational system in Poland at all levels, identifying its unquestionable achievements but also its weaknesses and making recommendations for reform. Research also results from current orders from the Ministry of Education and the Ministry of Science, Higher Education and Technology, which take into account the pressing requirements of these ministries — for example, the need to modernize programmes of instruction resulting from the reform of primary and secondary education instituted in 1973 (but subsequently suspended in 1981), or the change in recruitment of students for higher education in 1982 and 1983.

These research programmes thus cover a wide range of topics. They include educational research of a comparative nature which, identifying current trends in the development of education in other countries throughout the world, constitute a valuable system of reference for reform undertaken in Poland. One example among others of research of this kind is the analysis of educational changes in the world in the period 1945-80, conducted by the author of this chapter ('The educational changes in the world', 1980). Other examples of publications within this field of enquiry are listed in Note 1 at the end of the chapter.

The range of topics covered in Note 1 indicate that in Poland almost all important problems of education have been the subject of organized systematic enquiry. This assertion is not invalidated even if some areas — for example, methods of instruction and modern technological methods and materials, programmed texts, teaching machines, language laboratories and so on — have enjoyed greater interest among researchers than, say, the aims and content of education in contemporary schools. Obviously, not all the conclusions emerging from these enquiries have an equal chance of being accepted; not all are suitable for immediate application on a large scale in all schools, or, even more, throughout the entire system of institutionalized education. But a substantial part of this research has been utilized by education authorities and by teachers in their school practice, and the research has had a positive influence on this practice. It is appropriate to devote a separate section to this topic.

Research and educational practice

It follows from what has been said above that the results of educational research studies in Poland in the period 1945-80 have had a beneficial influence on educational practice. The impact of research is especially notable in a number of aspects which are listed in detail in Note 2; briefly, these include:

- the distribution of schools in specific areas, and manpower planning;
- new educational methods;
- improving textbooks for school and higher education;
- developing the lesson-system in schools;
- school failure and remedial education;
- child-rearing;
- methods of teaching languages and other subjects;
- linking school and work.

However, there are also instances where the findings of educational research have not been taken into account in preparing recommendations for action. One example is the attitude of education authorities to the programme of school reform recommended by the Committee of Experts in the 1973 report on the state of education in Poland, mentioned earlier. Instead of providing universal secondary education in the 11/12-year polytechnical school of general education, as recommended by the Committee of Experts on the basis of a comprehensive survey of national needs and analysis of steps to meet these needs, the Ministry of Education initiated a programme of reform of primary and secondary schools based on their own ideas, which were considerably different from the Committee's proposals. As a result, the reform which was started in 1973 with the main aim of universal 10-year secondary education, had to be stopped in 1981.

Not only was there no money for its continuation, but also the whole concept of the reform had not been sufficiently worked out.

It is also true that some recommendations based on research for modernizing the existing system of education cannot be realized in practice simply because the means of achieving this are not available. This is the situation in respect of attempts to reform school instruction by programmed texts in books or machines; attempts to individualize learning, relying less on what is termed 'frontal instruction' and more on group methods; trying to link school education more closely with what is called 'parallel education', principally through the mass media which in Poland are steadily increasing their educational activities, and finally in relation to continuing or lifelong education, by which every person should have the chance to learn what he or she wants to learn, at the time which is most convenient and in the style which will be most rewarding.

Expectations

Since 1980, Poland has been in a state of acute social and economic crisis, and this has affected education also at all levels. One manifestation of this crisis is a marked decrease in financial support for schools of various types and levels, and also a shortage of resources for education. To meet the needs and thus to create the necessary conditions for the proper functioning of educational institutions, would require over 1,000 'basic' (or 8-form) schools in new town settlements, 600 similar schools in villages, 400 vocational schools for students aged 15/16 to 18/20, 3,000 pre-school establishments, 200 special schools for children with mental and physical handicaps, 400 boarding schools, mostly in small towns and villages, 100 houses for children deprived of parental care, and finally over 35,000 flats for teachers. Only if these needs can be met will conditions be favourable for full implementation of the findings of educational research, within the school system or, more generally, both within and beyond the school provision, in formal and informal education. On the other hand, just because of these difficult conditions, educational research is all the more necessary. But the research must be oriented differently from what would be needed in non-crisis situations. Moreover, a crisis however long lasting comes eventually to an end, but education must go on in all circumstances.

What then are the priorities in Poland in the domain of educational research? In answering this question, one has to say first of all that education authorities have not abandoned the aim of providing universal secondary education for all, with full access to the Certificate of Maturity, whether in general or vocational education. What is wanted is a school which, more efficiently than the present school system, will prepare pupils for life, for professional studies and for higher education. Therefore this new school, the school of tomorrow, should in a rational way combine learning with work, formal with informal education, teaching with personal growth, and the needs of society with the needs of each individual. This is no easy task; but its difficulty makes it all the more challenging for the educational researchers.

This school of tomorrow, whose foundations must be established now, by research as part of a concerted plan, will have to educate differently from present practice. In particular, such a school must change from an institution in which knowledge is handed down, into an institution for cognitive development and self-education by pupils. The form of the new model of schools is well illustrated by slogans: 'teaching how to learn', 'learning to be', 'no limits to learning'. How could such slogans be realized in every-day school practice? How could it be achieved in the institutions of 'parallel learning'? And how could such school education be integrated with the idea of 'parallel education'?

These and similar questions could be answered most fully only by appropriate educational research. Consequently, the research should be initiated now so that its results can be utilized when conditions are more favourable for education than at present.

The history of education shows, without doubt, that the final effects of every educational reform, starting from small improvements in method and ending with the transformation of the whole structure of the educational system, depend largely on the teachers. Therefore, the prime task for education at present is to improve the provision for educating teachers – in particular, preparing them to fulfil, rationally and consistently, not only the role of informant but also that of adviser and guardian, encouraging the autonomous cognitive growth of children and teenagers and discreetly guiding this development. The achievement of this goal requires a sound theoretical foundation. But the creation of this basis depends entirely on well planned and well executed research, not limited to the domain of pedagogy.

In short, the most important research problems of today are the provision of universal and effective secondary education in Poland, how best to link school with work, and how to modernize the present system of educating teachers, preparing them to work in 'the school of tomorrow'. Alongside such enquiries, the topics of current research must also continue. These are concerned principally with how to implant in pupils of primary and secondary schools the inventive approach and the habit of heuristic, alternative thinking; how to free their minds from merely reproductive schemata; how to teach them responsible commitment to the highest humanistic, cultural and social values. Finally, there is the question of how to live in times characterized by the threat of nuclear apocalypse, by man's increasing devastation of the natural environment, by the rapid exhaustion of non-reproducible raw materials and sources of energy, by multifarious diseases of civilization, growing terrorism, the increase of juvenile delinquency, over population – in times when A-B-C, the traditional symbols of initiating children to education, have come to denote weapons of mass destruction, namely, Atomic, Biological and Chemical bombs.

Can organized disciplines find an answer to these questions, and in particular, can this be done by the disciplines of education?

Note 1

List of publications illustrating the range of topics covered in educational research in Poland:

Studies describing the goals and tasks of education in schools of various types and levels, eg *A model of an Educated Pole, ed* B Suchodolski, 1980; *Foundations of General Education,* W Okón, 1976;

Books on the organization and methods of teaching, eg *An Outline of the Theory of Education,* H Muszyński, 1976;

Exposition of methods of didactical work, eg *Technical Means of Instruction,* E Berezowski, 1982;

In addition, books on many monograph topics of which the following especially deserve mention:

Education for the Future, 1968 and *Problems of Education in Contemporary Civilization,* 1974 by B Suchodolski;

System of Instruction, 1971 by K Lech;

The Principles of Instruction, 1961 and *Education and Educationalists,* 1968 by B Nawroczyński;

The Essence and Aims of Education, 1973 and *The Theory and Means of Education,* 1973 by K Sosnicki;

Education and Industrialization, 1971 and *The Schooling of Polish Youth,* 1976 by M Kozakiewicz;

Solving Problems, 1969 and *Psychological Conceptions of Man,* 1977 by J Kozielecki;

Grasping the Content in the Process of Learning, 1978 by Z Włodarski;

The Method of First-year Instruction, 1962 and *Korczak,* 1978 by S Wołoszyn;

Reflections on Education, 1973 and *Essays on Higher Education,* 1976 by J Szcsepański;

Psychological Foundations of the Principles of Upbringing, 1972 by W Szewczuk;

Disturbances in the Development of Pupils and Failures in School, 1973 by H Spionek;

and finally, many manuals on didactics, general pedagogy, the history of education and educational theory, the psychology of child-rearing, and also the methodology of teaching various subjects.

Note 2

List of influential research studies and their authors:

'Developing the provision of primary and secondary schools in accordance with demographic changes to meet the manpower requirements of the job market' – M Falski and other authors on adjusting the network of vocational schools to economic needs in different regions of Poland;

'Modernizing educational methods, including research on the effectiveness of problem-solving approaches and group methods of instruction' – experimental educational research by Cz Kupisiewicz, K Lech, H Muszyński and W Okón;

'Modernizing instructional methods with particular reference to textbooks for school and higher education' – research by E Berezowski, Cz Kupisiewicz, L Leja and C Maziarz;

'Improving the lesson-system of school instruction' – studies by J Bartecki and T Lewowicki;

'Analysing the causes of school failure and developing means of counteracting it, such as specific remedial treatment, diagnosis and pedagogical therapy in schools of various kinds and at different levels' – studies by J Konopnicki, H Spionek and M Tyszko, and also over many years by the author of this chapter, summarized in

Didactic Failures: Causes and Remedies, 1972;

'A research project on an integrated system of child-rearing, including the activities of school, family and children's organizations' — H Muszyński;

'Developing methods of teaching Polish, English, French, German and Russian languages, and of teaching mathematics, biology, chemistry, physics, geography, history, technical subjects, aesthetic studies and music, and early education' — many researchers;

'Linking school and work, over a wide range, from simple practical activities such as working with cardboard and wood, to production work-experience for young people during school vacations.'

13. The promotion of educational research and development – Scottish style

Sally Brown

Summary: The Scottish Education Department's (SED) funded research programme plays a dominant part in educational research in Scotland. This programme includes developmental projects, but mainstream curriculum development has proceeded from documents produced by various national committees on which Her Majesty's Inspectorate are influential. Negotiations for research within the SED's programme are carried out by the Research and Intelligence Unit which mediates between the research community and the SED to promote mutual understanding. Funded projects are invariably designed to have some practical pay-off. During the 1970s the general funding increased steadily under both Labour and Conservative Governments. A sharp growth occurred from 1979 to 1981 as the Conservatives implemented designated programmes linked to their policies for education, but more recently the budget has had much smaller increases. Research has had a close relationship with practice and some influence on policy decisions, particularly in the programmes linked to government developments. The close links with practice have contributed to the rise of action-research approaches and facilitated dissemination of research ideas and findings in Scotland, but they have done little to communicate Scottish work to other parts of the world.

Introduction

It should come as no surprise that in Scotland's small and fairly centralized system of education (which is separate and different from that of the rest of the United Kingdom) a discussion of educational research and development should put strong emphasis on the role of the Scottish Education Department (SED). The current edition of its register of educational research (SED, 1983) shows that this executive branch of the government has provided support during 1983 for 116 projects in 20 institutions. Other bodies such as the Economic and Social Research Council (ESRC, formerly the Social Science Research Council), Scottish Health Education Group and various private foundations have investments in this area of research and development, but at a much more modest level. In their latest report (SSRC, 1983) the Education and Human Development Committee of the ESRC, for example, lists only seven projects currently supported in Scottish institutions which could be ambiguously classified as educational.

This is not to argue that all educational research and development in

Scotland is contained within the SED's funded research programme. There are many individuals in universities, colleges and schools who undertake a variety of independent enquiries. These, however, are necessarily small-scale projects which are less likely to find support for the dissemination of their findings or ideas and their impact on policy or practice is patchy.

More important, 'development' is seen by some as a separate activity from 'research' and not the responsibility of professional researchers or full-time curriculum developers within a programme of funded projects. Instead, the Consultative Committee on the Curriculum (CCC) was set up in 1965 with curriculum development as its main task (this 'mainstream' of Scottish curriculum development is discussed in the next section). The CCC's activities, however, provide only part of the 'development story'. Much of the SED's funded research programme could be termed development.

Mainstream curriculum developments

Over the past two decades curriculum development in Scotland has been largely a committee activity. First, the CCC, through its Committees on Primary and Secondary Education, has spawned central committees for particular subjects and working parties with concern for specific aspects of the curriculum. The reports and curriculum papers produced by these groups offer advice on course content, teaching approaches, materials, assessment and classroom activities but seldom present the teacher with a packaged course of the type emerging from conventional curriculum development projects (an exception is *Tour de France* for the first two years of French).

Second, the committees of experts constituting the subject or course panels of the Scottish Examination Board (SEB) are powerful in determining the way the curriculum in secondary school develops. Changes in the syllabus, guidelines and examination arrangements for awards in the Scottish Certificate of Education command immediate attention and galvanize teachers to implement the intended innovations.

Third, groups of Her Majesty's Inspectors (HMI) occasionally prepare reports identifying modifications or improvements in the curriculum which they deem desirable. For example, two such reports on primary education (SED, 1965, 1980a) offered frameworks within which schools were expected to develop their own curricula. Reports of this kind tend to be written in a prescriptive form, at a high level of generality and with little attempt to work through the awkward or conflicting implications they may have for classroom implementation.

In 1980 an interesting experiment was undertaken by the SED to explore a school-based development model as a replacement for the committee model. In a major initiative (entitled the 'Munn/Dunning' programme — SED, 1980b), on the curriculum and assessment of 14- to 16-year-olds, teachers from different schools cooperated with each other and, supported by HMIs and extra resources, generated and piloted new courses and assessment schemes. Six new courses for low achievers, including three which were multi-disciplinary, were developed in these 'extended feasibility studies' and 16 to 20 schools were involved in each development. There are questions to be asked about how truly 'school-based' this exercise was and to what extent the HMI 'support' would be better described as 'direction'. Nevertheless, there is ample evidence that teachers gained considerable professional satisfaction from producing high quality developments which were much more readily implemented in classrooms than were ideas from centrally-based committees.

It is, therefore, curious and disappointing to find a subsequent reversion to the committee model, where the feasibility studies' school-based procedures are replaced by joint working parties of the CCC and SEB for education from age 14 to 16 and by central task groups for development work post-16. It appears that the SED, after a brief relaxation, is now reinforcing the powerful influence it has traditionally exerted over decisions about the school curriculum. It does this through: first, the pivotal role accorded to HMIs on the committees, working parties and panels of the CCC and SEB, together with their privileged access to the SED's decision makers; second, the very close association between senior members of the SED and key officials of the SEB; and third, the patronage which operates so that other members of the committees, particularly teacher members, tend to be those whose ideas and work are most closely aligned with those supported by both SED and SEB.

In parallel with this broad front of curriculum development, and not always directly associated with it, the research programme has funded projects on a range of specific issues which, it was felt, could be more appropriately approached from a research perspective. In consequence, developmental projects concerned with curriculum innovations (eg multi-disciplinary courses or oral competence in English), assessment (eg diagnostic assessment or assessment of experiential learning), teaching strategies (eg mastery learning or pupil-centred methods) or resources (eg item banks or computer software) find a place in the SED's research programme. Before looking at the contents of that programme, however, let us consider how projects are initiated and negotiated.

Initiating and negotiating research

In 1973 the SED set up its Research and Intelligence Unit (RIU) with the intention that it should help the various SED divisions to identify their research needs and to have appropriate projects mounted. The RIU has no counterpart either in other departments of the Civil Service in Scotland or in the SED's opposite number in England (the Department of Education and Science). It functions as an intermediary between the executive branch of government concerned with education in Scotland and the educational research community. It is concerned, concurrently, with translating the government's areas of concern into general ideas for programmes of research which might be attractive to researchers, and with formulating researchers' initiatives into plans for projects which are likely to be seen by government as making a positive contribution to education or providing information relevant to decision making.

Over the decade of its existence, the RIU has endeavoured to maintain a broad research programme concerned with a range of educational matters and has endeavoured not to devote the general funds available solely to research issues ranking high in government priorities. (In the next section reference will be made to additional short-term research monies which are sometimes made available in respect of such priorities.) The view that research should relate to broad governmental areas of concern as well as to more specific policy-related issues has been accepted by the major decision makers within the SED. It has avoided the creation of conditions under which only projects directly supportive of policy, or intended to solve immediate and specific practical problems in education, are funded. In the first place, the RIU has seen it as more important that research is policy-informing rather than policy-directed and that involves the SED in being 'big' enough to accept criticism (a view less pervasive in some other parts of the SED than in the RIU). In the second place, the RIU doubts the capability of research to offer quick solutions to pressing problems; it sees the value of effective research as being manifest in the longer term, helping to develop greater understanding of educational matters, offering explanations of why things turn out the way they do and providing material which works 'its way into the woodwork of the organisation until the findings are eventually incorporated as part of the overall decision-making process' (Morris and Johnston, 1981, quoting Leigh, 1980).

The RIU has established negotiating practices which involve discussions with researchers, HMIs and SED divisions from the earliest stages in the research planning. It is, therefore, unusual for a researcher to present a completed proposal and then to have it summarily rejected; if agreement is unlikely, then this normally becomes clear during the preliminary conversations with the RIU. These procedures make it virtually impossible to distinguish unambiguously projects which are commissioned directly by central government from those initiated in their entirety by a researcher. However, in recent years researchers have gone to considerable trouble to find out what areas of concern are currently most likely to be funded before submitting their ideas for research. This implies that central influence on research is becoming stronger.

Most negotiations, particularly at the early stages of the discussions about projects, are carried out in the institutions where the work is to be done. This preference of the Unit for getting out into the field has several advantages: it avoids the atmosphere of government offices (which can be less than conducive to detailed discussion of research), enables the Unit to get to know the whole research team, offers others in research institutions opportunities to buttonhole Unit staff about research ideas and keeps the RIU informed about the availability of researchers, the conditions under which research is done and those educational activities or initiatives taking place under the auspices of other agencies.

This pattern of operation has established a fairly close and trusting relationship between the RIU and much of the relatively small research community. This relationship is nowhere more apparent than at the autumn meeting of the Scottish Educational Research Association, held annually at the University of St Andrews and an occasion for exchanging ideas and initiating research plans in both academic and social contexts. Furthermore, the Unit's efforts to retain and maintain contract researchers who, they believe, carry out competent and valuable research, are appreciated by many people. These somewhat cosy arrangements, however, are not viewed with approbation by everyone. There are researchers who look upon them as supporting a clique of SED favourites who toe the government line and receive funding for their research. In contrast, the disapproval of some within the SED arises because they see the RIU as being unduly influenced by an independently-minded research community.

Whatever the strengths and weaknesses in the Scottish system, envious glances are sometimes cast by those south of the border. After an annual conference of the British Educational Research Association, Murphy (1982) referred to:

> 'the extensive research programme that had been mounted in Scotland by the SED in connection with the recommendations of the Dunning Committee. English research eyes boggled and many reflected on the lack of co-ordinated post-Waddel 16+ examination research south of the border.'

Currently, however, there is uncertainty on the Scottish scene. The method of operation has evolved to a large extent through the efforts of two people: the first director of the RIU (a Chief Inspector now retired) and an HMI (nearing retirement) with a major responsibility over the last decade for designing, negotiating and managing the research programme. They have been manifestly successful in using their considerable knowledge of research and the research community to promote a successful and vigorous programme; but there are no obvious successors. The future of the principles and the mechanisms of research funding in the SED is under review and the research community is concerned that the commissioning and negotiating of research should continue to be in the hands of people with a good understanding both of its potential and of its limitations. Final funding decisions depend on the declared support of key SED administrators and are influenced by the views of HMIs with responsibility for relevant areas of education. Such individuals rarely have experience in research and their primary concerns are matters of general education and the requirements of politicians. Frequently, they have unrealistic expectations of quick simple solutions to complex educational problems or, alternatively, they fail to recognize the power of research to contribute to a general understanding of educational matters. The RIU has had a crucial role in promoting better understanding between researchers and these SED decision makers; it is essential that (a) such mediation should continue by some means within or outwith the SED, and (b) the research effort in Scotland should continue its current practice of avoiding concentration on a relatively small number of perceived government priorities (and much credit must go to the RIU for the development of that practice).

What counts as research?

If research is taken to be concerned with the extension of knowledge, and development is viewed as the utilization or application of accumulated knowledge for technological or other practical purposes, then the SED's funded projects cover both and, if anything, emphasize development. It is also clear that educational researchers in Scotland seldom receive financial support for an unencumbered search for truth; with few exceptions a practical pay-off is expected. That pay-off may include learning packages, computer programs, advisory services for teachers, item- or data-banks, exemplars of teaching strategies, assessment techniques or information which is relevant to educational policy decisions, teacher education or curriculum development.

A wide range of research methods from large-scale surveys to clinical or case studies is used and very few kinds of educational project appear to be unacceptable in principle. Among those rarities might be such things as arid statistical exercises, experimental/comparative studies which could be classified as 'pure' psychology or research into areas for which the SED has no responsibility, such as university teaching. In recent years the number of projects formulated as collaborative action-research has increased. The RIU sees action-research as having several advantages: it involves collaboration among teachers and between teacher and researcher in an empathetic partnership of equals; it is concerned with enquiries which are based on practice and on theory which is grounded in practice; it aims to initiate change to improve practice immediately and, at the same time, to generate knowledge about teaching; it calls for all participants, including teachers, to adopt a consciously reflective stance, make explicit their practice-based theories of teaching, formulate hypotheses about action to bring about desired change, test out those hypotheses and use their findings to revise their theories in a continuing cycle; and it accepts that any theory about teaching or prescription for action will be provisional and must be reexamined as the educational context changes or the teacher develops. This scenario promises some resolution of perennial problems identified in criticisms of conventional research (poorly communicated and little impact on practice), centralized curriculum development (low level of uptake), curriculum evaluation (seldom undertaken and certainly not sufficiently so on government developments) and teachers' attitudes to their work (unreflective and not at all enquiry-oriented).

The Scottish action-research studies show some prospect of offering these benefits, but there emerge a number of uncomfortable features associated with employing the approach (Brown, 1984). In particular, the model of the teacher as 'enquirer/researcher' appears not to be shared by everyone. There are many teachers, HMIs, SED administrators and politicians who support a 'top-down management' model where the 'wise' at the top hand down the curriculum to teachers and pupils. Even if the top of the educational hierarchy accepts that teachers should be research-oriented, there remains the question of how teachers are to be persuaded to adopt a reflective and enquiring stance towards their own teaching. Researchers tend to report on the developments achieved through action-research, but they are less forthcoming about methodological matters of how to persuade teachers effectively. Where persuasion has been effective, with teachers gaining insights through formulating and testing their own theories, there is no guarantee that their reappraised teaching aims will display the same priorities as the corporate aims of the school, local authority or government. How the system will respond to the conflict which emerges from this, and what the research programme will be able to tell us about how to disseminate or generalize knowledge acquired through action-research, are among the many interesting questions facing Scottish education.

A part of SED research funding is now earmarked for research and development in particular areas. Between 1967-68 and 1977-78 there was no such earmarking although monies were allocated under the following three heads: the general research programme; the grant to the Scottish Council for Research in Education (a semi-autonomous research agency); and research in the Scottish colleges of education. From 1978-79 money has been specifically used for projects in the Munn/Dunning developments for the curriculum and assessment of the 14 to 16 age group (SED, 1982); from 1979-80 funds have been allocated to the Scottish Microelectronics Development Programme (SMDP, 1981); and from 1980-81 funding has been available for national monitoring of achievement. Occasionally there is, within the general research programme, some emphasis on projects around a particular theme. Currently one such theme is 'the quality of teaching' which incorporates a series of heterogeneous studies covering teachers' entry to training institutions, pre-service education, the pro-bationary period and the career of the experienced teacher with in-service staff development.

The way in which the funding is shared among the various categories of project changes from time to time. However, the overall level of funds allocated to the SED's research programme has increased in real terms every year from 1967-68 to 1982-83. In that 15-year period the total nominal annual funding has grown from £67,000 to £1,677,000.

Who does the research and development?

The SED, largely due to the influence of the RIU, has avoided maintaining research as an elitist activity carried out only in universities and research institutes. Its aims include both the involvement of practising teachers (to encourage growth of reflective, self-critical, research-based approaches to teaching) and the development of research expertise and activity in colleges of education. The first of these has been only partially successful. The encouraging increase of teacher involvement in action-research and research-based post-graduate studies is now threatened by financial constraints, and only rarely these days are Scottish local authorities persuaded to second teachers to work with professional researchers.

The colleges, however, present a more optimistic picture. Of their staffing allocation 8 per cent is now assigned to research and, in addition to competing for general research money, they have specifically-designated funds (in 1982-83 about 7 per cent of the total SED research budget). Of the SED's funded projects, 46 per cent are currently based in colleges (SED, 1983).

The colleges' close associations with primary and secondary classrooms probably account for the emphasis their projects put on development rather than research. Many of their staff lack research training and, unfortunately, have not been encouraged to undertake university courses in research methodology. Despite a shortage of trained, competent researchers, the only full-time MEd research methodology course in Scotland has been discontinued because would-be students were unable to obtain secondment or sponsorship.

The universities probably stress research more than development. In the past, SED-supported research was often complemented by ESRC projects (particularly theoretical) and university-funded staff. Reduced finance for universities and social science research have changed that and have increased the insecurity of full-time researchers on short-term contracts. University researchers have better opportunities for research training than college researchers, but in either case bleak career prospects disrupt projects. The RIU's efforts to offer some continuity of employment for those it believes to be competent has reaped rewards on both sides.

Agencies such as the Scottish Council for Research in Education (SCRE) and the Scottish Microelectronics Development Programme (SMDP) lack the universities' and colleges' close contacts with teaching. They can, however, organize their activities more directly for the benefit of research and development. The SCRE's projects are more research-oriented than those of the SMDP which have concentrated on software development. Indeed, it is alarming how little of the SMDP's budget is used for research; this state of affairs may improve since from 1984 additional funds were made available specifically for the support of a microelectronics research programme.

SED-funded projects normally have associated advisory committees. These consist of individuals with expertise or interest in some aspect of education related to the research (eg teachers, local authority advisers, Examination Board officers, researchers, college/university lecturers, HMIs or people from other relevant occupations). They are invited by the RIU to meet about three times a year to offer advice and to comment on the project's progress and plans. There is, however, no obligation on the researchers to accept the advice; research decisions and reports remain their own responsibility. The purposes of advisory committees are twofold: first, members should offer critical and concrete support to the research and, second, the research should inform the committee and stimulate members to disseminate its ideas and findings to the wider educational community. One strength of these committees is that they maintain considerable autonomy for the project team while ensuring regular dialogue between researchers and practitioners about the relevance of the research. They can offer the SED an independent view in cases where difficulties are occurring or an extension to the research seems desirable. Their effectiveness varies and they appear to the author to work less well in circumstances where members are nominated by interested bodies (eg local authorities) rather than personally invited, or where *steering* committees replace the advisory group and attempt to control the research and development.

Research, policy and practice

While the detail of the government-sponsored research programme may be most easily explained by the power structures and practices within the education system, its general features must be linked to economic conditions and the political party in office. Under successive Labour and Conservative governments from 1967 to 1979, annual research funding grew fairly steadily from £67,000 to £547,000. In the financial years (1 April to 31 March) 1979-80 and 1980-81 this budget shot up by 75 per cent and 39 per cent respectively with the Conservatives coming to power in the spring of 1979. Part of the first of these increases may be attributed to decisions made under the previous Labour government, but most arises from the Conservatives' decisions to support the Munn/Dunning developments, the microelectronics programme and national monitoring of achievement. The government channelled funds into work which it saw as directly serving its policy goals of curriculum and assessment reform, introducing new technology into schools and raising standards. Labour had been reluctant to act decisively on the Munn and Dunning Reports (SED, 1977 a & b), because some of the major recommendations appeared divisive in the context of comprehensive education. In 1981-82 and 1982-83 overall levels of funding increased by 18 per cent and 7 per cent. This decrease in the growth rate of the research budget might be taken to reflect the Conservatives' commitment to cutting public expenditure, but in both years the increase was above the inflation rate and it is hard to imagine that any party could have maintained the previous rate of growth, given the country's economic circumstances.

About 44 per cent of the total budget is taken up by the three designated areas of policy-related work. A few projects within the current general research programme are also closely associated with Conservative policies such as 'parental choice of schools' provided for in *The Education (Scotland) Act 1981*. The general planning of projects within the different areas, however, is the responsibility of SED officials and only proposals of a particularly sensitive kind are submitted for Ministerial approval. It appears that Conservative Ministerial influence on educational research is less direct and more complex in Scotland than in England and Wales where the Secretary of State for Education keeps a firm hand on things. Perhaps the explanation for this lies in part in the very broad areas of responsibility which the Secretary of State for Scotland and his junior ministers have to shoulder, their substantial absence from Scotland in London, the domination by Labour of parliamentary representation for Scotland and of control of Scottish local authorities, and an absence of the English obsessions with controversial issues like selective schools or private education (something close to comprehensive state education has always had wide acceptance in Scotland).

The question of whether research influences policy decisions is always difficult to answer. My own belief is that individual projects tend to exert their influence, in the first instance, on educational practice. Insofar as they affect the thinking of the community of teachers, lecturers, advisers and HMIs, they may then become one influence on policy decisions. This process has been most apparent in the Munn/Dunning developments where research was made an integral part of the programme and a researcher was seconded as an adviser/consultant to the SED.

The work of several researchers in the programme was concerned with criterion-referencing and diagnostic assessment (eg Arnold and Simpson, 1982; Black and Dockrell, 1980; Brown, 1980 a & b) and this helped to change thinking about assessment. Subsequently, Inspectorate policy developed and now places emphasis on both diagnostic assessment as an integral part of teaching and on the use of criterion-referenced profiles for reporting pupils' attainments. The government's new proposals for certification in Scotland attempt a compromise (through 'grade-related criteria') between established, norm-referenced grades and criterion-referenced descriptions of performance. It is interesting, however, that although a research project was commissioned to explore the feasibility of a fully criterion-referenced certificate and a commitment was made to use the project's interim report (McCall *et al*, 1983) to inform decisions about the new certification, those decisions were taken before the date agreed for the production of the report. Perhaps research findings have to be mediated through other educators and cannot expect to have a direct effect on policy makers.

There are a number of other aspects of practice upon which the Munn/Dunning research has had an impact. In the associated developments teachers have had to address questions such as:

— How can practical skills in science, oral competence, reading among low achievers, communicative skills in French or affective learning in home economics be assessed?

— What teaching strategies are appropriate for mastery learning or learning through discussion?
— How do subject departments collaborate for multi-disciplinary courses?

The research projects have focused on the same issues and their products (material resources, conceptual clarifications, plans for action) are in demand. Researchers have become involved in the developments as consultants for working parties, action-researchers in schools, organizers of in-service courses, speakers at teachers' conferences and, in one case, the agency with responsibility for conceptualizing and piloting a new area of assessment for SEB certification. The problem has been to regulate these activities so that they reinforce rather than detract from the researchers' own research and development commitments. Despite effective researcher/practitioner collaboration, a tension remains between the short-term demands for solutions to practical problems and the long-term improved understanding of those problems to which research is best suited.

A close association of research with practice facilitates the dissemination of research findings but exerts pressure for them to be made available quickly. Perhaps this is the reason why commercial publication is used less than in other countries. Frequently universities, colleges, SCRE and the Scottish Curriculum Development Service (an agency of the CCC) publish or otherwise make available books, monographs, occasional papers or packages for teachers. This reduces delay in communication between researcher and practitioner but publicity outside Scotland is pitiful when compared with the major publishing houses. Perhaps we have only ourselves to blame for the rest of the world knowing so little about what is distinctive about Scottish educational research, assuming it to be just another corner of the UK.

References

Arnold, B and Simpson, M (1982) *Concept Development and Diagnostic Testing* Aberdeen College of Education: Aberdeen
Black, H and Dockrell, B (1980) *Diagnostic Assessment in Secondary Schools* Scottish Council for Research in Education: Edinburgh
Brown, S (1980a) *What Do They Know? A Review of Criterion-Referenced Assessment* HMSO: Edinburgh
Brown, S (1980b) *Introducing Criterion-Referenced Assessment: Teachers' Views* Stirling Educational Monographs, University of Stirling: Stirling
Brown, S (1984) Action research: problematic issues for its contribution to science teacher education, *Proceedings of Bat Sheva de Rotheschild Seminar on Science Teacher Education* Hebrew University, Jerusalem, January 1983 (in press)
Leigh, A (1980) Policy research and reviewing services for under fives *Social Policy and Administration* 14 162
McCall, J, Bryce, T, Gordon, P, Hewitt, C and Martin, P (1983) *Interim Report of the Criterion-Referenced Certification Project* Jordanhill College of Education: Glasgow
Morris, J G and Johnston, F H (1981) The impact of policy and practice on research *British Journal of Educational Studies* 29 209-217

Murphy, R (1982) Assessment *Research Intelligence* **12** 6

Scottish Education Department (1965) *Primary Education in Scotland* HMSO: Edinburgh

Scottish Education Department (1977a) *The Structure of the Curriculum in the Third and Fourth Years of the Scottish Secondary School* HMSO: Edinburgh

Scottish Education Department (1977b) *Assessment for All* HMSO: Edinburgh

Scottish Education Department (1980a) *Learning and Teaching in Primary 4 and Primary 7* HMSO: Edinburgh

Scottish Education Department (1980b) *The Munn and Dunning Reports: The Government's Development Programme* SED: Edinburgh

Scottish Education Department (1982) *The Munn and Dunning Reports: The Government's Development Programme, Interim Report on Research* SED: Edinburgh

Scottish Education Department (1983) *Educational Research: A Register of Current Educational Research Projects Funded by the Scottish Education Department* SED: Edinburgh

Scottish Microelectronics Development Programme (1981) *Strategy and Implementation Paper* SMDP: Glasgow

Social Science Research Council (1983) *Research Supported by the Social Science Research Council* SSRC: London

14. Pipers and tunes: research, policy and practice in Singapore

Sim Wong Kooi

Summary: The relation of research and policy in education often has to take into account some hidden agendas. The strategy adopted for research in Singapore is characterized as 'policy-oriented pragmatism', as compared with the other predominant strategy which has been labelled as 'enlightened opportunism'.

The Goh Report (Goh *et al*, 1979), which led to a major overall reform of the educational system, highlighted the shortcomings of earlier projects, and pointed out the limitations of existing arrangements for research and development projects. Trends in research at the Singapore Institute of Education are discussed, such as the move towards longer-term team research and the undertaking of commissioned studies, especially in curriculum evaluation and case studies.

Efforts to involve teachers systematically in research aimed at improving practice include publishing more interesting and readable abstracts for teachers and developing research aptitudes and attitudes through teacher education, at pre-service, induction, in-service as well as post-graduate stages. The case for promoting research wisdom, as distinct from research information or knowledge, is finally proposed.

Ideal versus actual scenarios

Ideally, research ought to be policy- and practice-oriented, policy ought to be research- and practice-oriented, and practice ought to be research- and policy-oriented. When confronted, most researchers, policy makers and practitioners in Singapore would probably avow that they are indeed approaching, if not approximating, the ideal situation. On close scrutiny, however, it usually becomes apparent that protean meanings are often associated with the different orientations.

Even for research studies that have not been commissioned by policy makers, nor have originated from practitioners' identification of their needs and problems, the researchers are likely to claim that, at least at the point of initiation, their studies were intended to provide illuminative insights into prevailing problems which were supposed to beset policy makers or practitioners. Likewise, policy makers who are politicians or politically-inclined, as is the case in Singapore, do take cognizance of practice and research but tend to apply a sieve which filters out the less immediately tangible aspects. While most practitioners do not actively conduct research, they are generally willing to cooperate with researchers, especially when they perceive the investigations as having possible links with policy, which they tend to accept without question.

Within the scope of this chapter, discussion will be confined to educational research in Singapore and its relation to policy and practice, rather than the other way round. Attention will be focused on the infrastructure and on issues related to educational research and development from the perspective of past, present and future scenarios.

The main organizations responsible for educational research and development are the Ministry of Education, especially its Research and Testing Division, and the Institute of Education. (The primary roles of the Institute of Education in Singapore are the professional training of teachers and the promotion of research in education: its management is academic, but it depends on government funding.) Other organizations, however, in particular the SEAMEO Regional Language Centre and the National University of Singapore, do conduct research in education even though the outcomes of their research have not been systematically tapped in relation to policy and practice. This is not to say that all research studies conducted under the aegis of the Ministry or the Institute would *ipso facto* be translated into policy or practice. As a matter of fact, apart from commissioned studies, a large proportion of the Institute's research has remained unnoticed by policy makers and practitioners. It is for this reason that recent attempts, to be discussed later, have been made by the Institute actively to follow up relevant research findings and also to invest in ongoing research on teacher education itself, since the articulation of outcomes from such studies with policy and practice in teacher education would be within the control of the Institute to a large extent.

As far as the Ministry is concerned, the main policy-making body is the fortnightly ministerial committee meeting, chaired by the Minister of Education or the Minister of State for Education, with all the directors, including the director of the Institute of Education, as members. Most of the policy decisions are based on discussions of research reports commissioned by the ministerial committee and are subsequently translated into educational practice.

In a meeting which lasts between two and two-and-a-half hours, 10 to 15 papers are normally discussed and it is not unusual for the more rigorous and sophisticated reports to be rejected. As a case in point, a painstaking validation study involving the adaptation of the Hall Occupational Orientation Inventory (Wong, 1983) was dismissed rather summarily, partly because the careful attempts to demonstrate construct validity through factor analytic and other techniques were not readily apprehended and partly because some members of the committee, which comprises mostly non-professionals, could not perceive the relevance of vocational guidance, let alone the use of tests for this purpose, in schools. A similar fate would have accompanied another report on 'A Study of the Criteria for Streaming Pupils into Secondary One' (Foo *et al*, 1983) which employed discriminant analysis as well as simulation studies to demonstrate the relative effects of weighting the different subjects at the primary school leaving examinations, which are used to stream pupils in secondary schools. However, when the paper was recast using simple, albeit somewhat questionable, statistics, it was readily accepted, even though the overall results and recommendations were the same as in the original paper.

The hidden agenda regarding the basis for acceptability or otherwise of research is unfortunately too attractive to be ignored. It is not unknown for some officers to begin an assignment by speculating on the types of findings as well as the types of presentation that they perceive as being more acceptable and to look selectively for confirmatory data. Even for contributions from the Institute of Education, researchers are often faced with the dilemma of either having to consider their efforts as an exercise in futility or else to present their report in a more acceptable way, even when it means having to underplay results that require more technical explanations or that run counter to what certain key members of the ministerial committee meeting have been advocating in public. For instance, Ng *et al* (1984) had to go to great lengths to provide some justification for the observed limitations of the phonics approach in early reading, while highlighting situations where this favoured approach would be more pertinent. The study was in fact intended to produce longitudinal data on the reading skills of children during the first three years of primary school. However, soon after it was started, not only were progress reports demanded, but the official deadline for completion of the study was reduced by half, so that adjustments to the design had to be made in order to produce meaningful cross-sectional data instead.

It should be apparent that if research is expected to have an impact on policy, some compromise in rigour and relevance is sometimes necessary, without unduly sacrificing professional standards. This strategy has been characterized as 'policy-oriented pragmatism', as compared to the other predominant strategy for research in Singapore, which has been labelled as 'enlightened opportunism' (Sim, 1983a). These two strategies might be said to correspond to the 'political model' and the 'enlightenment or percolation model' respectively, as suggested by Husen (1984) after examining the seven policy-related models advanced by Weiss (1979).

It would perhaps be useful at this juncture to trace some of the past situations which might have led to the present scenarios, especially in respect to the emergence of different 'tunes' that different 'pipers' are expecting to be played.

Past versus present scenarios

A major overhaul of the education system was brought about in 1979 with the implementation of the so-called Goh Report (Goh *et al*, 1979), which recommended, *inter alia*, a systematic, system-wide process of streaming at

different stages of schooling commencing at Primary 3. This was part of
the strategy for ameliorating the 'three main short-comings in the existing
system', namely 'education wastage, low literacy of many school leavers,
and non-attainment of effective bilingualism'.

In preparing the Report, Goh and his team scrutinized critically and
extensively a variety of earlier projects conducted by the Ministry of
Education, in terms not only of their findings but also the way in which
they were initiated, conducted and followed-up. Their dissatisfaction with
the then prevailing situation is evidenced by their criticisms and recommendations, some of which are quoted below:

'Ground level reactions seldom become the trigger for new projects.
Projects are usually initiated by the political leadership.

The ultimate objectives of projects are not always defined. If
defined, they are not always clear and specific.

The urgency of projects was not usually recognized ... Consequently, solutions to problems are often worked out by force of
circumstances and under pressure of time constraints.

A system of continual monitoring of and feedback from the
education system as a whole is lacking.

Projects should be systematically reviewed, properly perceived
and adequately evaluated, supported by effective feedback. Project
initiation from the ground level or middle management level should
be encouraged and recognized. All objectives should be clearly
defined, and the targets to be achieved should be specifically stated.
Through the systematic review of the education system and the
continuous monitoring of projects, problems will be identified more
efficiently and the urgency of projects will be recognized. To assist
in decision making, the Ministry of Education should also develop a
capacity to do basic social research.

Instead of relying on numerous committees to implement and
evaluate projects, delegation of jobs and responsibilities should be
more efficient. Most important of all, objectives and policies must not
be ambiguous; they must be completely understood by the implementing bodies and the ground level units. The implications of
new projects should be studied in depth and made known to the
ground level units who can then be made aware of their responsibilities. Possible outcomes should be predicted so that preventive
instead of remedial measures can be taken. Some new projects could
be experimented in pilot schools before being introduced in all the
other schools. This is to gauge ground level reactions and to identify
any implementation problems which might have been overlooked.'
(Goh *et al*, 1979)

The remarkable and unique fact is that none of the members of the team
responsible for this Report were members of the teaching profession;
many subsequently replaced some of the Directors of Divisions in the
Ministry who are educational professionals. While this has resulted in

greater analytical precision and cost-effectiveness, since they are mainly engineers and economists, research findings which are accompanied by caveats based on the review of the educational literature or which produce equivocal recommendations tend to be appreciated less, or are even unacceptable.

The infrastructure for generating policy-oriented research has indeed been streamlined, especially through:

(a) progressive refinements in establishing computerized data bases for school, teacher and pupil data;

(b) continuous monitoring of the movements and trends in streaming, including attrition rates for various cohorts of pupils; and

(c) commissioning a variety of *ad hoc* research studies, including pilot projects.

The *ad hoc* research studies have included validation studies of a general ability test, a 'survey of homework', a study of 'the effect of peer pressure on language learning', a 'survey of nutrition, television viewing and sleeping habits of school children in primary schools', and 'projections of teacher requirements'. Pilot projects normally precede the full-scale implementations of a new scheme, such as the open appraisal scheme in schools, the establishment of full-day schools and the 'gifted project'.

Because of the urgency to demonstrate success in the pilot projects, the need to establish controls is seldom appreciated, for the typical approach is to ensure that the best conditions obtain in the pilot situations and to obtain feedback from those associated directly or indirectly with the schools concerned through surveys. Thus, possible sources of internal or external invalidity would be extremely difficult to ascertain, especially since reasonably matched control groups cannot be established on a *post hoc* basis.

Although many of the changes arising from research studies could be regarded as manifestations of fine tuning in the implementation of the Goh Report, the rapidity and frequency of these changes have often been a concern not only to practitioners but also to parents as well as researchers. Referring to the Institute of Education, the writer (Sim, 1983b) pointed out that

'Individual staff or project teams have often been frustrated by the fact that by the time they completed their independent investigattions the critical issues they started with were no longer perceived as crucial. Those who resort to undertaking only assigned projects by means of less refined, but quick, methods appear to be reinforced, even though these were less professionally satisfying.'

Nevertheless, it was argued that, since the promotion of research in education is the other major objective of the Institute of Education, apart from the provision of teacher education at all levels, 'in order to promote research, IE should ... actively engage in research itself, (especially since) IE's track record in this field has so far been spotty and sporadic rather than systematic and systemic' (Sim, 1983b).

Arguing elsewhere for the stepping-up of research, especially on teacher education itself, the writer (Sim, 1983c) suggested that

> 'Since most of the research which has relevance to educational practice in Singapore has been conducted elsewhere, there is indeed a need to match some of the major studies with local research on a manageable scale before decisions are made with far-reaching consequences. There will, of course, be a need to take into account the usual time constraints which obtain in Singapore. But not to commit ourselves to at least a scaled-down replication of critical research is to abrogate the right to offer professional advice. It would similarly be suicidal if year-in and year-out IE carries on its business of teacher education without self-questioning and undertaking research on aspects of teacher education itself with the view to improved practices. Accountability and credibility will probably be enhanced through the juxtaposition of research and teacher education.'

Of particular significance are the four ongoing research projects on pre-service teacher education, which were begun over a year ago: (a) the development and validation of additional selection instruments for pre-service teacher education; (b) studies in innovative teaching methods in pre-service teacher education; (c) improving the reliability, validity and usability of instruments for the assessment of teacher trainees; and (d) follow-up studies of former students of the Institute of Education. It is hoped that the outcomes of each of these studies would help in the continual improvement of the Institute's pre-service teacher education programmes.

(a) Although the correlation between the academic criteria which are currently employed in the selection of teacher trainees and performance in the pre-service programme has been demonstrably poor, other alternative or additional criteria tend to be unacceptable without evidence of their possibly greater efficacy when employed with or without academic criteria in predicting performance. Thus, psychological instruments such as the MTAI and 16PF are being tried out and it is hoped that other measures, including principals' reports, especially regarding leadership qualities and other indicators of pedagogical ability, would also be explored in due course.

(b) As the only institution in Singapore which looks after teacher education, the Institute can only compare with itself in terms of the effectiveness of its programmes. Hence, it was considered essential that situations be set up for systematically comparing different innovative approaches in improving teaching, not only by student teachers during teaching practice, but also by lecturers in their various courses.

(c) In order to assess the effectiveness of these experiments as well as to provide criterion measures to compare the predictive validities of the different selection instruments, it would be necessary to consider ways of improving measures currently used for the assessment of performance. One approach, for example, involves the videotaping of classroom lessons, which are then viewed by groups of lecturers using different evaluation instruments and comparing inter-rater reliabilities.

(d) As a check on the relevance of the Institute's pre-service programmes, follow-up studies are being conducted with cohorts of graduates. Besides assessing the relevance of the pre-service curriculum to their roles at different stages of their careers, the studies also attempt to identify the problems these graduates face in schools initially and after a period of a few years.

The Institute of Education has also in recent years been conducting curriculum evaluation and case studies for the Ministry of Education. An ongoing commitment is the summative evaluation of various curriculum projects of the Curriculum Development Institute of Singapore. With minor variations, each evaluation project normally comprises four components: (a) intrinsic evaluation of materials (and methods); (b) classroom observation; (c) survey of teacher opinions; and (d) survey of pupil reactions and performance. So far, seven curriculum projects have been subjected to summative evaluation.

Numerous case studies have also been completed on behalf of the Ministry of Education. For example, pupils who performed well in subjects other than English Language at the Primary School Leaving Examinations (PSLE) were compared with another group who performed well in English Language and who were carefully matched with the earlier sample on selected home background characteristics (Ho et al, 1982). Another commissioned study involved an in-depth look into the home environment, intellectual abilities and academic performance of 38 pupils in mono-lingual classes, which are supposedly the weakest classes in upper primary school (Eng et al, 1984).

Apart from studies by post-graduate students in the Institute of Education and also in the SEAMEO Regional Language Centre or the Faculty of Arts and Social Sciences at the National University of Singapore, the emergent approach is to establish teams to conduct more sizeable research projects, some of which would invite students to participate in parts of the projects. For example, in the Second IEA Science Study which is being conducted in collaboration with the Ministry of Education, two graduate students are carving out manageable portions of the study for their own requirements. In the longitudinal Van Leer project on the social and cognitive development of pre-school children in Singapore, pre-service students who enrol in an elective course on the social and cognitive development of pre-school children are trained in administering the various instruments and take part in the discussion of the results.

Present versus future scenarios

The groundwork is hopefully being laid at present for a possible future scenario in which teachers would regularly be able to conduct classroom and other research aimed at improving practice. However, currently teachers are noted for their lack of professional reading, let alone reading of the research literature. It was with the view of encouraging teachers to read the relevant literature that in 1982 the bi-annual publication called *REACT* (Research and Evaluation Abstracts for Classroom Teachers) was published by the Institute of Education. By reducing technical jargon to an absolute minimum and using cartoons and simple illustrations, it is hoped to highlight those aspects of relevant research that are likely to be more useful and interesting to the classroom teacher. The Ministry of Education has supported this endeavour by making provisions for each teacher to be given a free copy of *REACT.*

At the pre-service level, individual lecturers are beginning to take the cue by involving their students in mini-studies as part of their assignment. Starting this year, as part of their induction to the profession during their period of probation, beginning teachers would also be supervised in undertaking an assignment aimed at helping them to develop propensities for professional problem finding and problem solving as well as the habit of reading widely in order to relate theory to practice.

Full-time in-service courses are also being introduced to equip future heads of departments and vice-principals or principals for their important leadership roles and responsibilities. In the Further Professional Certificate/Diploma in Education programme, prospective heads of departments are exposed to 'action research' as well as school appraisal and evaluation techniques. Similarly, for top-level school managers enrolling in the Diploma in Educational Administration programme, their school-based study as well as the educational evaluation course are meant to sensitize them to the need for empirical studies in attempting to improve their schools. In the meantime, wherever possible, aspects of research and evaluation are injected into in-service courses conducted by the Institute of Education. A senior member of staff has, for example, recently completed a series of seminars on research and evaluation of school-initiated projects, under the auspices of the Singapore Teachers' Union.

The Ministry of Education has been encouraging schools to undertake innovative projects and recently a project fund was set up in order to 'ensure that innovative ideas that enhance the education of our students are not hindered by the lack of funds'. It is hoped that, as the teaching profession becomes more research-oriented and sophisticated, the Ministry will also become more open towards access to its centralized data-bank by educational researchers. While it is fair that permission ought to be sought either to retrieve data from the data-bank or to collect data from schools, the tendency for projects which involve comparisons by race, language, religion or sex to be automatically rejected is rather unfortunate, especially since greater information and knowledge is required in order to plan more meaningfully for a multi-racial, multi-lingual, multi-religious and multi-cultural society like Singapore.

Following the hierarchy suggested by T.S. Eliot's verse, namely 'Where is the wisdom we have lost in knowledge? Where is the knowledge we have lost in information?', the writer has even argued for the progressive change 'towards promoting research wisdom'. The following excerpt might perhaps foreshadow a possible future scenario:

'What then are some likely desiderata for promoting research wisdom? It might be over-stating the obvious if we should stress that knowledge which is not useful is useless. But, the implication is that if research is conducted with little or no regard to whether and how the findings are expected to be applied, it is but an exercise in futility. Less obvious perhaps is the commitment to finding out not only what knowledge could be of use in improving educational practice, but more important, what knowledge, presented in what way, would be most likely to be usable. Characteristically, researchers, under the guise of pursuing knowledge for its own sake, have tended to abrogate this responsibility by being unconcerned with what happens after the study has been completed, sometimes without due regard to proper documentation and dissemination. The fallacious assumption is frequently made that policy-makers and practitioners can wait indefinitely for research studies to be concluded, that they would appreciate the jargon and technical details embodied in many a research report and that they are in fact ready to accept certain alternative courses of action which the researcher hopes to suggest but which could be construed as serious indictments of entrenched policies or practices.

Taking cognisance of the probable reactions of policy-makers and practitioners does not imply that the professional integrity of researchers would be sacrificed or compromised. On the contrary, what is being advocated is that the scope of researchers' concerns should extend beyond merely attempting to answer the specialised research questions to making plausible predictions of the extent to which the research findings are likely to be used, misused or unused. If the likelihood of a particular research having an impact on policy-makers and practitioners is estimated to be nil or negligible, it is wiser to abandon or drastically modify the study, unless we are prepared also to invest in more effective modes of promotion. Equally disturbing is the tendency, however inadvertently, for policy-makers and practitioners to over-generalise the results of a study which has, at the outset, delineated the limits of generalisability through its sampling design. For instance, a particular instructional approach might have been found to be most suitable for children of particular socio-economic backgrounds in a particular stream of a particular grade level in particular types of school when taught by teachers of particular expertise and experience, but the chances of these highly specific circumstances or conditions being overlooked when the particular findings are being applied are extremely great, even when the research report has incorporated appropriate cautions and caveats. For researchers to remain credible and responsible, it would therefore be advisable to widen the scope of generalisability either by undertaking a more comprehensive study through collaborative effort or by investing in follow-up or longitudinal studies. It would be unwise to be preoccupied only with one-shot studies of very narrow focus, however precise and sophisticated the methodologies that have been employed.' (Sim, 1984)

When a symbiotic relationship can be fostered between researchers on the one hand and policy makers and practitioners on the other, it is envisaged that the researchers would not only be able to become better pipers but also would be able to play the tunes they like.

References

Eng, S P et al (1984) *Report on Case Studies of 38 Monolingual Pupils* Institute of Education: Singapore

Foo, S K et al (1983) *A Study of the Criteria for Streaming Pupils into Secondary One* MCM Paper No 2158

Goh, K S and The Education Study Team (1979) *Report on the Ministry of Education 1978* Ministry of Education: Singapore (commonly referred to as the Goh Report)

Ho, W K et al (1982) I: *Case Studies of a Sample of Pupils whose Performance in English Language Usage in the 1981 PSLE was Poor in Comparison with their Performance in Other Subjects*; II: *A Follow-up Study of a Sample of Pupils who Performed Well in English Language in the PSLE* Institute of Education: Singapore

Husen, T (1984) Issues and their background *in* Husen, T and Kogan, M eds (1984) *Educational Research and Policy: How Do They Relate?* Pergamon Press: Oxford

Lun, C Y and de Souza, D (1983) *IEXperience: The First Ten Years* Institute of Education: Singapore

National Institute for Educational Research (1983) *Research and Educational Reform: Problems and Issues, and Strategies for Resolving Them* NIER: Tokyo

Ng, S M et al (1984) *Progress Report of Reading Skills Project* MCM Paper No 2313

Sim, W K (1983a) Research on the implementation and evaluation of reforms of educational content and methods in Singapore *in* National Institute for Educational Research (1983)

Sim, W K (1983b) IEXamining and IEXpanding IEXperience: Delineating IE's present and future roles *in* Lun, C Y and de Souza, D eds (1983)

Sim, W K (1983c) Research and teacher education: A Singapore perspective *Singapore Journal of Education* 5(2) 127-37

Sim, W K (1984) Guest Editorial: Towards promoting research wisdom *Singapore Journal of Education* 6(1) (in press)

Weiss, C H (1979) The many meanings of research utilization *Public Administration Review* September-October 426-31

Wong, E (1983) *Adaptation of the Hall Occupational Orientation Inventory — A Status Report* MCM Paper No 2119

15. Educational research in Sweden: reform strategies and research policy

Inger Marklund

Summary: During the last three decades the Swedish educational system has undergone a process of continuous reform from a system of parallel schools to a comprehensive school system. Several circumstances have contributed to the speed and extent of the changes, perhaps the most important of which is the fact that the Swedish educational system is highly centralized. Sweden is one of the very few countries that has a central non-political board, responsible for implementing political decisions and thus for the application of reform policy. This board – the National Board of Education (NBE) – is detached from the Ministry of Education and has central responsibility for primary, secondary and adult education. Although there are currently trends towards decentralization of decision making and responsibility for the educational system, the NBE will remain the central authority on educational matters and thus will be responsible for implementing two main educational principles in Sweden: uniformity of school structure and equality of educational opportunity.

Educational research and development (R & D) – as a consequence of this overall centralization – also has a centralized administration. This means that the NBE is responsible for a large part of educational R & D, and toward this end the Board has increasingly had funds at its disposal since 1962. A discussion of the impact of educational research therefore cannot be fully understood unless the reform strategies and the role of R & D within these strategies are described.

Educational R & D has been evaluated by a government-appointed committee, which presented its recommendations to the Minister of Education in February 1980. This article summarizes some of the conclusions drawn by that committee, especially as regards the impact of research.

Educational research and educational reform

In international literature, the importance of R & D for educational reform in Sweden has often been discussed. It has sometimes been contended that educational policy, and in particular the reform decisions taken, have been based on scientifically established results. This is not correct. Reform decisions have been based far more on general attitudes among the politicians regarding educational policy. However, one should not overlook entirely the fact that the Swedish community *has* succeeded in bringing about a dialogue between politicians, administrators and researchers so that research results have had at least some impact upon the making of educational policy (Marklund, 1966, 1971, 1973). By virtue of their independent status, researchers have been able to shed light on how educational issues interrelate with social, economic and cultural problems. Research projects have also contributed information about developmental psychology and the psychology of learning, in an often value-laden debate.

Educational policy making

The pathway to political decisions regarding education normally runs via government-appointed commissions. These commissions have in fact become a crucible for the creation of Swedish reform policy. They represent an essential ingredient in the central governmental system, and as such they operate somewhat differently from their counterparts in other countries.

The initial stage in this committee system is that the appropriate minister (in this case the Minister of Education) writes instructions for the particular committee's work and receives governmental authorization to appoint its members and secretariat. Educational committees are normally composed of:

   (a) parliamentary or other political party representatives;
   (b) representatives of interested parties within the educational system – usually teachers and school administrators; and
   (c) special experts in educational research and development work.

After investigative work usually lasting two to five years (although the above-mentioned committee on educational R & D completed its work in one-and-a-half-years), the committee publishes its final report including recommendations for action. This customarily includes both a timetable for putting into effect the proposed reforms and a cost estimate for these measures. The series of reports published by a committee often incorporates scientific and statistical studies of the issues covered. During the reform period since 1950, even a number of doctoral dissertations in education have been written as parts of committee reports on educational matters.

The committee presents it work to the Minister of Education, who is normally expected to send the final report and attached special studies to all public agencies affected by the work of the committee, as well as to organizations representing teachers, parents and students, and to special-interest and voluntary organizations of various kinds, including popular movements. Municipal authorities as well as colleges and universities affected by the committee's recommendations also require a copy of the report. The organizations to which these publications are circulated often put in a lot of work studying the report, the background material on which it is based, the recommendations it makes, the timetable proposed for the changes it recommends, and the amount the reform is expected to cost.

As a rule, the central government proposes a bill to Parliament based on the committee's recommendations and the comments subsequently made on them. It only seldom happens that a committee report does not result in a government bill being submitted to Parliament. It is thus characteristic of Swedish reform strategy that an issue which has been raised finally ends up before Parliament in one form or another. Another characteristic is that the lag between the presentation of a committee report and the subsequent Parliamentary decision on the same issue is comparatively short.

To illustrate how a committee can work, the above-mentioned committee on educational R & D may be taken as an example. The committee, which began its work in September 1978, comprised six members representing political parties, regional and local school authorities and educational research, with a professor of education as chairman. The Ministry of Education had one of its own experts serving on the committee, and a secretary-general was responsible for planning the work and for writing the report. The committee itself called in experts on various parts of its work. Thus, two experts worked on the problem of local educational development in the school and its relation to educational research. Two others, one of whom was a professor of education, made an evaluation of educational research conducted since 1962. A further expert prepared information on changes in Swedish society, especially in education, that were of importance for the recommendations to be made by the committee. Still another (also a professor of education) worked on the problem of how to strengthen links between Swedish and international educational R & D. All the experts prepared papers, which were discussed in the committee. Following this, the committee members decided what of this background material should be used, and how.

The report (SOU, 1980) was presented to the Minister of Education in February 1980, and was sent out to universities, regional and local school authorities and some organizations (teachers, students, parents, adult education organizations and special-interest groups). During autumn 1980, a bill was prepared in the Ministry of Education which was presented to Parliament in 1981. Thus, the time between initiation of the committee's work and the final decision made by Parliament was about two-and-a-half years. It is of special interest in this context to note that educational researchers were highly involved in the committee's work and, as such, were able to influence the recommendations finally made by the committee.

This brief description of reform strategies in education aims at highlighting the role of researchers who are regarded as playing a necessary and highly valued part in educational reform.

Resources for educational research

The resources for educational research are of two main kinds: fixed resources, allocated to research appointments and research departments at the universities; and flexible resources from the R & D funds of research councils and central educational authorities.

Most educational research is carried out in the ten education departments of the universities: three departments in Stockholm, two in Gothenburg and one in each of the universities of Linköping, Lund, Malmö, Umeå and Uppsala. Between these departments there are 18 professorial chairs in education, and to each chair is attached a certain resource-fund designated for research appointments. Furthermore, there are some research appointments which are usually held for a period of six years, alternating between different departments within the Faculties of Social Sciences. In economic terms, these fixed research resources amount altogether to approximately 6.5 million Skr. per year (about US $1.4 million). It should be noted, however, that these appointments also involve an obligation to teach, primarily to research students. To these responsibilities has been added during recent years an increasing amount of administrative work.

The flexible resources for educational R & D come from four main sources: the National Board of Education (NBE), the National Board of Universities, the Humanistic-Social Science Research Council and the Bank of Sweden Tercentenary Fund. These are often called the 'Big Four'. These four have a combined total of about 58 million Skr. per year at their disposal (about US $12.7 million) to allocate to research conducted on the educational system *as a whole*. If the university level is excluded, which it should be in this particular context, there remain about 40 million Skr. per year (about US $8.9 million) for educational R & D concerning primary, secondary and adult education (outside universities). The NBE funds account for 36 of these 40 million Skr.

Approximately 23.5 of the 40 million are allocated to the education departments of the universities for research projects, and the remaining 16.5 million are used by the NBE, regional boards, local school authorities, in-service teacher training centres and various kinds of adult education organizations for educational development work. (The figures given are valid for 1980.)

These figures can be used to show three important and frequently discussed relationships:

(a) that between running costs and developmental costs in education;
(b) that between fixed and flexible resources; and
(c) that between the members of the 'Big Four'.

The total NBE budget for education (excluding the universities) is 14,600 million Skr. (about US $3.2 billion). The development costs within this budget are 36 million Skr. Thus the development costs are 0.24 per cent of the total budget. It is customary to assume that at least 1 per cent of the running costs should be spent on R & D (though sometimes 2 per cent is thought more appropriate). There is a long way to go before either of these percentages is reached. The relation is somewhat better if one also includes some of the fixed resources for educational research. If we assume that about 50 per cent of the fixed resources of approximately 6.5 million Skr. are used for educational R & D of relevance here, the cost of development will be approximately 0.29 per cent of the total running costs.

The second relationship, which is even more debated, is the one between fixed and flexible resources. Again, according to my estimate above, 6.5 million Skr. is fixed and 40 million Skr. is flexible. There are, however, some fundamental uncertainties here about these 6.5 million Skr., for example regarding how much is actually spent on research. With these uncertainties in mind the relationship is still interesting. Eighty-six per cent of the R & D resources are flexible.

As the fixed resources are supposed to concentrate on basic research and the flexible are supposed to concentrate mainly on applied research (or more correctly on R & D), the question of balance arises. First, is it possible for professional researchers to take the scientific responsibility for applied research, and secondly, will there be enough resources available for more basic research? The committee which investigated these relationships strongly argued that the fixed resources should be increased. This was seen as a prerequisite also for an optimal use of the flexible resources.

Finally the third relationship is the one between the members of the 'Big Four'. As can be seen from the figures above, the R & D funds from the NBE comprise about 90 per cent of the flexible resources. It should be borne in mind, however, that the NBE is the responsible central authority for all primary, secondary and adult education. As NBE funds increased during the 1960s and early 1970s, the other three decreased their funding of educational research. So, in a way, this relationship reflects the view that, given the desirability of linking educational reform and research, NBE funds *should* be the main source for educational R & D.

With this background information in mind, I should now like to comment upon the impact of research on educational policy and practice.

Educational R & D: a short review

Since 1962 the NBE has been receiving the special R & D grant discussed above, of which about half is spent on research pursued at different university and college departments, primarily the departments of education (SOU, 1980; Estmer, 1976). From 1962 to 1980 the annual grant has grown from two million to 36 million, the total amount of money during these 18 years being approximately 325 million Skr. Between 150 and 175 of these millions have been allocated to research departments at universities and teacher training institutes. Bearing in mind the quotas between fixed and flexible resources for research, this means that most of these research departments of education have been built up with this money and have been engaged in policy-oriented research in education.

This brings us to the often discussed question of the 'steering' of educational research. The steering exercised by the NBE is of three kinds:

(a) delimitation of R & D problems;
(b) choice of research department; and
(c) determination of time and money frameworks for the projects.

Quite naturally, researchers often argue that their own preferences and qualifications should be decisive in determining priorities. The NBE has tried to overcome the problem of balance between researchers' and policy makers' wishes in this respect by referring plans for research projects to advisory groups of professors of education before the NBE reaches its decisions. The NBE has also taken the initiative in founding a research collegium which is comprised of all researchers acting as heads of departments and scientific leaders of research projects. This collegium meets twice a year and discusses with the NBE research issues of a more general kind. The scientific issues on research methods and procedures after the start of a project are left entirely to the researchers themselves.

This kind of policy-oriented or reform-oriented educational R & D has four attributes which distinguish it from what is usually termed discipline-oriented or basic research:

1. It is conducted in accordance with a *plan*, the budget for which covers a five-year period, with detailed budget planning spanning one year. The majority of large-scale R & D projects run for three to six years. The plan is officially adopted by the NBE after consultation with a group of educational researchers, as mentioned above.

2. The sub-programmes within this plan are based on *coordination of R & D*. In other words, the measures taken to use and apply the knowledge which research provides are often built into the research activity. Hence a great deal of R & D is not educational research in the traditional sense. The development segments often pertain to curriculum building, development of teaching aids, and development of evaluation instruments.

3. R & D is designed particularly to facilitate the *diffusion of results*. From the very beginning, means for transferring information to (among other things) the in-service training of teachers are built into the project. This is not so much intended as a method for identifying solutions to educational problems as a way of vitalizing the educational debate on a broad front. This debate is of great importance for decision makers on educational policy and in the administration of the educational system.

4. R & D of this kind is *examined and evaluated* against the goals established for educational policy. Such examinations and evaluations are made a number of times. First, the project activity is analysed by scientific observers. Secondly, it is rated by educational politicians and educational administrators. An Educational Advisory Council attached to the NBE, which includes representatives of the political parties, the municipalities, educational research, teachers and students, follows and passes judgement on R & D. It directs special attention to the evaluation issues. The committee then submits an annual report to the Minister of Education.

One of the largest problems with this reform-oriented and policy-oriented educational R & D lies in diffusion of research results, both the dissemination of information about them and their actual application. Therefore a considerable portion of R & D funds has been spent on measures which have been aimed at linking R & D with the in-service training of teachers and other school personnel. As will be discussed later, the measures taken have not been as successful as was hoped.

The educational R & D plan

The R & D plan of the NBE is currently constructed along two dimensions. It is both stage-oriented and problem-oriented. The problem areas identified for research vary over time in order to avoid rigidity in research approach. The *stages* follow those related to the areas of responsibility for the NBE, that is:

(a) pre-school education;
(b) primary school — ages 7-12;
(c) lower secondary school — ages 13-15;
(d) upper secondary school — ages 16-18 or 19, including vocational training; and
(e) adult education.

At the moment there are 18 problem areas prescribed for research:

- documentation and analysis of the Swedish educational system;
- educational systems and life-long learning;
- educational planning and educational evaluation — models and methods;
- school and physical environment;
- in-service training and personnel development;
- education and society;
- work in schools;
- cognitive development;
- communication skills;
- socio-emotional and physical development;
- tests and grading in educational evaluation;
- regional and local development work;
- the connection between pre-school and primary school;
- subject-oriented R & D;
- special populations (handicapped students);
- immigrants and national minorities;
- curriculum development work;
- teaching aids.

As can be seen, the problem areas are in no way mutually exclusive. The advantage of having problem areas as a complement to the stage structure lies in the subsequent anchoring of research planning to research conditions more than to administrative ones. In the future, this should continue to be one of the most preferred methods for planning research projects.

During the 18-year period studied by the above-mentioned committee, R & D projects have been carried out within all these problem areas and stages. However, an evaluation of the impact of research should not be made on the basis of individual projects. Accordingly, the committee chose to focus its attention upon conditions of impact rather than upon a detailed analysis of single research effects.

The impact of educational R & D

One important reason for the strong emphasis on the policy-orientation of educational R & D is the desire — and the belief — that the experiences and results gained can thus be more directly applied to everyday work at school and also more readily used as a basis for educational policy decisions. The expectations placed upon research are normally high, regardless of the research area. Research is often supposed to *solve* problems rather than enlighten the complexity of the problem in question. This is especially true for educational research in Sweden, largely because of the way educational R & D has been planned and carried out. The impact of research and development was one of the major questions in the above-mentioned committee's work. A fruitful way of examining the question of impact seemed to be to identify certain conditions for effective diffusion and use of research results and — by so doing — to find a more constructive and realistic way of examining the demands on research.

The committee classified the impact of research in two categories: first, the *effects per se*, and second, the *effect correlates*, ie those factors that increase or decrease the effects.

Effects can differ both in *kind* and *degree*. The kinds of effect can vary from very general to very specific. The degrees of effect can vary from very strong to very weak or even negative. Some possible and salutary *kinds of effect* are:

- attracting interest and creating a debate;
- influencing attitudes;
- giving rise to new organizational models;
- giving rise to administrative rules and routines;
- influencing the curriculum;
- introducing new working forms and new instructional methods;
- creating new teaching aids.

Each single effect can — as the committee stated — have a great, small or even negative influence.

Correlates can also be categorized according to kind and degree. Possible *correlates to the kinds of effect* are:

- problem area: from broad to narrow, from general to detailed;
- target group: from the general public to well-defined and small interest-groups.

Possible *correlates to the degrees of effect* are:

- the distinctness of the message (the results of research);
- information processes;
- the availability of efficient channels of communication (linkage personnel, interest-groups, organizations);
- the readiness to receive the results of research (awareness of need, etc);
- the increase of new knowledge, both practical guidance and theoretical insights.

The committee chose to analyse seven major problem areas: the links between pre-school provision and the primary school (the former is mainly the responsibility of the National Board of Social Welfare), the education of handicapped children, subject-oriented R & D (eg mathematics, foreign languages, Swedish), adult education, the development of teaching aids, educational planning and evaluation, and curriculum development. Some of the more important conclusions drawn will be summarized.

The kinds of effect

Although some quite immediate and obvious effects could be found, especially as regards teaching aids, the effects have mainly been of a general nature. Research results have started a debate on important educational issues and have influenced the attitudes held by those engaged in actual school work and those engaged in educational administration and policy. Thus the effects have been more indirect than direct, more long-term than immediate. This seems to be particularly true of research on basic reading and writing skills, on the teaching of foreign languages, on the integration of handicapped children in the comprehensive school, and of research on adult education. (Here we might find one of the most important reasons for the frequent complaints about the 'uselessness of educational research'. Indirect and long-term effects are seldom identified as effects of research, which they very well might be, but it is often difficult to trace back shifts of attitude or changes in methods of instruction to single research efforts.)

The degrees of effect

The most obvious effects were identified at levels above the actual school situation. This could be seen as a deficiency as well as a natural and acceptable condition. According to the first interpretation, it is unsatisfactory that research results are used mainly for changing administrative procedures, for revisions of curricula or for in-service training programmes. The other interpretation says that research results can only rarely be directly implemented in the everyday school situation but must be transformed before they can influence instructional practice. These two interpretations are not mutually exclusive but rather are complementary.

Effect correlates

The list of effect correlates above is not complete, and the factors listed are not mutually exclusive. Rather one can say that *if* (a) the results are distinct (univocal), and (b) there exist means of processing the information, especially through interest-groups or other well-defined and highly motivated target groups, and if finally, (c) the research problem is a new one, *then* impact is likely to occur. Such conditions, however, are very seldom found. The committee's analysis revealed that in one particular problem area — research on handicapped children — most of the effect correlates were at hand and hence research could be said to have had great impact on both educational policy and practice. This is especially true for research on deaf children where there has been a shift in attitudes and in instructional methods — from the earlier almost total dominance of oral methods to a 'total communication' method, combining oral and sign language. Research is of course not the only reason for this shift, but research has been sought, undertaken and applied.

In its conclusions, the committee argued that, in general, educational R & D had had impact on educational policy and practice to a greater extent than is usually stated. The value of R & D activities must always be related to the expectations put upon them. Strong belief in immediate and directly applicable results dominated the 1960s in Sweden as well as in other highly industrialized countries. One of the difficulties in discussing the impact of research lies in the fact that the demands placed upon it are often unrealistic. There have been few serious analyses of the kinds of problem that can actually be 'solved' or illuminated by educational R & D. The readiness to accept change is a first prerequisite for the use of outcomes from educational R & D. Research that tells the teacher or the school administrator that certain changes should be made in order to increase the fulfilment of politically-stated educational goals, will be 'used' only if the changes are in accordance with the opinions held by those responsible for their implementation.

In the main, there are very limited possibilities, if any, of guaranteeing a distinct message. There seems to be some doubt as to whether the correlate 'readiness' could ever be attained by every teacher and all those others who are responsible for teaching and for the administration of teaching. One can increase the possibilities for the use of research results, for example, by increasing information-processing efforts and by increased teacher in-service training programmes. The recommendations made by the committee also included several steps in this direction. But if the world of education is not inclined towards change nor oriented for it, and if the teachers, school administrators and politicians are reluctant actively to seek information and use it, then the question of the impact of educational research is academic.

Recent developments in educational and research policy

Decentralization is at present (1984) a central concept in Swedish politics and administration. This applies to practically all sectors of society. For various reasons, however, changes are particularly noticeable in the education sector.

Parallel to the Committee on Educational R & D described above, another committee studied questions of even greater fundamental importance. This committee, entitled the School Administration Committee, had the task of proposing changes in the role and duties of school administration in an increasingly decentralized education system. As was mentioned by way of introduction, the Swedish education system has been characterized by a high level of centralism by international standards. Organizationally this has been manifested through the existence of one central education authority, the NBE, with 24 regional boards subordinate to it.

Control of the school system can be summarized in three principal phases, beginning in 1946, ie the inaugural year of a continuous process of reform leading to the introduction of a nine-year comprehensive school.

Type of control	1946-1962	1962-1976	From 1976
Control through resources	Strong	Weak	Weak
Control through regulations	Weak	Strong	Weak
Control by objectives	Weak	Weak	Strong

Thus, control by means of earmarked resources predominated between 1946 and 1962. Following the decision, in 1962, to introduce the nine-year compulsory comprehensive school, control by means of an extensive code of regulations was stepped up, only to be superseded, from 1976 onwards, by a growing emphasis on management by objectives.

In a school system which is managed by objectives, the actual conduct of education and instruction and the use of the resources made available by society (the State) must to a great extent be determined by local conditions. One overriding objective, however, is still to ensure equivalent educational standards throughout the country. The recommendations made by the School Administration Committee and, in all essential respects, adopted by Parliament implied a radical reallocation of roles between the central, regional and local levels of the school system.

The NBE today is mainly concerned with strategic and long-range planning and with ensuring that the goals defined by Parliament and Government are actually achieved. The regional boards are required to exercise a certain measure of active supervision and also, above all, to encourage and support developments in local schools. Responsibility for the attainment of school objectives is vested above all in local education authorities or school boards and in the individual schools.

The two committees were active simultaneously, and this made it possible to coordinate their recommendations. The Educational R & D Committee recommended heavier emphasis on more long-range, basic educational and general social science research, while at the same time toning down more directly school-based R & D work to some extent; more of R and less of D, in other words. The Committee also underlined the need to broaden the scientific basis of educational research, which until then had mainly comprised pedagogical research. More general and basic educational research should also include such disciplines as political science, the economic sciences, cultural geography, humanistic disciplines and natural science. The view was also taken that more and more responsibility for educational development work should be given to the local authorities and that central development efforts, accordingly, should concentrate on supportive activities.

The Schools Administration Committee emphasized in its recommendations the links between long-range, strategic planning and research. The recommendations of both committees concerning the focus of research and the deployment of research resources were endorsed by Parliament. A successive transformation of the NBE Research Programme was begun in 1982, in keeping with the guidelines described above. The 'new' research programme has been published in English (NBE, 1983).

As has already been made clear, the research initiated and funded by the NBE can primarily be termed policy-oriented or decision-oriented (Marklund, 1982). Research initiated and funded by central authorities in various fields of policy makes up a relatively large portion of the total body of research conducted in Sweden. The past five years have also witnessed a number of important decisions of principle in the field of research policy.

In 1979 the Parliament passed a resolution accepting a 'sectoral principle' for research. This resolution was based on recommendations made by yet another governmental committee (The Research Council Commission). The principle states that central authorities (national boards, etc) should be responsible for the planning of R & D relevant to their respective areas, that they should have R & D funds at their disposal, and that this research as a rule should be carried out within research departments at the universities and normally not in research institutes outside universities. As far as education is concerned the decision can be seen as a confirmation of a policy that has actually been practised for nearly 20 years. It also means that the impact and diffusion of R & D results and experience must concern many parts of society and not exclusively the universities. Furthermore, the resolution makes the question of balance between fixed and flexible resources a crucial one. Qualitative requirements for this commissioned research must be just as high as the standards applied to other research activities, which means that there must be sufficient numbers of qualified researchers at the universities to assume scientific responsibility for the research assignments placed there by the various authorities. University representatives have argued strongly that the imbalance will threaten the quality of research and turn research departments into 'investigation departments'.

In the first national research programme presented by the then government in 1981, this sectoral principle was retained. National research programmes are to be submitted to Parliament every three years, and accordingly the second programme was presented in March 1984. This programme stresses the need for basic research and, above all, an expansion of fixed resources through the establishment of research appointments at intermediate level. It is also proposed that these appointments be partly funded by the various authorities having R & D funds at their disposal.

The NBE is already applying this system, albeit on a limited scale. There is likely to be a vigorous discussion in Sweden during the next few years concerning research priorities and the willingness and ability of universities to assume increased direct programming responsibility for the conduct of research which will also be capable of providing for the needs of social planning. The direction already taken in 1982 by educational research initiated and financed by the NBE is closely in line with current tendencies. This also puts the question concerning the relationships among the Big Four mentioned above in a somewhat different light. More and more major research projects are being jointly funded by two or more of these parties, which is also a sign that school research is coming to focus more on educational research.

Finally there is the not unimportant question as to whether politicians, educational administrators and practitioners will be patient enough to await the results of long-range research.

References

Estmer, B (1976) *Educational Research and Development at the NBE* National Swedish Board of Education: Stockholm

Marklund, I (1982) The sectoral principle in Swedish research policy *in (eds)* Kallen, D B P, Kosse, G B, Wagenaar, H C, Kloprogge, J J J and Vorbeck, M, *Social Science Research and Public Policy Making: A Reappraisal* London: NFER-Nelson

Marklund, S (1966) Educational reform and research in Sweden *Educational Research* 9 16-21

Marklund, S (1971) Comparative school research and the Swedish school reform *International Review of Education*, 17 39-49

Marklund, S (1973) Comprehensive schools: research and strategy and its links with educational policy *In Second Colloquium of Directors of Educational Research Organizations* Council of Europe: Strasbourg

NBE (1983) The research programme of the National Swedish Board of Education *School Research Newsletter*, 1983:2

SOU (1980) 2. Skolforskning och skolutveckling. Betänkande av Skolforsknings-kommittén (Educational research and educational development. Report of the Committee on Educational Research and Development, in Swedish.) Liber Förlag: Stockholm

Acknowledgement

The first part of this chapter is a revised version of a paper by Inger Marklund, 'Educational research in Sweden: reform strategies and research policy' which was published in the *International Review of Education*, 27, 107-17, 1981. Permission to use this material is gratefully acknowledged.

Part 2: New directions

16. Educational research: dissemination, participation, negotiation

Eric Hoyle

Summary: The dissemination of the findings of educational research in a form in which it can be readily utilized by practitioners is a perennial problem. Although the linear model remains the only practicable means of disseminating some forms of research data, alternative models have recently emerged which involve the creation of contexts in which both practitioners and researchers are active participants and in which the meaning of research findings is negotiated. A number of developments have precipitated this process including the growing influence in the social sciences of phenomenological approaches to knowledge, the recognition of the symbolic and political significance of research data, changing attitudes towards professional knowledge, the evidence of studies in communication and diffusion, and the technological developments in knowledge retrieval. These factors have led to the emergence of the knowledge-utilization movement which has had a particularly strong impact on curriculum development and an increasing influence on the relationship between researchers and practitioners. In the contexts which are created, research data rubs shoulders with experiential knowledge, resource constraints, policy positions and political beliefs.

The Rift Valley which has for so long existed in education between researchers and practitioners is a geological factor too well-known to require detailed description. For their part, researchers have tended to select their own problems to be investigated, choose their own methods, report their findings mainly to academic peers — and to bewail the fact that practitioners have failed to 'use' their findings. Practitioners — assumed here to include teachers, headteachers, advisors, administrators and elected representatives with educational responsibilities — have, in turn, claimed that although they would *like* to be able to draw upon research evidence for decisions concerning policy and practice, research fails to provide them with 'answers'. They have charged researchers with producing findings which are unintelligible, irrelevant or inconclusive. (A well-known chief education officer claimed to be hoping to find a one-armed researcher since he was frustrated by having direct questions answered in the form: 'On the one hand X. But on the other hand Y'.) The solution to the problem of a gap between researchers and practitioners has been sought in terms of 'better dissemination'. The problems tackled have hitherto been those of intelligibility, distribution and retrievability, but these solutions have been conceived in terms of a mechanistic one-way model: research, publication, dissemination and utilization. It is this simplistic model which has been increasingly challenged in recent years, with quite fundamental consequences not only for dissemination but for the nature of research itself, its epistemological assumptions and its linkage to practice.

Perhaps the major characteristic of attempts in recent years to close the gap between researchers and practitioners has been a loss of 'purity' (Douglas, 1966). Hitherto, there has been a strong boundary between researchers and practitioners. These separate categories, though one must emphasize that they still remain recognizably distinct, are less pure and definite than they were. The gap has been partly closed in three main ways. One has been the growth of roles intermediate between the researcher and the practitioner, the incumbents of which not only can speak the language of research but also are familiar with the substantive problems faced by educational institutions. Another is that styles of research have been evolving whereby the researcher and the teacher have entered into a more collaborative relationship in which 'dissemination' is inherent in the design. A third is the erosion of the boundary between research and practice, though such notions as 'the teacher-as-researcher' remain contested concepts.

Some precipitating factors

The erosion of the boundary between research and policy-practice, and the loss of purity between the two activities have been precipitated by a number of factors which can be broadly classified as technological, epistemological and professional.

Technological

In recent years the computerization and miniaturization of research data and library materials have immeasurably improved data retrieval. Of course, researchers and other academics tend to be the groups which most frequently have resort to data archives and undertake bibliographic searches. Nevertheless, the means now exist for practitioners to have reasonably easy access to sources of data, materials and references. Undoubtedly the most advanced system is ERIC which produces Research in Education (RIE), the Current Index to Journals in Education (CIJE), microfiche and paper copies from the Document Reproduction Service (EDRS) and computer tapes. Additionally, materials are available in ten areas of educational practice (eg science education, counselling and guidance) from clearinghouses in various American Universities. The ERIC system is decentralized, with access from 2268 locations in the US and internationally. A survey of use over a ten-year period indicated that ERIC resources had been used 2.7 million times annually; that 63 per cent of users were students or persons promoting educational services, with the other 37 per cent being researchers; and that one third of the people employed within the American education system had used ERIC resources, of whom 80 per cent were teachers employed in primary or secondary schools (Burchinal, 1983). Although ERIC is by far the most extensive and sophisticated system, other systems exist in various countries; potential access of practitioners to research and developmental materials is considerable. The advance of information technology and particularly the spread of microcomputers will considerably augment practitioner access to data. However, technological systems are neutral and can only fulfil a *perceived* professional need; their utilization depends on the support of *social* systems.

Epistemological

Developments in various fields have served to challenge the rationalistic, mechanistic model of dissemination of a body of objective, neutral knowledge from researchers to practitioners. Researchers point to the limits of objective knowledge in the social sciences, the different meanings attached to bodies of knowledge by occupants of different roles in the educational system, and the active, transforming response of the would-be user of such knowledge. A number of such trends can be identified.

One is the phenomenological perspective which has become influential in the social sciences in the past 20 years. Its epistemological assumptions are essentially idealist and hold that, at least in the sphere of social life, objective knowledge is either inherently unattainable, or, where attainable, trivial. Knowledge is held to be, for the most part, a social construct. A phenomenological sociology of knowledge perceives knowledge as being the outcome of the inter-subjective relations within particular groups and hence relative. Thus the proper activity of the social scientist is not the testing by empirical methods of general theory but the understanding through observation, interview and the analysis of natural speech of the process by which knowledge is constructed, negotiated and transformed in social contexts. On this view the generalizing summary data of experimental and survey research are otiose, and it thus follows that sociologists adopting this perspective question the validity of official statistics. Although the thoroughgoing idealism of this approach may be accepted by relatively few social scientists — and it is vigorously and fundamentally rejected by others — it has served to induce a degree of caution amongst many and to generate an awareness of the limitations of knowledge acquired through methods approximating to those of the natural sciences. It has also instilled the value of interpretative approaches to understanding and the negotiable nature of much of what counts as knowledge.

A second challenge to the objectivity of knowledge is given impetus in political and policy studies. One does not have to adopt an extreme subjectivist stance to accept that research data are embedded in a socio-political context to a degree which renders their objectivity difficult to establish.

This is not to deny the potentiality of objectivity, but simply to accept that their embeddedness is such that the data will remain essentially contested. Data become inextricably linked with interests. Their influence on policy and practice rarely springs directly from their compelling nature *sui generis*. Their influence is shaped by their association with interests. Data become salient and influential when they are timely and when they are appropriated by a powerful interest group. It is a truism that the same data are capable of quite different interpretations by policy makers and practitioners. This applies to statistical as well as to documentary material. Not only laymen, but academics, differ in their interpretation of the same data. A classic study which demonstrates the diversity of interpretations which the same data can generate is Allison's (1971) study of the Cuban missile crisis in which he shows that the same documentary material can be used to support three quite different explanations.

These issues have been explored in relation to educational research and policy in a number of recent publications, notably Nisbet and Broadfoot (1980) and Husen and Kogan (1984).

A third challenge has been the influence of research in the communication of knowledge. Essentially, there has been a growing emphasis on the active role of the recipient of a communication such as a piece of research whereby the recipient *brings* meaning to the information which is thus neither neutral nor accepted passively in terms of the meaning attached by the reader. An early, sometimes challenged, but still significant finding of communication research was the concept of *two-step flow* which indicates that the majority of people are not directly influenced by impersonal media: the media influence directly only a few key people (the 'influentials') who in turn influence many others through social interaction. In short, most people are influenced by other people. Research on the diffusion of innovation has shown that most new ideas and practices spread through social systems and are taken up at various points of an S-shaped adoption curve by categories of adopters: *innovators, early adopters, early majority, late majority, laggards* (Rogers and Shoemaker, 1971). The evidence of this research on the communication of ideas has generated a number of initiatives seeking to ensure that educational knowledge is disseminated via individuals occupying roles with this as a specific task (see also Feller, 1981).

In sum, a number of very different approaches to an understanding of the nature of knowledge and its transmission have undermined earlier simplistic notions of a rational sequence whereby the product of educational research is transmitted as a neutral body of knowledge via impersonal modes of communication to passively-accepting practitioners who will apply it in undiluted form to their practical problems. Whatever the ultimate degree of 'objectivity' which research data might have, there is little doubt that it will be interpreted, negotiated and transformed by the social systems through which it is diffused.

Professional

One aspect of the professional development of teachers is linked with the knowledge issues raised above. Conventional theory about the professions holds that through a lengthy period of training they acquire a body of cognitive knowledge, including research findings, which they bring to bear on practice. Some teacher educators continue to accept the possibility of a substantial direct influence of theory-and-research on practice. Many others now recognize that its influence is indirect and simply one of a number of contextual factors. Critics of the conventional view of professional knowledge point out that practice is based much more on experience, intention, folk-ways and interpersonal understandings which are not easily codified into a body of cognitive knowledge (cf Halmos, 1971). Critics of teachers have long dismissed the relevance of theory and research to practice, but thoughtful observers within the education profession (eg Jackson, 1968; Macnamara, 1976) have posed questions about the direct influence of cognitive knowledge. Similar questions have been asked about the knowledge-base of the medical profession, the profession most commonly assumed to be based firmly on research knowledge (Freidson, 1970). Again, the growing recognition of the professional integration of theoretical knowledge and research data has led in recent years to a number of innovations in patterns of professional development. Elsewhere I have summarized these trends as follows:

'Initial training has come to involve more school experience particularly of kinds other than that of block teaching practice. This experience is utilized in both subject work and educational studies as the basis for the discussion of both practical and theoretical problems. As this experience must necessarily be limited, it is augmented by simulations, case material and other resources which focus on the practical problems and the teaching contexts which teachers are likely to encounter. Students are led from these experiences and associated materials to a consideration of the theoretical issues which they generate through group discussion. Insofar as lectures are part of the programme, these are increasingly more concerned with providing material on particular problems and issues as a further resource for group discussion rather than as part of a course which presents a systematic and sequential body of theory. Students are encouraged to take a reflexive stance towards their own school experience and to try to convert personal problems into more general issues. To a greater degree than in the past, assignments require students to reflect on particular problems of teaching rather than to reproduce a body of theory under examination conditions, and the assessment of students is based on the insights which they bring to this task and the degree to which they can marry these insights to relevant parts of educational theory.

The nature of in-service work has also been changing. Non-award bearing courses have become more problem-oriented and workshop-based and there has been some move toward school-focused in-service work whereby schools have sought to identify their particular in-service needs and the providing agencies have sought to meet their needs by providing special courses, through consultancy work in the school, and through facilitating visits of staff to other institutions. Advanced work, not unexpectedly, has changed to a lesser degree and continues to provide systematic, theoretical and discipline-based courses. Nevertheless, there have been some developments here with a trend towards courses in curriculum, pedagogy and administration with students having the opportunity to present, in lieu of conventional research dissertations, curriculum evaluations, reports of some form of innovation in their school or various other modes of applied or action research which engage with the substantive problems faced within their institutions.

Educational research has itself been changing somewhat in character with a trend towards more action and applied projects. There has also been a growing concern amongst researchers in institutions of higher education to help teachers to conduct research on their professional problems via the establishment of teacher research groups. This has involved educational researchers engaging with problems which are rather difficult to handle according to conventional research protocols.' (Hoyle, 1982)

(See also Hoyle and Megarry, 1980 for a wider discussion of some of these developments.)

The knowledge-utilization movement

This movement, which now has its own journal in *Knowledge: Creative, Diffusion, Utilization,* is concerned with developing ways of bridging the gap between the production of educational knowledge and its incorporation into educational practice. Its concerns have been to formulate and implement strategies which would bridge the gap including the establishment of new institutions, roles, networks, technologies and modes of presenting material. The 'knowledge' involved has not been primarily research data. It has included curriculum materials and accounts of good practice. The emphasis is on problems-to-be-solved rather than knowledge-to-be-transmitted. Hence conventional research data may form an element in a body of knowledge relative to the solution of a problem and will be weighed along with other kinds of knowledge by practitioners and their advisers. Thus the boundary between forms of knowledge is somewhat blurred.

Havelock, a key-figure in the knowledge-utilization movement development, identifies four strategies in the use of knowledge to effect educational changes, only the fourth of which met the criteria for effective transmission (Havelock, 1969). The *diffusion* or *social-interaction* model is the relatively unplanned spread of knowledge through social networks of individual practitioners via various messages (advisors, lecturers), media (word of mouth, professional publications) and sittings (conversations, courses, conferences). The disadvantages of this model is its slowness, its haphazardness and its dependence upon individual rather than work-group interest. The *research, development* and *dissemination* model proposes a more rational, systematic, large-scale process involving a division of labour between researchers, developers, disseminators and practitioners. The disadvantages of this model are that it assumes a 'rational but passive consumer' (Havelock) who receives the package and implements the necessary changes; it takes little account of local circumstances; and it is applicable mainly to curriculum materials rather than research data. The *problem-solving* model rejects the centre-periphery assumptions of the other two and sees innovation as springing from perceived needs and problems experienced. The school, or other unit, searches for solutions to these problems and in doing so will take account of different kinds of knowledge: the experience of other schools, the advice of experts, and research evidence. The major disadvantages of the problem-solving approach are that the institution concerned may lack expertise in identifying relevant sources of knowledge, in understanding such knowledge, in converting this knowledge to the needs of the particular situation and in actually implementing change. The strength of the fourth model, the *linkage* model, is that although the problem-solving approach remains central, the resources of the school are supplemented by external resources which can be called upon to help the institution to understand and negotiate change. Those involved in this support are researchers, curriculum specialists, organizational consultants etc and the institutions are research and development units, university departments, and advisory services who work with individual schools as linkages in networks of institutions (Hoyle, 1976).

Various linkage models are reviewed by Bolam, 1982, and Paisley and Butler, 1983. One significant North American example is the Pilot State Dissemination Programme (PSDP) which was initiated in the 1970s (Louis, 1983, provides a summary and a bibliography of reports of the project; see also Louis and Sieber, 1979). The purpose of the programme was to link bodies of educational knowledge such as ERIC, Current Index to Journals in Education (CIJE) and Research in Education (RIE) to potential users in educational institutions by means of intermediate institutions. Havelock's linkage model provided the theoretical base. Louis writes:

'the primary goal of the PSDP was to stimulate consumption of research-based information of any type among a broad group of educators ranging from individual teachers with concerns about supplementing classroom materials, to entire school boards interested in policy change. Responsiveness to client definitions of need was paramount, and limited emphasis was placed on setting expectations for what the requestors of information should actually do with it.'

The projects which constituted the programme each had a district project office with facilities for information retrieval, field agents whose functions were to stimulate interest in using information and who were generalists and facilitators understanding both the practical problems of teachers and the data available to them, and back-up resources consisting of specialist consultants to whom the field agents could refer teachers and administrators for specific advice. Louis summarizes the *modus operandi* as follows:

> 'When an educator expressed interest in obtaining information on a topic, the field agent would communicate this, via a printed form conveying minimal information about the request and the requestor, to the project headquarters. In most instances, a computer search of ERIC (and the CIJE/RIE files in two states) would be initiated, sometimes supplemented by a "manual" search through available catalogs. In some instances, additional library searches were coordinated and state specialists contacted. However, most requests were serviced through more routine searches of the available national databases.'

The major characteristics of a linkage structure are as follows:

1. the initiative comes from the practitioner;
2. the impetus is stimulated by the presence of external expertise;
3. the linking agent makes available relevant knowledge;
4. this knowledge is interpreted in the light of the particular problem or state of the institution;
5. the knowledge is one component only in a process of innovation which must take into account a wide range of other contingent factors.

Thus, although knowledge may be 'objective' its impact on practice is mediated by a social process which takes particular considerations into account.

Research styles

A simple typology of research styles will help the argument at this point.

1. *Basic Research.* The problem is identified by the educational researcher and arises less out of practice than out of the developing body of social science theory. The researcher will undertake such research as part of his university duties or be supported by a funding agency such as a research council which allocate at least some funds to this kind of research. Apart from a report to any sponsor the findings will be disseminated via academic publications and read largely by academics.

2. *Objective Research.* The problem is identified by the researcher or by a sponsoring body. It is a practical problem of general concern, eg a problem relating to learning, the grouping for interaction, school organization. However, the style is objective. Data are gathered

in a detached manner. Again a report may be made to the sponsor who, if it is a government agency, may use the data in policy-making procedures. Otherwise dissemination will be via academic publications to be read mainly by academics, students and a small number of interested practitioners. However, if it is newsworthy it will be disseminated in an edited form through the mass media.

3. *Summative Evaluation*. Projects of this kind are concerned with evaluating the outcome of some change in practice. The unit of the analysis may vary considerably from samples of children to curricular practice and institutional structures. The style is objective. The potential sponsors will vary from, say, a research council committed only to making the evidence available to a government department who has sponsored the research in relation to specific policy considerations. Dissemination will be by report to the sponsors, to the unit evaluated, or to both. Otherwise, where broader dissemination occurs this will be as for objective research, ie academic publications and the media.

4. *Formative Evaluation*. Here the data selected in the process of evaluation are fed back to the unit of evaluation during the period of the research in order that they can make changes to practice. Two patterns of dissemination are possible. One passes directly from the researcher to the participant. In practice, the relationship, and hence the mode of dissemination, can vary from an objective reporting of data to a pattern of reporting involving the discussions and negotiations of the meaning of the data and its consequence for action. The other pattern of dissemination is the report to the sponsor plus perhaps reports in publications to be read by academics or practitioners. These can themselves vary from reporting the data and the changes made in the light of the data (findings subject to summative evaluation) to accounts of the *process* of negotiation.

5. *Action*. As with the other categories many variants occur within this style, but essentially it involves the researcher in taking a problem experienced by one institution, gathering data relevant to the problem, negotiating possible solutions with staff, and undertaking formative evaluations of those solutions. Styles of action researchers vary from the non-directive resource person to solution-proposing participant. The sponsors of this kind of research might be the institutions themselves, or funding agencies, but, of course, such research is likely to be ineffective unless the demand comes from the institution itself. Dissemination is again of two kinds: immediate data feedback to participants and accounts written in reports to sponsors or in academic journals.

All five forms of research and associated patterns of dissemination flourish. They serve different functions and have their own inherent validity. However, there has been a growing emphasis on action-oriented research. The undoubted advantage of such approaches is that the problem of how research reaches the practitioner ceases to be a 'dissemination' problem.

However, two other kinds of problem arise. One is that subjectivity is likely to be increased because the data will be system-specific and therefore not objectively validated and the researcher is that much more easily — and often deliberately — pulled into the action. This is not a great problem for those who question the objective status of research data since any data produced will be the subject of negotiation between researchers and practitioners. The other major problem is that of generalizability. Action research which is reported for a wider audience can necessarily only offer a portrayal of a particular instance. However, the interpretive social scientist would argue that circumstances are never identified and thus the experience of one action project cannot be directly transposed to another. Thus the portrayal of a case is available for participants in other institutions to interpret in the light of their own circumstances. There remains, however, the problem of disseminating case material to a wider readership.

Participation and negotiation

This chapter has so far reviewed some changes in how knowledge is perceived and how both dissemination and utilization of knowledge and styles of research are changing. From this review it would seem that two principles governing the acquisition, dissemination and utilization of educational knowledge are emerging. These are *participation* and *negotiation*.

By *participation* one means that two categories of hitherto passive and inert groups in the educational system are becoming increasingly more participative. These groups are the *subjects* of research and the *consumers* of research knowledge. The two groups, of course, sometimes — perhaps increasingly — overlap. This impetus to greater participation stems, as indicated, from changing views of knowledge and its effective utilization but perhaps, even more fundamentally, from the change in the socio-political climate in the 1960s with its emphasis on the participation of those affected by decisions in the decision-making process itself. The research correlate is that the subjects of research should be involved in the research process. (Insofar as this broader socio-political climate is influential it may be that more recent changes in that climate which have, for example, led to a growing emphasis on accountability and more direct political control of education, at least in Britain, could have an impact on the nature of research process with a greater emphasis on objective-detached summative styles.) However, the trend has been towards greater participation. For example, a number of universities have established teacher research groups whereby the problems to be investigated have been determined by the teachers themselves who have undertaken such research under the guidance of university staff and with the support of other teachers in the group. The 'problems' identified by teachers tend to be substantive problems experienced in daily professional work and tend to be different from the 'problems' identified by researchers which tend to arise from a pre-existing theoretical base.

By *negotiation* is meant that in various ways the 'knowledge' which is the product of research becomes, as it were, an agenda item for discussion, hence yielding potentially different interpretations. The nature and settings of such negotiation are varied and it would be impossible to explore a typology in detail in this chapter. At one extreme is the situation in which knowledge is regarded as inevitably relative and the researcher and participant researchers negotiate an agreed outcome. This is legitimated by a phenomenological approach to knowledge. One of the best-known techniques is that of 'triangulation' developed notably at the Centre for Applied Research in Education at the University of East Anglia: the data gathered by the researcher through subvention and interview are fed back to the researched (say teachers) and third-party participants (say pupils) who offer their interpretations of the data. The process is obviously capable of an infinite regression of accounts of accounts and the investigator must at some time decide when to 'go public' (Adelman and Walker, 1975).

At another level, negotiation occurs through steering committees established by funding agencies. Here the data may be treated as 'objective' in epistemological terms but attachment of 'meaning' will differ according to different sets of participants.

Contexts of dissemination and negotiation

One is almost tempted to summarize some of the changes of the past 15 years as 'from dissemination to negotiation'. The implication of such a slogan would be that traditional patterns of dissemination from researcher to non-involved consumers largely through the medium of print had given way to a situation in which research, consumers of research and researchers interact more directly and sometimes verbally. However, it has to be conceded that much of the dissemination of research conforms to earlier patterns, that there are no alternatives to these patterns if research is to be *widely* disseminated, and that participation and negotiation have occured only on a limited scale. Nevertheless, there remains a strong case for evolving new contexts of negotiation wherein both producers and consumers are brought together. In this section we can give some examples.

In 1978 the Social Science Research Council (SSRC) for the United Kingdom resolved to initiate a research programme in early childhood education. Jerome Bruner, then at Oxford University, was invited to submit a proposal. The proposal submitted, and accepted for funding by SSRC whose positive support matched an imaginative bid, was not for a programme of data collection but for a rolling seminar which would involve not only researchers but members of the medical, teaching and social work professions with early childhood responsibilities. The object was to explore the implications for policy and practice of existing research and to carry out small-scale action projects to test the effectiveness of particular interventions. The obvious problem of this kind of activity is that its effectiveness is difficult to assess, and it would be against the spirit of the enterprise to invest further research funds in evaluating it (Bruner, 1980).

A major experiment in participation has been mounted by Andrew McPherson at the Sociology of Education Research Centre at the University of Edinburgh, again supported by a substantial commitment from SSRC. McPherson's achievement has been to create the Scottish Education Data Archive (SEDA), a facility which can be used by practitioners, policy makers, community groups and other stakeholders in the educational system. The data on which this facility is based is essentially the patterns of pupil achievement and progress through school and into employment or higher education. The facility enables the various consumers of such know-ledge to gain direct access to the data and to interrogate it using the SPSS statistics packages. However, a first stage in this process was the creation of awareness of the potentialities of the data base and the programme included a research fellow with special responsibilities for making known the potentiality of the data. The project also included short sessions of training in the use of SPSS programs for potential consumers (McPherson, 1975).

A third example of the creation of a context for negotiation is the national conference approach built into two recent projects undertaken at the Bristol University School of Education under the direction of Dr Ray Bolam. Essentially the strategy is, at different points in the life of a policy-oriented project, to involve in a conference the researchers, the practitioner-participants and sets of 'influentials' from various constituencies in the educational system who could have a potential role in disseminating further and, in some cases, implementing the good practice which had emerged from the project. Two conferences were held in relation to the Teacher Induction Pilot Scheme (TIPS) Project. The first was concerned with the results of the first year of operation. Its immediate aim was 'to facilitate the exchange between the participants of practical information, ideas and materials about the organization and implementation of various kinds of induction scheme'. A second aim was 'to assist in the creation of an informal communication rationale of people and institutions engaged in mounting induction programmes' (Bolam and Baker, 1975). A second conference was held in 1977 (Bolam et al, 1977), again including researchers, participants in the research programme and 'influentials'. In particular, conference members included members of the Induction and In-service Training Committee (INIST) of the Advisory Committee for the Supply and Training of Teachers (ACSTT) which had the task of advising the government on all aspects of teacher education including induction. The members of this committee took the role of 'interrogators' and assessed the 'evidence' presented at the conference. Mr Pat Milroy, the sub-committee chairman, summarized the lessons of the project which would be taken on board in their advance to the government. The 'influentials' also included members of Her Majesty's Inspectorate, administrative staff from the Department of Education and Science, and LEA advisors. A similar approach was taken with respect to the Schools and In-Service Teacher Education (SITE) Project (Baker *et al*, 1982). The final conference again involved researchers, participants and 'influentials' and on this occasion used a 'fish-bowl' technique as a means of sharpening up the policy implications and encouraging a critical exchange of views: a small group of participants debated the findings in a plenary session at which members of the 'audience', ie conference participants, could interject statements and ask questions.

A final example is the provision of membership service by the National Foundation for Educational Research. Since its establishment in 1947 the Foundation has undertaken research on its own initiative, and in response to requests from a variety of agencies has disseminated findings largely through publications. In recent years, however, it has begun to provide advice and consultancy directly to member bodies, largely Local Education Authorities, on presenting their own particular enquiries. This service includes (NFER Research Information 1):

- discussion of a problem or innovation to relate its features to background research and define specific objectives;
- preparation of a programme for a project in line with the resources needed or available;
- drafting questionnaires, schedules or tests; proposing methods for data analysis; clarifying aspects of report-writing;
- undertaking pilot studies in collaboration with the organization concerned;
- advising on formulating research and development proposals, including rationale, design, instrumentation, costing, techniques for analyses and reporting.

Of course, this is not providing *data* directly to a consumer but enabling consumers to formulate their own research from within the problems which they face. To this degree there is negotiation between those with expertise and those confronting substantive problems.

Conclusion

Essentially the argument of this chapter is that the way to improve the dissemination of educational knowledge to practitioners is to create contexts for participation and negotiation. Individuals learn best from other individuals and they learn best when they play an active part in the learning process. After all, this has been an axiom of educational theory and we have no reason to believe that it applies any less to adult professionals than to children. Without taking a phenomenological view of knowledge, it would nevertheless seem that the meanings which people attach to the social world and to accumulated knowledge are to some extent shaped by social contexts. The chapter has sought to predicate the nature of the support for the importance of social contexts in dissemination and to cite a few of the more interesting examples. Developments in microelectronics will undoubtedly greatly facilitate access to data and reports of research findings. This may mean that when the majority of practitioners have direct access to data from their own homes the two-step flow of communication will be less significant. But that remains to be seen. Even though interactive strategies of dissemination may be more effective than the 'spray and pray' mode of conventional approaches they are limited in scope and pervasiveness by logistical and cost factors. Thus dissemination via publication will remain an important means of reaching practitioners. It is therefore vital that innovations continue within this strategy such as the readable but authoritative reviews of the state-of-the-research-art in a particular field. Notable examples include *Early Childhood Education* (Tizard, 1974) produced by the Social Science Research Council and the brief but informative literature on research currently being produced by the National Foundation for Educational Research.

References

Adelman, C and Walker, R B (1975) Developing pictures for other frames: action research and case study *in* Chanan, G and Delamont, S eds *Frontiers in Classroom Research* London: NFER Publishing Co
Allison, G T (1981) *Essence of Decision: Explaining the Cuban Missile Crisis* Little Brown: Boston
Baker, K, Sikora, J, Davies, J P, Hider, A T (1982) *The Schools and In-Service Teacher Education (SITE) Evaluation Project* University of Bristol School of Education: Bristol
Bolam, R (1982) *Strategies for School Improvement: a Report of OECD* OECD/CERI: Paris
Bolam, R and Baker, K eds (1975) *The Teacher Induction Pilot Scheme (TIPS) Project: 1975. National Conference Report* University of Bristol School of Education: Bristol
Bolam, R, Baker, K, McMahon, A, Davis, J and McCabe, C (1977) *The Teacher Induction Pilot Scheme (TIPS) Project: National Conference Papers* University of Bristol School of Education: Bristol
Bruner, J S (1980) *Under Five in Britain* Grant McIntyre: London
Burchinal, L G (1983) ERIC: The international educational information system *in* Paisley, W J and Butler, M eds *Knowledge Utilization Systems in Education* Sage Publications: Beverly Hills
Douglas, M (1966) *Purity and Danger* Routledge, Kegan Paul: London
Feller, I (1981) Three coigns of diffusion research *in* Rich, R E ed *The Knowledge Cycle* Sage Publications: Beverly Hills
Freidson, E (1970) *The Profession of Medicine* Dodd Mead: New York
Halmos, P (1971) Sociology and the personal service professions *in* Freidson, E ed *The Professions and their Prospects* Sage Publications: London
Havelock, R G (1969) *Planning for Innovation through Dissemination and Utilization of Knowledge* Institute of Social Research: Ann Arbor, Michigan
Hoyle, E (1973) *Strategies of Curriculum Change* Open University Course E203 Unit 23 Open University Press: Bletchley
Hoyle, E (1982) The professionalization of teachers: a paradox *British Journal of Educational Studies* 30(2) 161-71
Hoyle, E and Megarry, J (1980) *World Yearbook of Education, 1980: The Profes-

sional Development of Teachers Kogan Page: London

Husen, T and Kogan, M eds (1984) *Educational Research and Policy: How Do They Relate?* Pergamon Press: Oxford

Jackson, P W (1968) *Life in Classrooms* Holt, Rinehart, Winston: New York

Louis, K S (1983) Dissemination systems: some lessons from programs of the past *in* Paisley, W J and Butler, M *Knowledge Utilization Systems in Education* Sage Publications: Beverly Hills

Louis, K S and Sieber, S D (1979) *Bureaucracy and the Dispersed Organization* Ablex Publishing Corp.: Norwood, N J

Macnamara, D (1976) On returning to the chalk face: theory not into practice *British Journal of Teacher Education* **2** (2)

McPherson, A F (1975) Methodological aspects of collaborative research *Research Intelligence* **2**

Nisbet, J and Broadfoot, P (1980) *The Impact of Research on Policy and Practice in Education* Aberdeen University Press: Aberdeen

Rogers, E and Shoemaker, F (1971) *Communications of Innovations* New York: Free Press

Tizard, B (1974) *Pre School Education in Great Britain* London: Social Science Research Council (now the Economic and Social Research Council)

17. Educational research and educational change: the case of Sweden

Ulf P. Lundgren

Summary: Educational research may be viewed as a scientific activity for various reasons: because it is based in scientific institutions, or because it uses scientific procedures, or because it is seen as a process of 'mapping' reality. Each of these perspectives is to be found in the history of the scientific approach to educational issues in Sweden. Initially, the creation of a specific discipline of education was legitimated by the need for a scientific basis for teacher education and the protection of the educational system from the influence of special interest groups.

The use of educational research in the comprehensive reorganization of Swedish schools demonstrated its value in the public sphere, and secured increased funding for an institutional structure for educational research. The tradition of large-scale empirical statistical psychological studies for which Sweden is internationally known was thus established.

Research activity, however, extended beyond these limits to include evaluation and development, to implement further organizational reforms and to construct new teaching materials on an individualized-learning model appropriate to the comprehensive school. More recently, problems, both social and pedagogical, within the educational system and new perspectives from sociology, combined with financial cut-backs, have tended to challenge the positivist assumptions in the traditional Swedish model of research. The thread of continuity throughout recent changes is the legitimation of educational research as a rational basis for decision making in education.

Educational research is more difficult than other social science research to delineate and analyse out of its national context. One reason for this is that the language used in education is everyday language and lacks specificity.

> 'In education, then, it is not the language that is distinct and special but rather its users. The language of education is the common familiar language of daily affairs as used by a specific identifiable group of persons in the conduct of a distinct set of tasks.' (Komisar, 1971:328)

The language used by educational researchers working within an educational system reflects the patterns of thinking built into that system. Analyses of educational research traditions presented for an international audience must therefore build on translations which do not take terms for granted, but try to bring out the essential meanings.

One example is the term 'curriculum', a key concept in educational research (cf Kallos and Lundgren, 1979), yet used differently by different authors. Dottrens (1962) notes that the term curriculum in early writings seems to have meant a *document* showing a detailed plan for the school year: today the term syllabus conveys this meaning, in French plan d'études, in German Lehrplan. The Swedish term Läroplan is translated as curriculum, but this covers both meanings, a plan for schools decided by parliament, and the more general meaning of curriculum as a structured series of learning outcomes (cf Johnson, 1967). This example indicates the complexity of translation among the web of threads that link educational research to its object of study. In explaining how a specific research tradition has developed it is necessary then to explain not only the educational system which is its object, but also the cultural context within which the research tradition in question is formed and has its legitimacy.

The formative years

Education may be described as a scientific activity from three points of view. The first point of view is institutionally oriented. From this aspect scientific work is the work carried out within institutions established for scientific studies. The second point of view relates scientific work to the methods used in acquiring knowledge: science here implies the proper use of accepted methods. Education as a science is frequently defined in this way in handbooks and textbooks (cf Kallos and Lundgren, 1975, 1979). On this definition scientific work can be carried out outside scientific institutions, as long as the methods used are accepted as scientific. The third point of view relates science to the real world and the attempt to categorize or 'map' the world. Research is then

> '... sequences of transformations of complexes composed by know-
> ledge, problems, and instruments. The term instruments refers to
> hard-ware tools used in laboratories and to soft-ware tools such as
> mathematical and statistical techniques. It will be assumed that
> research is concerned with a part of the real world. Knowledge may
> then be described as an authorized map of the territory'(Tornehohm,
> 1971:2).

What is scientific knowledge here is a question of how knowledge is created in relation to a specified part of the reality. The delineation of the territory that is to be mapped and the validity of the maps created then determine the scientific quality. These three points of view overlap and are of course simplifications, but they serve as a useful framework for the following analysis of the emergence of educational research in Sweden on the scientific model.

In Sweden, as in most of the nations of Northern Europe, education — or pedagogy — was formed within philosophy and followed thus a specific

220 ULF P. LUNDGREN

philosophical tradition, mainly Herbartian. Herbart saw pedagogics as consisting of two parts: moral philosophy, the determination of goals and content of education; and principles of instruction, for which psychology was the necessary base. The psychology advocated by Herbart was based on his apperception theory, which he claimed could be refined into a logic-mathematical structure. Within this tradition pedagogics or education as a science had two main tasks. One was normative in character, and covered pedagogics as a part of the cultural reproduction of society. The other task was to explain the limits and possibility of pedagogics as a transformation process. In the development of Herbartian pedagogics, we can see the emergence of a distinction between a theoretical side of pedagogics – including the two aspects mentioned above – and a practical side. According to Herbart, science would never be the sole base for practical pedagogics. He writes:

'Of those responsible for upbringing I have demanded science and intellect. For others, science serves merely as spectacles; for me it is an eye – the best eye for viewing our affairs ... The first, but far from the complete, science for the educator is psychology. I think I know the possibilities of such a science; it will take a long time before we possess it, still longer before we can demand it of the educator. But never would it replace the observation of a pupil; an individual can only be discovered, never deduced.' (Herbart, 1806: 33, our translation)

The linkage between the theoretical side and the practical side of pedagogics was, within this tradition, not a simple rational relation. Theoretical pedagogics could deliver a conceptual framework, an understanding of the social meaning of upbringing and education, and specify the limits for these processes. The practical side of pedagogics had to be built on the knowledge and ability of the teacher. In this way Bertil Hammer – the first professor of pedagogics in Sweden – characterized, in his inauguration lecture, the nature of education:

'... a life process, a developmental process, the new generations that grow up and live in a society and culture; it is a piece of history, the history of the transmission of the cultural heritage from generation to generation. For theoretical pedagogics then, upbringing will not in reality be an activity for which one will write laws, but a process, a developmental process, which one has to describe and understand. This does not mean that theoretical pedagogics will not have practical value, since it will be a theoretical research into causality; the more we know the powers of educational activity the more we will be able to intervene in it.' (Hammer, 1910, from Lindberg and Lindberg 1983:20, our translation)

As early as 1780 lectures in pedagogy were held at the University of Uppsala and the Academy of Abo in Finland (then part of Sweden), covering 'Foundations for systems of private and public education', and amalgamating ancient pedagogic ideals with the ideas of the Enlightenment (cf Sjöstrand, 1961:25, 184, 224). More regular teaching in pedagogics was offered from 1803 in Uppsala, Lund and Åbo. The 1842 law on compulsory education made it necessary to organize the education of teachers, both for teachers for the common public schools in specialist colleges (seminars) and for teachers in the academic schools for whom university graduation was required, including (from 1875) 2 one-year courses in pedagogics, one theoretical and one practical. In 1910 the first chair in pedagogics was established. In the inauguration lecture the new professor described education as a science in this way:

'In order to understand what a science is and wants, answers are demanded to the following three questions: What is the object of the discipline, what problems are dealt with, what kind of research methods are used to solve the problems?'

He specified three main areas of education as a science:

'(1) to enquire into the objects of upbringing ... this is the task for the philosophy of education or a theological oriented pedagogy;
(2) to study in depth the educational process as it forms the individual; in other words, to investigate the biological and psychological conditions that determine the development of the child; educational psychology or individual pedagogy;
(3) to study education at large as a social phenomenon, whose historical and social conditions have to be pointed out; social pedagogics (including the history of education.' (Hammer, 1910, from Lindberg and Lindberg, 1983:20, our translation)

In 1905 a proposal had been submitted in parliament to establish a chair in pedagogics, in which pedagogics as a science was likened to medicine, and the relation between theory and practice was discussed on the analogy of medicine and medical practice. The argument was that pedagogy had left the speculative era, and had become a science of its own with established scientific methods.

'The pedagogy of our time is not a branch of speculative philosophy; it has been transformed into a modern scientific study, not only by drawing on the safe results of experiential psychology but also, for its own purpose, by applying strict experimental methodology.' (AK no 152, 1905, from Richardson, 1983:54, our translation)

What we see is a struggle, in the early years of this century, to establish pedagogy as a distinct science separate from philosophy and adjusted to the methods of the growing behavioural sciences. The basic argument for this development was the need for a modern science as a basis for teacher education. This has to be seen in relation to changes in the school systems. As the State intervened in the educational sphere, education became more associated with production, and was viewed as an instrument for social change. This in turn raised the questions and problems of how to transfer the goals and content of education from the agenda of the researcher to the agenda of the politicians. Thus the Herbartian tradition was disowned, and the study of how the transmission process was brought about and could be governed became the main focus. Consequently, the problems for researchers to deal with were identified as problems relating to the individual learner, and educational psychology came to dominate the stage. No chairs existed in psychology until the 1950s when existing chairs in pedagogics were divided into two — psychology and pedagogics. Prior to this the growing interest among researchers in psychological problems had to be developed within pedagogics.

In this way up to the end of the Second World War the idea of education as a science was established, and teacher education was closely linked to this idea. Doctorates were awarded for studies in education and a labour market existed for these graduates as lecturers in teacher education, as school inspectors, as administrators and as school psychologists. New chairs in pedagogics were established, in Lund in 1912, in Göteborg in 1919 and in Stockholm in 1937. With the establishment of teachers' colleges in the 1950s new education research departments were created.

The school reforms

With increasing industrialization and urbanization the demands on public education changed. The established educational provision was insufficient to meet these demands. In particular, public education was expected to provide a qualification for all citizens — a qualification related partly to society's demands for basic skills and partly to demands for vocational skills as a preparation for working life. There was also a change in attitude to the responsibility of public institutions for children's upbringing. Public education was more generally seen as fostering personal development as well as providing an education of value on the labour market. A more rational and pragmatic code was established in which education was looked upon as an instrument for social change. A rationally planned and implemented education was intended actively to change society. Reform of schooling was considered possible with the aid of science. Education became a democratic right but at the same time it was more closely related to production. In this development there is a paradox. In creating a school system that gives the same possibilities for all, irrespective of social background, the educational process must be independent of the production structure in its values, knowledge and skills. On the other hand a more pragmatically oriented school system must be dependent on the production structure for its content. This paradox was resolved by separating the content of education from the methods for transmission. The pattern of thinking was built on the ideas that the school system should give knowledge and skills of importance for social life and for production, but in the process of instruction the individual would be central. This instruction was to be built on a scientific understanding of the psychology of the child, thereby giving a guarantee of fair treatment of the child. Methods of instruction were separated from content, a separation mirrored even in teacher education, in which some teacher educators became responsible for subject matter and others for techniques of instruction.

After the Second World War most of the countries of the Western World reconstructed their educational systems. In general, there was a trend towards a comprehensive school system, moving from highly selective and differentiated systems towards open systems to which all had access, and where differentiation was postponed as far as possible. During the 1950s a number of economists tried to establish relationships between educational investment, research and economic growth. The increased demand for education which resulted required increased intervention from the State. In turn this created a situation which called for increased planning and control over educational investment.

The work of reforming the Swedish school system which led to the establishment of the nine-year comprehensive school, was begun by the School Committee appointed by the 1940 parliament. The purpose of this committee of experts was to take an overall view of the existing school system and propose necessary changes. Directly after the war the committee was replaced by a parliamentary commission, the 1946 School Commission. The committee of 1940 had not then finished its work, and was unable to deliver an agreed proposal on differentiation in the school. The experts representing the academic schools argued for early differentiation and the experts from the public schools demanded a late differentiation. When the 1946 School Commission delivered its final report in 1948 (SOU, 1948:27), a heated debate was triggered off, as the proposals were considered too radical. What the School Commission proposed were new goals for the compulsory school system — a widening of the responsibility of the school to care for the child as a person, an education for democracy. The school was to encourage personal development, critical thinking, independence and cooperative ability. Constant change in society, the Commission said, required not only factual knowledge but also ability to assimilate and discover new knowledge. Methods of instruction had to be revised and the individual child was to be the focus of instruction. A compulsory nine-year school system was to replace the old differentiated system.

However it was difficult to find a politically acceptable answer to the question of when differentiation was to be made. Economic and political developments in society during this century had changed the conception of schooling and the function of education. The reforms amalgamated three factors: the need to organize a uniform school system in order to control practical administration; the need to create a school system that gave equal opportunities regardless of social background, sex and geographical location; and the need to modernize curricula and adjust the goals and the content of education to modern social life and to the world of work. Thus we can talk about an administrative, a political and a curriculum factor. The paradox in creating a school system that on the one hand was independent of the structure of society and production by giving the same opportunities to all, but at the same time was dependent on and responsive to changes in cultural life and in the world of work, was articulated in the politically heated discussions on when differentiation of the children was to occur. Early differentiation meant better adjustment to a differentiated labour market; late differentiation opened up better opportunities for children to choose careers. The political decision of the 1950 parliament to solve this dilemma in a rational way, was to test the consequences of different organizational solutions after a period of experimentation. And this called for pedagogical research and evaluation.

The school reforms and educational research

The School Commission of 1946 implemented a programme of research and development to be administered by the National Board of Education. The problems involved in planning the school reform were seen as answerable by means of research. The development of advanced statistical methods made it possible to analyse extensive data and make comparisons. Although pure experiments were impracticable, statistical techniques gave the promise of delivering results that came close to the situation of a pure experiment. One classical example is the Stockholm study (N-E Svensson, 1962), later followed up by another large survey, the Göteborg study (Bengtsson and Lundgren, 1968, 1969). In 1955 the council of Stockholm divided the city into two school districts. In the south of Stockholm various types of comprehensive schools were implemented and in the northern part of the city the old traditional school system continued. Using this 'natural' experiment, Svensson (1962) conducted a study in which the achievements of the pupils in these two districts were compared. A covariance method was used in order to control differences between districts in the social background of the pupils. The results showed small or no differences between the two districts (cf Dahllöf, 1971).

The Stockholm study illustrates the type of problems that were specified and the type of research called for. From the politicians the demand was to have answers to broad questions, such as, which system produces the best results – selective or non-selective classes? This question did not call for any theoretical explanation: preference for one organization over another was embedded in political ideology. In the terms of our discussion of the three aspects of education as a science, the institutional, the methodological and the territorial aspects, we can see here how economic support to research encouraged an educational science which had its identity in the research methods used. The problems were specified in the political and public debate: the researcher had to deliver a scientifically acceptable answer.

In this way the school reforms set the framework for educational research. The problems specified demanded answers that could be delivered in psychological terms using statistical methods. Translating this discussion into epistemological terms, it can be said that the problems specified needed answers that were given within a logical-empirical or positivistic research tradition. In turn these answers were valuable for the decision makers. The Stockholm study, for example, delivered results that indicated that late differentiation would not hazard scholastic achievement. In that sense educational research delivered arguments to support a specific educational policy: research demonstrated a pragmatic value and was looked upon as a necessary part in the rational development of the school system.

During the 1950s a series of research studies was carried out in relation to the planning of the school system. Härnqvist (De Wolff and Härnqvist, 1962, SOU 1958:11) conducted a survey of the 'pool' of ability, a survey which was influential in the planning of the reform of the gymnasium. Härnqvist (1960) also carried out a study of individual differences which was used in the development of study patterns in the upper stages of the comprehensive school and the gymnasium. Dahllöf (1960, 1963) conducted a curriculum study on the mother tongue and mathematics in the compulsory school, and later another study on curriculum demands in the gymnasium.

The implementation of the reform

The school reform led to a shift of interest from research directly linked to teacher education — didactic-oriented research — to research which served the reform of the school system. New funds were allocated to educational research. A major part of these resources were administered by the National Board of Education, which was responsible also for implementing and evaluating the reform. Thus, during the 1950s and the 1960s educational research was established on a large scale. New chairs were established in the research institutes at the new Teachers' Colleges. The new professors and researchers qualified by mastering large-scale data collection and advanced statistics. What we see here, then, is an amalgamation of the methodological aspect and the institutional aspect. It was by mastering a scientific methodology that educational research could respond to public and political demands, which resulted in resource expansion and the establishment of research institutes. Thus education as a science was legitimated by the methodology used, thereby responding to questions that were raised in connection with the reforms. And educational research then was linked to the planning and evaluation of the reforms, thereby giving economic support, which firmly institutionalized pedagogics.

Having a legitimate institutional structure and a rapid growth rate, educational research changed character with the implementation of the reforms. Knowledge was acquired from follow-up studies based on large-scale projects, and longitudinal studies produced statistics on the effects of schooling. Härnqvist, for example, followed a sample of students through the school system to adult life (cf A Svensson, 1971). The Göteborg study conducted by Andersson (1969) made an important contribution to understanding the relation of schooling to changes in attitudes and behaviour among students. The Västmanland-study (Lundman, 1979) and the Örebro-study (Magnusson *et al*, 1967) are other examples. These large-scale projects can be seen as consequences of the knowledge developed within research on the reforms. After the implementation of the reforms, however, resources were allocated to developing instruments for carrying out the new policies, in the form of tests for the new school system and materials for instructional systems. Test construction followed the established pattern but the development of instructional material was something new. Research money was allocated to develop materials for individual instruction within the framework of comprehensive classes. These were pure developmental projects, but the fact that they were carried out within established research institutes made them legitimate as research both financially and academically. Few of these projects were implemented, but substantial resources were allocated to constructing instructional materials during the 1960s. What we thus see is a renewal of the links between educational research, teacher education and school practice but now mediated through an educational technology.

The establishment in the 1950s of teacher colleges with research institutes was part of a reform which aimed to base the education of teachers more clearly on scientific knowledge. As research money was allocated for producing new instructional materials for the new school system, the result was a transformation of parts of educational research to developmental projects legitimated as research by the fact that they were carried out within established research institutes and departments. Thus, we can see how educational research was legitimated by its research methods and how these methods were developed and used, and also how the establishment of institutionalized research programmes gave space for development work, which was legitimated as research. As this latter research had no firm base it declined with changes in the school debate and changes in perception of school problems.

Evaluation of the reform

When the decision was taken in parliament on the comprehensive school system a decision was also taken to follow up the reform. The long planning and committee period from 1940 to 1962 was considered too slow a strategy for the continuous development of the school system. The National Board of Education was given the task of following up the implementation and of suggesting changes to the government and parliament (cf Lundgren, 1977). The first reform of the curriculum for the comprehensive school was suggested in 1969 in a proposal from the National Board of Education.

The school reform had led to new school units. These new schools had to be rather large in order to provide the necessary range of options for grades seven to nine. The 1962 reform had been a political compromise, with a comprehensive system up to grade seven followed by a progressive differentiation of courses and a clear differentiation of study in grade nine. This system of various options demanded large school units. During the 1960s demographic changes, with increasing immigration and urbanization, resulted in new suburbs on the outskirts of cities and in industrial areas. In these new housing areas new schools were situated. As a result school problems tended to be concentrated in certain areas. In 1970 internal problems in the school system surfaced in a parliamentary debate. A parliamentary committee on 'The Inner Work of the Schools' (SIA) was set up and reported in 1974 (SOU 1974:53). This report documented the way in which the persistent difficulties of teaching heterogenous classes were being tackled. Comprehensive school practice recommended the use of self-pacing instructional materials, but instead forms of remedial teaching were being introduced outside the regular classroom. Statistics from 1963 on demonstrated that this solution was increasingly applied: the Committee noted in 1972 that approximately 40 per cent of all students received some remedial teaching. Thus to some extent a parallel school system was being established within the comprehensive school by the introduction of remedial teaching. The Committee initiated experiments in which resources were allocated differentially to schools with specific problems. Evaluation of these trials demonstrated quite clearly that experimental schools often used the liberal rules for resource allocation in a way which in effect meant a differentiation of the students (Kilborn and Lundgren, 1974). This transformation, recreating a differentiated school within the comprehensive school framework, illustrates the new types of problem which were identified in the 1970s and which began to influence educational research.

Evaluation of the reforms showed that many of the aspirations of the reform movement had not been fulfilled. Interest slowly shifted from broad questions about the effects of organizational change to focus more on questions concerning work in the classroom. There was criticism from teachers that educational research was of no use to them in their work. Although teacher education was supposed to be based on educational research and teachers were supposed to master educational psychology, to diagnose children's problems and build up individualized teaching, educational research had instead been linked to the educational administrators' need to estimate parameters for planning and following up the reforms. Organizational changes were offered as solutions to the social problems of the classroom. With criticism of the centralized, bureaucratically controlled school system and of educational research, there was growing interest in new approaches to teaching.

At the same time radical changes within social science resulted from criticism of positivistic-oriented research. Within education there was a renewed interest in basic epistemological questions and research into the teaching process itself (cf Lundgren, 1977). In 1967 Dahllöf published a new analysis of the Stockholm study using data on how the teaching process had developed in the different types of schools in the Stockholm study. Dahllöf made a new interpretation. He showed that though there were small differences between selected and unselected classes, there were large differences in the time taken to reach a given standard (Dahllöf, 1971). In explaining this new interpretation of results on the effects of ability grouping he developed a theoretical model (cf Lundgren, 1972, 1977) that had an important influence on the research in the 1970s. Again we can see two lines of research interest develop. One of these was directed towards studies of the classroom process following Dahllöf's earlier work and broadened into a series of studies which could be labelled as the sociology of teaching. This research line represented what Hammer in his inaugural lecture in 1910 had called social pedagogy, the interest in understanding how social and historical conditions shape the educational process, and thus it can be seen as a renewed interest in the classical research tradition within education. The other line was a development of educational research within the field of educational psychology with an orientation back to didactics, the study of the learning process, the content of learning, and the structure of school subjects, studies of the basic skills of reading and spelling and arithmetic and also of subjects like physics (cf Marton, 1975; Lybeck, 1981; Säljö, 1982). Behind this development are other currents: the new sociology of education in England, a renewed Marxist influence, criticism of the positivistic research tradition, influences from the development of curriculum theory in the USA, phenomenologically directed research, and so on. The underlying factors, however, are changes in society.

With the decrease in economic resources towards the end of the 1970s, the State needed a better basis for cutting back expenditure. The period of expansion was ended and in recession the decision base changed. The relation between policy makers and researchers also had to change. Previously, the link took the form of a programme formulated by politicians and tested by researchers. Now this was replaced by a situation where each step of change had to be done in a context of resistance. The question now was how to put resources to better use, not simply a matter of additional resources to deal with problems. At the end of the 1970s a commission (the Dahllöf Commission) was set up to review the in-service training of teachers and the use of educational research. It is significant that the commission proposed that research and development were to be separated and that research should be linked more to planning: R & D was replaced by R & P.

At present educational research in Sweden is suffering financial cutbacks. Public debate is concerned with 'back to basics' and the academic outcomes of teaching. Research in education shows a fragmented picture. Its various emphases represent different traditions established in earlier phases, but these traditions can never be understood within the research context alone. We have to see them in relation to changes in Swedish society and the consequences of these changes for the educational system. The thread of continuity during this development is the legitimation of educational research as the rational basis for decision making in education.

References

Andersson, B-E (1969) *Studies in Adolescent Behavior* Almqvist and Wiksell: Stockholm

Bengtsson, J and Lundgren, U P (1968) *Modellstudier i utbildningsplanering och analyser av skilsystem* (Model Studies in Educational Planning and Analyses of School Systems) Licentiatavhandling, Department of Education, University of Göteborg: Göteborg

Bengtsson, J and Lundgren, U P (1969) *Utbildningsplanering och jämförelser av skolsystem* (Educational Planning and Comparisons of School Systems) Studentlitteratur: Lund

Dahllöf, U (1960) *Kursplaneundersökningar i matematik och modersmålet* (Research on the Curricula for Mathematics and Mother Tongue) Statens offentliga utredningar SOU 1960:15: Stockholm

Dahllöf, U (1963) *Kraven på gymnasiet* (The Demands on the 'Gymnasium') Statens offentliga utredningar SOU 1963:22: Stockholm

Dahllöf, U (1967) *Skoldifferentiering och undervisningsförlopp* (School Differentiation and Teaching Process) Almqvist and Wiksell: Stockholm

Dahllöf, U (1971) *Ability Grouping, Content Validity and Curriculum Process Analysis* Teachers College Press, Columbia University: New York

De Wolff, P and Härnqvist, K (1962) Reserves of Ability: Size and Distribution *in* Halsey (1962)

Dottrens, R (1962) *The Primary School Curriculum* UNESCO (Monograph on Education II): Paris

Halsey, A H (1962) *Ability and Educational Opportunity* OECD: Paris

Hammer, B (1910) Om pedagogikens problem och forskningsmetoder (About problems and research methods in education) *Svensk Lärartidning* 42:940-43

Härnqvist, K (1960) *Individuella differenser och skoldifferentiering* (Individual Differences and School Differentiation) Statens offentliga utredningar SOU 1960:13: Stockholm

Herbart, J F (1806) *Allgemeine Pädagogik* Bochum

Johnson, M Jr (1967) Definition and models in curriculum theory *International Review of Education* 19 187-94

Kallòs, D and Lundgren, U P (1975) Educational psychology: its scope and limits *British Journal of Educational Psychology* 45 111-21

Kallòs and Lundgren, U P (1979) *Curriculum as a Pedagogical Problem* Gleerup/ Liber: Lund

Karabel, J and Halsey, A H (1977) *Power and Ideology in Education* Oxford University Press: London

Kilborn, U and Lundgren, U P (1974) *Skolans inre arbete* (The Inner Work of the School) P A Nordstedt and Sö-nerö Stockholm

Komisar, B P (1971) Language of education *in* Deighton, L C *ed The Encyclopedia of Education* Vol. 5 327-34, MacMillan and The Free Press: New York

Lindberg, G and Lindberg, L (1983) *Pedagogisk forskning i Sverige 1948-1971* (Educational Research in Sweden 1948-1971) Institute of Education, University of Umeå: Umeå

Lundgren, U P (1972) *Frame Factors and the Teaching Process* Almqvist and Wiksell: Stockholm

Lundgren, U P (1977) *Model Analysis of Pedagogical Processes* Liber: Lund

Lundman, L (1979) *Socioekonomisk differentiering i grundskolan* (Socio-economic differentiation in the Comprehensive School) Liber: Lund

Lybeck, L (1981) *Archimedes i klassen* (Archimedes in the Classroom) Acta Universitatis Gothenburgensis: Göteborg

Magnusson, D Dunér, A and Beckne, R (1967) *Anpassning, beteende och prestation* (Adjustment, Behaviour and Achievement) Department of Psychological Research, University of Stockholm: Stockholm

Marton, F (1975) On non-verbation learning *Scandinavian Journal of Psychology* 16

273-79

Richardson, G (1983) Från ekologi till pedagogik: en förändring inom svensk skola — och en avhandlingsutveckling (From Ecology to Pedagogics: a change within the Swedish School — and the development of a thesis) *Forskning om utbildning* 10 47-55

Säljö, R (1982) *Learning and Understanding* Acta Universitatis Gothoburgensis: Göteborg

Sjöstrand, W (1961) *Pedagogikens historia III:1* (Educational History Part III:1) CWK Gleerup: Lund

SOU 1948:27 *1946 års skolkommissions betänkande med förslag till riktlinjer för det svenska skolväsendets utveckling* (Report of the 1946 School Commission with Suggestions and Guidelines for the Development of the Swedish School System) Statens offentliga utredningar: Stockholm

SOU 1958:11 *Reserver för högre utbildning. Beräkningar och metoddiskussioner* (Resources for Higher Education. Estimations and Methodological Discussions) Ecklesiastikdepartementet: Stockholm

SOU 1974:53 *Skolans arbetsmiljö* (The Work Environment in the Schools) Utbildningsdepartementet: Stockholm

Svensson, A (1971) *Relative Achievement. School Performance in relation to Intelligence, Sex and Home Environment* Almqvist and Wiksell: Stockholm

Svensson, N-E (1962) *Ability Grouping and Scholastic Achievement* Almqvist and Wiksell: Stockholm

Törnebohm, H (1971) *Reflections on Scientific Research* Institute for the Theory of Science: Göteborg

18. Educational action-research

John Elliott

Summary: This paper explores the relationship between a process model of curriculum design and the view of the theory-practice relationship embodied in the idea of educational action-research. It concludes with an exploration of the problem of establishing an appropriate form of organization for action-research in educational institutions.

The paper covers four major themes:

1. the nature of educative action and its relationship to educational knowledge;
2. the development of teachers' professional knowledge through action-research;
3. educational research and educative practice; and
4. the institutionalization of action-research in schools.

In developing each theme the author draws together a variety of relevant theoretical work, and illustrates his exposition with examples of action-research projects with which he has been personally involved.

Introduction

In the educational field action-research has developed into an international movement. Collaborative networks of classroom teachers, teacher educators, and educational researchers have been established in the United Kingdom, Australia, Canada, Germany, Austria, and Iceland and there are signs of the movement spreading in the USA and Spain. The Classroom Action-Research Network (CARN) based at the Cambridge Institute of Education in the United Kingdom was established in 1976 to disseminate ideas about the theory and practice of educational action-research and keep individuals and groups in touch with each other on a regular basis. CARN publishes a bulletin (see Holly and Whitehead, 1984) which includes an updated membership list, and convenes conferences.

A major formative influence on the development of the movement was the notion of 'teachers as researchers' propounded by the late Lawrence Stenhouse at the Centre for Applied Research in Education in the University of East Anglia (see Stenhouse, 1975). Early exemplars of Stenhouse's idea were his own Humanities Curriculum Project (see Stenhouse, 1970; Elliott, 1983a; Ruddock, 1983) and the Ford Teaching

Project which I directed (see Elliott, 1976). Both these early examples of educational action-research, involving collaborative investigations of practical teaching problems were based in the Centre for Applied Research in Education (CARE) at the University of East Anglia.

As the movement has spread and developed it has spawned a considerable amount of second-order theoretical reflection and discussion on the following themes:

(a) the nature of educative action and its relationship to educational knowledge (see Stenhouse, 1983; Elliott, 1980);
(b) educational action-research and the development of professional knowledge (see Carr and Kemmis, 1983; Elliott, 1983b);
(c) problems in facilitating and institutionalizing educational action-research (see Nixon, 1983; Elliott and Ebbutt, 1984; Brown *et al*, 1982; Holly, 1984); and
(d) methods of data collection and analysis (see Elliott, 1976; Adelman, 1981; Burgess, 1981; Winter, 1982; Elliott and Ebbutt, 1984).

In this chapter I shall explore the first three themes in a fairly personal manner, drawing on other writing when it appears relevant. Whenever possible I will illustrate concepts and ideas with examples drawn from the action-research projects I have been involved with.

The nature of educative action and its relationship to educational knowledge

Stenhouse (1975) quite explicitly designed his Humanities Project on what he described as a 'process model' of curriculum development and sharply contrasted it with 'the objectives model' that was becoming fashionable in the curriculum field during the late 1960s in the United Kingdom. He claimed that the latter was inappropriate to the central curriculum problem he faced; namely, how can teachers be helped to handle controversial human issues in an educationally worthwhile way with adolescent students in schools. Since much of the content of a contemporary relevant humanities curriculum consists of human acts and social situations which are morally or politically controversial in our society, teachers have no public mandate to promote their own views about right and wrong courses of action. In the absence of agreed public criteria for settling human issues the idea of designing a curriculum in the light of precise specifications of learning outcomes did not appear feasible. So Stenhouse defined a general aim of 'understanding human acts, social situations and the controversial issues they raise' and from it derived a set of procedural principles which he believed to be *logically consistent* with the aim. (I would personally replace 'logically' with 'ethically'.)

Before commenting on Stenhouse's idea of analysing educational aims into procedural principles, it is necessary to deal with the view that the aim of 'understanding' could have been analysed into more specific and measurable learning outcomes. To my knowledge, Stenhouse did not directly deal with this potential criticism of the design of the humanities project. However, he did take it into account in his more general discussion of the limitations of the objectives model when applied to knowledge-based as opposed to skills-based curricula (see Stenhouse, 1975, chapter 7).

His general view was that the objectives model distorted the nature of educational knowledge. He argued that the major ideas and concepts of a discipline of knowledge were intrinsically problematic and open to divergent and novel interpretations. They constituted dimensions of meaning for students to explore creatively, a dynamic cultural medium to assist imaginative thought, rather than inert objects to be mastered.

On this view human understanding is the quality of thought which progressively unfolds *within* the learning process. As such it is impossible to describe learning outcomes independently of processes. The outcomes are simply qualities of mind progressively realized in-process. They are not pre-specifiable, standardizable, and fixed end-states of learning. To regard learning as a process which is directed towards some fixed end-state is to distort its educative value, because what makes it educative is not its instrumental effectiveness in producing 'knowledge' outcomes that can be independently defined, but the quality of thinking realized in-process.

This quality cannot be exhaustively defined with any degree of precision. It constitutes an ever-receding standard, inasmuch as what counts as 'understanding' rather than 'misunderstanding' is something thoughtful teachers continue to learn as they reflect upon the way their students learn. They evolve criteria for assessing students' work but these are never conclusive. Such criteria provide a basis for critical dialogue with students rather than a definitive verdict on their competence as learners, and are in turn open to modification in the light of that dialogue. Students are given the opportunity to influence their teachers' assessments of the quality of their work. Thus for Stenhouse the educational aim of 'understanding' supports a *critical* as opposed to a *marking* model of assessment.

I have argued elsewhere (see Elliott, 1983a) that Stenhouse's process theory of understanding is very similar to Gadamer's theory of hermeneutic interpretation with respect to historical texts. Gadamer (1975) argues that there is no such thing as grasping the objective meaning of an historical text. The interpreter brings to the text a particular frame of reference — beliefs, values, and attitudes — which have been developed through his or her experience at a particular time and social location. It is impossible for the interpreter to stand outside these subjective biases or prejudices to grasp what the text objectively means. There is no ahistorical understanding. But this does not imply that the development of understanding is an undisciplined process.

For Gadamer, insights are developed in the space between the objective text, or artifact, and the subjective frame of reference the interpreter brings to it. Understanding is the outcome of interaction between the

objectively existing text and the subjectivity of the interpreter. This interaction will not happen if the interpreter simply selects from the text that
which confirms his or her own prejudices. Yet the prejudices must be
brought into play, rather than attempt a bias-free stance, because the
creative interaction between text and interpreter stems from the experience
of being unable to fit the evidence of the text into the framework imposed
on it. It is out of this experience that the interpreter becomes open to the
text and the emergence of new insights. What checks the tendency to fit
the meaning of the text to the prejudices of the interpreter is an awareness
of alternative ways of interpreting it. The interpreter is forced to question
his or her own initial interpretation by becoming aware of alternative
interpretations. The initial interpretation is tested against the evidence of
the text in the context of a discussion about the validity of alternative
interpretations.

Stenhouse claimed that one can *logically* derive teaching principles
from the educational aim of 'understanding'. Such a claim, the basis of his
process model of curriculum design, is only intelligible in terms of a
process account of 'understanding' as an educational aim. Once this aim is
viewed as an extrinsic product of learning, then the selection of teaching
strategies is governed by questions concerning their causal efficacy in
bringing the aim about, rather than their logical consistency with it. With
respect to the Humanities Project, Stenhouse claimed that the following
procedural principles were logically consistent with the project's aim:

1. discussion rather than instruction should be the core activity in the
   classroom;
2. that divergence of view should be protected;
3. procedural neutrality should be the criterion governing the teacher's
   role; and
4. that teachers have responsibility for quality and standards in learning,
   ie by representing criteria for critiques of viewpoints.

It is not difficult to see how these teaching principles pre-suppose a
process theory of understanding, and reflect the sort of account of this
process provided by Gadamer. Stenhouse envisaged a discussion- rather
than instruction-based classroom, in which students were given the
freedom to express their views on a variety of human acts and social
situations. The principle of discussion legitimated the free expression of
prejudice, and that of procedural neutrality reminded teachers to refrain
from using their authority position to promote their own prejudices as
objective truths. However, Stenhouse believed that prejudices ought to be
subjected to the test of critical standards and it was the responsibility of
teachers to represent them in the classroom. This was done by introducing
evidence documenting human acts, social situations, and the issues they
raised when it was relevant to the views being expressed. Such evidence
came in the form of historical, sociological, literary and artistic material in
a variety of media. Teachers would ask students to assess their views in the
light of the evidence before them, to justify their interpretations of the

evidence, or to pose alternative interpretations.

Finally, the principle of protecting the expression of divergent views and interpretations is derived from the need to encourage students to explore the subject matter, and evidence relevant to it, from a variety of angles.

Another example of a process model is provided by the Ford Teaching Project (see Elliott, 1976). The project involved 40 teachers from different curriculum areas and stages of schooling in East Anglia, undertaking action-research into problems of enquiry/discovery teaching. The central team (Clem Adelman and myself) helped teachers to clarify an agreed aim of enquiry/discovery teaching; namely 'to enable pupils to reason independently in classrooms'. We then logically analysed this aim into its constitutive values and derived from them a set of teaching principles.

The analysis was as follows:

Aim: to enable independent reasoning
Values implicit in aim: that pupils should be free to:
1. initiate problems for enquiry
2. express and develop their ideas
3. test their ideas against relevant and sufficient evidence
4. discuss their ideas with others
Teaching principles:
1. teachers should refrain from preventing pupils doing 1 to 4 (above)
2. teachers should intervene to help pupils do 1 to 4 (above)

The first set of principles specified *negative* and the second set *positive* enabling conditions. It should be noted that the teaching principles overlap with those specified by Stenhouse. This is because 'independent reasoning' is a constitutive element in the development of understanding. Conceptions of educational aims embody clusters of values and principles which are selected out through analysis and the way they are formulated will depend on the analyst's own anticipations about which values are being neglected in practice, and what needs to be changed in the light of customary practice in relation to particular subject-matters.

In both the Humanities and Ford Teaching Projects, the analysis of process values and principles was performed by 'outsiders' although they remained open to modification in the light of subsequent reflection by the teachers involved. More recently the Schools Council TIQL (Teacher-Pupil Interaction and the Quality of Learning) project, which involved teacher groups in ten schools undertaking action-research into problems of teaching for understanding (see Elliott and Ebbutt, 1984), left the explication of values and principles to the teachers involved as an integral part of the research. I shall return to the question of who theorizes about the values and norms of educative practice later.

We are now in a position to clarify the view of *educative action* implicit in the process as opposed to the objectives model of curriculum design. A process model specifies teaching and learning activities which are judged to be educative in terms of their ethical consistency with the 'development of understanding', conceived as a learning process which progressively manifests a certain intrinsic quality of mind. Criteria of ethical consistency can be logically derived from a conception of this process.

By way of contrast an objectives model of curriculum design will specify teaching and learning activities which are judged to be educative in terms of their instrumental or technical effectiveness in producing pre-specifiable, quantifiable, and standardizable knowledge outcomes. From the point of view of the process model, educative action is ethical in character. From the point of view of the objectives model it is largely technical in character: ethical considerations entering into questions of curriculum design purely in the selection of ends rather than means.

The development of professional knowledge through action-research

In the previous section I explored the relationship between educational knowledge and educative action from the point of view of the process model of curriculum design in contrast to the objectives model. In this section I want to explore the implications of the process model for the nature and development of teachers' professional knowledge and its relationship to educative practice.

I have argued elsewhere (see Elliott, 1983c) that the idea of a professional practice can be analysed into two components. First, it involves a commitment to ethical values; hence the term 'profession'. Second, it involves the possession of expert knowledge. The crucial question is how the relationship between these two components of professional practice is conceived.

Donald Schon (1983) has claimed that scholarly literature on the professions is dominated by a particular view of the relationship between professional practice and expert knowledge. He calls it the model of technical rationality. From the standpoint of this model professional practice involves the application of science and technology to practical problems. The model assumes that practical problems are essentially technical in nature, ie problems of discovering the most efficient and effective means of bringing about pre-defined states of affairs (objectives). For it is only when problems are defined in these terms that scientific principles and technology can be applied to their solution.

Schon suggests that from the standpoint of technical rationality the expert knowledge of professionals will consist of:

1. a knowledge of theoretical principles specifying the causal conditions which optimize the production of the desired states of affairs;
2. a knowledge of specific techniques (technology) for manipulating the problem situation so that it conforms to the conditions specified by the principles; and
3. the skills required to apply these principles and techniques to the problem situation.

Schon calls these three elements of expert knowledge implicit in the model of technical rationality the basic science, applied science, and skill components respectively. If teaching is a profession according to the model of technical rationality, then teachers need to know the theoretical principles governing the conditions of learning, and the techniques which can be employed to optimize those conditions. But the generation of the relevant theoretical principles and technology are specialist tasks for educational researchers and curriculum planners respectively. The professional practitioner's task is to apply the relevant principles and technology skilfully rather than develop them. This does not imply that teachers should not be involved in basic educational research and curriculum development, but that from the standpoint of technical rationality such involvements are not essential elements of professional practice.

The possibility of expert knowledge as it is posited by the model of technical rationality assumes that the practical problems it can be applied to are susceptible to general solutions. Schon cites Wilbert Moore's (Moore and Rosenblum, 1970) view that there must be 'sufficient uniformities in problems and in devices for resolving them to qualify the solvers as professionals'. Only if such uniformities exist can relevant scientific knowledge and technology be developed. The model of technical rationality assumes the generalizability of problem situations and solutions.

This considerably restricts what can count as a truly professional practice and results, according to Schon, in the kind of distinction drawn by Glazer (1974) between major and minor professions:

> 'The major professions are "disciplined by an unambiguous end — health, success in litigation, profit — which settles men's minds", and they operate in stable institutional contexts. Hence they are grounded in systematic, fundamental knowledge, of which scientific is the prototype, or else they have a high component of strictly technological knowledge based on science in the education which they provide. In contrast, the minor professions suffer from shifting, ambiguous ends and from unstable institutional contexts of practice, and are *therefore* unable to develop a base of systematic, scientific professional knowledge. For Glazer the development of a scientific knowledge base depends on fixed, unambiguous ends because professional practice is an instrumental activity. If applied science consists in cumulative, empirical knowledge about the means best suited to chosen ends, how can a profession ground itself in science when its ends are confused or unstable?' (Schon, 1983)

From the standpoint of the model of technical rationality the values the professional professes reside in the realm of fixed, unambiguous ends. Values enter into the selection of ends but not into the selection of means. The latter is entirely based on technical rationality, ie the selection of means purely in terms of their instrumental efficiency and effectiveness.

Now the emerging of a hierarchy of educationists — educational researchers based in universities developing a relevant body of theoretical principles, curriculum planners defining unambiguous knowledge outcomes and translating research findings into a technology of teaching, and teachers applying this technology in classrooms – indicates an aspiration towards the status of a major profession as it is defined from the standpoint of technical rationality.

The kind of process theory of educational knowledge articulated by Stenhouse does not fit the model of technical rationality at all. From the standpoint of such a model, the claim that educational values cannot be defined in terms of fixed and unambiguous ends and that they furnish criteria for the selection of means, only serves to diminish the status of education as a profession and efforts to develop a body of professional knowledge grounded in systematic scientific research. What those blinkered by the model fail to see is that there is an alternative model of professional practice that suggests an entirely different relationship between expert knowledge and values. Schon calls this model reflection-in-action.

He draws our attention to the fact that many practices involve knowing-in-action. Practitioners do not always act according to the model of technical rationality, ie apply theoretical and technical knowledge to instrumental decisions. Rather they act spontaneously without prior thought, and yet the purposefulness of the actions they perform suggests they are grounded in intuitive or tacit understandings of the nature of the problem, its causes, and ways of dealing with it. Here, knowledge is not applied to action but tacitly embodied in it. The practitioner may not even be able to articulate what he or she knows-in-action. People often know more than they can say. In this kind of practice, thought and action are fused together. Schon (1983) recalls Gilbert Ryle's account (1949) of intelligent action:

> 'When I do something intelligently ... I am doing one thing and not two. My performance has a special procedure or manner, not special antecedents.'

and then puts the same idea in the words of Andrew Harrison:

> 'when someone acts intelligently, he "acts his mind" '. (Harrison, 1978)

Knowing-in-action contains numerous tacit assumptions which might be described as theories-in-action. By way of example Schon describes Inhelder and Karmiloff-Smith's (1974-75) experiment, requiring children aged six to seven to balance wooden blocks, some conspicuously or inconspicuously weighted at one end, on a metal bar. The researchers discovered that all the children began the task in the same way. All the blocks were systematically first tried at their geometric centre. They explained this persistent and universal behaviour in terms of a tacit theory in action; namely, 'things always balance in the middle'. The observers redescribe what the children may experience as 'a feel for the blocks' in terms of a 'geometric centre' theory-in-action.

An account similar to Schon's of the theory-practice relationship with specific reference to educational practice has been worked out in some philosophical detail by Carr and Kemmis (1983). Their major conclusion is:

'Since educational practitioners must already have some understanding of what they are doing and an elaborate if not explicit set of beliefs about why their practices make sense, they must already possess some "theory" that serves to explain and direct their conduct.'

But, as both Schon and Carr and Kemmis argue, it is not just observers who can reflect about practitioners 'knowing-in-action'. The latter can do it themselves and thereby recover and describe their own tacit theories-in-action. Self-reflection of this kind is divided into two sub-categories by Schon: reflection-on-action and reflection-in-action. The former consists of a retrospective account of 'the understandings they have brought to their handling of the case'. The latter consists of reflection alongside action and the pace and duration of its episodes will vary with the pace and duration of the situations in which the professional is performing.

Both these types of self-reflection may be activated by the experience of surprise based on a felt inconsistency between action and situation. In reflection the practitioner will begin to examine this lack of fit between act and situation. It will involve consciously recovering his or her theories-in-action and examining them in relation to the facts of the situation. In this way an ill-defined problem area becomes clearer and the practitioner is required to develop a new theory of the situation which can then be tested in subsequent action.

The processes of reflection-on and reflection-in action arise precisely because the situation at hand defies the familiar categories of problems and problem-solutions, which the practitioner has tacitly employed in the past when spontaneously acting in and reacting to situations. They are processes which presuppose, contrary to technical rationality, that the contexts of action are not always stable, and that the practical problems which arise from them can be novel and unique in certain respects:

'When the phenomenon at hand eludes the ordinary categories of knowledge-in-practice, presenting itself as unique or unstable, the practitioner may surface and criticise his initial understanding of the phenomenon, construct a new description of it, and test the new description by an on-the-spot experiment.' (Schon, 1983)

It is interesting that in his accounts of the experience of 'fit' between act and situation Schon suggests that professional practices are tacitly guided by norms which give *form* to conduct. The realization of these norms is not an extrinsic consequence of professional activity but the realization of certain qualities in the activity itself. The ends of professional practices are qualities to be realized in the form of the practice itself rather than quantities to be produced as a result. Moreover, Schon suggests that ends of this kind may be intuitively sensed rather than consciously articulated. They provide a sense of the form to be realized in action rather than clearly pre-defined objectives to be brought about as a result.

> 'Chris Alexander in his *Notes Towards a Synthesis of Form* considers the knowing involved in design. He believes that we can often recognize and correct the "bad fit" of a form to its context, but that we usually cannot describe the rules by which we find a fit bad or recognize the corrected form to be good.
>
> Ruminating on Alexander's example, Geoffrey Vickers points out that it is not only artistic judgements which are based on a sense of form which cannot be fully articulated: "Artists, so far from being alone in this, exhibit most clearly an oddity which is present in all such judgements. We can recognize and describe deviations from a norm very much more clearly than we can describe the norm itself." For Vickers, it is through such tacit norms that all of us make the judgements, the qualitative appreciations of situations, on which our practical competence depends.' (Schon, 1983)

It is not difficult to link Stenhouse's process model of curriculum design with this general view of professional practice as guided by 'a sense of form' rather than specific objectives. In fact Stenhouse often presented the design of the Humanities Project as a specification of a *form* of practice to be realized in the classroom (see, for example, Stenhouse, 1970). His procedural principles constituted an articulation of his sense of the form of teaching appropriate to the handling of controversial issues in class-rooms.

We are now in a position, from a knowledge-in-action model of professional practice, to articulate an alternative view of the relationship between professional knowledge and professional ethics. Professional knowledge will consist of practical theories or conceptual frameworks — categorizations of practical problems, their explanations, and solutions — which underpin professional practices. These practical theories, often tacitly embodied in rather than consciously applied to practice, do not consist of general causal principles from which technical means-ends rules of action can be derived. They are not conditioned by an interest in achieving technical control, but by an interest in realizing a form of practice which is ethically consistent with professional values. Professional values are not so much a source of terminal objectives which are to be achieved as a result of practice, as a source of norms to be realized in practice. The practical knowledge-in-action of the professional is ethical rather than technical in character, ie a knowledge of how to realize an ethical form in action rather than of how to bring about certain pre-conceived end-states as a result of it.

Since practical situations are potentially unstable the professional's knowledge-in-action (acquired as a result of past experience of uniformities in problems, their explanations, and solutions) can never provide an infallible guide to future conduct. It helps the professional to anticipate rather than predict future possibilities, and he/she always needs to be open to the experience of surprise, to the need to recover and consciously reflect upon the appropriateness of their knowledge for the present situation. It is through such reflection that the individual's stock of professional knowledge is extended and enriched.

But the learning of individuals can also be shared with fellow-professionals, so that what is developed is not simply the private knowledge of an individual but also the common stock of knowledge available to all the practitioners of a profession. The professional development of individuals, as indicated by an increasing capacity to act consistently with professional values in a variety of practical situations, depends on a fruitful interaction between the development of shared and private knowledge. The more individuals share what they have learned with each other the more the common stock of professional knowledge is extended and enriched. And the more this common stock is developed in response to the changing contexts of professional practice the greater is the individual's capacity to diagnose the problem situations encountered and to respond appropriately.

In the process of developing professional knowledge through reflection-in-action, ends and means cannot be treated separately. As Schon argues, the professional's enquiry:

'... is not limited to a deliberation about means which depends on a prior agreement about ends. He does not keep means and ends separate, but defines them interactively as he frames a problematic situation.' (Schon, 1983)

Any practical theory about how to act consistently with professional values will presuppose a normative theory, ie an understanding of the norms implied by these values, and in terms of which ethically consistent practice is judged. Now professionals deepen their understanding of the norms they profess by reflecting about the concrete strategies they employ to realize them in practice. In other words normative theory — a theory of practical ends — is developed through reflection upon means, and as this happens new possibilities for the selection of means emerge in the form of practical theories. Practical and normative theory cannot be developed independently of each other (see Elliott, 1983b). Teachers cannot develop practical theories of teaching independently of developing their educational theories, ie their theories about the nature of educational values and processes. It is only from the perspective of technical rationality that the activity of educational theorizing is differentiated from that of educational research, and both from the activity of teaching.

In this section I have tried to show how Stenhouse's process model of curriculum development implies a view about the nature and development of teachers' professional knowledge and its relationship to educative practice which is radically different from the model of technical rationality. It is a view which gives teachers, rather than specialist researchers and theorists, responsibility for generating their own expert knowledge. This is why the 'teachers as researchers' movement emerged in the UK in the context of process-focused curriculum development projects. What Schon has recently described as a process of reflection-in/on-action in relation to the development of professional knowledge more generally, is now being increasingly characterized in educational settings as action-research. Both the Ford and TIQL Projects were explicitly described in these terms. In the next section of this chapter I want to argue that the action-research paradigm enables us to bridge the present gulf between what currently passes for educational research and the intuitive practice of teaching.

Educational research and educative practice

The term 'action-research' was first coined by Kurt Lewin (1947) to describe a mode of enquiry which has the following characteristics:

1. It is an activity engaged in by groups or communities with the aim of changing their circumstances in ways which are consistent with a shared conception of human values. As a means of realizing 'the common good' − rather than a merely individual good − it strengthens and sustains a sense of community. It is not to be confused with a solitary process of 'self-evaluation' in the light of some individualistic conception of the good.

2. It is a reflexive social practice in which there is no distinction to be drawn between the practice being researched and the process of researching it. Social practices are viewed as 'research acts'; as 'theories-in-action' or 'hypothetical probes' to be reflectively assessed in terms of their potential for realizing worthwhile change. From this perspective, teaching is not one activity and research-into-teaching another. Teaching strategies embody practical theories about ways of realizing educational value in particular situations, and when they are reflectively implemented they constitute a form of action-research. If one views a social practice like teaching as a reflexive activity the division of labour between practitioners and researchers vanishes. Lewin's idea of action-research has its roots historically in the Aristotelian tradition of a moral or practical science concerned with the realization of shared human values and ideals (see Elliott, 1983b).

When a social practice is viewed as a moral science it can be contrasted with two other ways of viewing it. Some might view it as a craft which is informed by the intuitive and tacit know-how acquired by its practitioners through experience. Others might view it as a set of techniques for achieving quite specific objectives which can be pre-specified in measurable terms.

Maurice Holt (1981) has argued in favour of a view of teaching as an intuitive craft. He is sceptical of the reflective stance on the grounds that it inhibits spontaneity and de-skills teachers. I would argue that as long as the tacit theories are embodied in intuitive teaching work, then there is no need for the practitioner to reflectively examine and test them through action-research. But the situations teachers find themselves confronting today are constantly changing in ways which make previously established habits and routines of teaching redundant. They require a continuous development of 'theories-in-action' through action-research, and one condition of such development will be that previously established patterns of teaching will need to be inhibited. In order to develop new skills teachers will have to increasingly tolerate the experience of being de-skilled.

However, as the work of Schon and Carr and Kemmis indicates, the idea of teaching as a reflexive practice is not inconsistent with the idea that it is also an intuitive practice involving tacit knowledge-in-action. The former presupposes the latter. Action-research focuses on problematic aspects of practice, but it can only do so if other aspects operate at the level of tacit knowledge. Not every aspect has to be recovered and consciously reflected on. And when new knowledge has been consciously developed, its implementation in concrete action will reach a stage where it becomes once more spontaneous, intuitive action. Action-research not only renders some tacit professional knowledge obsolete but it also helps to replenish the store available to the practitioner.

Central government within the UK now appears to be moving towards a conception of teaching based on the model of technical rationality. Sir Keith Joseph's recent Sheffield speech (Joseph, 1984) emphasized the clear specification of learning outcomes and the extensive use of criterion-referenced testing to measure them. On these assumptions good teaching becomes a matter of technical effectiveness, and one can expect an increasing sponsorship of applied research in a search for the means-ends rules which specify the 'skills' as 'techniques' teachers need to acquire.

Once teacher education becomes viewed as a matter of training teachers to become technical operatives there is little room for the idea of teaching as reflection-in-action, action-research, or a moral science. Nor is there much room for a view of teaching as a moral craft (see Tom, 1980) involving tacit knowledge-in-action. Whereas a moral craft underpins a moral science it is undermined by a conception of professional practice as a matter of technical rationality.

In my view educational research needs to be reconstructed within a moral science or action-research paradigm. What makes research *educational* is the aim of realizing educational values in practice. It is guided by values. The aspiration to make educational research value-free is a contradiction in terms. One might contrast *educational research* with *research on education* which uses educational processes as a context in which to explore and develop basic theories within the behavioural science disciplines, and implies a division of labour between teachers and researchers. The theories developed in these academic disciplines may have value in helping teachers to diagnose their practical situations, but this value can only be determined through practitioner-based action-research and not internally within the disciplines themselves.

Objections to a reconstructed paradigm of educational research as a form of action-research or moral science usually cluster around the issue of objectivity. The research process must be kept separate from the practices it focuses on if it is to avoid being biased by the values of practitioners. However, this view that researchers can detach themselves from their moral and social values has now been convincingly shown to be untrue by social theorists and philosophers of science (see Carr, 1983). They have shown how values enter into the very way in which the subject-matter is viewed, the kinds of evidence the researcher believes it is important to collect and the methods by which that evidence is analysed. Objectivity is better conceived of as an awareness of one's value-biases, a willingness to make them explicit, and an open attitude towards evidence which is inconsistent with them. In the context of action-research, objectivity involves being open to evidence of inconsistency between one's practices and values, and a willingness to modify one's understanding of the latter as one reflects about the problems of realizing them in the former. Given the possibility of objectivity viewed in this light, and the view that social practices embody 'theories-in-action', there is no reason why the scientific method cannot be applied as rigorously in reflective practice as it is in the natural and behavioural sciences.

Lewin mapped out a disciplined process of action-research which has parallels with scientific method in other disciplines. His model specifies a spiral of activities in the following sequence:

1. clarifying and diagnosing a problem situation for practice;
2. formulating action-strategies for resolving the problem;
3. implementing and evaluating the action-strategies; and
4. further clarification and diagnosis of the problem situation (and so into the next spiral of reflection and action).

Whereas the natural and behavioural scientist will begin with a theoretical problem defined by his or her discipline, the action-researcher begins with a practical one. But there is a sense in which the latter's problem is also a theoretical one. It emerges in the experience of a mismatch between his or her practical theories and the situation confronted. The only difference between the practitioner and the natural or behavioural scientist is that the former's theory is often implicit in his or her practice and not consciously articulated. An important part of the action-research process is therefore the clarification of the problem by making the practitioner's 'theory-in-action' explicit, and showing how the situation in which it operates cannot accommodate it.

Stage one may, with respect to educational action-research for example, involve developing explanatory theories which focus on the constraining influences of institutional, system, and societal factors on teachers' freedom to foster educational values in classrooms. The process of action-research can bring the realization that certain gaps between theory and practice cannot be closed until something has been done to change these contextual factors. In this case, action-research may move from reflection on pedagogical strategies into reflection on political strategies undertaken to change 'the system' in ways which make educative action possible.

The political dimension of educational action-research has been highlighted particularly in the work of Stephen Kemmis and his colleagues at Deakin University of Australia. He and Carr (see Carr and Kemmis, 1983) view educational action-reserach as more than simply a practical or moral science. It should also be a critical science within the critical theory paradigm of the social sciences developed by the members of the Frankfurt School (see, for example, the works of Habermas, 1971, 1976, 1978, 1979). According to Carr and Kemmis, any adequate or coherent educational science:

> '... must be concerned to identify and expose those aspects of the existing social order which frustrate rational change, and must be able to offer theoretical accounts which enable teachers (and other participants) to become aware of how they may be overcome ...'

In this chapter I have deliberately avoided going too deeply into this political dimension of educational action-research. But it is important. Within the UK the work of the TIQL Project teachers (see Ebbutt and Elliott, 1984) embodied a critique of the present examination system and the social ideologies which underpin it. Nevertheless, I am of the opinion that teachers always have an area of freedom within which they can continue to improve the educative quality of their practices in classrooms, and that action-research can help to clarify the possibilities for, as well as the limitations on, their freedom of action.

Stage two of the action-research process is equivalent to the formulation of scientific hypotheses. A new practical theory is required to change the situation, as it is now understood, in a way which is more consistent with the practitioner's values. Such a theory will specify action-hypotheses, ie strategies the practitioner believes are worth testing to see if they work. The third stage of the action-research spiral, the implementation and evaluation of action-strategies, is a form of hypothesis-testing. The outcome may suggest the need for further problem clartification and subsequent modification and development of action-hypotheses. And so, through spirals of action-research, practitioners develop their practical theories by a similar method to that employed by natural and behavioural scientists.

I am not going to describe the specific techniques that have been developed for collecting and analysing qualitative data in action-research. They are very similar to those employed in qualitative research in the social sciences and the illuminative paradigm of educational evaluation, and an extensive methodological literature already exists in these areas (see, for example, Hamilton *et al*, 1977; McCormick and James, 1983; and Hammersley and Atkinson, 1983).

The institutionalization of action-research in schools

The action-research paradigm of professional practice is not an easy one to realize within educational institutions as they are organized at present. Attempts by central governments to control the process of schooling bureaucratically by defining and standardizing its inputs and outputs leads to a form of organization which Handy (1984) has described as a *role culture*:

> 'The "organizational idea" behind this type of organization is that organizations are sets of *roles* or job-boxes, joined together in a logical and orderly fashion so that together they discharge the work of the organization. The organization is a piece of construction engineering, with role piled on role, and responsibility linked to responsibility. Individuals are "role-occupants" with job descriptions which effectively lay down the requirements of the role and its boundaries.
>
> The communications in these cultures are formalized, as are systems and procedures. The memoranda go from role to role (Head of X Department to Deputy Head) and are copied to roles, not individuals. The place abounds in procedures for every eventuality in rules and hardbooks. There are standards, quality controls and evaluation procedures. It is all organized and *managed* rather than led.'

This form of school organization facilitates technical control over learning processes to produce pre-determined objectives. The increasing dominance of the role culture in schools is underpinned by the view that professional practice is a matter of technical rationality. It can be contrasted with another form of professional organization described by Handy — the *person culture*:

> 'The person culture puts the individual first and makes the organization the resource for the individual's talents ... The "organizational idea" behind this culture is that the individual talent is all-important and must be serviced by some sort of minimal organization. They do not in fact like to use the word organization but find all sorts of alternative words (practice, chambers, partnership, faculty etc.) instead, nor do they talk of managers but of secretaries, bursars, chief clerks etc., indeed the managers of these organizations are always lower in status than the professionals ... Stars, loosely grouped in a cluster or constellation, is the image of a person culture.' (Handy, 1984)

This form of organization has dominated academic institutions in the past. It is highly congruent with the idea of teaching as a craft grounded in intuitive, tacit, knowledge-in-action. From this culture, the claim of teachers to be autonomous experts who cannot tolerate external interference with their individual judgement flows. It is a culture that is

currently being threatened by the emergence of a role culture to facilitate
political and bureaucratic control over the process of schooling.

The educational action-research paradigm of professional practice
presupposes a third form of organization cited by Handy; the *task culture*.

'The task culture evolved in response to the need for an organizational form that could respond to change in a less individualistic way
than a club culture, and more speedily than a role culture.

The "organizational idea" of this culture is that a group or team
of talents and resources should be applied to a project, problem or
task ...

It is the preferred culture of many competent people, because
they work in groups, sharing both skills and responsibilities; they are
constantly working on new challenges since every task is different,
and thus keep themselves developing and enthused. The task culture
is usually a warm and friendly culture because it is built around
co-operative groups of colleagues without much overt hierarchy.
There are plans rather than procedures, and reviews of progress
rather than assessment.

These cultures thrive in situations where problem-solving is the
job of the organization.'

The speed of social change in contemporary society creates unstable
contexts for professional practice. The individualistic person culture
cannot develop the new professional knowledge required to resolve
increasingly complex practical problems. Handy claims that some professions are responding to such complexity by 'grouping themselves into task
cultures and submitting themselves to more organizational disciplines'. The
emergence of the action-research movement in the sphere of education is
in effect this kind of response. The projects I have cited in this chapter all
sought to establish a novel organizational framework in the educational
system. They attempted to implement teams of teacher-researchers in
schools under a coordinator (rather than a manager), and to link the
teams together in local, regional and even wider networks. They redefined
the roles of specialist theorists, researchers, teacher trainers, and local
inspectors as consultative and facilitating tasks involving dialogue with
practitioners.

But such attempts have not only encountered the resistance of those
who wished to maintain their identities within the person culture. They
have collided with the development of role cultures, particularly in large
secondary schools. The school-based teams were founded in the hope of
promoting collaborative problem solving through free and open
communication between individual practitioners. But they tended to
collapse when confronted with a role culture designed to facilitate
hierarchical control through upward information flow, the avoidance of
error in following rules and regulations, and rigid role specialization. The
frequently-cited problem of 'lack of time', for individual and shared
reflection-on-action, simply reflected the demands teachers were required

to meet if they were to function satisfactorily within the increasingly dominant role culture of their schools.

The emergence of the role culture represents a political/administrative response to the complexity of schooling. This response attempts to re-establish a stable context for professional practice by treating the problems of schooling as technical problems amenable to social engineering, and thereby reducing their complexity.

For those who believe that the development of role cultures within the educational system distorts and constrains educative practice, there is no escape from the obligation of attempting to institutionalize task cultures in schools. This does not necessitate the total overthrow of the role culture. In every educational institution there are problems for which technical solutions are entirely appropriate. The establishment of administrative routines and roles to carry them out can create zones of stability that enable the institution to concentrate its energy and effort on the more fundamental problems of improving the quality of teaching and learning processes.

As Handy argues, what makes an organization successful is not the achievement of a pure form but getting the right mix. The problem of institutionalizing a task culture which supports educational action-research is not one of overthrowing the emerging role culture, but of discovering how to graft the former into the organization so that it continues to live within it in a fruitful dialectic with the latter, rather than simply being killed off by it.

In my view the increasing 'threat' of the role culture to the traditional person culture of schools is a major reason for the spread of the action-research movement. Faced with the bureaucratic erosion of their traditional person culture the teaching profession has increasingly come to realize that the only way to maintain control over their professional practices is to embrace the action-research paradigm and the organizational form appropriate to it. If I am right, then the future prospects for the action-research paradigm of educative practice are promising.

What is now required is more systematic reflection-on-action by all those attempting to facilitate the institutionalization process. We have come to call this kind of reflection the practice of facilitating action-research *second-order action-research*.

References

Adelman, C (1981) On first hearing *in* Adelman (1981)

Adelman, C ed (1981) *Uttering, Muttering* Grant McIntyre: London

Alexander, C (1968) *Notes Toward a Synthesis of Form* Harvard University Press: Cambridge, Massachusetts

Brown, L *et al* (1982) Action research in education: notes on the national seminar (Australia) *Bulletin No. 5 of the Classroom Action-Research Network* Cambridge Institute of Education

Burgess, R (1981) Keeping a research diary *Cambridge Journal of Education* 11, 1 Lent Term

Carr, W (1983) Can educational research be scientific? *Journal of Philosophy of Education* **17**, 1

Carr, W and Kemmis, S (1983) *Becoming Critical: Knowing through Action Research* Deakin University, Victoria

Ebbutt, D and Elliott, J eds (in press) *Issues in Teaching for Understanding* The Schools Curriculum Development Committee (formerly The Schools Council of England and Wales)

Elliott, J (1976) Developing hypotheses about classrooms from teachers' practical constructs *Interchange* **7**, 2 2-22, 76-77

Elliott, J (1980) Implications of classroom research for professional development *in* Hoyle, E and Megarry, J eds (1980) *Professional Development of Teachers, World Yearbook of Education* Kogan Page: London

Elliott, J (1983) A curriculum for the study of human affairs: the contribution of Lawrence Stenhouse *Journal of Curriculum Studies* **15**, 2 105-23

Elliott, J (1983a) Self-evaluation, professional development and accountability *in* Galton, M and Moon, R eds *Changing Schools ... Changing Curriculum* Harper and Row: London

Elliott, J (1983b) *Teacher Evaluation and Teaching as a Moral Science* Mimeo, Cambridge Institute of Education

Elliott, J and Ebbutt, D eds (1984) *Facilitating Educational Action-Research in Schools* The Schools Curriculum Development Committee (formerly the Schools Council of England and Wales) (in press)

Elliott, J and Whitehead, D (1982) *Bulletin No. 5 of the Classroom Action-Research Network* Cambridge Institute of Education

Gadamer, H (1975) *Truth and Method* Sheed and Ward Stagbooks: London

Glazer, N (1974) *The Schools of the Minor Professions* Minerva

Habermas, J (1971) *Toward a Rational Society* Heinemann: London

Habermas, J (1976) *Legitimation Crisis* Heinemann: London

Habermas, J (1978) *Knowledge and Human Interests* Heinemann: London

Habermas, J (1979) *Communication and the Evolution of a Society* Heinemann: London

Hamilton, D *et al* eds (1977) *Beyond the Numbers Game* Macmillan Education: London

Hammersley, M and Atkinson, P (1983) *Ethnography: Principles in Practice* Tavistock Publications: London and New York

Handy, C (1984) *Schools as Organizations* The Schools Curriculum Development Committee (formerly The Schools Council of England Wales)

Harrison, A (1978) *Making and Thinking* Hackett: Indianapolis

Holly, P (1984) Institutionalising action-research in schools *Cambridge Journal of Education 14.2* Summer Term

Holly, P and Whitehead, D (1984) *Bulletin No. 6 of the Classroom Action-Research Network* Cambridge Institute of Education

Holt, M (1981) *Evaluating the Teachers as Evaluators* Hodder and Stoughton: London

Inhelder, B and Karmiloff-Smith, A (1974-75) If you want to get ahead, get a theory *Cognition* **3**, 3 193-212

Joseph, Sir Keith (1984) Speech to the North of England Conference, Sheffield, January 6. Department of Education and Science

Lewin, K (1946) Action research as minority problems *Journal of Social Issues* **2** 34-46

Lewin, K (1947) *Field Theory in Social Science* Harper: New York

McCormick, R and James, M (1983) *Curriculum Evaluation in Schools* Croom Helm

Moore, W E and Rosenblum, G (1970) *The Professions* Russell Sage Foundation: New York

Nixon, J ed (1983) *A Teacher's Guide to Action Research* Grant McIntyre: London

Rudduck, J ed (1983) *The Humanities Curriculum Project: an Introduction* Revised edition. University of East Anglia, Norwich for The Schools Curriculum Development Committee (formerly the Schools Council of England and Wales)

Ryle, G (1949) Knowing how and knowing that *in The Concept of Mind* Hutchinson: London

Schon, D (1983) *The Reflective Practitioner: How Professionals Think in Action* Temple Smith: London

Stenhouse, L (1970) Some limitations on the use of objectives in curriculum research and planning *Paedagogica Europaea* 6 73-83

Stenhouse, L (1971) The humanities curriculum project: the rationale *Theory Into Practice* 10.3 154-62

Stenhouse, L (1975) *An Introduction to Curriculum Research and Development* Heinemann Educational Books: London

Stenhouse, L (1983) Curriculum research and the art of the teacher *in Authority, Education and Emancipation* Heinemann Educational Books: London

Tom, A R (1980) Teaching as a moral craft; a metaphor for teaching and teacher education *Curriculum Inquiry* 10.3

Winter, R (1982) Dilemma analysis *Cambridge Journal of Education* 12.3 Michaelmas Term

19. Curriculum development – from RDD to RED: review, evaluate, develop

Malcolm Skilbeck

Summary: The impact on curriculum development of the educational change model of RDD (research-develop-disseminate) has been debated over several decades. From an early interest in development conceived as research-related and leading to change through the systematic dissemination of curriculum products and processes, the curriculum agencies set up teams of specialists to implement the model. However, other factors and forces intervened. Not only were there criticisms of the relevance of this style of thinking and acting to school curriculum change, but the agencies responsible for promoting and supporting curriculum development were not, on the whole, research centres and they lacked the resources needed to undertake serious RDD on a substantial scale, appropriate to the size and complexity of their client school system.

The focus of curriculum development has shifted, over time, from the central team approach embracing research and development in specific topics and areas of the curriculum to more diffuse, local or 'grass roots' forms of school improvement. The quest for improvement in the quality of learning in schools, in student participation and in the effects and outcomes of learning, like the team-based research and development approach, is faced with serious challenges. Still lacking are comprehensive strategies and, no less important, goals, criteria and values for assessing 'improvement'. How, then, is improvement in the curriculum to be effected?

The Schools Council has been a major national curriculum development centre during a period of unprecedented growth and activity in educational research and development. Its experience, aims and dilemmas are explored and reference is made to other curriculum agencies to illustrate the central argument of this chapter: that the older version of RDD needs to be revised and reconstructed in order to meet the requirements of teacher professionalism, local initiatives, school autonomy, and participatory decision making, and in response to new social and cultural demands. The chapter argues for a transition from RDD to what is termed RED (review-evaluate-develop): that is, to a situation where local groups, working collaboratively and within broad policy frameworks, themselves participate in the basic processes of research and development in the curriculum.

Changing perceptions and roles of research in relation to curriculum development

In this chapter I shall discuss some of the problems we have encountered and lessons learnt in building research into the programmes and agencies of curriculum development which have been such a marked feature on the educational landscape since the mid 1950s. From a consideration of this experience we may better appreciate the linkages between research and development (R & D) in the curriculum field, especially the uses of research in the current interest in qualitative methods and programmes of school improvement. In illustrating my argument I shall draw very largely from the experience of the Schools Council for Curriculum and Examinations for England and Wales (SC), but shall refer also to R & D in some other settings.

The period I am considering is from the early 1960s to the early 1980s, a time when noteworthy shifts have occurred in the relationships between educational research and different kinds of development, and school practitioners have become more involved in R & D than ever before. Indeed, practitioner and other forms of local involvement are one of the keys to understanding the changing relations between research and development: 'views from below' as Farrar *et al* (1980) graphically term it. Nor can we overlook the focusing of public and political interest on R & D through ambitious claims or aspirations for projects and what they could achieve by way of improving conditions of learning and pupil learning outcomes. Also, it was during this period that in the curriculum field, R & D progressed from its early preoccupations with linear development models and scientistic theories of knowledge to eclecticism with respect both to methodologies (qualitative as well as quantitative designs and techniques) and epistemologies (eg relativist theories of truth by agreement and action by mutual consent).

From the mid 1960s into the early 1980s SC was the principal curriculum R & D agency in the United Kingdom and one of the most productive and influential bodies of its kind anywhere in the world. In addition to considering the SC, however, I shall refer to selected activities in other curriculum agencies, in particular the Australian Curriculum Development Centre (CDC) and North American and international programmes for school improvement.

Early in the period under review, attempts or recommendations were strongly made to structure curriculum development by applying the research-development-diffusion/dissemination model (RDD), which initiates action through a research study and terminates it by planned dissemination of products whose need is indicated by research and whose quality is tested through research-structured field trials. This model has its most powerful applications in science-based industries, such as chemicals, where product competition is extremely strong in the market place and where, consequently, product development through closely guarded research work in company laboratories is crucial in maintaining a company's competitive edge. In education, its relevance has never been generally accepted and indeed in curriculum development its early advocacy quickly gave way, in the face of practical experience and criticism. Some of its critics were perhaps overhasty in condemning it, although their criticisms were often well-judged in relation to exaggerated claims and neglect of practitioner participation (Stenhouse, 1975: 219-23).

Not all the assumptions and aspirations of the model were abandoned, most notably the belief that research solves problems and that dissemination is a discrete, end-on process which can be made more effective by the adoption of pre-planned strategies (eg in-service teacher education (INSET), or the construction of information systems or by salesmanship).

Dissemination, under various guises, is one of the central themes in contemporary school improvement programmes (Bolam, 1982; Fullan, 1983; OECD/CERI, 1983). Alternative or complementary models began to be proposed almost as soon as RDD was adopted by curriculum agencies — for example, the well known social interaction and problem-solving models of Havelock (Havelock, 1971a, b). The general inclination to condemn curriculum projects which are predicated on a centre-periphery set of relations, with central agencies controlling the flow of information and resources to perimeter groups, is another example of the hostility to what were taken to be basic RDD assumptions and the scepticism about the dissemination capability of single centres (Nisbet, 1971; Schon, 1971; Stenhouse, 1975).

My main argument in this chapter is that, despite the sceptics, there is still a case to be made out for a strong research component within and in relation to curriculum development and school improvement and that in making out this case we can and indeed ought to recast the RDD model into what I term review, evaluate, develop (RED). Related points are that through this recasting we can resolve the dissemination issue, bring evaluation more effectively into play in the development process and strengthen relationships between the more established development and improvement programmes and local curriculum development and review movements which have often been proposed as alternatives to RDD. This seems useful at a time when school reviews are being actively fostered by central and local authorities and when there is still an over-sharp dichotomy between national strategies for development as practised by such agencies as SC (until 1984), the Australian CDC and other national level bodies, and local action groups.

The expression review, evaluate, develop (RED) in this chapter refers to inter-related activities whereby practitioners and the institutions in which they work (including schools) participate consciously and deliberately in R & D — they are not merely recipients of its products but collaborate actively with research specialists and may be regarded as co-owners of R & D processes and outcomes. There are several consequential and related points:

— development of the curriculum and other forms of school improvement are seen as reflective, critical processes entailing systematic review and appraisal of current practice by those directly involved (practitioners participate in research);
— school review is now familiar to many teachers and is gaining acceptance as a means whereby the school community assesses itself perhaps with outside assistance and with reference to external criteria and makes its findings available to others (research is evaluative in

function);

— evaluation, including institutional self-evaluation, is pointless unless it leads to action and preferably action that is experimental in character, can be monitored and is subject to further modification — examples are curriculum revision, organization development and in-service training programmes (evaluation is for change, development);

— the processes of review, evaluation and development, if carried out at the institutional level, enjoy a number of advantages over the older style of RDD but need not preclude use of or participation in large-scale research and development projects (research styles are not mutually exclusive);

— one of the positive outcomes of the accountability movement is a greater school-level awareness of the need for and the nature of evaluation (accountability can foster RED); and

— school reviews are being actively fostered in many education systems and can provide a basis for more extended use of R & D processes and findings in school practice (RED can be a platform for larger R & D projects).

Examples of RED are most readily found in the literature of school-based curriculum development, curriculum evaluation including institutional self-evaluation and action research (Kemmis *et al*, 1981; Simons, 1981; Skilbeck, 1984a, b).

The chapter title should not be read as inferring that during the past three decades there has been a simple progression in curriculum agencies and school improvement programmes from an early adoption of RDD to its subsequent rejection and the adoption of RED or some other orientation towards research and development. Although some kind of displacement has occurred it has not been complete nor has it taken the form of a simple process of initial adoption of a model followed by its abandonment, and eventual replacement. It is necessary to mention this, as especially among advocates of school-based curriculum development and of the movements of teachers-as-evaluators and teachers-as-researchers there is a tendency, first, to treat RDD and its attendant centre-periphery strategies as having failed in their purpose and, second, to overlook the school-based curriculum development, local initiative and teacher participation in development of the 1960s and before.

The situation has always been more complex than the simple opposition between central and local strategies suggests. In SC for example, from the very beginnings in 1964, the role of the teacher as an applied researcher was implicit, although not spelt out, in the oft-repeated principle of the teacher choosing, assessing and adapting curriculum project materials. This is an unsophisticated version of RED, and I shall say more about it below, when I indicate the various ambivalences and ambiguities in the Council's attitude towards both the teacher's role in selecting materials and the uses of RDD in project work. It is as though, from the very beginning of large scale project-based curriculum development, there were underlying tensions between those forces giving prominence to diversity, localism and practitioner-based R & D, and the centralized, expert models through which research-based products were made available to large markets. These became explicit quite early in the literature of the period under consideration with costly results. Entangled were wide-ranging criticisms of the use of 'industrial models' which somehow combined RDD with management-by-objectives, of central dominance of curriculum decision making (the teacher as object), of research as hypothesis testing by specialists instead of problem solving by practitioners. As the arguments among researchers and developers raged throughout the 1960s and 1970s, administrators and policy makers decided that, in all this turbulence, research in education was yielding little of value to them (Atkin, 1979; Callahan, 1962; Lawton, 1980; Pile, 1976; Schwab, 1969; Stenhouse, 1975).

In reviewing the changes that have occurred in styles and applications of research in relation to curriculum evaluation and development we must not overlook the rapidity of change. Projects and programmes came on line rapidly in the 1960s and 1970s in curriculum agencies around the world. Indeed this was a period of creation: of national curriculum centres in the newly emerging countries of Africa and Asia as well as in England, Ireland (the Curriculum Development Unit in Dublin, for example), the USA (the regional laboratories and research centres in universities), Australia, New Zealand and Western Europe (the Dutch SLO, for example). Within ministries of education and through private foundations, large-scale projects were floated, alike in centralized and decentralized education systems. There was very little time − or inclination − to make lengthy preliminary appraisals. The notion of curriculum development as R & D, with a dissemination phase to follow in due course, and under the direction of a small project team, was quickly taken up. Discussion of the models and styles followed and almost at once RDD came under fire. It was challenged, modified and to a degree supplanted but never abandoned completely. Since the early 1970s we have seen many efforts to bring about closer, more productive relationships among research, development and related processes of innovation with strong participant involvement. Good examples of this are the literature reporting, evaluating and assessing the American school improvement programmes, academic analyses which attempt to reformulate the categories of knowledge production and utilization and projects of international agencies, including UNESCO and OECD (Berman and McLaughlin, 1975; Farrar et al, 1980; Fullan, 1982; Louis and Rosenblum, 1981; OECD/CERI, 1983; Rhine, 1981; UNESCO, 1983; Emrick and Peterson, 1978).

The uses made of R & D in education have become intertwined with government policies and programmes. Not only is the government now the principal funding source; the policies for curriculum, teacher education and school organization adopted by governments have proved to be a major influence in the adoption of styles and modes of development. This point is strikingly illustrated in Britain in the 1980s in the highly centralized and directive strategies for change in 14+ education adopted by the heavily funded Manpower Services Commission. By contrast, also in

Britain, the adoption of comprehensive schooling as a form of organization was not, at first, accompanied by a move towards new types of curricula specifically for comprehensive schools. Her Majesty's Inspectorate have taken up this matter and carried out development programmes to give shape to new curriculum models (Department of Education and Science, 1981a, 1981b). Adoption by the British Government of the Rothschild customer-contractor principle, discussed below, is a particularly significant illustration of a trend towards the use of research as contributory to sponsored development.

Educational research and the quest for school improvement

Since the mid-1950s in the USA and some 10 to 15 years later in the UK, Holland, Sweden, Germany, Australia, Canada and many other countries around the world, there has been a marked expansion of educational research supported from the public purse. Less often commented on has been the channelling of public funds for educational research into development work, initially mainly curriculum development, then wider forms of school improvement. The lines between research, evaluation and development are often quite blurred, as indicated by the currency of terms like research for development, research for better schools, professional development (INSET), organization development, the self-evaluating school, or school-based curriculum development. Attempts to construct strategies and models in which research, development, evaluation, improvement, innovation and so forth intermingle have been popular throughout the whole period.

The founding of the new agencies, for example the American National Institute of Education, the Australian CDC and a number of national curriculum centres in Europe, Asia and Africa, has given wide coverage to the concept of development — development *in* the curriculum and *of* the curriculum for the sake of nation building (curriculum *for* development) (Skilbeck, 1981, 1982; UNESCO, 1983). Research devoted to building up knowledge and understanding without any particular implications for action has grown during this period, but not at the same rate (Dockrell and Hamilton, 1980; Nisbet and Broadfoot, 1980; Oldham, 1982). The emphasis has gone towards practical applications, evaluations, policy and dissemination and utilization studies in an effort to ascertain the effectiveness or otherwise of innovations.

This widespread concern among policy makers, developers and many researchers for relevance, effect and applications cannot be reduced to a clearcut distinction between 'pure' and 'applied' research. Since education is itself a form of intervention, directed towards practical ends which embody aims and values, educational research — unless it is purely historical or factual — tends to be explicitly or implicitly action-oriented, accumulating knowledge about the normative activity of educating. Hence the overwhelming predominance of problem solving, evaluative and

policy studies, the frequent discussions of theory-practice relations and
the criticism of research that appears to lack a practical significance. None
of this, of course, brings into question the role of research in contributing
towards understanding and knowledge; rather it is in education that
understanding and knowledge are thought to be for the sake of practical
action (Carr, 1983; Nisbet and Broadfoot, 1980).

'Improvement', a favourite term in the 19th century tradition of self-
help, has once again come to the fore in educational discussion. However,
improvement is now taken to mean not individualistic self-help types of
changes but ascertainable and goal or value directed changes in educational
systems and programmes. This, too, has its antecedents in the 19th and
early 20th century views of education as a science: knowledge 'rightly'
gained and 'properly' applied will ensure a 'better' education (Connell,
1980, part 1).

'Improvement' now includes higher levels of student performance in the
curriculum, enhanced teacher professionalism, the display of managerial
skills by school principals, and evidence of greater efficiency in the use of
resources (Basic Studies National Field Task Force, 1974; OECD/CERI,
1983). Public funding agencies see themselves as custodians of 'improvement' and allocate research and development budgets accordingly. In the
UK the adoption of the Rothschild customer-contractor principle by
central governments marks a shift from research for the sake of knowledge
to research to meet problems and priorities high on the policy agenda of
the government of the day (Nisbet, 1981; Rothschild, 1971, 1972). In
education, this is reflected, for example, in the rise of the Assessment of
Performance Unit all of whose funded research (mainly for test construction and administration and analysis of results) is conducted on the
customer-contractor principle — by universities and the National
Foundation for Educational Research (NFER).

It is interesting to see Lord Rothschild, whose name is most closely
associated with the customer-contractor principle through his 1971 and
1972 reports, challenging its applicability in applied social science when
reporting (favourably) on the Social Science Research Council. He argued
that the main purpose of applied social research is to provide material for
informed debate and decision making and hence, in a democratic society,
for research of a more independent nature than the government controlled
customer-contractor principle allows (Rothschild, 1982: 11-12).

Why has the shift towards research sponsored by government in pursuit
of its policies occurred and what has resulted from it? The answers lie
embedded deep in modern culture: an era of rapid change, of experimentation, expansion and optimism about the effectiveness of large-scale,
knowledge-based enterprise in achieving social amelioration. A full
consideration of all this would take us too far from the theme of the
chapter but a brief listing of some of the reasons helps in elucidating the
movements with which we are concerned. Public schooling has been
commonly treated as one of the instruments of planned social, cultural
and economic development and its functions therein need to be under-

stood. This has given rise not only to surveys of provision and performance and the growth of educational statistics but also to the large-scale action research projects in which specific interventions were trialled for their effects upon defined types of social or economic deprivation: in England, for example, the educational priority area projects (Halsey, 1972). The large budgetary increases for public schooling during the 1960s and 1970s with their implications for fiscal policy and planning also meant increased interest by the public, politicians and administrators in studies of the effects of schooling and barriers to attaining educational goals. Put very crudely, could educational budgets be stabilized or cut without loss of performance? Interestingly, this was the period of maximum criticism of the public school for alleged falling or static standards of student attainment – criticism in part ideologically inspired, in part itself research-based (Black Papers 1-5, 1969-77). Was schooling, or in particular were increased school budgets, producing better learning? This question proved a challenge to claims made by educators and others about the role of education in social, economic and cultural change. Were there, after all, clear links between investment in schooling and improved educational standards? Was not research, as for example in the case of the widely publicized Coleman Report in the USA, bringing forth evidence of the ineffectiveness or limited returns from large-scale provision and programme development? (Coleman et al, 1966).

School improvement programmes and curriculum development agencies have been at the centre of these controversies about the relationship of performance outputs to financial inputs. Some have been closed in the mid to late 1970s and early 1980s, many substantially restructured or scaled down, including many of that pioneering group of agencies, the American Regional Laboratories and University R & D Centres. The middle ground, between direct government sponsorship and ultimate direction of R & D on the one hand and small-scale localized activities on the other, has become vacated in the late 1970s and early 1980s. The very agencies which from their inception set as their target the construction of educational R & D programmes specifically to bring about qualitative improvements in education have been reduced, eliminated or brought under ever-closer government control. In Australia, for example, in 1981 CDC was first heavily cut (at the same time as the national Education Research and Development Committee was eliminated) and then, after a lengthy freeze, reactivated – but under the Federal Government's principal school financing agency, the Schools Commission. In Britain, the Schools Council was closed and replaced by two smaller, mainly nominated bodies (the School Curriculum Development Committee and the School Examination Council).

Over and above all other claims by the agencies it has been their claim that increased funding for educational R & D will result in qualitative improvements in the educational system that has resulted in the sharp questioning of these agencies by academics and researchers as well as by the press and politicians. Yet it was through a coalescing of the several interests mentioned — government policies, social amelioration, economic development, community aspirations, the expansion of the educational base and the rapid growth of professionalism within education — that the idea of large-scale, qualitative improvement emerged and the agencies were themselves created. It seems as if, by staking out large claims, seeking large-scale public funding and adopting highly visible strategies, the national level 'improvement' agencies over-reached themselves almost before they were under way. There were, it is true, other factors at work and they cannot be discounted. The explanation of the decline of the regional and national development agencies particularly in North America, Australia and the UK is no doubt complex and cannot be dissociated from political ideology and bureaucratic rivalries. But part of it is undoubtedly a consequence of the difficulties the agencies and their programmes encountered in satisfying external demands, demands which they themselves helped to generate — for example, their inability to handle the problems of dissemination and utilization of resources and materials they had themselves fostered. In adopting RDD or variants of it, by establishing production and diffusion teams which offered to provide teachers with usable, educationally beneficial resources and by generally committing themselves to the thesis that R & D could, if on a large scale and with a strengthened infrastructure (eg networks of local teachers' centres), effect significant changes in schools, the agencies invited — and received — the most vehement criticism. Sometimes the critics disliked the values of a project, and mounted community campaigns against it — as happened in Australia with the CDC Social Education Materials Project and as has happened frequently in England in the press attacks on individual projects. At other times, professional and official criticisms were made of the plethora of demands being made on schools, or of the lack of evidence of project take-up. Combined with the criticism, ironically and as subsequent research showed, the vast majority of teachers in England and Wales were indifferent to or unaware of what the programmes and projects were all about (Steadman *et al,* 1978-81). These criticisms and problems had their parallels in other countries but seem to have been most prominent in the English-speaking world, especially Canada, Australia, USA and England. Was there, in all this, a fundamental difficulty with the basic proposition: that through structured enquiry (research) a problem could be identified, in a development phase solutions could be produced (development) and, finally these could be effectively diffused throughout a system (dissemination)? Is it significant that in the countries mentioned, the agencies were generally not part of the governmental-bureaucratic apparatus but were as a rule heavily funded through it (hence 'accountable' but not 'controllable')?

RDD and the project team

Given the perceived success of RDD in other fields of social endeavour, eg agricultural innovations or the adoption of new industrial processes, it is not surprising that it should seem to offer a prospect of successful problem-resolution in education, provided, that is, certain assumptions were made about curriculum processes — assumptions which often proved in the event to be false. The RDD model was available in the late 1950s and early 1960s, it had demonstrated success, or so it was believed, and it was readily advocated in an environment where big science and big technology were widely admired (Callahan, 1962). In curriculum development, the small project team, a kind of task force of specialists who would undertake RDD programmes, was also adopted, perhaps on the wartime military, bureaucratic and industrial models of small task forces to undertake well-defined, limited projects to solve specific problems.

The adoption of RDD in education and of the project team in curriculum development was not a consequence of a disinterested, Baconian valuing of knowledge and its possible practical applications. Instead, it was a response, using the language, values and instruments available at the time and conditioned by prevailing practices outside education, to strong criticism of shortcomings in the quality of education, criticisms which in the USA were especially strong throughout the 1950s (Bestor, 1953). Educational researchers were themselves among the advocates of the model and the curriculum development team was an educational creation, not something imposed from without.

Another point relevant to an understanding of how RDD and the well-funded project team for a time came to dominate curriculum development and how the notions of school improvement already referred to blossomed during the 1960s and 1970s is the buoyancy of the economies of industrial societies. Conceptually as well as organizationally, development and improvement have been tied into large and expanding educational budgets. An interesting illustration of this is the practice of Schools Council officers of selectively under-budgeting projects and, in the expectation of 'budget flexibility', returning several times for additional funds for 'essential extensions' and 'dissemination'. ('Realistic' budgeting, in the first instance, would have been unacceptable to the Council committees.) More significant, perhaps, is that all of the processes referred to under the headings of development and improvement — even teacher self-evaluation and school-based curriculum development — when seen in system-wide terms, require additions to educational budgets; they have not been achieved, generally, by a redistribution of existing budgets (which would in any case be a serious problem since such budgets are mainly for salaries which in turn reflect fixed conditions-of-service agreements between employers and unions). RDD in the service of school improvement was large scale — and expensive, at least relative to previous levels of research funding. Readiness to accept its costs has declined with economic downturn and this is another reason for the move away from the earlier, large-scale programmatic versions of RDD.

We have seen that RDD was itself justified in part as a means of effecting large-scale school improvement, that this was translated into a team model of curriculum development and that uncertainty as to whether some of its flag-carrying programmes had succeeded in this respect was a factor in the search for alternatives. Later in this chapter these points will be explored in more detail in the context of SC programmes and policies. I have suggested, also, that from a very early stage in the modern curriculum development movement variants and alternatives to RDD were actively canvassed. We need now to consider 'improvement' a little more closely.

School improvement

The term 'school improvement' has gained currency during the 1970s but, by itself, it tells us nothing about the aims of improvement, the aspects or processes to be improved, the methods to be used or the criteria for evaluation. A general weakness of the self-styled school improvement programmes is their preoccupation with *processes* of change — first RDD and more recently implementation questions — at the expense of a consideration of the *substance* of goals and values and the *content* of school education. Moreover, it is proving extraordinarily difficult to bring about productive and mutually supportive relationships among specific, small-scale projects loosely grouped together in broad improvement programmes.

Lacking clear definitions, we might say that 'school improvement' is not even a mission or a strategy but a question-begging term as likely to give rise to difficulties for the professional R & D people as did the earlier adoption of the RDD model. No doubt conscious of this danger, educational development agencies including international bodies like the Centre for Educational Research and Innovation of the OECD have begun to take a more critical and analytical stance towards the whole notion of 'improvement'. Qualitative issues in education cannot be resolved by the study of change processes, and 'improvement' in education, like another popular catchcry 'good practice', brings into question both the nature of the activity that is to be improved and the standards against which it is to be judged — and by whom (White, 1969, 1983).

'Improvement' is a blanket term commonly referred individually or collectively to the processes of curriculum development, teacher professionalism in and out of the classroom, school organization and aspects of administration and planning, especially those to do with implementation of policy. These processes have been identified as crucial among those major factors affecting student learning which are amenable to action by educators (as social environment for example may not be). The aim is not to 'improve' any of them as an end in itself but as a means to bring about some desirable changes in student learning. As to whether school improvement programmes have achieved this, there is room for doubt. As indicated, the qualitative issue is usually avoided; there is also an inherent difficulty in establishing causal relationships, and changes in student learning may well post-date improvement programmes by several years.

Some studies have addressed the latter problem (Tamir and Amir, 1981), but it remains a problem for development agencies which are publicly funded and under constant challenge to demonstrate 'effects'.

School improvement programmes are usually innovatory, although there is no necessary connection between innovation and improvement, as defined. Some of the most recent designated improvement programmes consist of a collection of loosely related small-scale projects, focused more on workshops, observation studies, field visits and meetings than on identifiable innovation in classroom practice. They may be regarded as background to classroom and school innovation and, in that respect — as in their claims to be able to bring about system-wide changes — they are quite similar to the earlier large-scale curriculum development projects. The major differences seem to be: (1) an orientation towards the institutions of education and schooling, as social processes; (2) small budgets; (3) analysis of a wide repertoire of processes from curriculum to resource allocation; and (4) avoidance of the linearity of RDD (Bolam, 1982).

School improvement has thus neither a clear-cut and definite orientation towards specific or particular ways and means of effecting desirable innovations in schools nor does it specify any particular forms or modes of research and development. It is a kind of gathering together of the residue of the large-scale development programmes, and the alternatives and counter-programmes (eg action research) that they fostered.

In order to avoid the difficulties encountered by, and the very damaging cricitism of, the RDD-inspired movements, supporters of school improvement programmes in the 1980s will need to be ready with answers to several questions:

1. What is the character of the student learnings that school improvement programmes aim to change or foster?
2. How high do these learnings rate in priorities of public authorities and where they are not high what efforts are being made to influence those policies?
3. Of the several dimensions and processes of improvement commonly identified are there any that can claim priority, what do we know of their track records and how do they relate to one another (eg could school-based curriculum development provide a focus for school-based INSET and institutional self-evaluation)?
4. What kinds of research are most relevant to school improvement programmes and who should undertake it? How has research played a part in the design and initiation of school improvement programmes?
5. Is school improvement research primarily policy-oriented? evaluative? descriptive? If it is all of these what are the specific roles of the research?
6. What are we learning from school improvement programmes about the relationships of research to development?
7. What prospects do school improvement programmes have of achieving professional and public understanding and support?

8. What contribution, if any, can research make to determining values and criteria which are embedded in the concept of improvement?

These are very general questions which need to be applied differentially to specific programmes and there are others that might be asked. What is necessary, in the light of our experience of several decades of large-scale educational development and professional, public and political responses, is that sponsors and participants in the new wave of improvement programmes and in research in the customer-contractor mode do raise and answer these questions. Since improvement of any situation, in the sense of bringing about changes of a desirable and valuable kind, requires knowledge of that situation, some views about its dynamics, and an understanding of causal relations, research must have a crucial part to play, but research of what kind? Equally, we need to have aims and values to relate our assessment and interpretation of that situation, and any changes will involve people, their attitudes and relations (Pitman, 1981; Richardson, 1975; Rudduck, 1976).

'School improvement' as an aspiration by external groups, even when collaborating closely with personnel within the school, raises many questions, in which research, normative analysis, strategic planning, human relations and resource allocations will play a part. It is fair to conclude that the RDD model was not adequate (and probably was not intended to be) for handling these and related questions. Will current and recent moves towards programmes of school improvement fare better? The experience of the Schools Council is salutary since all of the trends in R & D and the issues thus far identified in this chapter are in some form exemplified in its 20-year history. What has been learnt from SC curriculum projects is a much bigger story than can be recounted here, but I can perhaps outline some of the most decisive changes insofar as they relate to changing perceptions of the role of research in curriculum development.

The Schools Council: rise and fall of RDD?

The Council was founded in 1964 amidst controversy, as Taylor points out in Chapter 5. Its political-administrative origins are demonstrated by the decision by the government of the day to abandon its own plan for an internal curriculum agency and to adopt instead the recommendation of the Sir John Lockwood Committee for a tripartite body, representing teachers' associations, local education authorities and the Department of Education and Science (Lockwood, 1964). With successive modifications, including revised constitutions, the Lockwood scheme lasted until 1984 when, due to the Government's unilateral withdrawal of funds (by then it shared funding with the Local Education Authorities), the Council collapsed.

The Council was destined to fulfil three functions as an educational R & D agency:

1. *The conduct of educational research.* The research function of SC
   was very clearly stated in its Constitution where one 'object' was
   enunciated: 'The object of the Schools Council shall be in the
   promotion of education by carrying out research into and keeping
   under review the curricula, teaching methods and examinations in
   schools, including the organisation of schools so far as it affects their
   curricula' (Schools Council, 1978).
2. SC was to serve as a widely *representative forum.* The structure and
   composition of the Council were designed — and redesigned — to
   facilitate discussions and debate and possibly resolution of national
   issues in curriculum and examinations. Its publications contain many
   examples of views about schooling, educational policies and social
   issues (but very few about 'whole' curriculum questions) and its
   examinations programmes, although generally abortive in respect of
   government acceptance of structural reform proposals, are a 20-year
   history of attempts to resolve fundamental defects in the public
   examinations system. As a forum, the Council was assuming an
   avowedly political role, as one of its first Joint Secretaries acknowledged (Caston, 1971).
3. Teacher representatives were always in a majority in the Council,
   and the Council saw itself as the guardian of *teacher autonomy* in
   the curriculum. Its one and only 'general principle', of the right of
   teachers to choose — or reject — whatever was proposed for the
   curriculum (including the Council's own proposals), was affirmed by
   the then Chairman Dame Muriel Stuart in 1970: the Council, she
   said, 'does not lay down what teachers must teach, but seeks to
   provide for them the choice of ideas, methods and even materials, so
   that teachers can exercise their professional freedom and responsibility' (Stuart, 1970).

We can find many examples of this principle, in the writings of the
Council's architect, Derek Morrell, in the teachers' centre movement, in
the frequent reiteration of the teacher's role in project design and development and, during the Council's final period following the 1978
Constitution, in the construction of programmes which aspired to provide
support and encouragement for activities directly arising from teacher-
defined needs and problems (Morrell, 1962; Schools Council, 1979).

For the purposes of this chapter there is no need to trace the working
out of these declared SC functions. Some examples are given by Taylor in
Chapter 5. We may note, however, two important sets of contradictions
which marked the Council's work from the start. First, the Council was
not in and of itself in a position to provide 'choice' for teachers. Since it
was but one agency in the business of materials production and other
aspects of curriculum, on this point it was at most *extending* the choice
available to schools. The constitutional principle of each school having the
fullest possible measure of responsibility for its own curriculum and the
curriculum and teaching methods being evolved by the school staff does
not in fact entail choice in any and all aspects of the curriculum. Thus

school-level curriculum making can include the adoption of a common curriculum framework, its adaptation to local circumstances and pupil needs, and the selection or adaptation of limited sets of externally devised materials. In practice, 'autonomy', 'choice' and 'variety' masked a proliferation of materials projects for which the Council for much of its life had no general strategies and no means of interrelating in a coherent general programme of development and reform. The difficulty of achieving such strategies in a large, diverse and politically active, national body cannot be ignored. Parallels in this respect, can be drawn with the National Institute of Education in the USA and in the relationship between the Australian CDC (a federal agency) and the State school system and their controlling governments and agencies.

In its own official statements about the style of research and development it was promoting, the Council frequently committed itself to a version of RDD, even though it lacked the capacity to follow through in the way the model requires. Thus, the curriculum development process was held to require the assembling of a team, perhaps an inter-disciplinary team of teachers, researchers, evaluators and administrators to:

1. study a body of practice and make a systematic review of relevant literature;
2. give a clear statement of aims (sometimes operationalized);
3. design materials in accordance with the aims;
4. test and modify materials in pilot schools;
5. diffuse materials through publication, publicity and in-service courses; and
6. evaluate: by testing to see whether aims had been achieved. (Nisbet, 1973, 1979)

As practised in the large-scale, centrally organized project usually located in a higher education institution which served as a national centre in association with the Council, this approach may seem to conform to Schon's concept of a centre-periphery model of change (Schon, 1971). However, we must bear in mind the Council's relatively small budgets (for a large and populous school system), the range and diversity of projects, the emergence of multiple-site projects in teachers' centres, and the participation, sometimes of very large numbers, of teachers in a problem-solving mode (Nisbet, 1973; Schools Council, 1974: 24; Wrigley, 1981). It would be a mistake to suppose that SC ever functioned as a single, homogeneous national centre beaming out the products of its research-grounded design and development projects and backing them with heavy funding for utilization and take-up. In its organization, it never could establish structures that would have made this possible; in research terms, it never built up a comprehensive, coherent set of projects from which development flowed inexorably into dissemination. The Council, or rather some of its officers, did, like other educational R & D agencies and funding bodies, seek out and back promising individuals whose ideas might subsequently prove fruitful.

The best example is Lawrence Stenhouse.

It would not be difficult, by sampling the variety of Schools Council projects, to produce examples of every one of the major forms of innovation strategy analysed in the standard texts on the subject. This array of styles and approaches could have given the Council excellent guidance for future action, had they ever been collectively and systematically analysed, as American development projects were by Havelock, Fullan, Berman and McLaughlin and others.

In spite of diversity in practice, the Council, in its earlier years, declared an adherence to RDD through its projects. The similarity of the declared SC mode to the classic American version of RDD is evident if we compare the Council's own formulation of how a project should function (see above) with the steps of RDD as outlined by one of its leading US exponents, R. N. Bush. Bush's steps are as follows: a team (usually interdisciplinary) assembles and undertakes

- needs assessment
- specification of objectives
- analysis of alternative strategies and treatments
- choice among alternatives in field situations
- continuing evaluation and refinement
- production
- dissemination and installation (Bush, 1976).

In both formulations of the strategy, it is to be noted that the testing and modification of experimental curricula are an essential step. Through the elaboration of this step as personnel were recruited to project teams to undertake it, the modern curriculum evaluation movement has emerged. We can find examples from curriculum development centres in many different parts of the world: the models transcended national and ideological considerations — for a while. So-called formative evaluation within the curriculum development projects became in the UK the principal mode of experience, training and subsequent professionalization of educational evaluators (Tawney, 1973, 1976; Harlen, 1978) just as, in the US, the condition of Title 1 of the Elementary and Secondary Education Act, that all projects be evaluated, was the largest single factor in the emergence of contemporary educational evaluation.

There can be no doubt that, in its early official statements on how curriculum projects would or should in general proceed, SC was formally adopting RDD as a strategy. But this is not quite how things worked out in practice. As already indicated, the Council did not see curriculum innovation as other than a partnership — a partnership of a political kind in reaching decisions and a partnership in which teachers could decide whether or not to use the materials produced: they were not merely the targets of skilful and well-funded dissemination campaigns but could, both within and outside the Council, introduce a quite different set of considerations. Consistency of approach was not possible and — as many said — not desirable either. Structurally, then, the Council could not adopt a uniform strategy and there are good reasons for supposing that its early avowal of RDD was not a thought out response to its own situation but a consequence of that train of events whereby the American initiative in curriculum reform of the 1950s was picked up by the Nuffield Foundation and then transferred to the Council. In addition to these considerations, a comment by Jack Wrigley, the Council's longest serving Director of Studies, shows that even the large-scale centrally organized project did not always function in the way to be expected from the RDD model: 'In some projects the development would begin first based upon hunches, ideas, ideals, and the thoughts of creative people ... such a development would throw up problems which might themselves call for careful research so that in some cases we would begin with the development aspect and eventually carry out research projects.' (Wrigley, 1981). In his chapter, Taylor shows how, out of this blurring of 'research' and 'development', the Council played down its significance in research funding.

Wrigley suggested that, in education, research and development were never linear but always interactive, and that teachers and researchers intermingled in SC development teams (Wrigley, 1973a, b). This interpretation is borne out in an early publication where, after discussing plans for basic and very wide ranging research needed *before* full five-year (post-Newsom) courses of secondary education were introduced, the Council says that development work must begin 'at once, on the basis that the results of research and enquiry will progressively inform and refine the development work' (Schools Council, 1968).

A further set of considerations, to prove crucial in leading the Council away from the notion of the large-scale central project, quickly emerged within the experience of some of the project teams. The best known but by no means the only one of these teams to cast doubt upon the model was Lawrence Stenhouse's Humanities Curriculum Project (Stenhouse, 1975). Stenhouse's work was especially significant in challenging at least three of the postulates of RDD:

1. that substantial, specialist research precedes a major phase of development;
2. that the proper outcome of a curriculum project is a research-based product which should be disseminated and installed; and
3. that teachers can be appropriately viewed as clients and recipients (Skilbeck, 1983).

Despite the verbal and at times ideological promulgation of RDD, in the UK setting it is difficult to find examples of large-scale curriculum projects where there is at the beginning a substantial research phase out of which emerges a design which ultimately provides a product for widespread dissemination. This is true of educational R & D as a whole, not only of the Schools Council's activities. Even where one can point to such examples (notably in secondary science projects) a very substantial part of the research component of the project is to be found in the evaluation phase where not only are the materials assessed but the whole activity of the project is brought under review. Several of the best known and most interesting researches arising from the whole curriculum development movement are of this type (Shipman, 1974).

It is clear then that, despite its early proclamation of adherence to a RDD strategy, the SC approach to curriculum development was in practice more diverse than this and that research played a variety of roles, by no means all of them expert and specialist. This has been the case generally in curriculum development agencies. A good example is Scotland's Consultative Committee on the Curriculum where the Inspectorate plays a leading role in sponsoring, coordinating and supporting action programmes which usually have a defined research component but not a dominating research motif, or where working parties and action groups plan and implement studies, perhaps calling on academics and researchers to perform particular tasks within them (see Chapter 13).

Most of the Schools Council's curriculum projects were brought to a kind of culmination in trialled and evaluated material products intended for classroom use. If the research role in their production was problematic, the dissemination one was no less so. It was widely believed both inside and outside the Council that some use by schools of their products was desirable, notwithstanding the principle of unfettered teacher choice.

It was exceedingly difficult for the Council to claim substantial public funding for its projects whilst ostensibly remaining indifferent to their impact in schools under the principle of teacher choice. Such indifference was a real factor insofar as it inhibited a hardheaded analysis of just what kind of response to its initiatives would have satisfied the Council. When in 1975, for example, the Programme Committee reviewed achievements in curriculum R & D it concluded that despite much good work many projects were still 'insufficiently used'. It complained that it had 'little authentic information about how the Council's projects actually come to the notice of teachers, and are considered, and are adopted or rejected by them' (Schools Council, 1975). Nevertheless, the Council resolved only to establish 'more effective' ways of meeting the needs of schools — it did not declare as a high priority the determination of the criteria by which its own success or otherwise in R & D were to be assessed. Existing projects, numbering some 160, were to be more vigorously disseminated but neither quantitative nor qualitative guidelines or timelines were set.

As early as 1970-71 the Council was turning its attention to dissemination and the relationship of its work to in-service teacher education. A working party on dissemination was set up by the Programme Committee in 1972, reporting in October 1977. In addition to the spread of teachers' centres (where inter alia Council materials were presented and displayed) several studies on dissemination were funded, regional centres and a national information service featuring Council activities were established and the Council's major general study of dissemination, the Impact and Take-Up project, was commenced. Moreover, evaluation studies associated with particular projects were showing up weaknesses in the design of projects and pointing to the conditions that needed to be satisfied if projects were to have an effect on teaching. In the latter part of the 1970s, in the SC as elsewhere in the educational world, accountability pressure led to an even closer interest in dissemination.

From the foregoing, however, it may be seen that three rather different kinds of problems were emerging for a dissemination strategy. First, by declaring as an article of faith the teacher's right to choose, the Council could scarcely go beyond a dissemination strategy that brought its products and ideas to the notice and attention of teachers. Uptake would always remain an unambiguous matter in such a situation.

Second, by never declaring or attempting to define conditions for success for its projects and programmes, the Council left it open to its critics to condemn a 'lack of success' in dissemination and uptake. There were not, as in industry, commercial criteria to refer to, nor were other criteria available, except somewhat vague (and certainly not agreed) qualitative standards referring to the 'educational value' of project materials or the processes whereby they were created. Much use was made of anecdotal evidence, committee or staff opinions and a tacit understanding of what is 'educationally sound'.

The Council's concern to know who was using its products was focused, in the mid 1970s, by the Impact and Take-Up project. The authors of the project's three reports concentrated on a narrow definition of materials take-up (not on the response of the educational system to a new approach to curriculum renewal). They argued that the large project strategy had been generally successful, but by this time the Council's own reluctance or inability to declare how it wished its projects to be judged had proved a serious disadvantage in the public and political debate. There are other reasons, too, to suppose that even before Impact and Take-Up the Council had lost the confidence of its major sponsor, the DES (Lawton, 1980: 74-76).

A third point, which relates generally to the large project-based approach to curriculum development and deserves fuller treatment than is possible here, is that the 'dissemination problem' is a function of the project itself.

The curriculum development project, as we have experienced it over some three decades, has made many assumptions which we must now question. These relate to such items as: how to define a need or task to which development efforts are to be addressed; whether a linear, chronological progression of episodes of research, development, trialling, evaluation, rewriting, and disseminating captures the essence of educational processes and institutions; and the nature of professional choice and decision making in the curriculum.

It is quite possible for an interventionist strategy to produce insoluble problems for itself and it is my contention that that is precisely what the combination of a linear concept of RDD and the curriculum development project team has produced. By setting as a goal the production of materials — or procedures — for widespread dissemination to a large and diverse educational service where power, authority and resources are widely diffused, and where the development agency is itself grossly underfunded in relation to the scale of the task, curriculum developers in a very real sense have created the problem of dissemination which, in recent years, they have been at some pains to try to resolve. More attention to and more funds for dissemination, even if they could be procured, in these circumstances may simply result in a highlighting of the fundamental weaknesses of the strategy. For reasons already given the issue of 'implementation' of projects *could not* be resolved. Once the decision had been taken to produce materials or procedures for adoption by others, rated as free choosing professionals, a dissemination problem was born. In a market system this then becomes a challenge to promotions and sales staff. But curriculum agencies like SC are not in a market system. The Council's response to its own difficulties, insofar as it incorporated a new concern for dissemination, was unlikely to prove satisfactory and events of the late 1970s showed this to be the case. However, heightened dissemination activity was only one strand. The others were the reconstitution of the Council (which falls outside the purview of this chapter) and the move 'from projects to programmes'.

Review, evaluate, develop: an alternative strategy?

In 1978, as Taylor points out in Chapter 5, a major change occurred in the SC when, following a lengthy review and self-evaluation, a new Constitution was adopted. From this review and through the new committees there emerged, alongside the projects, a mode of work claimed to be very different from what had preceded it. Space does not permit an appraisal of this claim in any detail. Since strategies involve people, we must not overlook a significant change in personnel. In its last years, the Council had in position of Chairman, Secretary and Deputy Secretary, three local education authority officials. The so-called programme phase — its last as events turned out — of SC was summed up by the outgoing chairman, Sir Alex Smith, in an oblique but telling reference to the 'dissemination crisis': 'Perhaps the Council, in more of its work, should be aiming less at final publication and concentrating more on processes of involvement and feedback' (Tomlinson, 1978). In the same speech the Chairman made a revealing comment about where he perceived the Council's emphasis in the past to have lain: 'Should the Council be primarily a research and development funding body, leaving implementation entirely to others — or should it explore the implications of its work and follow through the consequences?' (ibid: 4). These remarks, despite capturing the essence of one of the crucial problems in the whole RDD approach, do not clearly point towards anything dramatically different. They are indicative of a widespread belief in curriculum R & D in the late 1970s: something had gone wrong with the strategies and styles of the two previous decades; alternatives were needed; nothing clear and definite seemed to have emerged; it was time not only for reappraisal but for new exploratory ventures, incorporating the experience of earlier work and picking up on what might seem to be practical alternatives to RDD and the centralized project team (Short, 1983; Tomlinson, 1981). In the English experience, as in that of several other countries that had been active in curriculum development, what was available included:

1. local development groups and units with strong teacher and local education authority adviser involvement;
2. a diversity of institutions, agencies and groups with interest and experience in curriculum development;
3. the philosophies of school-based curriculum development and INSET and of localized action research.
4. a style of negotiated agreements in evaluation and development under a general rubric of democratic decision making;
5. a wide and varied set of individual curriculum development projects which could be quarried for ideas and promising practices; and
6. critiques and analyses of strategies of curriculum development.

In England and Wales, at about the same time as the Council was undergoing a metamorphosis, another style of curriculum R & D was emerging, through official, central government sponsorship. By the agency of Her Majesty's Inspectorate and officials in the Department of Education and Science three fundamental changes occurred. The changes in mode of sponsorships, combined with the decline of the large development project model, the continued vitality of small-scale, unsponsored, teacher-centred development, and the developments already referred to in SC, have brought us to a new era of curriculum R & D. The changes at the level of official, government sponsorship that I have in mind are, first, the Inspectorate's own style of curriculum research, through a succession of reviews and reports on curriculum practice in the schools; second, the goverment's production of a general policy, outlining a framework for the whole curriculum; third, the emergence of within-school and within-local-education-authority reviews (Clift, 1982; Department of Education and Science 1981a, b; Skilbeck, 1982, 1984b). The last of these has to be seen alongside the movements, independent of central government, of institutional self-evaluation, teachers as researchers and action research which are discussed in other chapters.

Let us see, in conclusion, what the oscillations in curriculum R & D over three decades and through the interventionist and responsive strategies adopted by national agencies have yielded us by way of promising modes for the future. Although, in these concluding remarks, I cannot re-open the question of the role of government in all this, there can be no doubt that any discussion of changing perspectives in educational R & D, in the curriculum field, that omits this role will be seriously handicapped. The first point, then, is that government is not only the chief sponsor and the main source of funds but increasingly a direct factor in the styles and modes of research and development that are adopted. Curriculum R & D has suffered a great deal from its inadequate relations with government, its limited grasp of political processes and its tendency to define goals and procedures as if they were very largely autonomous educational entities. As against this and especially during the past decade, the curriculum development movement has shown great sensitivity to local structures and issues, building up a comprehensive apparatus ('networks') of local and regional institutions and relationships. The attempt to consolidate all this in the SC in the post-1978 programmes of work was frustrated by the central government's abandonment of the Council at a crucial stage in the evolution of the new strategies and by the lengthy hiatus between the run-down of SC and the establishment of new, separate agencies for curriculum development and examinations (which are themselves both government sponsored and centralized).

Second, the curriculum development movement, in Britain and in its central agency, SC, as in other countries, has been equivocal and ambiguous in its stance towards research and has never succeeded in resolving some quite basic questions about the relationship of research to development. On the other hand it is through the working out of Council-type projects that most of the significant curriculum research in this country has been undertaken. This is also the case in several other countries, although the situation is now changing as governments sponsor more work of their own choosing. A research platform, evident in evalua-tion research, for example, has been provided. It has potential, too, for future development processes. The most interesting newer (or revived) styles of educational research, such as naturalistic methods, case study, localized action research and participatory R & D, are all a direct outcome of curriculum projects.

Third, despite the critical onslaughts, the RDD model has not been shown to have no further uses in curriculum development. However, its hypostatizing as a linear sequence of discrete activities, has been shown to be inappropriate and its application has proved an unsatisfactory means of effecting change on the scale and of the type thought to be needed.

The analysis of RDD into a large number of distinct activities, the incorporation into that analysis of a study of professional roles and decision-making processes in education, of the changing circumstances in school and local education authority curriculum reviews and of the growing public interest in educational innovation can, perhaps, yield up for the future another style of R & D in curriculum and in education generally. This style I have characterized as review, evaluate, develop, a natural outgrowth of school-based curriculum development, action research and other curriculum initiatives of the 1960s and 1970s (OECD/ CERI, 1975; Skilbeck 1984b). 'Review' is a normal professional, reflective, stock-taking activity; 'evaluate' requires the determination of criteria, goals, and processes; and 'develop' constitutes a series of responsive actions undertaken to effect desirable (ie criteria-directed) changes. Widespread participation — by parents, community and students as well as teachers — opens RED up as a public enterprise with strong professional structures. RED activities can be small-scale or nation-wide and may themselves constitute a kind of research and embody research findings. From a curriculum perspective, RED will still be defective as long as it evades the issue of what is to be taught and learnt in schools. The curriculum development movement has given a partial answer. I have suggested elsewhere (Skilbeck, 1984b) that if we accept the school as the ultimate curriculum-making body we can greatly strengthen its hand — and its credibility — by adopting a national framework which includes generally agreed aims, criteria — and a broadly defined core curriculum. Research in curriculum needs to be school-focused and in some respects school-based, but this does not preclude the continued use of large-scale R & D of which the RDD model, for all its limitations and adaptations in practice has given us useful experience.

References

Atkin, J M (1979) Education accountability in the United States *Educational Analysis* 1 1

Basic Studies National Field Task Force (1974) *Final Report and Recommendations* US Department of Health, Education and Welfare: Washington, DC

Berman, P and McLaughlin, M (1975) *Federal Programs Supporting Educational Change* Vol IV *The Findings in Review* Rand Corporation: Santa Monica, California

Bestor, A E (1953) *Educational Wastelands* University of Illinois Press: Champaign-Urbana

Black Papers 1-5 (1969-77):
    Cox, C B and Dyson, A E (1969) *Fight for Education* The Critical Quarterly Society
    Cox, C B and Dyson, A E (1969) *The Crisis in Education* The Critical Quarterly Society
    Cox, C B and Dyson, A E (1970) *Goodbye Mr. Short* The Critical Quarterly Society
    Cox, C B and Boyson, R (1975) *The Fight for Education* Dent: London
    Cox, C B and Boyson, R (1977) *Black Paper 5* Temple Smith: London

Bolam, R (1982) *Strategies for School Improvement: a Report for OECD* OECD/CERI: Paris (mimeo)

Bush, R N (1976) *Educational Research and Development: the Next Decade* Occasional Paper No 11 Stanford Center for Research and Development in Teaching: Stanford, California

Butcher, H J and Pont H B eds (1973) *Educational Research in Britain 2* University of London Press: London

Callahan, R E (1962) *Education and the Cult of Efficiency* Chicago University Press: Chicago

Carr, W (1983) Can educational research be scientific? *Journal of Philosophy of Education* 17 1:35-43

Caston, G (1971) The Schools Council in context *Journal of Curriculum Studies* III 1

Clift, P (1982) LEA schemes for school self-evaluation *Educational Research* 24 4: 262-71

Coleman, J S, Campbell, E Q, Hobson, C J, McPartland, J, Wood, A M, Weinfield, F D and York, R L (1966) *Equality of Educational Opportunity* Department of

Health, Education and Welfare, Washington, DC

Connell, W F (1980) *A History of Education in the Twentieth Century World* Canberra. Curriculum Development Centre

Department of Education and Science (1981a) *The School Curriculum* Her Majesty's Stationery Office: London

Department of Education and Science (1981b) *Curriculum 11-16: a review of progress* Her Majesty's Stationery Office: London

Dockrell, W B and Hamilton, D eds (1980) *Rethinking Educational Research* Hodder and Stoughton: London

Emrick, J A and Peterson, S M (1978) *A Synthesis of Findings Across Five Recent Studies in Educational Dissemination and Change* Far West Educational Laboratory: San Francisco

Farrar, E, Desanctis, J E and Cohen, D K (1980) Views from below: implementation research in education *Teachers College Record* 82 1:77-100

Fullan, M (1982) *The Meaning of Educational Change* Teachers College Press: New York

Fullan, M (1983) Evaluating program implementation: what can be learned from follow through *Curriculum Inquiry* 13 2:215-27

Halsey, A H (1972) *Educational Priority* Vol 1 Her Majesty's Stationery Office: London

Harlen, W ed (1978) *Evaluation and the Teachers' Role* Macmillan Educational for the Schools Council: London

Havelock, R (1971a) *Innovations in Education: Strategies and Tactics* Institute for Social Research University of Michigan: Ann Arbor Michigan, (mimeo)

Havelock, R (1971b) The utilization of educational research and development *British Journal of Educational Technology* 2 2:84-98

Kemmis, S et al (1981) *The Action Research Planner* Deakin University Press: Geelong, Victoria

Lacey, C and Lawton, D eds (1981) *Issues in Evaluation and Accountability* Methuen: London

Lawton, D (1980) *The Politics of the School Curriculum* Routledge and Kegan Paul: London

Lockwood, J (1964) *Report of the Working Party on the Schools' Curricula and Examinations* Her Majesty's Stationery Office: London

Louis, K and Rosenblum, S (1981) *Linking R and D with Schools: a Program and its Implications for Dissemination* National Institute of Education: Washington

Morrell, D H (1982) The freedom of the teacher in relation to research and development work in the area of curriculum and examinations *Educational Research* 5 2:85-89

Nisbet, J (1973) *The Schools Council* Case Studies of Central Institutions for Educational Change OECD/CERI: Paris

Nisbet, J (1979) An international perspective in Ramsay, P (1979)

Nisbet, J (1981) Educational research and educational practice in Simon, B and Taylor, W eds (1981)

Nisbet, J and Broadfoot, P (1980) *The Impact of Research on Policy and Practice in Education* The University Press: Aberdeen

OECD/CERI (1975) *Handbook on Curriculum Development* OECD/CERI: Paris

OECD/CERI (1983) *International School Improvement Progress Report* OECD/CERI: Paris, (mimeo)

Oldham, G (1982) *The Future of Research* Society for Research in Higher Education: Guildford, Surrey

Pile, W (1976) in *House of Commons 10th Report from the Expenditure Committee* Her Majesty's Stationery Office: London

Pitman, A (1981) The necessary distortion of disseminated innovations *Journal of Curriculum Studies* 13 3: 253-56

Ramsey, P ed (1979) *Issues in Curriculum Development* Institute of Education Auckland: New Zealand

Rhine, R ed (1981) *Making Schools More Effective: New Directions from Follow Through* Academic Press: New York

Richardson, E (1975) *Authority and Organization in the Secondary School* Macmillan Educational: London

Rothschild, Lord (1971 and 1972) The Organisation and Management of Government Research and Development (Cmd 4814). A Framework for Government Research and Development (Cmd 5046) Her Majesty's Stationery Office: London

Rothschild, Lord (1982) *An Enquiry into the SSRC* Her Majesty's Stationery Office: London

Rudduck, J (1976) *Dissemination of Innovation: the Humanities Curriculum Project* Evans/Methuen for the Schools Council: London

Schon, D (1971) *Beyond the Stable State* Penguin Books: Harmondsworth, Middlesex

Schools Council (1968) *The First Three Years 1964-67* Her Majesty's Stationery Office: London

Schools Council (1974) *Schools Council: the First Ten Years 1964-1974* The Council: London

Schools Council (1975) Minutes of Programme Committee (SC 75/558)

Schools Council (1978) *Constitution* The Council: London

Schools Council (1979) *Schools Council Principles and Programmes* The Council: London

Schwab, J J (1969) The practical: a language for curriculum *School Review* Nov 1-23

Shipman, M (1974) *Inside a Curriculum Project* Methuen: London

Short, E C (1983) The forms and use of alternative curriculum development strategies *Curriculum Inquiry* 13 1:43-64

Simon, B and Taylor, W eds (1981) *Education in the Eighties* Batsford: London

Simons, H (1981) Process evaluation in schools in Lacey, C and Lawton, D eds (1981)

Skilbeck, M (1981) Curriculum issues in Australia 1970-1990 *Compare* II 1:59-76

Skilbeck, M (1982) *Curriculum Development* APEID Occasional Paper No 9 UNESCO: Bangkok

Skilbeck, M (1982) *A Core Curriculum for the Common School* University of London Institute of Education: London

Skilbeck, M (1983) Lawrence Stenhouse: research methodology *British Educational Research Journal* 9 1:11-20

Skilbeck, M ed (1984a) *Evaluating the Curriculum* Hodder and Stoughton: London

Skilbeck, M (1984b) *School Based Curriculum Development* Harper and Row: London

Steadman, S et al (1978-81) *Reports to the Schools Council on Impact and Take-Up* The Council: London

Stenhouse, L (1975) *An Introduction to Curriculum Research and Development* Heinemann: London

Stuart, Dame Muriel (1970) The Schools Council: a mechanism for change *School and Innovation 1870-1970* Supplement to *Dialogue* (Feb) The Council: London

Tamir, P and Amir, R (1981) Retrospective curriculum evaluation: an approach to the evaluation of long term effects *Curriculum Inquiry* 11 3:259-78

Tawney, D ed (1973) *Evaluation in Curriculum Development: Twelve Case Studies* Macmillan: London

Tawney, D ed (1976) *Curriculum Evaluation Today* Macmillan: London

Tomlinson, J (1978) *Report of the Review Body: Chairman's Statements to Schools Council Governing Council* GC Minutes 1/78

Tomlinson, J (1981) *The Schools Council: a Chairman's Salute and Envoi* Address to British Association for the Advancement of Science The Schools Council: London

UNESCO (1983) *Final Report of Eighth Regional Consultation Meeting on the Asian Programme of Educational Innovation for Development* UNESCO: Bangkok

White, J P (1969) The curriculum mongers: education in reverse *New Society* 6 March

White, J P (1983) *The Aims of Education Revisited* Routledge and Kegan Paul: London

Wrigley, J (1973a) The Schools Council *in* Butcher, H J and Pont H B *eds* (1973)

Wrigley, J (1973b) Lecture 1 *A breakthrough in curriculum development — far reaching innovations by the Schools Council* University of Melbourne: Melbourne (mimeo)

Wrigley, J (1981) *Confessions of a Curriculum Man* Jack Kerr Lecture University of Leicester School of Education: Leicester (mimeo)

20. Case study

Robert E. Stake

Summary: Case study is becoming more widely accepted as a research approach. Defined as the study of a single case or bounded system, it observes naturalistically and interprets higher-order interrelations within the observed data. Results are generalizable in that the information given allows readers to decide whether the case is similar to theirs. Case study can and should be rigorous. Whereas experimental design has checks built into its methods, in case study the responsibility lies more with the researcher. While other styles of research aim to elicit general relationships, case study explores the context of individual instances.

Within the domain of educational research, perhaps nothing recently has changed as much as the acceptability of case study. In contrast to the situation just ten years ago, descriptive materials on individual cases now are well received, not just as illustrative examples but as a principal vehicle of observation and analysis.

The new popularity seems partly a matter of taste, perhaps a fad. But there are reasons why sponsors and consumers of research, as well as practitioners, restored respectability to case study, and reasons why this form of study offers something unique and potentially useful, even while problematic.

Disappointment

Since the mid 1950s a social activism has been alive throughout the world. It was stimulated by United Nations efforts and world trade, but was influenced probably even more by new communication sophistications. The new 'media' permitted every governor to see into every ghetto and village, and permitted every resident there to behold the many moves of government. To an almost Orwellian degree, everybody's business became everybody's business.

The ideological and political response of ministries of education, reflecting an enthusiasm similar to that of American schoolmasters a generation earlier, was to enlist the aid of educational research and technology (Travers, 1983). New curricula, pedagogies, pupil personnel services, and the like would bring great economic and social benefit. Researchers were funded to find those general explanations of learning that permitted uniform attacks on ignorance and unreadiness.

It did not work. Laws of learning could be shown valid in the abstract and en masse, but were seldom indicative of factors determining what would happen in the particular classroom (Hamilton, 1981). Slow learners remained slow, the misbehaving misbehaved. The governors and commissioners of education lost their enthusiasm too, not for the technology of mass education, but for the provision of a handsome budget for formal research.

Partly in reaction to disappointing experiments and surveys, civic and educational leaders looked around for alternative ways of understanding educational problems. Disregarded earlier for looseness and subjectivity, the case study seemed worthy of new attention. Perhaps oversold on education as a science, the world swung somewhat more again toward research as historical record (Stenhouse, 1977). Thus there was a move from grand theory to grounded theory (Glaser and Strauss, 1967) and from explanation of underlying forces to description of cases (von Wright, 1971), a move backward, some would say, from a Galilean to an Aristotelian view.

The case

Case study is the study of a single case — whether simple and specific, such as Miss Valdez, last year's teacher of geography, or abstract and complex, such as all the legislation in Nordic countries to keep small rural schools open. It is a case, a bounded system. The case is usually an entity of intrinsic interest, not merely a sample from which to learn about the population. It is similar to others, yet distinct, and each of the cases is to be noted for a certain unity within, a certain systemic character (Goode and Hatt, 1952). When it is time to understand a particular case, not just to compare it to others or to know the collective, we design a case study.

In some discussions, case study has been presumed identical to naturalistic enquiry. Naturalistic research is the study of objects in their own environment, with a *design* relatively free of intervention or control. This work is often organized around issues of interest to lay people (as opposed to specialists) and perhaps reported in ordinary (rather than technical) language. Some case studies are naturalistic, others are not. A researcher's report of observations of a school board, covering what has been important to the board, is usually naturalistic, whereas the school psychologist's report of special tests undertaken by a child is a case study, formal (abstract, discipline-based) rather than naturalistic. Other case studies not usually naturalistic are medical case histories, so-called 'n=1 studies', biographies, many policy studies and some institutional research. Many educational case studies are naturalistic, but not all; many naturalistic studies are not case studies because they do not concentrate on a particular case.

Contextuality

These distinctions are important epistemologically. Case study researchers seek to learn a great deal about a single case, examining events and measurements, trying to fit them all together. Sometimes they seek *grand* understanding, a generalization, one that perhaps has not emerged from studying many cases all at once. Our views of general truth fade off to the left into circumstantial uniqueness, but also to the right, into the obscurity of mass representations. The case study worker works harder to avoid the latter.

Case study data have been called 'thick data', not necessarily stacked high, but 'thick like spaghetti', highly interconnected (Geertz, 1973). In the language of statistical analysis, the higher-order interactions are thought worthy of study. In their search for grand generalization, other researchers hope to work free of complicating interaction effects, contextuality, the situation. The case study researcher, particularly the naturalistic case researcher, appreciates the milieu (Parlett and Dearden, 1977) and anticipates that critical understandings will depend on interactions between figure and ground (Wehlage, 1981). For example, MacDonald *et al* (1982: 139), noted Juliana, a teacher, admonishing the whole class: 'There's no Spanish speaking in here.' 'I just can't help it', answered one of the girls, giggling.

Each case, of course, is embedded in historical, social, political, and other contexts. The social context is often pre-emptive. The lesson may be grammar, but viewers record who misbehaves and who does the work. Observations of curricular or philosophical issues may require extraordinary preparation to carry the observers' attention beyond the social processes before them. Of course, case study need not rely primarily on interpersonal methods or phenomena.

Generalizability

As school administrators and government officials lost patience with the educational researchers' quest for grand generalization, they increasingly supported evaluation studies of national-programme demonstrations — then became discouraged there too. Lee Cronbach has pointed out (1982) that most programme evaluation studies should be thought of as case studies. Evaluation researchers hope to generalize to other cases, but cannot 'control' the countless programme or contextual features so as to learn which are vital and which not. Programme evaluation studies frequently identify conditions under which a programme failed or succeeded. We often draw causal inference, eg 'Without a coordinator to follow-up subsequent classroom practice, these in-service training results are not enduring.' But even the best studies do not yield functional equations identifying zones or gradients of generalizability. Such a sophisticated technology is not available to the programme developer.

Most evaluation designers have continued to rely on an inference model whereby samples, even of size one, are studied in order to refine general rules, in the hope of guiding the management of cases belonging to the same population. An alternative inference model is implicit in case literature. The researcher optimizes reader opportunity to relate the case described directly to their own cases, to infer particularistic understandings not necessarily mediated by general rules (Polanyi, 1958), eg 'Perhaps *our* coordinator should do more "follow-up".' If there is epistemological reference to populations at all, it is to that collection of cases with which *the reader* is already acquainted, rather than to a population formally established by the researcher. Stake (1978) has called the generalizations 'naturalistic', contrasting them in form and substance to the formal generalizations emphasized in statistical inference.

A researcher who relies on statistical inference to identify generalizations for the management of education usually tries to anticipate key independent variables, those that consistently co-vary with criterion variables. A researcher who tries to promote reader-made naturalistic generalizations usually tries to provide the elaborate information on which readers decide the extent to which the researcher's case is similar to (and thus likely to be instructive about) theirs. The pursuit of contextuality then is not only for consideration of interactions but also for clarification of possible use.

There is a political aspect to this choice. Research aimed at generating grand generalization increases the authority of and dependence upon the specialist. Case research aimed at enabling users to increase understanding through naturalistic generalization offers a greater possibility of facilitating the autonomy and sense of responsibility of the practitioner. Epistemologically again, with case study the researcher may be attempting to provide information that facilitates the reader's own analysis more than to deliver statements of generalization (Walker, 1980).

One of the objections to case study is often voiced in the question, 'But is this case typical?' (Of course it only makes sense to talk about typicality if a population, a reference group, is agreed upon.) It is contended by Kemmis (1980) and others that understanding the general can often be enhanced by studying the atypical. The atypical can alert us to variables or happenings that we regularly overlook. And the atypical case long-watched may inform us better than briefly-watched more typical cases. Our philosophy of science fails to tell us how much to expect complex social processes to be correlated with the demographic characteristics by which we usually define typicality. For demographic representation a typical case needs to be studied. For problem solving, typicality may be of relatively small importance. Of course we usually would like to know how similar this case is to others.

Rigour

It is often supposed that there is artistry but little discipline to case study, as if neither rules nor preparation were needed. Accomplished ethnographers, historians, and journalists of course have both rigour and routine. True, the rules and processes are not as accessible to newcomers or critics as we would like. As illustrated below, methodological improvement often can be sought in the foci of study, in the interpretations of observations, and in the validation of findings.

The boundaries that define the bounded system (the case) are only sometimes indicative of the foci of the study. Many forces pry into the researcher's agenda of issues (Smith, 1981). Time and costs demand delimitation. Rigour requires iterative, integrated choices, only some of which are identified here.

The terms 'etic' and 'emic' are often used to identify the conceptual structure: etic issues being those brought in by and belonging to the research community or other outsiders and emic issues being those that emerge from the study or belong to the case. An etic issue in Howard Becker's *Boys in White* (1961) was the orientation of medical school to the teaching of science; an emic issue was the social and administrative constraint that never really allowed the medical student to assume primary responsibility for care of a patient.

These issues, preordinate or emergent, are essential to the development of rigorous studies. A capability for recognizing data pertinent to chosen issues obviously depends on experience in the field and acquaintance with specialized writings, ie on preparation. In emic studies especially, the issues are reworked in successive refinement (Dewey, 1938) or progressive focusing. As in all educational research, the case researcher is given great leeway in deciding what questions are worthy of study.

Interpretation

In all research, the interpretation of collected observations is problematic, but especially so with case study, and more especially so with naturalistic case study. Content analysis (Andre, 1983) will often be invoked to convert qualitative data into quantitative, particularly as data holdings overflow, but the uniqueness and contextuality of case data may be quickly lost.

Particularly when the researcher is already a recognized authority, the opportunity to advance personal views is great, and the external checks against it are weak. With little obligation to declare issues and criteria in advance, with little demand for operational definition, and with no effective way of obligating interpretations to be submitted to critical review, the case study can easily become a minstrel's song.

But subjectivity and especially disciplined criticism (Lakatos and Musgrave, 1970) are sometimes the power of educational case study.

Processes not anticipated can be discovered; the full intuitive and rational powers of the researcher can be brought directly to bear on phenomena. The report is recognized not as veridical representation of reality but as interaction — hopefully a meaningful, useful and rich interaction — between observer and observed, a 'constructed' reality.

Validity

It is possible for case research to be rigorous, but the initiative is largely that of the researcher, not that of the research community. The checks and balances of random sampling and double blind treatments are absent; often instruments are not standardized and validated. Missing are the longer-term purges of publication and review in the professional literature — case reports are seldom suitable for refereed journals. Mainly available are the 'techniques' of triangulation (Denzin, 1978), those various ways of cautiously looking again and again, plus the commitment to seek deliberately to disconfirm one's own interpretations. Negotiating drafts with key actors is more than a courtesy; it becomes essential to accuracy and completeness (Rist, 1981). Lacking fixed model and coefficient, the able case researcher indicates the validity of the report by giving an elaborate account of how he/she carried out the study.

As with tests, the validity of case study depends on the use to which it is put. For representation of a case of intrinsic interest, the researcher assumes the primary burden for selecting appropriate descriptors and writing valid interpretations. For building theory, the casework would be found by scholars to have a different validity. (Much of the literature on social science field methods reflects this aspiration. For other aims these methods ought not automatically to be considered the best.) For contributing to a reader's vicarious experience and readiness for decision making, the validation burden is shared with readers, all dependent on what the researcher tells about context and method, each having to infer the quality of contributions to their own interpretations.

Case study reporting commonly features *vignettes* to illustrate key issues or moments. Vignettes are powerful explanatory devices, but they overstate. These illustrative examples are selected not only because they capture a certain essence, but because they arrest attention. They have a power that moves even the steadfast rationalist. When Stake *et al* (1976) finished their massive collection of science teaching case studies for the National Science Foundation, the director of that agency was debriefed. He responded with a vignette illustrating how science was taught in his daughter's classroom. And now *this* vignette has repeatedly been used to indicate the power and pervasiveness of vignettes. Of course they are too facile, too easily accepted (or rejected), denying the complexity of the situation, partially undoing the major justification for case study. They are essential to our reports, but if not carefully circumscribed they constitute threat to the validity of our study.

Common problems

Two additional problems of case study are cost and difficulty of training. For most applied research, the *time* and *cost* of doing proper ethnographic case studies* are prohibitive, and even the short-term observations (derided by Rist, 1980, as 'blitzkreig studies') often cost-out at more than $1000 per day on site. It is reasonable to suppose some sponsors will look for researchers who already intend doing such a study, who will contribute time, student help, and their own institution's resources to the project.

As for training, courses on case study research have emerged at graduate schools of education. Issue identification, observation and interview skills, gaining access, coding and winnowing, ethical questions, all are brought up. But scholarship and experience are needed as much as technical skill. The demands of case research are sometimes incompatible with the demands of dissertation research, especially the quest for generalizability and theory-building. Also, good fieldwork requires the most able researchers be in-the-field making observations, thus permitting some opportunity for apprenticing, but not for large numbers of researchers-in-training. Asked how to go about training case researchers, Arne Trankell expressed doubt that one should offer to do so (personal communication, 1973).

Musing on reasons not to do case studies, Rob Walker (1981) cited the inevitable *personalization*. He noted that case ethic calls for penetrating the facades and ruses of bureaucracies — set up for good reason: to avoid disabling conflicts and to by-pass immovable obstacles. The good of their enterprise, and its clients, may or may not be served by the investigative researcher. The case study researcher is a small but sometimes important part of 'the media' which compromise everyone's privacy. But David Jenkins (1980) reminded us that protection of personal feelings may not justify perpetuation of social injury due to information denied.

A few who know well the promise of case study research, and its price, conclude that, in the aggregate there is more of hurt (or nuisance) than help (Miles and Huberman, 1984). Others increasingly see more of help.

The history of case research is long, yet its explicated method remains immature. Its assurances of validity do not match its potential for embracing thematic and contextual complexities. But the choice to do or not to do case study, as indicated at the outset, is more an epistemological than a methodological choice. If educational research can satisfy its patrons' 'need to know' by describing formal relationships among variables, by presenting generalizations and theory, then it need seldom confront the problematics of case study. But if they need to know about the complexity and contextuality of individual cases, then case study is necessary.

*As Wolcott, 1975, made clear, most naturalistic case studies are not ethnographies.

References

Andre, M E D A (1983) Use of content analysis in educational evaluation: doing prose analysis *Discourse* **4** 1

Becker, H S (1961) *Boys in White* University of Chicago Press: Chicago

Cronbach, L J (1982) *Designing Evaluations of Educational and Social Programs* Jossey-Bass

Dalin, P (1976) *Guidelines for Case Studies* IMTEC, University of Oslo (mimeo)

Denzin, N K (1978) *The Research Act* McGraw-Hill: New York

Dewey, J (1938) *Logic: The Theory of Inquiry* New York

Geertz, C (1973) *The Interpretation of Cultures* Basic Books

Glaser, B and Strauss, A L (1967) *The Discovery of Grounded Theory: Strategies for Qualititative Research* Aldine Publishing

Goode, W J and Hatt, P K (1952) *Methods in Social Research* McGraw-Hill: New York

Hamilton, D (1981) Generalizations in the educational sciences: problems and purposes *in* Popkewitz and Tabachnick (1981)

Jenkins, D (1980) An adversary's account of SAFARI's ethics of case study *in* Simons (1980)

Kemmis, S (1980) The imagination of the case and the invention of the study *in* Simons (1980)

Kenny, W R and Grotelueschen, A D (1984) Making the Case for case study. *J. Curriculum Studies* **16** 1:37-51

Lakatos, I and Musgrave, A eds (1970) *Criticism and the Growth of Knowledge* Cambridge University Press

MacDonald, B, Adelman, C, Kushner, S and Walker, R (1982) *Bread and Dreams* University of East Anglia, Centre for Applied Research in Education, Occasional publication No 12

Miles, M B and Huberman, A M (1984) *Analyzing Qualititative Data* Sage Publications

Nisbet, J and Watt, J (1978) Case Study. Nottingham University School of Education, Rediguide 26

Parlett, M and Dearden, G eds (1977) *Introduction to Illuminative Evaluation: Studies in Higher Education* Cardiff-by-the-Sea, California: Pacific Soundings Press

Polanyi, M (1958) *Personal Knowledge* Harper and Row

Popkewitz, T S and Tabachnick, B R eds (1981) *The Study of Schooling* Praeger

Rist, R C (1980) Blitzkrieg ethnography *Educational Researcher*

Rist, F C (1981) On what we know (or think we do): gatekeeping and the social control of knowledge *in* Popkewitz and Tabachnick (1981)

Simons, H ed (1980) *Toward a Science of the Singular* University of East Anglia, Centre for Applied Research in Education, Occasional Publication No 10

Smith, L M (1981) Accidents, serendipity, and making the commonplace problematic: the origin and evolution of the field study 'problem' *in* Popkewitz and Tabachnick (1981)

Stake, R E (1978) The case study method in social inquiry *Educational Researcher* 5-8, February 1978

Stake, R E, Easley, J et al (1978) *Case Studies in Science Education* CIRCE, University of Illinois

Stenhouse, L (1977) *Case Study and Case Records: Toward a Contemporary History of Education* University of East Anglia, Centre for Applied Research in Education (mimeo)

Travers, R M W (1983) *How Research has Changed American Schools: A History from 1840 to the Present* Kalamazoo: Mythos Press

von Wright, G H (1971) *Explanation and Understanding* Routledge and Kegan Paul

Walker, R (1980) Making sense and losing meaning *in* Simons (1980)

Walker, R (1981) Three good reasons for not doing case study research BERA paper, September 1981 (mimeo)

Wehlage, G (1981) The purpose of generalization in field-study research *in* Popkewitz and Tabachnick (1981)

Wolcott, H (1975) Criteria for an ethnographic approach to research in schools *Human Organization* **34**: 111-27

Part 3: Bibliography and biographical notes

Bibliography

John D. Wilson

The bibliography is divided into four sections; the first covers published chapters and articles in books, including whole books and booklets, by individual authors, the second lists publications (books and documents) issued by official and corporate bodies, and the third includes articles, periodicals and working papers. These three sections include nearly all of the references cited in individual chapters: unpublished manuscripts and a few specialized references have been omitted.

In section IV a number of key references from sections I, II and III and some other important recent publications have been annotated. An asterisk (*) beside a particular entry in the first three parts of the bibliography indicates that it is among those annotated in section IV.

Section I: Books and pamphlets

Abramson, M A (1978) *The Funding of Social Knowledge Production and Application: A Survey of Federal Agencies* National Academy of Sciences: Washington, DC

Adair, J G and Davidson, R (1981) *Research Activity of Social Scientists* Report to the Social Science Federation of Canada: Ottawa

Adams, R S and Biddle, B J (1970) *Realities of Teaching* Holt, Rinehart and Winston: New York

Adams, R S and Chen, D (1981) *The Process of Educational Innovation: An International Perspective* Kogan Page: London and the UNESCO Press: Paris

Adelman, C ed (1981) *Uttering, Muttering* Grant McIntyre: London

Alexander, C (1968) *Notes Toward a Synthesis of Form* Harvard University Press: Cambridge, Mass

Allison, G T (1981) *Essence of Decision: Explaining the Cuban Missile Crisis* Little Brown: Boston

Andersson, B-E (1969) *Studies in Adolescent Behavior* Almqvist and Wiksell: Stockholm

Arnold, B and Simpson, M (1982) *Concept Development and Diagnostic Testing* Aberdeen College of Education: Aberdeen

Ausubel, D P (1961) *Maori Youth* Price Milburn: Wellington

Averch, H A, Carrol, S J, Donaldson, T S, Kiesling, H J and Pincus, J (1974) *How Effective is Schooling? A Critical Synthesis and Review of Research Findings* Educational Technology Publications: Englewood Cliffs, NJ

Bailey, S K, Frost, R T, Marsh, P E and Wood, R C (1962) *Schoolmen and Politics* Syracuse University Press: Syracuse, New York

Baker, K, Sikora, J, Davies, J P, and Hider, A T (1982) *The Schools and In-Service Teacher Education (SITE) Evaluation Project* University of Bristol School of Education: Bristol

Beaudelot, C and Establet, R (1971) *L'école capitaliste en France* (The capitalist school in France) Maspero: Paris

Becker, H S (1961) *Boys in White* University of Chicago Press: Chicago

Beeby, C E (1979) *Assessment of Indonesian Education: A Guide in Planning* NZCER Wellington

Bengtsson, J and Lundgren, U P (1968) *Modellstudier i utbildningsplanering och analyser av skolsystem* (Model Studies in Educational Planning and Analyses of School Systems) Licentiatavhandling, Department of Education, University of Göteborg: Göteborg

Bengtsson, J and Lundgren, U P (1969) *Utbildningsplanering och jämförelser av skolsystem* (Educational Planning and Comparisons of School Systems) Studentlitteratur: Lund

Benton, R (1981) *The Flight of the Amokura: Oceanic Languages and Formal Education in the Pacific* Educational Research Series No 63, NZCER: Wellington

Bergendal, G ed (1983) Knowledge and higher education: report from a series of colloquia held in 1981-82. Stockholm: National Board of Universities and Colleges, Almqvist and Wiksell

Berman, P and McLaughlin, M (1975) *Federal Programs Supporting Educational Change* Vol IV *The Findings in Review* Rand Corporation: Santa Monica, CA

Bestor, A E (1953) *Educational Wastelands* University of Illinois Press: Champaign-Urbana

Black Papers 1-5 (1969-77):
  Cox, C B and Dyson, A E (1969) *Fight for Education* The Critical Quarterly Society
  Cox, C B and Dyson, A E (1969) *The Crisis in Education* The Critical Quarterly Society
  Cox, C B and Dyson, A E (1970) *Goodbye Mr Short* The Critical Quarterly Society
  Cox, C B and Boyson, R (1975) *The Fight for Education* Dent: London
  Cox, C B and Boyson, R (1977) *Black Paper 5* Temple Smith: London

Black, H and Dockrell, B (1980) *Diagnostic Assessment in Secondary Schools* Scottish Council for Research in Education: Edinburgh

Bolam, R (1982) *Strategies for School Improvement: A Report for OECD* OECD/CERI: Paris (mimeo)

Bolam, R and Baker, K eds (1975) *The Teacher Induction Pilot Schemes (TIPS) Project: 1975 National Conference Report* University of Bristol School of Education: Bristol

Bolam, R, Baker, K, McMahon, A, Davis, J and McCabe, C (1977) *The Teacher Induction Pilot Schemes (TIPS) Project: National Conference Papers* University of Bristol School of Education: Bristol

Bourdieu, P and Passeron, J C (1964) *Les héritiers* (The heirs) Les editions de Minuit: Paris

Bowles, S and Gintis, H (1976) *Schooling in Capitalist America: Educational Reform and the Contradictions of Economic Life* Basic Books: New York

Brookover, W B and Lecotte, L W (1977) *Changes in School Characteristics Coincident with Changes in Student Achievement* Michigan State University, College of Urban Development: East Lansing, MI

Brown, S (1980a) *What Do They Know? A Review of Criterion-Referenced Assessment* HMSO: Edinburgh

Brown, S (1980b) *Introducing Criterion-Referenced Assessment: Teachers' Views* Stirling Educational Monographs, University of Stirling: Stirling

Bruner, J S (1980) *Under Five in Britain* Grant McIntyre: London

Buch, M B ed (1974) *A Survey of Research in Education (Up to 1972)* Centre for Advanced Studies in Education M S University of Baroda: Baroda

Buch, M B ed (1979) *Second Survey of Research in Education (1972-1978)* Society for Educational Research and Development: Baroda

Burke, S F and Keeves, J P eds *Literacy and Numeracy in Australian Schools, Vols I, II and III* AGPS: Canberra

Burrell, G and Morgan, G (1979) *Sociological Paradigms and Organisational Analysis* Heinemann Educational Books: London

*Bush, R N (1976) *Educational Research and Development: The Next Decade* Occasional Paper 11 Stanford Center for Research and Development in Teaching: Stanford, CA

Butcher, H J and Pont, H B eds (1973) *Educational Research in Britain 2* University of London Press: London

Callahan, R E (1972) *Education and the Cult of Efficiency* Chicago University Press: Chicago

Capelle, J (1974) *Education et politique* (Education and Politics) PUF: Paris

Caplan, N, Morrison, A and Stambauch, R J (1975) *The Use of Social Science Knowledge in Policy Decisions at the National Level* University of Michigan Press: Ann Arbor, MI

Carey, J T (1975) *Sociology and Public Affairs* Sage Publications: Beverly Hills, CA

Carr, W and Kemmis, S (1983) *Becoming Critical: Knowing through Action Research* Deakin University, Victoria

Chitnis, S (1970) *Sociology of Education in India — A Review* Tata Institute of Social Sciences: Bombay

Clark, M ed (1981) *The Politics of Education in New Zealand* Studies in Education No 29, NZCER: Wellington

Clay, M M (1979) *Reading: The Pattern of Complex Behaviour* Heinemann: Auckland

Cohen, L, Thomas, J and Manion, L eds (1982) *Educational Research and Development in Britain 1970-1980* NFER-Nelson: Windsor

Coleman, J S, Hoffer, T and Kilgore, S (1982) *High School Achievement: Public, Catholic and Private Schools Compared* Basic Books: New York

*Connell, W F (1980) *The Australian Council for Educational Research, 1930-80* ACER: Hawthorn (Vic)

Connell, W F (1980) *A History of Education in the Twentieth Century World* Canberra: Curriculum Development Centre

Coons, J E and Sugarman, S D (1978) *Education by Choice: The Case for Family Control* University of California Press: Berkeley, CA

Cronbach, L J et al (1980) *Toward Reform of Program Evaluation* Jossey-Bass: San Francisco

Cronbach, L J (1982) *Designing Evaluations of Educational and Social Programs* Jossey-Bass: San Francisco

*Cros, L (1981) *Quelle école, pour quel avenir?* (What school, for what future?) Casterman: Paris

Dahllöf, U (1960) *Kursplaneundersökningar i matematik och modersmalet* (Research on the Curricula for Mathematics and Mother Tongue) Statens offentliga utredningar SOU 1960: 15: Stockholm

Dahllöf, U (1963) *Kraven på gymnasiet* (The Demands on the 'Gymnasium') Statens offentliga utredningar SOU 1963: 22: Stockholm

Dahllöf, U (1967) *Skoldifferentiering och undervisningsförlopp* (School Differentiation and Teaching Process) Almqvist and Wiksell: Stockholm

Dahllöf, U (1971) *Ability Grouping, Content Validity and Curriculum Process Analysis* Teachers College Press Columbia University: New York

Dalin, P (1976) *Guidelines for Case Studies* IMTEC, University of Oslo (mimeo)

Deal, T E and Kennedy, A A (1982) *Corporate Cultures: The Rites and Rituals of Corporate Life* Addison-Wesley: Reading, MA

Denzin, N K (1978) *The Research Act* McGraw-Hill: New York

Deutscher Bildungsrat (1970) *Strukturplan für das Bildungswesen* (Structure plan for education) Bundesdruckerei: Bonn
Deutscher Bildungsrat (1974) *Aspekte für die Planung der Bildungsforschung* (Aspects of educational research planning) Bundesdruckerei: Bonn
Dewey, J (1938) *Logic: The Theory of Inquiry* New York
Di Iorio, F ed (1983) *Innovazione educativa e riforma dell'insegnamento primario* (Educational innovation and the reform of primary education) Centro Europeo dell'Educazione: Frascati, Italy
*Dockrell, W B and Hamilton, D eds (1980) *Rethinking Educational Research* Hodder and Stoughton: London
Doeringer, P and Piore, M (1971) *Internal Labor Markets and Manpower Training* D C Heath: Lexington, MA
Dooley, P A, Graham, N C and Whitfield, R C et al (1981) *Survey of Educational Researchers in Britain* Aston Educational Enquiry, Occasional Paper No 4, The University of Aston: Birmingham
Dottrens, R (1962) *The Primary School Curriculum* UNESCO (Monograph on Education II): Paris
Douglas, M (1966) *Purity and Danger* Routledge and Kegan Paul: London
Dubnick, M J and Bardis, B A (1983) *Thinking about Public Policy, a Problem-solving Approach* Wiley: New York
Dye, T R (1972) *Understanding Public Policy* Prentice Hall: Englewood Cliffs, NJ

Ebbutt, D and Elliott, J eds (1984) *Issues in Teaching for Understanding* The Schools Curriculum Development Committee (formerly The Schools Council of England and Wales) (in press)
Elliott, J (1983b) *Teacher Evaluation and Teaching as a Moral Science* Cambridge Institute of Education (mimeo)
Elliott, J and Ebbutt, D eds (1984) *Facilitating Educational Action-Research in Schools* The Schools Curriculum Development Committee (formerly The Schools Council of England and Wales) (in press)
Emrick, J A and Peterson, S M (1978) *A Synthesis of Findings Across Five Recent Studies in Educational Dissemination and Change* Far West Educational Laboratory: San Francisco
Enfance, nº spécial 5 (1952-53) *La psychologie scolaire* (Academic psychology) PUF: Paris
Eng, S P et al (1984) *Report on Case Studies of 38 Monolingual Pupils* Institute of Education: Singapore

*Farquhar, R H and Housego, I E eds (1980) *Canadian and Comparative Educational Administration* Education-Extension, University of British Columbia: Vancouver
Foo, S K et al (1983) *A Study of the Criteria for Streaming Pupils into Secondary One* MCM Paper No 2158
Fourastié, J (1963) *Le grand espoir du vingtième siècle* (Great expectations of the 20th Century) Gallimard: Paris
Freidrick, C J (1963) *Man and His Government; An Empirical Theory of Politics* McGraw-Hill: New York
Freidson, E (1970) *The Profession of Medicine* Dodd Mead: New York
Freire, P (1972) *Pedagogy of the Oppressed* Penguin Books: Harmondsworth
Führ, Ch (1979) *Education and Teaching in the Federal Republic of Germany* Carl Hanser Verlag: München/Wien
*Fullan, M (1982) *The Meaning of Educational Change* Teachers College Press: New York

Gadamer, H (1975) *Truth and Method* Sheed and Ward Stagbooks: London
Gage, N L, Husén, T and Singleton, J W (1980) *Report of the Task Force on the Impact of the Research, Development and Field Activities of The Ontario Insti-

tute for Studies in Education: Summary and Conclusions Ontario Institute for Studies in Education: Toronto

Galpin, R and Wright, C eds (1964) *Scientists and National Policy Making* Columbia University Press: New York

Garz, D and Kraimer, K eds (1983) *Brauchen wir andere Forschungsmethoden? Beiträge zur Diskussion interpretativer Verfahren* (Do we need other research methods? Contributions to the discussion of interpretative procedures) Scriptor: Frankfurt am Main

Geertz, C (1973) *The Interpretation of Cultures* Basic Books

Géminard, L (1977) *L'enseignement éclaté* (The education explosion) Casterman: Paris

Glaser, B and Strauss, A L (1967) *The Discovery of Grounded Theory: Strategies for Qualitative Research* Aldine Publishing

Glazer, N (1974) *The Schools of the Minor Professions* Minerva

Goode, W J and Hatt, P K (1952) *Methods in Social Research* McGraw-Hill: New York

Gosden, P (1983) *The Education System since 1944* Martin Robertson: Oxford

Habermas, J (1971) *Toward a Rational Society* Heinemann: London

Habermas, J (1976) *Legitimation Crisis* Heinemann: London

Habermas, J (1978) *Knowledge and Human Interests* Heinemann: London

Habermas, J (1979) *Communication and the Evolution of Society* Heinemann: London

Hall, C (1981) *Grandma's Attic or Aladdin's Cave: Museum Education Services for Children* Studies in Education No 30, NZCER: Wellington

Halsey, A H (1962) *Ability and Educational Opportunity* OECD: Paris

Hamilton, D et al eds (1977) *Beyond the Numbers Game* Macmillan Educational: London

Hammersley, M and Atkinson, P (1983) *Ethnography: Principles in Practice* Tavistock Publications: London and New York

Handy, C (1984) *Schools as Organizations* The Schools Curriculum Development Committee (formerly The Schools Council of England and Wales)

Harbison, F and Myers, C (1964) *Education, Manpower, and Economic Growth* McGraw-Hill: New York

Harlen, W ed (1978) *Evaluation and the Teacher's Role* Macmillan Educational for the Schools Council: London

Härnqvist, K (1960) *Individuella differenser och skoldifferentiering* (Individual differences and school differentiation) Statens offentliga utredningar SOU 1960: 13: Stockholm

Harrison, A (1978) *Making and Thinking* Hackett: Indianapolis

Havelock, R G (1969) *Planning for Innovation through Dissemination and Utilisation of Knowledge* Institute of Social Research: Ann Arbor, MI

Havelock, R (1971a) *Innovations in Education: Strategies and Tactics* Institute for Social Research University of Michigan: Ann Arbor, MI (mimeo)

Herbart, J F (1806) *Allgemeine Pädagogik* Bochum

Ho, W K et al (1982) *I: Case Studies of a Sample of Pupils whose Performance in English Language Usage in the 1981 PSLE was Poor in Comparison with their Performance in Other Subjects; II: A Follow-up Study of a Sample of Pupils who Performed Well in English Language in the PSLE* Institute of Education: Singapore

Holdaway, E A and Friesen, D (1980) *Canadian Society for the Study of Education: Development and Challenge* Department of Educational Administration, University of Alberta: Edmonton

Holt, M (1981) *Evaluating the Teachers as Evaluators* Hodder and Stoughton

*House, E R (1980) *Evaluating with Validity* Sage Publications: Beverly Hills, CA

Hoyle, E (1973) *Strategies of Curriculum Change* Open University Course E203 Unit 23 Open University Press: Bletchley

Hoyle, E and Megarry, J (1981) *World Yearbook of Education, 1980: The Professional Development of Teachers* Kogan Page: London
*Husen, T and Kogan, M eds (1984) *Educational Research and Policy: How Do They Relate?* Pergamon Press: Oxford

Iannaccone, L and Lutz, F W (1970) *Politics, Power, and Policy: The Governing of Local School Districts* Charles E Merrill: Columbus, OH
Ingenkamp, K ed (1980) *Forschung and Lehre sind frei* ... (Research and teaching are free ...) Beltz Verlag: Weinheim/Basel

Jaccard, P (1957) *Politique de l'emploi et de l'éducation* (The politics of employment and education) Payot: Paris
Jackson, P, Reid, N A and Croft, A C (1982) *SWOT: Study WithOut Tears* NZCER: Wellington
Jackson, P W (1968) *Life in Classrooms* Holt, Rinehart and Winston: New York
Johns, R L, Morphet, E L and Alexander, K (1983) *The Economics and Financing of Education* (fourth ed) Prentice Hall: Englewood Cliffs, NJ

*Kallen, D B P, Kosse, G B and Wagenaar, H C et al eds (1982) *Social Science Research and Public Policy-Making: A Reappraisal* SVO-NFER Nelson: Windsor
Kallòs and Lundgren, UP (1979) *Curriculum as a Pedagogical Problem* Gleerup/Liber: Lund
Karabel, J and Halsey, A H (1977) *Power and Ideology in Education* Oxford University Press: London
Kemmis, S et al (1981) *The Action Research Planner* Deakin University Press: Geelong, Victoria
Kilborn, U and Lundgren, U P (1974) *Skolans imre arbete* (The inner work of the school) P A Nordstedt & SöherÖ: Stockholm
Klafki, W (1976b) *Aspekte kritisch-konstruktiver Erziehungswissenschaft* (Aspects of critical-constructive educational science) Beltz Verlag: Weinheim/Basel
Knorr, K D, Strasser, H and Zilian, H G eds (1975) *Determinants and Control of Scientific Development* Reidel: Dordrecht, Holland
Kuhn, T (1962) *The Structure of Scientific Revolutions* University of Chicago Press: Chicago, IL

Lacey, C and Lawton, D eds (1981) *Issues in Evaluation and Accountability* Methuen: London
Lakatos, I and Musgrave, A eds (1970) *Criticism and the Growth of Knowledge* Cambridge University Press
Lambright, W H (1976) *Governing Science and Technology* Oxford University Press: New York
Lawton, D (1980) *The Politics of the School Curriculum* Routledge and Kegan Paul: London
*Legrand, L (1977) *Pour une politique démocratique de l'éducation* (A democratic approach to education) PUF: Paris
Lemberg, E (1963b) *Das Bildungswesen als Gegenstand der Forschung* (Education as the object of research) Quelle und Meyer: Heidelberg
Lerner, D and Lasswell, H D eds (1951) *The Policy Sciences* Stanford University Press: Stanford, CA
Lieberman, A and McLaughlin, M W eds (1982) *Policy Making in Education* Eighty-First Yearbook of the National Society for the Study of Education, Part I, University of Chicago Press: Chicago, IL
Lindberg, G and Lindberg, L (1983) *Pedagogisk forskning i Sverige 1948-1971* (Educational research in Sweden 1948-1971) Institute of Education University of Umeå: Umeå
Louis, K and Rosenblum, S (1981) *Linking R and D with Schools: A Program and its Implications for Dissemination* National Institute of Education, Washington

*Louis, K S and Sieber, S D (1979) *Bureaucracy and the Dispersed Organization* Ablex Publishing Corp: Norwood, NJ

Lun, C Y and de Souza, D (1983) *IEXperience: The First Ten Years* Institute of Education: Singapore

Lundgren, U P (1972) *Frame Factors and the Teaching Process* Almqvist and Wiksell: Stockholm

Lundgren, U P (1977) *Model Analysis of Pedagogical Processes* Liber: Lund

Lundman, L (1979) *Socioekonomisk differentiering i grundskolan* (Socio-economic differentiation in the comprehensive school) Liber: Lund

Lutz, F W and Iannaccone, L (1978) *Public Participation in Local School Districts* D C Heath: Lexington, MA

Lybeck, L (1981) *Archimedes i klassen* (Archimedes in the classroom) Acta Universitatis Gothenburgensis: Göteborg

McCall, J, Bryce, T, Gordon, P, Hewitt, C and Martin, P (1983) *Interim Report of the Criterion-Referenced Certification Project* Jordanhill College of Education: Glasgow

McCormick, R and James, M (1983) *Curriculum Evaluation in Schools* Croom Helm

MacDonald, B, Adelman, C, Kushner, S and Walker, R (1982) *Bread and Dreams* University of East Anglia, Centre for Applied Research in Education Occasional Publication No 12

McDonald, G (1981) *Working and Learning: A Participatory Project on Parent-Helping in the New Zealand Playcentre* Studies in Education No 32, NZCER: Wellington

McLaughlin, M (1975) *Evaluation and Reform: Elementary and Secondary Education Act of 1965, Title I* Ballinger: Cambridge, MA

Machiavelli, N (1981) *The Prince and Other Political Writings* (translated by B Penman) Dent: London

Madaus, G F, Airasian, P W and Kellaghan, T (1980) *School Effectiveness: A Reassessment of the Evidence* McGraw-Hill: New York

Magnusson, D, Dunér, A and Beckne, R (1967) *Anpassning, beteende och prestation* (Adjustment, behaviour and achievement) Department of Psychological Research, University of Stockholm: Stockholm

Majault, J (1981) *Comptes, mécomptes, descomptes* (Accounts, miscounts, discounts) Casterman: Paris

Malmquist, E in co-operation with Grundin, H (1975) *Educational Research in Europe Today and Tomorrow* CWK Gleerup: Lund, Sweden

*Malpica, C ed (1983) *The Generalisation of Educational Innovations: the Administrator's Perspective* International Institute for Educational Planning: Paris

Mann, D (1975) *Policy Decision Making in Education* Teachers College Press: New York

Mann, D (1976) *The Politics of Administrative Representation* D C Heath: Lexington, MA

Mercurio, J A (1972) *Caning, Educational Rite and Tradition* Syracuse University: Syracuse, NY

Mialaret, G (1954) *Nouvelle pédagogie scientifique* (A new scientific pedagogy) PUF: Paris

Miles, M B and Huberman, A M (1984) *Analyzing Qualitative Data* Sage Publications.

*Mitchell, D E (1981a) *Shaping Legislative Decisions: Education Policy and the Social Sciences* D C Heath: Lexington, MA

Mitter, W and Weishaupt, H ed (1977) *Ansätze zur Analyse der wissenschaftlichen Begleitung bildungspolitischer Innovationen* (Preliminary analyses of the monitoring of educational-political innovations) Beltz Verlag: Weinheim/Basel

*Mitter, W and Weishaupt, H eds (1979) *Strategien und Organisationsformen der Begleitforschung* (Strategies and organizational forms of monitoring research) Beltz Verlag: Weinheim/Basel

*Mitzel, E ed (1982) *Encyclopedia of Educational Research* The Free Press: New York

Moore, W E and Rosenblum, G (1970) *The Professions* Russell Sage Foundation: New York

*Myers, R (1981) *Connecting Worlds: A Survey of Developments in Educational Research in Latin America* IDRC-TS35: Toronto

Nagel, S ed (1980) *Handbook of Policy Studies* D C Heath: Lexington, MA

Ng, S M et al (1984) *Progress Report of Reading Skills Project* MCM Paper No 2313

Nisbet, J (1973) *The Schools Council* Case Studies of Central Institutions for Educational Change OECD/CERI: Paris

*Nisbet, J and Broadfoot, P (1980) *The Impact of Research on Policy and Practice in Education* Aberdeen University Press: Aberdeen

Nisbet, J and Watt, J (1978) *Case Study* Nottingham University School of Education Rediguide 26

Nixon, J ed (1983) *A Teacher's Guide to Action Research* Grant McIntyre: London

Nuthall, G A and Lawrence, P J (1965) *Thinking in Classrooms* NZCER: Wellington

*Oldham, G ed (1982) *The Future of Research* Leverhulme Programme of Study into the Future of Higher Education, Monograph 4 Society for Research in Higher Education: Guildford, Surrey

Olson, R D ed (1971) *Selected Readings for Educational Psychology* McCutcheon Publishing: Berkeley, CA

Osborne, R J (1982) *Learning Science: A Generative Process* Graduate School of Education: UCLA

Ouchi, W (1981) *Theory Z How American Business Can Meet the Japanese Challenge* Addison-Wesley: Reading, MA

*Paisley, W J and Butler, M (1983) *Knowledge Utilisation Systems in Education* Sage Publications: Beverly Hills, CA

Parkyn, G W (1967) *Success and Failure at the University* Vol 1 1959, Vol 2 1967 NZCER: Wellington

Parlett, M and Dearden, G eds (1977) *Introduction to Illuminative Evaluation: Studies in Higher Education* Pacific Soundings Press: Cardiff-by-the-Sea, CA

Pareek, U and Kumar, V K (1966) *Behavioural Science Research in India (1925-65) — A Directory* Behavioural Science Centre: Delhi

Pareek, U and Sood, S (1977) *Directory of Indian Behavioural Science Research* Acharan Sahkar: Delhi

Patton, M Q (1978) *Utilization Focused Evaluation* Sage Publications: Beverly Hills, CA

Peters, T J and Waterman, R H Jr (1981) *In Search of Excellence: Lessons from America's Best-Run Companies* Harper and Row: New York

Piéron, H (1963) *Examens et docimologie* (Examinations and assaying) PUF: Paris

Pile, W (1976) *in House of Commons 10th Report from the Expenditure Committee* Her Majesty's Stationery Office: London

Polanyi, M (1958) *Personal Knowledge* Harper and Row

Popkewitz, T S and Tabachnick, B R eds (1981) *The Study of Schooling* Praeger

Purkey, S C and Smith, M S (1982) *Effective Schools — A Review* Wisconsin Center for Education Research, University of Wisconsin: Madison, WI

Radford, W C (1973) *Research into Education in Australia* AACRDE Report No 1, AGPS: Canberra

Ramsey, P ed (1979) *Issues in Curriculum Development* Institute of Education: Auckland, New Zealand

Reuchlin, M (1954) *L'orientation scolaire et professionnelle* (Academic and professional orientation) PUF: Paris

Rhine, R ed (1981) *Making Schools More Effective: New Directions from Follow Through* Academic Press: New York

Richardson, E (1975) *Authority and Organization in the Secondary School* Macmillan Educational: London

Ripley, R B ed (1966) *Public Policies and their Politics* New W W Norton: New York

Rist, R C and Anson, R J eds (1977) *Education, Social Science, and the Judicial Process* Teachers College Press: New York

Rivlin, A (1971) *Systematic Thinking for Social Action* Brookings Institution: Washington, DC

Robinson, D S (1947) *The Principles of Reasoning* (third edition) Appleton-Century-Crofts: New York

Rogers, E and Shoemaker, F (1971) *Communications of Innovations* Free Press: New York

Roth, L ed (1976) *Handlexikon zur Erziehungswissenschaft* (Handbook of educational science) Ehrenwirth Verlag: München

*Roth, L ed (1978) *Methoden erziehungswissenschaftlicher Forschung* (Educational research methods) Verlag W Kohlhammer: Stuttgart

Rudduck, J (1976) *Dissemination of Innovation: The Humanities Curriculum Project* Evans/Methuen for the Schools Council: London

Rudduck, J ed (1983) *The Humanities Curriculum Project: An Introduction* Revised edition University of East Anglia: Norwich for The Schools Curriculum Development Committee (formerly The Schools Council of England and Wales)

Ryan, D W (1983) *Sponsored Research in OISE: A Report to the OISE Board of Governors* Ontario Institute for Studies in Education: Toronto

Ryle, G (1949) Knowing how and knowing that *in The Concept of Mind* Hutcheson: London

Säljö, R (1982) *Learning and Understanding* Acta Universitatis Gothoburgensis: Göteborg

Scheerens, J (1983) *Het sectoronderzoek: onderwijsonderzoek in de marge van beleid en wetenschapp?* SVO-Flevodruk: Harlingen

Schiefelbein, E (1983) *The Role of Educational Research in the Conception and Implementation of Educational Policies: The Latin American Experience* IIEP-UNESCO: Paris

Schiefelbein, E and Garcia Huidobro, J (1980) *La investigacion educacional en America Latina, situacion y perspectivas* CIDE-REDUC: Santiago

Schon, D (1971) *Beyond the Stable State* Penguin Books: Harmondsworth, Middlesex

*Schon, D (1983) *The Reflective Practitioner: How Professionals Think in Action* Temple Smith: London

Schulman, L and Sykes, G eds (1983) *Handbook of Teaching and Policy* Longman: New York

Scribner, J ed (1977) *The Politics of Education* The Seventy-sixth Yearbook of the National Society for the Study of Education, Part II, University of Chicago Press: Chicago

Shaeffer, S and Nkinyangi, J A (1983) *Educational Research Environments in the Developing World* International Development Research Centre: Ottawa

Shipman, M (1974) *Inside a Curriculum Project* Methuen: London

Simon, B and Taylor, W eds (1981) *Education in the Eighties* Batsford: London

*Simons, H ed (1980) *Towards a Science of the Singular* University of East Anglia, Centre for Applied Research in Education Occasional Publication No 10

Skilbeck, M (1982) *Curriculum Development* APEID Occasional Paper No 9 UNESCO: Bangkok

Skilbeck, M (1982) *A Core Curriculum for the Common School* University of London Institute of Education: London

Skilbeck, M ed (1984a) *Evaluating the Curriculum* Hodder and Stoughton: London

Skilbeck, M (1984b) *School Based Curriculum Development* Harper and Row: London

Snow, C P (1959) *The Two Cultures and a Second Look: Expanded Version of the Two Cultures and the Scientific Revolution* Cambridge University Press: London

SOU 1958:11 *Reserver för högre utbildning. Beräkningar och metoddiskussioner* (The Resources for Higher Education. Estimations and Methodological Discussions) Ecklesiastikdepartementet: Stockholm

SOU 1974:53 *Skolans arbetsmiljö* (The Work Environment in the Schools) Utbildningsdepartementet: Stockholm

Stake, R E, Easley, J et al (1978) *Case Studies in Science Education* CIRE, University of Illinois

Steadman, S et al (1978-81) *Reports to the Schools Council on Impact and Take-Up* Schools Council: London

*Stenhouse, L (1975) *An Introduction to Curriculum Research and Development* Heinemann Educational Books: London

Stenhouse, L (1977) *Case study and case records: Toward a contemporary history of education* University of East Anglia, Centre for Applied Research in Education (mimeo)

Stewart, F (1974) *Once More unto the Breach* Report of the Executive Director of the Canadian Education Association for 1973-74: Toronto

Stufflebeam, D L ed (1981) *Standards for Evaluations of Educational Programs and Materials* (Joint committee on standards for educational evaluation) Holt Rinehart and Winston: New York

*Suppes, P ed (1978) *Impact of Research on Education: Some Case Studies* National Academy of Education: Washington, DC

Svensson, A (1971) *Relative Achievement. School Performance in relation to Intelligence, Sex and Home Environment* Almqvist and Wiksell: Stockholm

Svensson, N-E (1962) *Ability Grouping and Scholastic Achievement* Almqvist and Wiksell: Stockholm

Tawney, D ed (1973) *Evaluation in Curriculum Development: Twelve Case Studies* Macmillan: London

Tawney, D ed (1976) *Curriculum Evaluation Today* Macmillan: London

*Taylor, W ed (1973) *Research Perspectives in Education* Routledge and Kegan Paul: London

Tizard, B (1974) *Pre-School Education in Great Britain* Social Science Research Council (New Edition published as *Early Childhood Education: A Review and Discussion of Current Research in Britain*) NFER: Windsor

Tomlinson, J R G (1981) *The Schools Council: A Chairman's Salute and Envoi* Schools Council: London

Törnebohm, H (1971) *Reflections on Scientific Research* Institute for the Theory of Science: Göteborg

Toro, B (1983) *Diffusion and Use of the 'Resumenes Analíticos en Educacion (RAE)' and Increasing 'REDUC Network' Capacity* OISE: Toronto (mimeo)

Travers, R M W ed (1973) *Second Handbook of Research in Teaching* Rand McNally: Chicago

Travers, R M W (1983) *How Research has Changed American Schools: A History from 1840 to the Present* Mythos Press: Kalamazoo

von Wright, G H (1971) *Explanation and Understanding* Routledge and Kegan Paul: London

Ward, V (1973) *Resources for Educational Research and Development* NFER Publishing Co: Windsor

*Weiss, C H ed (1977) *Using Social Research in Public Policy Making* D C Heath: Lexington, MA

Weitman, D R, Horst, P, Taber G M and Whaley, J S (1973) Design of an evaluation system for NIMH *Contract Report 962-7* The Urban Institute: Washington, DC

White, J P (1983) *The Aims of Education Revisited* Routledge and Kegan Paul: London

Wirt. F M and Kirst, M (1982) *Schools in Conflict* McCutchan: Berkeley, CA

Wise, A (1967) *Rich Schools, Poor Schools* University of Chicago Press: Chicago

Wong, E (1983) *Adaptation of the Hall Occupational Orientation Inventory — A Status Report* MCM Paper No 2119

Wrigley, J (1973b) Lecture 1 *A Breakthrough in Curriculum Development — Far Reaching Innovations by the Schools Council* University of Melbourne: Melbourne (mimeo)
Wrigley, J (1981) *Confessions of a Curriculum Man* Jack Kerr Lecture University of Leicester School of Education: Leicester (mimeo)

Yates, F (1972) *The First Twenty-five Years: A Review of the NFER* The Foundation: Slough

Section II: Official and corporate publications

Alberta Department of Education (1981) *Seventy-Sixth Annual Report, 1980-81:* Edmonton
Andrews, J H M and Rogers, W T eds (1982) *Canadian Research in Education: A State of the Art Review* Social Sciences and Humanities Research Council of Canada: Ottawa
Association of Indian Universities (1983) *Information Handout 1983-84:* New Delhi
Australian Government Commission of Inquiry into Poverty (1976) *Poverty and Education in Australia* 5th Report AGPS: Canberra

Basic Studies National Field Task Force (1974) *Final Report and Recommendations* US Department of Health Education and Welfare: Washington, DC
Bund-Länder-Kommission für Bildungsplanung und Forschungsförderung (1979) *Evaluation schulischer Neuerungen* (Evaluation of school innovations) CERI-Seminar Dillingen 1977 Klett-Cotta: Stuttgart
Bund-Länder-Kommission für Bildungsplanung und Forschungsforderung (1981) *Dimensionen und Grenzen der Evaluation schulischer Neuerungen* (Dimensions and limits of the evaluation of school innovations) CERI-Seminar Neusiedl am See 1979 Klett-Cotta: Stuttgart

*Carraz, R (1984) *Recherche en éducation et socialisation de l'enfant* (Report on the education and socialization of the child) Rapport au Ministre de la Recherche et de la Technologie, la Documentation Française: Paris
Central Advisory Council for Education (1959) *Sixteen to Nineteen* (Crowther Report) HMSO: London
Centro de Investigacion y Desarrollo de la Educacion (CIDE) (1983) *Indice de Resumenes Analiticos sobre Educacion* 1 1-281
Cliche, Y (1982) *Rapport annuel, 1981-82* Fonds FCAC pour l'aide et le soutien à la recherche: Quebec
Coleman, J S, Campbell, E Q, Hobson, C J, McPartland, J, Wood, A M, Weinfield, F D and York, R L (1966) *Equality of Educational Opportunity* Government Printing Office: Washington, DC
Crozier, M, Eide, J, Hamm-Brücher, H, Noah, H and Vanbergen, P (1976) *Reviews of National Policies for Education: Canada* Organization for Economic Co-operation and Development: Paris

Department of Education and Science (1981a) *The School Curriculum* HMSO: London
Department of Education and Science (1981b) *Curriculum 11-16: A Review of Progress* HMSO: London

Eddy, W P (1982) *Annual Research Highlights* Alberta Department of Education: Edmonton
Estmer, B (1976) *Educational Research and Development at the NBE* National Swedish Board of Education: Stockholm

Goh, K S and The Education Study Team (1979) *Report on the Ministry of Education 1978* Ministry of Education: Singapore (commonly referred to as the Goh Report)

Government of India, Ministry of Information and Broadcasting, Research and Reference Division (1983) *India 1983* Government of India Press: Faridabad

Halsey, A H (1972) *Educational Priority* Vol 1 HMSO: London

Indian Council of Social Science Research (1982) *Information Handout 1982*: New Delhi

Institut National de Recherche Pédagogique et Centre National de la Recherche Scientifique (1980-82) *Répertoire des organismes français de recherche en sciences de l'éducation* (List of French educational research organizations) INRP-CNRS: Paris

International Development Research Centre (1983) *Review of IDRC Activities 1982*: Ottawa

Karmel Report (1973) *Schools in Australia* Australian Schools Commission, Australian Government Printing Service: Canberra

Legrand, L (1983) *Pour un collège démocratique* (Towards a democratic secondary school) Rapport au Ministère de l'Education Nationale, La Documentation Française: Paris

Lockwood, J (1964) *Report of the Working Party on the Schools' Curricula and Examinations* HMSO: London

Montgomerie, T C (1982) *Telidon Distance Education Field Trial* Alberta Department of Education: Edmonton

National Academy of Education (1969) *Policy Making for American Public Schools* National Academy of Education: New York

National Center for Educational Statistics (NCES) (1982) *Digest of Educational Statistics* Government Printing Office: Washington, DC

National Council of Educational Research and Training (1966) *Educational Investigations (PhD) in Indian Universities (1939-66)* NCERT: New Delhi

National Council of Educational Research and Training (1968a) *Educational Investigations (MEd) in Indian Universities (1939-66)* NCERT: New Delhi

National Council of Educational Research and Training (1968b) *Third Indian Yearbook of Education (Educational Research)* NCERT: New Delhi

National Council of Educational Research and Training (1983) *Annual Report 1982-83*: New Delhi

National Council of Educational Planning and Administration (1983) *Annual Report 1982-83*: New Delhi

National Institute for Educational Research (1983) *Research and Educational Reform: Problems and Issues, and Strategies for Resolving Them* NIER: Tokyo

*New Zealand Association for Research in Education (1980) *Research in Education in New Zealand: The State of the Art* NZARE/Delta: Palmerston North

OECD/CERI (1975) *Handbook on Curriculum Development* OECD/CERI: Paris

OECD/CERI (1983) *International School Improvement Progress Report* OECD/CERI: Paris (mimeo)

*OECD (1983) *Reviews of National Policies for Education: New Zealand* OECD/CERI: Paris

Office of Management and Budget (OMB) (1982) *Budget of the United States Government: Fiscal Year 1983* Government Printing Office: Washington, DC

Rothschild, Lord (1971 and 1972) The Organisation and Management of Government Research and Development (Cmd 4814). A Framework for Government Research and Development (Cmd 5046) HMSO: London
Rothschild, Lord (1982) An Enquiry into the SSRC (Cmd 8554) HMSO: London

Schools Council (1968) The First Three Years 1964-67 HMSO: London
Schools Council (1974) Schools Council the First Ten Years 1964-1974 The Council: London
Schools Council (1975) Minutes of Programme Committee (SC 75/558)
Schools Council (1978) Constitution The Council: London
Schools Council (1979) Schools Council Principles and Programmes The Council: London
Schools Council (1980) Annual Report for 1978-79 The Council: London
Science Council of Canada (1983) Annual Report, 1982-83: Ottawa
Scottish Education Department (1965) Primary Education in Scotland HMSO: Edinburgh
Scottish Education Department (1977a) The Structure of the Curriculum in the Third and Fourth Years of the Scottish Secondary School HMSO: Edinburgh
Scottish Education Department (1977b) Assessment for All HMSO: Edinburgh
Scottish Education Department (1980a) Learning and Teaching in Primary 4 and Primary 7 HMSO: Edinburgh
Scottish Education Department (1980b) The Munn and Dunning Reports: The Government's Development Programme SED: Edinburgh
Scottish Education Department (1982) The Munn and Dunning Reports: The Government's Development Programme, Interim Report on Research SED: Edinburgh
Scottish Education Department (1983) Educational Research: A Register of Current Educational Research Projects Funded by the Scottish Education Department SED: Edinburgh
Scottish Microelectronics Development Programme (1981) Strategy and Implementation Paper SMDP: Glasgow
Sheffield, E ed (1982) Research on Postsecondary Education in Canada Social Sciences and Humanities Research Council of Canada: Ottawa
Social Sciences and Humanities Research Council of Canada (1982) 1981-82 Annual Report: Ottawa
Social Sciences and Humanities Research Council of Canada (1983) Research Grants: Guide to Applicants: Ottawa
Social Science Research Council (1975) Annual Report for 1974-75 SSRC: London
Social Science Research Council (1976) Annual Report for 1975-76 SSRC: London
Social Science Research Council (1983) Research Supported by the Social Science Research Council SSRC: London
SOU 1948:27 års skolkommissions betänkande med förslag till riktlinjer för det svenska skolväsendets utveckling (Report of the 1946 School Commission with suggestions and guidelines for the development of the Swedish school system) Statens offentliga utredningar: Stockholm
SOU (1980) 2. Skolforskning och skolutveckling. Betänkande av Skolforskningskommittén. (Educational research and educational development. Report of the Committee on Educational Research and Development) Liber Förlag: Stockholm (in Swedish)
Stapleton, J J, Allard, M, MacIver, D A, MacPherson, E D and Williams, T R (1982) Education Research in Canada: Aims, Problems and Possibilities Social Sciences and Humanities Research Council of Canada: Ottawa

Tomlinson, J (1978) Report of the Review Body: Chairman's Statements to Schools Council Governing Council GC Minutes 1/7
Tomlinson, J (1981) The Schools Council: A Chairman's Salute and Envoi Schools Council: London

UNESCO *International Colloquium: Research and Practice in Education* held in Bucharest (Romania) in November 1980

UNESCO (1983) *Final Report of Eighth Regional Consultation Meeting on the Asian Programme of Educational Innovation for Development* UNESCO: Bangkok

University Grants Commission (1982) *Annual Report 1981-82*: New Delhi

United States Comptroller General (1977) *Social Research and Development of Limited Use to National Policy Makers* General Accounting Office: Washington, DC

Wisenthal, M (1982) *Education Research: Future Expectations and Past Performance* Social Sciences and Humanities Research Council of Canada: Ottawa

Section III: Articles, periodicals and working papers

Adelman, C (1981) On first hearing *in* Adelman (1981)

Adelman, C and Walker, R B (1975) Developing pictures for other frames: action research and case study *in* Chanan, G and Delamont, S *eds Frontiers in Classroom Research* NFER Publishing Co: London

Andre, M E D A (1983) Use of content analysis in educational evaluation: doing prose analysis *Discourse* 4 1

*Atkin, J M (1979) Education accountability in the United States *Educational Analysis* 1 1

Aurin, K (1969-70) The role of empirical research in educational planning and policy-making *Western European Education* 1 74-92

Bancroft, Lord (1984) Whitehall and management: a retrospect *Journal of the Royal Society of Arts* 132 5334 371

Beckman, N *ed* (1977) Policy analysis in government: alternatives to 'muddling through' *Public Administration Review* 27 221-64

Berliner, D C *ed* (1980) *Review of Research in Education* Vol 8, American Educational Research Association: Washington, DC

Berliner, D C *ed* (1981) *Review of Research in Education* Vol 9, American Educational Research Association: Washington, DC

Bundi, H (1983) Quoted in: Research funding scrutinized. *Times Educational Supplement* 19 August 1983

Boyd, W L (1979) Changing politics of curriculum policy making for American schools *Review of Educational Research* 48 577-628

Brahan, J W (1983) *CAL Technology — Decade Past, Decade Present* Paper presented at Fourth Canadian Symposium on Instructional Technology, Winnipeg

*Brahm, L and Gutierrez, G (1983) REDUC: an educational documentation network serving development in Latin America *UNESCO Journal of Information Science, Librarianship and Archives Administration* 5 89-94

Bresson, F (1965) Langue et communication (Language and communication) *in* Fraisse et Piaget *eds Traité de psychologie* T VIII PUF: Paris

Brown, L *et al* (1982) Action Research in Education: Notes on the National Seminar (Australia) *Bulletin No 5 of the Classroom Action-Research Network* Cambridge Institute of Education

Brown, S (1984) Action research: problematic issues for its contribution to science teacher education *Proceedings of Bat Sheva de Rotheschild Seminar on Science Teacher Education* Hebrew University Jerusalem, January 1983 (in press)

Burchinal, L G (1983) ERIC: The international educational information system *in* Paisley, W J and Butler, M *eds Knowledge Utilization Systems in Education* Sage Publications: Beverly Hills, CA

Burgess, R (1981) Keeping a research diary *Cambridge Journal of Education* 11 1 Lent Term

Caplan, N (1976) Factors associated with knowledge use among federal executives *Policy Studies Journal* 4 229-34

Caplan, N (1981) Social research and public policy at the national level *in* Kallen *et al* (1982)

Carelli, D (1983) Review of Seminario 80 *International Review of Education* **29** 101-2

Carlson, K (1979) Ways in which research methodology distorts policy issues *The Urban Review* **11** 1-16

Carr, W (1983) Can educational research be scientific? *Journal of Philosophy of Education* **17** 1 35-43

Caston, G (1971) The Schools Council in context *Journal of Curriculum Studies III 1*

Castro, C and Bordignon, G (1980) Da pesquisa a toamada de decisao: existem caminhos privilegiados? *in* Shiefelbein and Garcia Huidobro (1980)

Clift, P (1982) LEA schemes for school self-evaluation *Educational Research* **24** 4 262-71

Coleman, J S (1976) Policy decisions, social science information and education *Sociology of Education* **49** 304-12

De Wolff, P and Harnqvist, K (1962) Reserves of Ability Size and Distribution *in* Halsey (1962)

Deiseach, D (1979) *Educational Research in Canada: The Sum of the Parts is Greater than the Whole* Paper presented at Canadian Society for Studies in Education Conference, Saskatoon

Dockrell, W B (1981) The contribution of national surveys of achievement to policy formation *in* Kallen *et al* (1982)

Dreyfus, D (1972) Limitations of policy research in congressional decision making *Policy Studies Journal* **1**

Drezek, S, Monkowski, P G and Higgins, P S (1982) Current versus perceived-ideal procedures for determining educational program-evaluation budgets: a survey of school evaluators *Educational Evaluation and Policy Analysis* **4** 97-108

Dror, Y (1967) Policy analyst: a new professional role in government *Public Administration Review* **13** 197-203

Dunn, S S (1965) Educational research in the light of Australian experience *in* M Young *ed Innovation and Research in Education* Routledge and Kegan Paul: London, 157-74

Dworkin, R (1977) Social sciences and constitutional rights — the consequences of uncertainty *in* Rist, R C and Anson, R J (1977)

Edmonds, R R (1979) Effective schools for the urban poor *Educational Leadership* **37** 17-23

Elliott, J (1976) Developing hypotheses about classrooms from teachers' practical constructs *Interchange* **7** 2 2-22, 76-77

Elliott, J (1980) Implications of classroom research for professional development *in* Hoyle, E and Megarry, J eds (1980) *Professional Development of Teachers World Yearbook of Education* Kogan Page: London/Nichols Publishing Co: New York

Elliott, J (1983) A curriculum for the study of human affairs: the contribution of Lawrence Stenhouse *Journal of Curriculum Studies* **15** 2 105-23

Elliott, J (1983a) Self-evaluation, professional development and accountability *in* Galton, M and Moon, R eds *Changing Schools . . . Changing Curriculum* Harper and Row: London

Elliott, J and Whitehead, D (1982) *Bulletin No 5 of the Classroom Action-Research Network* Cambridge Institute of Education

Etzioni, A (1982) *in American Education* (November and December volumes, US Department of Education)

Farrar, E, Desanctis, J E and Cohen, D K (1980) Views from below: implementation research in education *Teachers College Record* **82** 1 77-100

Feller, I (1981) Three coigns of diffusion research *in* Rich, R E ed *The Knowledge Cycle* Sage Publications: Beverley Hills, CA

Flather, P (1982) Conspiracies and counterplots *Times Higher Educational Supplement* 22 January

Florio, D H, Behrmann, M M and Goltz, D L (1979) What do policy makers think of educational research and evaluation? Or do they? *Educational Evaluation and Policy Analysis* 1 6 61-87

Fullan, M (1983) Evaluating program implementation: what can be learned from follow through *Curriculum Inquiry* 13 2 215-27

Gilliss, G C (1979) *Increasing Teacher Knowledge and Appreciation of Research* Paper presented at Canadian Education Association Conference on Research and the Classroom Teacher, Winnipeg

Glass, G V (1976) Primary, secondary, and meta-analysis of research *Educational Researcher* 5 5-8

Glass, G V (1978) Integrating findings: the meta-analysis of research *Review of Research in Education* 5 American Educational Research Association: Washington, DC

Glynn, E H (1971) University of Toronto, Classroom Applications of self-determined Reinforcement *in* Olson (1971)

Gordon, E W ed (1983) *Review of Research in Education* Vol 10, American Educational Research Association: Washington, DC

Gréco, P (1963) Apprentissage et structures intellectuelles (Industrial training and intellectual structures) *in* Fraisse et Piaget, *Traité de psychologie* T VIII PUF: Paris

Greenfield, T B (1979) *Research in Educational Administration in the United States and Canada: An Overview and Critique* Paper presented to British Educational Administration Society, Birmingham

Hall, G E and Loucks, S F (1982) Bridging the gap: policy research rooted in practice *in* Lieberman and McLaughlin 1982

Halmos, P (1971) Sociology and the personal service professions *in* Freidson, E ed *The Professions and their Prospects* Sage Publications: London

Hamilton, D (1981) Generalizations in the educational sciences: problems and purposes *in* Popkewitz and Tabachnick (1981)

Hammer, B (1910) Om pedagogikens problem och forskningsmetoder (About problems and research methods in education) *Svensk Lärartidning* 42 940-43

Havelock, R (1971b) The utilization of educational research and development *British Journal of Educational Technology* 2 2 84-98

Havighurst, R J (1982) Philanthropic foundations *in* Mitzel 1982

Hersom, N (1980) Twenty-five years of research in education: 1955 to 1979 *Alberta Journal of Educational Research* 26 262-75

Heyns, B L (1981) Policy implications of the public private school debates *Harvard Education Review* 5 519-25

Hofstee, W K B (1982) Evaluatie: een methodologische analyse *Tijdschrift voor Onderwijsresearch* 5 (in Dutch)

Holdaway, E A (1976) The organization of educational research: some European issues relevant to Canada *Canadian Journal of Education* 1 5-17

Holdaway, E A (1980) Educational administration in Canada: concerns, research and preparation programs *in* Farquhar and Housego (1980)

Holly, P (1984) Institutionalising action-research in schools *Cambridge Journal of Education* 14.2 Summer Term

Holly, P and Whitehead D (1984) *Bulletin No 6 of the Classroom Action-Research Network* Cambridge Institute of Education

Hoyle, E (1982) The professionalization of teachers: a paradox *British Journal of Educational Studies* 30 2 161-71

Hunka, S (1978) *Prospectives in Educational Research* Opening Address to Canadian Educational Research Association: London, Ontario

Husen, T (1984) Issues and their background *in* Husen, T and Kogan, M *eds* (1984) *Educational Research and Policy: How Do they Relate?* Pergamon Press: Oxford

Inhelder, B and Karmiloff-Smith, A (1974-75) If you want to get ahead, get a theory *Cognition* 3 3 193-212

Jenkins, D (1980) An adversary's account of SAFARI's ethics of case study *in* Simons (1980)
Johnson, M Jr (1967) Definition and Models in Curriculum Theory *International Review of Education* 19 187-94
Joseph, Sir Keith (1984) Speech to the North of England Conference, Sheffield, January 6 Department of Education and Science

Kallòs, D and Lundgren, U P (1975) Educational psychology: its scope and limits *British Journal of Educational Psychology* 45 111-21
Keeves, J P (1981) Societal change and its implications for educational research in Australia *in* Karmel, P *ed Education, Change and Society* ACER: Hawthorn (Vic) 239-53
Kemmis, S (1980) The imagination of the case and the invention of the study *in* Simons (1980)
Kenny, W R and Grotelueschen, A D (1984) Making the Case for Case Study *Journal of Curriculum Studies* 16 1 37-51
Kirkland, J, Deane, F and Brennan, M (1983) About CrySOS: a clinic for people with crying babies *Family Relations* 32 4
Klafki, W (1976a) Erziehungswissenschaft als kritisch-konstruktive Theorie: Hermeneutik, Empirie, Ideologiekritik (Educational science as critical-constructive theory: hermeneutics, empirics, ideology) *in* Klafki (1976b)
Klein, R (1976) The rise and decline of policy analysis: the strange case of health policymaking in Britain *Policy Analysis* 2 458-75
Knorr, K D (1975) The nature of scientific consensus and the case of the social sciences *in* Knorr, Strasser and Zilian (1975)
Komisar, B P (1971) Language of education *in* Deighton, L C *ed The Encyclopedia of Education* Vol 5 327-34 MacMillan and The Free Press: New York

LaNoue, G R (1982) Political science *in* Mitzel (1982)
Lasswell, H D (1951) Introduction *in* Lerner and Lasswell (1951)
Leigh, A (1980) Policy research and reviewing services for under fives *Social Policy and Administration* 14 162
Lemberg, E (1963a) Von der Erziehungswissenschaft zur Bildungsforschung: Das Bildungswesen als gesellschaftliche Institution (From educational science to educational research: education as a social institution) *in* Lemberg (1963b)
Lindblom, C E (1959) The science of 'muddling through' *Public Administration Review* 19 79-88
Louis, K S (1983) Dissemination systems: some lessons from programs of the past *in* Paisley, W J and Butler, M *Knowledge Utilization Systems in Education* Sage Publications: Beverly Hills, CA
Lynch, P (1979) Public policy and competency testing *Education and Urban Society* 12 65-80

Macnamara, D (1976) On returning to the chalk face: theory not into practice *British Journal of Teacher Education* 2 2
McPherson, A F (1975) Methodological aspects of collaborative research *Research Intelligence* 2
McPherson, A (1977) What is collaborative research? *Collaborative Research Newsletter* 1 1. Centre for Educational Sociology: Edinburgh University
Marklund, I (1982) The sectoral principle in Swedish research policy *in* Kallen, D B P, Kosse, G B, Wagenaar, H C, Kloprogge, J J J and Vorbeck, M *eds Social Science Research and Public Policy Making: A Reappraisal* NFER-Nelson: London

Marklund, S (1966) Educational reform and research in Sweden *Educational Research* 9 16-21

Marklund, S (1971) Comparative school research and the Swedish school reform *International Review of Education* 17 39-49

Marklund, S (1973) Comprehensive schools: research and strategy and its links with educational policy *in Second Colloquium of Directors of Educational Research Organizations* Council of Europe: Strasbourg

Marton, F (1975) On non-verbatim learning *Scandinavian Journal of Psychology* 16 273-79

Mitchell, D E (1981b) Social science utilization in state legislatures *in* Berliner (1981)

Mitchell, D E (1982) Governing schools *in* Mitzel (1982)

Mitchell, D E, Kerchner, C T, Erck, W and Pryor, G (1981) The impact of collective bargaining on school management and governance *The American Journal of Education* 89 147-88

Mitter, W (1983) Le recenti ricerche sulla scuola primaria nella Repubblica Federale Tedesca (Recent researches on the primary school in the Federal Republic of Germany) *in* Di Iorio (1983)

Morrell, D H (1962) The freedom of the teacher in relation to research and development work in the area of curriculum and examinations *Educational Research* 5 2 85-89

Morris, J G and Johnston, F H (1981) The impact of policy and practice on research *British Journal of Educational Studies* 29 209-17

Murphy, R (1982) Assessment *Research Intelligence* 12 6

NBE (1983) The Research Programme of the National Swedish Board of Education *School Research Newsletter, 1983* 2

Nash, R (1981) Ideology and the ideological effects of educational practice *Delta* 29 November 1981

Nisbet, J (1979) An international perspective *in* Ramsay, P (1979)

Nisbet, J (1981) Educational research and educational practice *in* Simon, B and Taylor, W *eds* (1981)

Nuthall, G A (1973) Contemporary models of teaching *in* Travers *ed* (1973)

Oléron, P (1963) Les activites intellectuelles (Intellectual activities) *in* Fraisse et Piaget *Traité de psychologie* T VIII PUF: Paris

Pitman, A (1981) The necessary distortion of disseminated innovations *Journal of Curriculum Studies* 13 3 253-56

Rich, R F (1976) Uses of social science information by federal bureaucrats: knowledge for action vs knowledge for understanding. A paper presented at the annual meeting of the Midwest Political Science Association, Chicago, Illinois, April 1976

Richardson, G (1983) Från ekologi till pedagogik: en förändring inom svensk skola — och en avhandlingsutveckling (From Ecology to Pedagogics: a change within the Swedish school — and the development of a thesis) *Forskning om utbildning* 10 47-55

Rist, R C (1980) Blitzkrieg ethnography *Educational Researcher*

Rist, R C (1981) On what we know (or think we do): gatekeeping and the social control of knowledge *in* Popkewitz and Tabachnick (1981)

Rogers, W T (1982) *Research in Canadian Education: Contributions to Canadian Society* Unpublished paper, University of British Columbia: Vancouver

Rossell, C H (1980) Social science research in equity cases: a critical review *in* Berliner (1980)

Roth, H (1963) Die realistische Wendung in der pädagogischen Forschung (Realistic change in pedagogic research) *Die deutsche Schule* 55 109-19

Ryan, D W and Butler, L F (1982) Effectiveness of teaching: the Canadian experience *Studies in Educational Evaluation* 7 247-62

Schiefelbein, E (1978) Educational research networks in Latin America *International Review of Education* 24 483-500

Schiefelbein, E (1981) Research, policy and practice: the case of Chile *International Review of Education* 27 153-62

Schilling, W R (1964) Scientists, foreign policy, and power *in* Galpin and Wright (1964)

Schon, D (1977) *in* Weiss, *op cit*

Schwab, J J (1969) The practical: a language for curriculum *School Review* Nov 1-23

Sheffield, E (1979) *Policy-oriented Research on National Issues in Higher Education* Discussion paper for the colloquium on data needs for higher education in the eighties, Statistics Canada: Ottawa

Short, E C (1983) The forms and use of alternative curriculum development strategies *Curriculum Inquiry* 13 1 43-64

Sim, W K (1983a) Research on the implementation and evaluation of reform of educational content and methods in Singapore *in* National Institute for Educational Research (1983)

Sim, W K (1983b) IEXamining and IEXpanding IEXperience: delineating IE's present and future roles *in* Lun, C Y and de Souza, D eds (1983)

Sim, W K (1983c) Research and teacher education: a Singapore perspective *Singapore Journal of Education* 5 2 127-37

Sim, W K (1984) Guest Editorial: Towards promoting research wisdom *Singapore Journal of Education* 6 1 (in press)

Simons, H (1981) Process evaluation in schools *in* Lacey, C and Lawton, D eds (1981)

Sjöstrand, W (1961) *Pedagogikens historia III: 1* (Educational History Part III: 1) CWK Gleerup: Lund

Skilbeck, M (1981) Curriculum issues in Australia 1970-1990 *Compare* II 1 59-76

Skilbeck, M (1983) Lawrence Stenhouse: research methodology *British Educational Research Journal* 9 1 11-20

Smith, L M (1981) Accidents, serendipity, and making the commonplace problematic: the origin and evolution of the field study 'problem' *in* Popkewitz and Tabachnick (1981)

Stake, R E (1978) The case study method in social inquiry *Educational Researcher* 5-8

Stenhouse, L (1970) Some limitations on the use of objectives in curriculum research and planning *Paedagogica Europaea* 6 73-83

Stenhouse, L (1971) The humanities curriculum project: the rationale *Theory into Practice* 10.3 154-62

Stenhouse, L (1983) Curriculum research and the art of the teacher *in Authority, Education and Emancipation* Heinemann Educational Books: London

Stuart, Dame Muriel (1970) The Schools Council: a mechanism for change *School and Innovation 1870-1970* Supplement to *Dialogue* (Feb) The Council: London

Tamir, P and Amir, R (1981) Retrospective curriculum evaluation: an approach to the evaluation of long term effects *Curriculum Inquiry* 11 3 259-78

Taylor, W (1981) Education research and development in the UK *International Review of Education* 27 179-96

Terhart, E (1982) Interpretative approaches in educational research *Cambridge Journal of Education* 12 141-60

Tom, A R (1980) Teaching as a moral craft: a metaphor for teaching and teacher education *Curriculum Inquiry* 10.3

Tomkins, G, Connelly, F M and Bernier, J-J (1981) *State of the Art Review of Research in Curriculum and Instruction* Submission to the State of the Art Review of Educational Research for the Canadian Society for the Study of Education

Ukeles, J B (1977) Policy analysis: myth or reality? *Public Administration Review* 23 221-28

Walker, R (1980) Making sense and losing meaning *in* Simons (1980)

Walker, R (1981) Three good reasons for not doing case study research BERA paper (mimeo)

Wehlage, G (1981) The purpose of generalization in field-study research *in* Popkewitz and Tabachnick (1981)

Weiss, C H (1979) The many meanings of research utilization *Public Administration Review* September/October 426-31

Weiss, C H (1981) Policy research in the context of diffuse decision-making *in* Kallen *et al* (1982)

Weiss, J (1976) Using social science for social policy *Policy Studies Journal* 4 234-23

White, J P (1969) The curriculum mongers: education in reverse *New Society* 6 March

Winter, R (1982) Dilemma analysis *Cambridge Journal of Education* 12.3 Michaelmas Term

Wirt, F M (1980) Comparing educational policies: theory, units of analysis, and research strategies *Comparative Education Review* 24 174-91

Wirt, F (1982) Neo-Conservatism and national school policy *Educational Evaluation and Policy Analysis* Nov/Dec 6

Wirt, F M and Mitchell, D E (1983) Social science and educational reform: the political uses of social research *Educational Administration Quarterly* 18 1-16

Wolcott, H (1975) Criteria for an ethnographic approach to research in schools *Human Organization* 34 111-27

Wood, N (1984) Exams Council answers Sir Keith's call *Times Educational Supplement* 13 January

Wright, E N (1982) *Role and Function of Research Units in Boards of Education in Ontario* Paper presented to Association of Educational Research Officers of Ontario, Toronto

Wrigley, J (1973a) The Schools Council *in* Butcher, H J and Pont, H B *eds* (1973)

Yeakey, C C (1983) Emerging policy research in education research and decision-making *in* Gordon (1983)

Section IV: Annotated bibliography

Atkin, J M (1979) Educational accountability in the United States *Educational Analysis* 1 1 5-22
A review of schemes for accountability employed in the United States is presented in the context of a discussion of their origins. Factors cited include concern about school effectiveness, the failure of schools and other public institutions to be agents of social reform, distrust of specialists and fragmentation of community. The implications are explored in terms of the demise of public schooling in the USA.

Brahm, L and Gutierrez, G (1983) REDUC: an educational documentation network serving development in Latin America *UNESCO Journal of Information Science, Librarianship and Archives Administration* 5 89-94
An account of the origins, objectives, organization and output of REDUC — the Latin American Educational Documentation Network — which has been functioning in various countries in the region since 1972 as a disseminator of information and its products. Information is defined by REDUC as 'the relationship established between a set of data and a set of problems with a view to making appropriate decisions designed to understand and solve these problems', and its activities include training educational personnel in ways of using scientific data and applying them to the problems they are facing.

Bush, R N (1976) *Educational Research and Development: the Next Decade* Occasional Paper No 11, Stanford Center for Research and Development in Teaching: Stanford, CA
Bush, director of the Stanford Center for Research and Development in Teaching from 1965-76, defines research and development as the 'discovery of new knowledge and its application in the solution of problems' and 'the relating of theory and practice'. This paper outlines the history of R & D in the USA with special reference to the period since 1960. In general, the effects of educational R & D upon educational practice have been disappointing because the effort has been too small, the trained researchers too few, and the resources too limited, An 11 point agenda for educational R & D during the next decade includes: (1) building a constituency; (2) broadening the collegial base; (3) strengthening all parts of the R & D enterprise; (4) recognizing that education is a total system; (5) shifting emphasis from correlational studies and single-variable experimental studies to more complex experimental studies, interventions and clinical analyses; (6) making more modest claims; (7) building a better national educational R & D agenda; (8) effectively advancing the interdisciplinary claims of educational R & D; (9) strengthening university participation in educational R & D; (10) increasing attention to cost/benefit considerations; (11) re-establishing the upward trend of expenditures for educational R & D.

Carraz, R (1984) *Recherche en éducation et socialisation de l'enfant* (Report on research in the education and socialization of the child) Rapport au Ministère de la Recherche et de la Technologie, La Documentation Française: Paris
A recent synthesis of the state of educational research in France with recommendations for its development. This report is the work of a large commission which has produced several reports synthesized by the author.

Connell, W F (1980) *The Australian Council for Educational Research (ACER) 1930-80* ACER: Hawthorn (Vic)
A detailed history of the growth of ACER, the personalities who shaped it and the programmes which were undertaken. Includes a select list of research and development activities and publications by ACER.

Cros, L (1981) *Quelle école, pour quel avenir?* (What school, for what future?) Casterman: Paris
A synthesis of research studies fully documented with numerous unpublished references. The author, who was director of the National Institute of Pedagogy and director of the central administration of the national Ministry of Education, has made an exhaustive review of educational policy and educational research in France over the past 30 years.

Dockrell, W B and Hamilton, D eds (1980) *Rethinking Educational Research* Hodder and Stoughton: London, UK (index)
Eleven essays mostly from the mid 1970s (some revised for publication in this volume) on the nature of educational research, and its relationship to practice. Their main thrust is towards explaining how educational research has developed and the need to devise models and approaches which will help understanding of practice and provide the means to influence it. Several of the authors have since developed more sustained treatments of the themes touched upon. Contributors include Nisbet, Dockrell, Bruner (on the role of the researcher as an adviser to the educational policy maker), Walker (on case studies), Becher, Stake (on responsive evaluation), Westbury, Bernstein, Kallos and Matthew, Smith and Connolly (on nursery education). The editors do not attempt to explain the significance of the contributions.

Farquhar, R H and Housego, I E eds (1980) *Canadian and Comparative Educational Administration* Education-Extension, University of British Columbia: Vancouver (index)
This collection relates to the contemporary role of the educational administrator as a mediator among various internal and external forces that influence the formulation

and implementation of policy. It is based on papers prepared for an International Intervisitation Program in Education Administration (IIP '78) held in Canada during May 1978. It is organized in seven sections. The Prologue relates specifically to leadership for educational administration in Canada. Section two focuses on policy issues drawing upon both theoretical foundations and illustrative cases from several countries. Section three includes papers on problems and trends in the field of educational administration with reference to England, Canada, Australia and Sri Lanka. Section four deals with training of educational administrators, with papers on the South American and South-east Asian contexts as well as America, Britain and Australia. Sections five and six deal with planning (including a paper on Nigeria) and 'prospects' which comprise two papers on the future study of educational administration. The final section — Epilogue — comprises a paper by Housego on Administration and Policy Making in Education: the contemporary predicament. Papers have been edited and revised to sustain the focus outlined above, and some new papers specially commissioned have been included.

Fullan, M (1982) *The Meaning of Educational Change* Teachers College Press: New York (index)
Many people do not have a clear coherent sense of meaning of what educational change is for, what it is and how it proceeds. Yet unless change is understood at the subjective level (how people actually experience it), and at the sociopolitical level, the problem of deciding the direction of change and the means of realizing it will not be appreciated. These issues are explored with the assistance of a wide range of examples of externally and internally initiated educational innovations which have affected primary and secondary schools and were implemented at school, district and national levels. The bulk of the examples are from Canada and USA, although some are from UK.

Part I provides the overall framework. Its six chapters consider such issues as the sources of educational change, its meaning, the causes and processes of adoption, implementation and maintenance, and issues in planning, managing and coping with change. Part II focuses on roles of the various participants in change. Six chapters review the role of teachers, the principal, the student, the district administrator, the consultant, the parent and the community. Part III focuses on three issues: the role of federal, state and provincial governments, the professional preparation and development of teachers, and the future of educational change. An appendix defines 15 selected major innovative programmes and research studies in the United States.

An impressive distillation of knowledge; as Seymour Sarnson rightly observes, 'Professor Fullan has written a most comprehensive analysis of discrete studies of efforts at educational change. He puts this analysis in a most thoughtful theoretical framework and manages extraordinarily well to make it interesting to the reader. That is no small feat!'

House, E R (1980) *Evaluating with Validity* Sage Publications, Beverly Hills, CA
House aims to make evaluators more reflective about what they do. The book presents a clear and impressively comprehensive conceptualization of modern evaluation, ranging from the major approaches, to the standards and principles such a practice must entail, to a critique of those approaches by those standards.

There are four parts. Part I characterizes modern evaluation efforts. A summary of basic evaluation approaches is presented and the underlying epistemological, ethical and political assumptions are explicated against a background which assumes that evaluators, irrespective of approach adopted, are operating rationally.

Part II suggests that truth, beauty and justice are the 'standards for evaluation'. Truth entails more than merely 'scientific' truth; beauty, manifested in coherence and imagery in the evaluation, influences the credibility of the evaluation for a particular audience; sense of justice has important consequences for the type of evaluation one undertakes and for the results of the evaluation.

Part III attempts to derive the political and moral principles on which an evaluation should be based. Evaluation is seen as rational persuasion; the conditions necessary for 'fair' evaluation are explained.

Part IV is a critique of federal evaluation policy in the USA and of the major evaluation approaches discussed in Part I. No approach serves for all occasions. The nature of valid evaluation is discussed: such evaluation should be true, credible and normatively correct.

The three appendices include an analysis of the logic of an evaluation, a discussion of naturalistic evaluation, and an example of an evaluation agreement.

Husen, T and Kogan, M eds (1984) *Educational Research and Policy: How Do They Relate?* Pergamon Press: Oxford, UK (index)
This is a record of a symposium held in 1982 to mark Husen's retirement. It has three parts: first, Husen himself reports interviews with leading policy makers and researchers in Sweden, Germany, Britain and USA; second, Kogan, who acted as rapporteur, provides in seven sections (52 pages) a penetrating analysis and concise summary of research-policy issues; third, the 12 papers are reproduced, including one by Mats Hultin on the role of the World Bank. Other contributors include Coleman, Dahllöf, Postlethwaite and Trow.

Issues highlighted by Kogan include the relation of research to policy, and of policy to research; the importance of considering the role of different types of research (eg fundamental v *ad hoc*) on policy for different aspects of the education system (eg school v higher education) in different contexts (eg developed v developing countries) which reflect different social, political and ideological systems and traditions. *Accounts* of 'impact' are distinguished from *explanations* which are subsumed within different types of models, which themselves reflect the different orientations of researchers to context and the perception of the role of research by policy makers in different contexts. Interaction between researchers and policy makers may be on a consensual or linear basis, as brokers (eg World Bank) on a pluralistic model which emphasizes multidimensional viewpoints, or as agents of falsification of policy makers' assumptions. The models in use reflect institutional relationships between researchers and policy makers, and the nature of the knowledge seeking and using systems developed by policy makers: in some situations policy makers and researchers may interchange roles; in others, house R & D units within government may facilitate communication. The nature of the knowledge base relevant for different kinds of policy making, and the concept of what counts as knowledge, are also problematical. Within government the nature of the policy field, the stage of intervention (viz policy formulation, legislation, implementation) and the extent to which the government is the primary user of the knowledge requested, or a secondary user which channels development ideas towards practitioners, are further considerations which help explain the conclusion that the knowledge-policy relationship is indeterminate and unsystematic, and that diffusion and enlightenment are the main ways in which 'impact' is to be seen.

International Review of Education XXVII (1981) 101-206 A Special Issue on the Provision for Educational Research and Development in countries across the world, edited by J D Nisbet.
This special issue includes an editorial, seven country reviews, and an extensive review article by R J W Selleck of Weiss (1977), Suppes (1978), Dockrell and Hamilton (1980) and Nisbet and Broadfoot (1980). The reviews cover Sweden (I Marklund's chapter is the basis of the contribution to the present yearbook), USA (Gideonse), Upper Volta (Damiba (in French)), Thailand (Ketudat and Fry), Chile (Schiefelbein), Poland (Okon) and UK (Taylor).

Following an attempt to classify research as 'free', 'policy-oriented' and 'developmental', Taylor's payer reviews the relatively modest growth of such research in the UK from the mid 1960s. Research 'impact' is discussed in terms of duration, audience and generalizability. The conclusion reviews problems, future prospects and requirements.

Kallen, D B P, Kosse, G B, Wagenaar, H C, Kloprogge, J J J and Vorbeck, M (1982) *Social Science Research and Public Policy-Making: A Reappraisal* SVO-NFER-Nelson: Windsor (no index)
SVO (Foundation for Educational Research in the Netherlands) organized a symposium in 1981. The issues discussed are clearly presented in a helpful introduction and the 11 papers, which deal with both general issues and experience in developed western countries, are reproduced. The essential impact of research on policy making is seen to be in its capacity to redefine the problem facing policy makers. This, however, raises the question of the political dimension in research in terms of what is permitted to be investigated, the selective perception of issues and policy alternatives by researchers, and the willingness and ability of administrators and politicians to modify dogma in the light of research evidence. In short, the problem of the relationship between social science research and policy making is seen less in terms of a gap to be bridged and more in terms of how the wisdom of policy making can be improved and the role of research in improving it.

Contributors include Wagenaar, Caplan, Dockrell, de Groot, Klabbers, Legrand, Marklund, De Mey, Sheerens, Suppes, Timpome, Weiss. Caplan's and Weiss' papers are of particular interest. Caplan reports on empirical data regarding the utilization of knowledge for the social sciences. He suggests that knowledge has a *life cycle* within an organization: it both survives and changes. A life cycle approach by definition encompasses more than input-output stages. Once attention is given to the throughput stage organizational variables become pre-eminent over the customary variables such as timeliness, relevance, etc.

Weiss shows how generalizations and ideas from numbers of studies come into currency in an indirect way: the main influence is *enlightenment*. She illustrates this in the context of political decision-making processes.

Legrand, L (1977) *Pour une politique démocratique de l'éducation* (A democratic approach to education) Presses Universitaires de France: Paris
The author is Research Director of the National Institute for Educational Research in Paris. He takes as the basis of this work the undeniable sickness of the present education system after 15 years of innovations which have failed, and questions the reasons for these failures.

The first part of his book comprises nine chapters. Drawing on the archives of the National Institute for Educational Research, as well as his own objective study, he points out the hierarchical and bureaucratic forces at work in an effort to neutralize innovation, while the technical and economic evolution of society gradually changes the structure of a school system which resists change. Chapter titles include 'the failure of transition and practical classes', 'the proliferation of exams', and 'innovations in content and methods in (a) mathematics and (b) French in the elementary school: the reasons for failure'.

The second part comprises four chapters in which he tries to point the way to effective reform. Such reform is inseparable in his eyes from political and social transformation. But he also insists on the need to break the weight of hierarchy and bureaucracy by giving freedom to local initiative, and responsibility to teachers, parents and pupils, without which no positive evolution of the education system is possible. An annexe includes three papers: the first is an example of evaluated innovation in secondary education (the CES), the second is reflections on the organization of educational research, while the third discusses the nature and conditions of innovation.

Louis, Karen S and Sieber, S D (1979) *Bureaucracy and the Dispersed Organisation: the Educational Extension Agent Experiment* Ablex Publishing Corporation: New Jersey (index)
Set in the context of 'bridging the gap between research findings and practitioner use' this volume provides an account of a pilot experiment in the USA in the introduction of seven educational 'extension agents' — field workers with a role parallel to that in agriculture — whose remit was to assist schools in three states to modify practice. In addition to considering issues in the development of an innovative dispersed organization (ie goals, functions, roles and levels of support), the authors highlight the effectiveness of intervention to promote clients' needs and problem centred analysis.

Malpica, C ed (1983) *The generalisation of educational innovations: the administrator's perspective* International Institute for Educational Planning: Paris, France (mimeo)
This report of a 1980 IIEP seminar comprises an introductory note, three background papers, three national experiences (Ghana, Peru and Malaysia) and a selective bibliography. It represents a follow up to a research project reprinted in Adams and Chen (1981)*.

The introductory note (Malan and Rassekh) contrasts *innovation* — 'more isolated efforts to improve or change certain aspects of the educational process' — with *reform* which is whole system, involves non-educational considerations such as economic development, equality of opportunity, etc and reflects a decision taken at the centre of the system. In his background note Adams, drawing on case study evidence, identifies the mechanisms of reform, the structures through which different systems are realized, and the functions (eg monitoring and implementation) to be filled and the different administrative components which are relevant. Malan identifies administrative problems in the generalization of reform, including attitudes and styles, the balance of power between different levels of an administration and its related agencies, the financial consequences of the generalization of innovations and the human factor (eg volunteers v conscripts). Havelock and Huberman, on the basis of research on the nature of 65 innovations, identify six themes which explain issues in generalization. To these they give the acronym ORACLE in which O = object, R = relevance, A = authority, C = consensus, L = linkage, E = environment. In addition they provide four model patterns of generalization of projects, viz 'the alternative of grandeur', 'controlled expansion', the crusade, and small-scale and local. They also illustrate 'long' and 'short' cycle patterns of problem solving.

Country experiences comprise an account of the Ghana experiment in continuation schools (Anim), introduction of innovations in Peruvian education in 1972 to make it broader in scope and more democratic (by CIPE (the Centre for Investigation and Promotion of Education)) and the integrated curriculum project in Malaysia (Ahmed).

Mitchell, Douglas E (1981) *Shaping Legislative Decisions: Education Policy and the Social Sciences* Lexington Books D C Heath and Company: Lexington, Mass (index)
An analysis of the ways in which legislative policy makers in three states in the USA (California, Oregon and Arizona) develop policies in the context of lobbies and pressures. Part I develops an overall perspective for interpreting state legislative policy making in terms of previous research, the nature of the decision-making situation affecting legislation, and the principal elements in each policy actor's orientation toward decision-making responsibilities.

Part II reports the results of the analysis of field data which demonstrate the role of social science evidence in the three stages affecting the development of legislation,

* Adams, R S and Chen, D (1981) *The Process of Educational Innovation: An International Perspective* Kogan Page: London and the UNESCO Press: Paris

viz articulation (problem definition), aggregation (problem solving by providing evidence for a proposed line of action) and allocation (evidence assessment to win the debate on the consequences of the policy). At the stage of 'oversight' of existing policies, social science provides performance evaluation, principally for the mobilization of criticism. Mitchell's findings lead him to conclude that 'social science expertise is more widely used than generally appreciated', and that 'policy-makers differ in both their inclinations and their capacities to utilise social research and evaluation findings', that 'intellectually social-science serves to conceptualise and interpret cause and effect relationships', while 'socially, it shapes the development of support groups or coalitions and controls access to legislative debate'.

Part III is a summary in which seven major recommendations for improving legislative decision making and social science utilization are presented. These include that 'sponsors, disseminators and interpretors of social science should self consciously discriminate between *policy* research and evaluation (intended for immediate utilisation in decision making) and *social* research and evaluation (intended to expand general knowledge about social behaviour)', and that 'state legislatures should develop procedures for *systematically* monitoring social research in order to assess its implications for current policy decisions; and these include training opportinities to upgrade skills in locating and interpreting social science findings'.

Mitter, W and Weishaupt, H eds (1979) *Strategien und Organisationsformen der Begleitforschung* (Strategies and organizational forms in associated research) Beltz Verlag: Weinheim/Basel (Deutsches Institut für Internationale Pedagogische Forschung): Frankfurt-am-Main
The papers in this volume were presented at a conference organized by the Society for the Promotion of Educational Research in 1976. They provide a review of research on a number of experiments and developments in education undertaken by the Länder and by the Federal Commission for Educational Planning. They illustrate the whole spectrum of present-day associated research practice and problems. The following case studies (with critical commentary by colleagues in some cases) are included: (i) Three case studies of differentiated teaching in comprehensive schools (Baumert); (ii) Innovation and evaluation in regional teacher further education and neighbourhood curriculum development in Hessen 1972-77 (Heymann); (iii) Case studies of organizational patterns and research perspectives in academic initiatives in reform at Secondary Level II (Seidl); (iv) Three case studies in the academic accompaniment to innovations at Secondary Level I (Teschner).

Mitzel, H E ed (1982) *Encyclopaedia of Educational Research* Fifth Edition (Four Volumes) The Free Press: New York
Sponsored by the American Educational Research Association and begun in 1979 there are 12,000 index entries and 317 contributors most of whom discuss the policy implications of the research reviewed in the US context. Volume 1 includes the organizing scheme with entries classified under 18 broad headings. Major articles are also listed.

Myers, R (1981) *Connecting worlds: a survey of developments in Educational Research in Latin America* IDRC – TS35: Toronto
The situation of educational research in developing countries (with special reference to Latin America, Sub-Saharan Africa and India) is contrasted with that which pertains in the industrialized countries. Based on extensive and considered personal experience and insight, the author explores the question of how these 'two worlds of research' may be brought into closer interaction. A useful list of 'lessons learned' about the climate and organization of research, research themes and methods, and the communication and impact of research results is included.

Nisbet, J D and Broadfoot, P (1980) *The Impact of Research on Policy and Practice in Education* Aberdeen University Press: Aberdeen (index)
This clearly structured and widely quoted review was commissioned by the UK

SSRC (now Economic and Social Research Council). Based on a literature review and interviews with leading figures in the UK and USA, it focuses on 'research . . . directed towards advancement of knowledge', ie excluding curriculum development and evaluation. Four chapters are aimed at a general audience and review the North American and the European scenes and the personal perspectives of administrators and researchers on the meaning of 'impact'. One chapter examines theoretical frameworks and perspectives that might be used for empirical studies seeking to explain impact. The final chapter is aimed at policy makers and practitioners and discusses policy for promoting 'research into research'. The introduction includes an overview in which the authors conclude that the contribution of research to education is more often in establishing appropriate questions to be asked by those who have to decide and act than in providing them with ready-made answers. Includes an extensive bibliography.

New Zealand Association for Research in Education (1980) *Research in Education in New Zealand: The State of the Art* Research Monograph No 3 NZARE Wellington and Delta: Palmerston North
This is a collection of 15 state-of-the-art papers and seven commentaries given at the first NZARE (New Zealand Association for Research in Education) conference. Each article surveys a single field including aims, methods and significance of the studies reviewed. Topics include early education, child development, education of Maori children, special education, guidance and counselling, sociology of education, women and education, history of education, measurement and testing, classroom studies, behaviour analysis, reading, science education, mathematics education and continuing education. Bibliographies and names of scholars working in these fields are also provided. Overall the book gives the most comprehensive and substantive picture available of research in New Zealand prior to 1980.

Organisation for Economic Co-operation and Development (1983) *Reviews of National Policies for Education: New Zealand* OECD: Paris
An up-to-date commentary on New Zealand education organized round five main themes: school structures, curriculum and examinations, preparation for the transition to working life, access and resources, and educational policy making.

A brief chapter on research reviews its development, the issues under investigation and the problems currently being faced. The latter include funding and coordination with other kinds of social inquiry and decision making.

Oldham, G (1982) *The Future of Research: Programme of Study into the Future of Higher Education* Vol 4 Research into Higher Education Monographs, Society for Research into Higher Education: Guildford, Surrey
A volume of background papers and discussion notes on one of the 1982 SRHE/ Leverhulme Seminars. It focuses on the specific role of institutions of higher education (especially universities) in the UK in research against a background of the changing conception of the function of research. Since higher education contributes only 10 per cent of the research and development activity in the UK, one question explored is the particular role the higher education system should seek to play. Chapters on research in the natural sciences, social sciences and the humanities contrast and illuminate differences in the concept, nature and context of research, and review such factors as the balance between teaching and research, the role of Research Councils, sources of funding, and the extent to which institutions can and should develop and pursue their own research policy. One chapter discusses issues in postgraduate research training. The 14 final recommendations are related to the longer-term health of higher education research by suggesting means whereby priorities can be identified and funding can be managed to ensure that these are adequately tackled.

Paisley, W J and Butler, M (1983) *Knowledge Utilisation Systems in Education* Sage Publications: Beverly Hills, CA
This volume claims to provide 'the most comprehensive overview of educational

knowledge utilisation (eku) yet to appear'. Knowledge utilization refers to communication of new knowledge within and between the different groups in education with a need or interest in acquiring and acting on it. Its 16 chapters and nine short case studies describe the history, current status and future prospects of eku systems in the USA. Each chapter is clearly structured.

Part I – *Origins* – comprises two chapters. One is by the senior editor which discusses trends in enrolment and educational finance between 1965 and the late 1970s, and describes the educational and political preconditions for the flowering of dissemination, technical assistance and networking programmes. A second chapter outlines the role of federal government in coordinating and promoting change.

Part II -– *Approaches* – comprises eight chapters which review the development and role of systems such as ERIC, the National Diffusion Network, extension experiments, state and regional initiatives, and inter-organizational arrangements.

Part III — *Issues* – comprises five chapters which examine the costs of extension systems, the equity of topic coverage and distribution in information systems, advances in dissemination practice (a much cited review by Peterson and Emrick) and in diffusion theory. The editors contribute a 'futures' chapter on eku in 2001.

Part IV comprises succinct authoritative case studies written by those directly involved and describes traditional information dissemination services (journals and resource centres) as well as newer developments such as networks and information exchange centres for women, technical assistance and other specialist interests. The concluding example describes the role of electronic technology in providing information about technology.

Roth, L ed (1978) *Methoden erziehungswissenschaftlicher Forschung* (Educational Research Methods) Verlag W Kohlhammer: Stuttgart, W Germany
Leading German experts survey methods of undertaking educational research in different fields using a wide range of techniques. Each essay attempts to be comprehensive and includes suggestions for further reading. Chapter headings (and authors) are: (1) Educational research, its methods, topics and difficulties (Roth); (2) Research in terms of its practice, concepts, strategies and financing (Merkens); (3) Methods in the humanities (Beckmann); (4) Empirical research methods (Roth); (5) Research planning and design (Rollett); (6) Research statistics (Fricke and Rützel); (7) Methods in comparative education (Schiff); (8) A critique of ideology (Klafki); (9) Action research (Straka). (10) Methods of teaching business management in the educational system (Schönwalder).

Schon, D A (1983) *The Reflective Practitioner: How Professionals Think in Action* Temple Smith: London (index)
Schon's concern is with an 'epistemology of practice'. He considers how professionals interpret, seek for and find solutions to the problems which confront them in their work. He compares this performance to that of the artist: intuitive or unconscious selection is made from the models of practice, techniques and strategies that represent their expertise. His analysis challenges the concept of professionalism based on 'technical rationality'. It conceives of professional practice as straightforward application of scientific theory and technique to new problem cases. Schon argues that practice involves the professional in finding solutions by means of 'reflection-in-action'. This is a research activity involving experimentation and testing the 'fit' of solutions before adoption of the most satisfying as the 'best resolution' of the problem.

Part I of this clearly and economically written text comprises chapters on the 'crisis of confidence in professional knowledge' and 'from technical rationality to reflection-in-action'. Part II comprises seven chapters five of which illustrate the analysis of practical problems in such fields as design, psychotherapy, engineering design and scientific research, town planning and management. Reference is also made to a study of the professional development of teachers through in-service experiences at MIT.

Two of the chapters stand back from the cases. One of these describes 'the structure of reflection-in-action' in terms of how the reflective practitioner interacts with a problem. He seeks to redefine it, and to evaluate the quality of successive attempts to understand its nature and to prescribe ways of best solving it. Such experimentation is conducted in a 'virtual world' of the office or the personal tutorial, where everyday impediments to vigorous reflection-in-action can be suspended or controlled. Another chapter examines 'patterns and limits of reflection-in-action across the professions'.

Part III examines the nature of reflective research and considers the implications of reflection-in-action for the future of the professions and the bureaucratic structures within which professions operate. Reflective research involves *frame analysis* (of the ways in which problems and roles are perceived), *repertoire building* on the basis of the analysis of complex cases, precedents and exemplars which illuminate the link between theory and practice, applications of *methods of inquiry and overarching theories* held by practitioners and which help them interpret and restructure new problem cases, and focusing on the *process of problem solving* so that practitioners can be helped to articulate the basis for their actions, and thus be made more conscious of the operation of the reflective process.

Reflection-in-action creates tension between the individual (eg the teacher) and the structures of his institution and its operational assumptions; the stability of the institutional structure is challenged. Yet reflection-in-action is a prerequisite for sophisticated professional performance, and for the viability of professions within society. This conception of role is essential to the health, effectiveness and relevance of the institution: the problem for the institution is to develop a learning system capable of coping with such tensions and converting them into productive channels.

Simons, H ed (1980) *Towards a Science of the Singular* Centre for Applied Research in Education, University of East Anglia Occasional Publication No 10, 1980: Norwich, UK
Eleven seminal papers prepared for a 1975 conference in the UK on 'Case Study Methods in Educational Research and Evaluation'. An excellent introductory chapter by the editor highlights the main themes which include the theory-practice issues, epistemology of case study, issues in problem definition, evidence collecting and reporting, ethical issues, political contexts, and dissemination. She also provides a helpful introductory note to each contribution summarizing key points and connecting the different papers, all of which reflect an 'illuminative' approach to empirical enquiry drawing on the seminal thinking of Stenhouse and Parlett and Hamilton.

The authors include Barry MacDonald and David Jenkins (the ethics and politics of case study), Adelman, Kemmis and Jenkins (the contribution of case study to educational research), Stake (the nature of generalization in case study — a widely quoted reference also published in *Educational Research* (1978) 5-8), Hamilton (assumptions underlying case study research), Kemmis (the conception of 'the case' and the nature and justification of case study), Graef and Smith (the ethics of conducting and reporting case studies), Walker (on making sense of the data), Walker and Wilby (on parallels with documentary film making and journalism), and Parlett (on training for case study research and evaluation).

In his paper Stake argues that people understand events and situations on the basis of personal experience (tacit knowledge) which is the basis for generalization. In educational matters the way to understanding is through cases which are helpful for defining the focus of enquiry. Cases can take a variety of forms and provide a means of testing hypotheses. Case studies provide a more sure basis for generalization from naturalistic evidence.

Stenhouse, L (1975) *An Introduction to Curriculum Research and Development* Heinemann Educational Books: London (index)
'A central problem in the improvement of education is the gap between accepted

policy and practice' (p218). The late Stenhouse was a seminal writer. This book is a classic for the scope of its discussion on the role of the teacher, the nature of curriculum, and the conceptualization of the process of innovation, reflecting primarily the UK context. Stenhouse argues that schools should be conceived as research and development institutions rather than as the clients of external, support agencies, that there should be collaboration and partnership between staff on projects and teachers, reflecting the different skills they bring to the analysis of practice, that the classroom is the context for developing understanding of the processes of teaching and learning and that classroom teachers can be assisted to become researchers of their own practice and agents in its development. For Stenhouse research is 'the means towards a "disciplined institution", fusing creativeness and self criticism' (p223). His work has been an important influence on the development of the thinking of a number of contributors to the present volume.

Suppes, P *ed* (1978) *Impact of Research on Education: some Case Studies* National Academy of Education: Washington, DC (index)
This volume comprises nine chapters which review research findings in terms of their effect on school practice. The focus is not on the scientific validity of the ideas presented but on the impact of these ideas on educational practice. Several chapters adopt an historical approach. They focus on use of psychological tests (Carroll), vocabulary research and the written materials used in schools (Clifford), behaviour modification and the influence of B F Skinner (Glazer), implications of Piaget's theories (Groen), the influence of psychoanalysis in American elementary education (Suppes and Warren), language research applications in second language acquisition (Stern, Wesche and Harley), the relationship between basic research and practice, with special reference to the architectural design of classrooms (Getzels), educational research and educational reform in Sweden (Husen), social science research, the law and school finance reform (Bressler and Berks).

Getzels' paper argues that basic research has more long-term influence than applied research: it alters the paradigm cumulatively. He defines basic research as 'studies in which the investigator fomulates his own problem regarding a phenomenon or issue, and his aim is primarily to conceptualise and understand the chosen phenomenon or issue, and only secondarily, if at all, to do anything about'. Basic research − or 'theoretical inquiry' or 'conclusion oriented' investigations − deals with 'discovered' problems, while applied research deals with 'presented' problems. The crucial function the university performs is formulating and pursuing apparently impractical problems which otherwise might remain imprisoned for being unformulated. He quotes the Nobel Prize physicist Feynmann: 'the truth is discovered first, and the beauty or "necessity" of that truth only seen later'. The dangers of avoiding theory are factualism, reliance on 'experts', adherence to pat techniques, lack of a professional language, and 'subjectivity'.

Taylor, W *ed* (1973) *Research Perspectives in Education* Routledge and Kegan Paul: London (index)
One of the first UK attempts to analyse the conceptual foundations and organization and management of educational research. Part I contains useful chapters by Taylor (organization of educational research in UK) and Härnqvist (training and career structures of educational researchers). Part II consists of somewhat dated 'disciplinary perspectives' by Peters and White (philosophy), Nisbet and Entwistle (psychology), Simon (history), Musgrove (sociology of the school and of teaching), and Swift (sociology and educational research). Part III is on 'research and practice' and comprises chapters by Taylor (knowledge and research) and by Glennerster and Hoyle (research and education policy).

Weiss, C H *ed* (1977) *Using Social Research in Public Policy Making* Lexington Books D C Heath and Company: Lexington, USA (index)
A seminal reader with a succinct and penetrating introduction by the editor. She summarizes the conventional wisdom on research utilization and identifies in the

reported studies the range of different meanings which the term may have and the actual uses to which research is put in policy formulation. She emphasizes the important role of research in problem conceptualization.

Four of the remaining 15 chapters discuss obstacles to transforming social research results into policy decisions. These include the differences in experience and outlook of policy makers and researchers, divergence in values, and the unstable and ambiguous nature of social research knowledge. Another four chapters deal with the relationship between research and policy in executive agencies, legislation and the courts in the USA. Six chapters present quantitative evidence on the relationship between research and government policy in such fields as health and policy making. A final chapter by Rheim and Schon examines the metaphors, stories, maps and models within which social 'problems' are framed, and reframed, and suggests criteria against which problem setting may be evaluated.

The papers reflect European as well as North American perspectives: the editor points out that the issues of the relationship of policy to research are international. Weiss offers six models of using research: (1) *problem solving: the classical, linear model* (research provides empirical evidence that will help to solve a policy problem); (2) *knowledge-driven: knowledge exists and is harnessed by society* (basic research is applied to meet a practical need, eg the pill); (3) *interactive model* (researchers contribute as one lobby to the pool of ideas and views on how a problem should be resolved); (4) *research as political ammunition: political model* (research used as ammunition for the side in a policy debate that finds its conclusions most congenial and supportive); (5) *miscellaneous uses: the tactical model* (research to delay action, as a training ground for researchers, to generate more research); (6) *research as conceptualization* (research, often undertaken at some remove from the immediate policy issue, used to reconceptualize the character of policy issues or even to redefine the policy agenda).

Biographical notes on contributors and editors

Raymond S Adams (Chapter 11), after academic service in universities in New Zealand, Australia and the USA, became Dean of Education at Massey University in 1980. He has been Chairman of the New Zealand Council for Educational Research for four years and has written books on classroom research and research on educational innovation. He has a number of research publications in British, American, Australian and New Zealand journals. He was for two years seconded to UNESCO's International Institute for Educational Planning in Paris.

Sally Brown (Chapter 13) is a Senior Research Fellow in the education department at the University of Stirling where she has been since 1970. From 1980 she was seconded for four years as Research Adviser/Consultant to the Scottish Education Department with responsibilities mainly for negotiating and managing a programme of 25 research projects associated with developments in the curriculum and assessment of 14- to 16-year-olds. Her research interests have been broadly in the areas of science education, curriculum innovation and assessment. She has published articles and books on pupils' and teachers' attitudes, integrated science, cognitive preferences, factors affecting the effectiveness of curriculum innovations, classroom observation, action-research, criterion-referenced assessment and assessment in a variety of areas of the curriculum. Before joining an education department, she taught physics at school, college of education and university levels, and spent nearly five years in Nigeria.

John Elliott (Chapter 18) is currently Tutor in Curriculum Studies at the Cambridge Institute of Education. From 1972 to 1974 he directed the Ford Teaching Project while at the Centre for Applied Research in Education in the University of East Anglia. This teacher-based project was one of the early examples of educational action-research to appear in the UK. Subsequently John Elliott has directed funded action-research projects into school accountability (1978-80) and teacher-pupil interaction and the quality of learning (1981-83).

Edward Holdaway (Chapter 5) is Professor of Educational Administration and Director of Institutional Research and Planning at the University of Alberta, Edmonton, Canada. He obtained his undergraduate education at the University of Melbourne and his MEd and PhD at the University of Alberta, where he has been on the staff since 1968. His experience includes teaching at secondary schools and post-secondary institutions in Australia and Canada. During sabbatical leaves in 1974-75 and 1981-82, when he was affiliated with the University of London, the University of Melbourne and Monash University, Professor Holdaway studied the organization of educational research in several Western countries. From 1976 to 1978 he was President of the Canadian Educational Researchers' Association and from 1978 to 1980 was Chairman of the Research Policy Committee of the Social Science Federation of Canada. His teaching and research interests include administrative behaviour, research organization, administrative structures, job satisfaction and evaluation. Professor Holdaway has published extensively in refereed journals and served on the Editorial Board of *Educational Administration Quarterly* from 1976 to 1981.

Eric Hoyle (Chapter 16) has been Professor of Education at the University of Bristol since 1971. His previous posts included teaching in two secondary schools, a college of education and a university. His interests and published works are in the areas of educational administration, the process of innovation, the professional development of teachers and the relationship between research and policy.

He is also interested in the sociology of knowledge and the sociological study of organizations and of the professions. He was founding co-editor of *Research in Education* and is on the editorial boards of a number of other journals including the *British Journal of Teacher Education*. He was research consultant to the Donnison Commission on direct grant schools, vice-chairman of the Educational Research Board of the Social Science Research Council and is currently a member of the Executive Committee of the Universities Council for the Education of Teachers, and a co-opted member of Avon Education Committee. He has lectured in various colleges and universities in Africa, Australia, North America and Malaysia.

Czeslaw Kupisiewicz (Chapter 12) is a member of the Polish Academy of Sciences and Professor at the University of Warsaw. His main fields of scientific activity are learning and instructional theories, and comparative education. Among his publications are: *Niepowodzenia Dydaktyczne* (Failure in School); *Podstawy Dydaktyki Ogolnej* (The Foundations of General Didactics); *Nauczanie Programowane* (Programmed Learning); *Przemiany Edukacyjne w Swiecie* (Educational Changes in the World); *Szkolnictwo w Procesie Przebudowy* (School Systems in Transition); and *Paradygmaty Reform Oswiatowych* (Paradigms of School Reforms). Apart from these books, his many articles have also been published in English, French, German, Spanish and Russian.

Louis Legrand (Chapter 6) has been a primary school teacher, a teacher of philosophy, a departmental inspector for the Ministry of Education from 1951 to 1962, an inspector for the Academie from 1962 to 1966, and Research Director and Head of Department at the Institut National de Recherche Pédagogique from 1966 to 1980. Since 1980 he has been Professor at Strasbourg University. He holds the Degree of Docteur es Lettres (Etat) 1958. He is the author of numerous articles which have appeared in specialist reviews between 1960 and 1982. His main works are: *L'influence du positivisme dans l'ouvre scolaire de Jules Ferry*; *Pour une pédagogie de l'etonnement*; *Psychologie appliquée a l'éducation intellectuelle*; *L'enseignement du français a l'école elementaire*; *Une methode active pour l'école d'aujourd'hui*; *Pour une politique démocratique de l'éducation*; *L'école unique, à quelles conditions?*

Ulf P Lundgren (Chapter 17) is Professor of Education at Stockholm Institute of Education, where he is the scientific leader for a research group for curriculum theory and cultural reproduction. He is chairman for the Society for the History of Swedish Education. In his research Professor Lundgren developed the frame factor theory, concerning limits for public education. He has worked for several commissions with evaluations of school experiments and was governmental expert for the recently implemented curriculum for the comprehensive school system in Sweden. He has also conducted an evaluation on the Portuguese school system for the government in Portugal.

Inger Marklund (Chapter 15) is Head of the Research Division of the National Board of Education in Sweden. She has also held the post of Professor in the Department of Education at Uppsala University. From 1978 to 1980, she was Secretary-General of a government-appointed commission on educational research and development.

Jacquetta Megarry (Series Editor) is an author, journalist and freelance consultant. After a first degree in maths and psychology at Cambridge University she trained and practised as a teacher in Glasgow. She took an MEd degree in 1972 and became a lecturer in education first at Glasgow University then at Jordanhill College of Education (1973-80), where she also produced distance learning materials in a variety of media. From 1973 to 1984 she was a leading figure in the UK Society for the Advancement of Games and Simulations in Education and Training.

Since 1981 she has worked freelance, specializing in computers and information technology. Recent books include *Computer World* (Pan/Piccolo Factbook, 1983), *Computers Mean Business* (Kogan Page and Pan, 1984) and *Inside Information: Computers, Communications and People* (BBC Publications, forthcoming).

She has acted as a consultant on computer education to the Microelectronics Education Programme, on information technology to the Council for Educational Technology and the BBC Computer Literacy Project, on general education and the information society for OECD/CERI in Paris and on distance learning in Bhopal, India. Currently she is developing open learning systems for vocational education involving interactive video.

Douglas E Mitchell (Chapter 2) is Professor of Education and Associate Dean, School of Education, University of California, Riverside. He received his PhD in political science from Claremont Graduate School in 1973. His major research works include studies of state-level policy formation, local school district politics, the impact of teacher unions on school organization and governance, and how rewards and incentives affect teacher work performance. An emphasis on alternative social science paradigms, individual work orientations, and interpersonal authority systems pervades Professor Mitchell's research and writing. He has examined the role of ideological and belief systems in controlling both individual and group behaviour.

Wolfgang Mitter (Chapter 7) is Professor of Education and Director of the Department of General and Comparative Education at the German Institute for International Educational Research at Frankfurt am Main. He did his undergraduate work at the University of Mainz and was awarded his doctorate by the Free University in Berlin in 1954. He was a Gymnasium (secondary school) teacher until 1964 when he became Professor of Education at the Luneburg College of Education. At the same time he began to give lectures at the University of Hamburg. Since 1972 he has been Director of the Department of General and Comparative Education and permanent member of the Research Board at the German Institute for International Educational Research at Frankfurt/Main, and between 1978 and 1981 he held the elective office of Director of the Research Board of this Institute. He also lectures at the University of Frankfurt/Main. He is the author or editor of many books and has published many journal articles. His main areas of research are comparative education (especially comparing educational systems in Eastern and Western Europe), structural and curricular issues of the Eastern European systems and conceptual studies on educational research. Since the beginning of the 1970s he has worked on various occasions as consultant to UNESCO, OECD and the Council of Europe. Between 1977 and 1981 he was one of the two vice-presidents of the Comparative Education Society in Europe. In 1981 he was elected President of this Society and in 1983 confirmed in this function until 1985.

Peter W Musgrave (Chapter 4) is Professor of Education at Monash University. From 1949 to 1956, he worked in industry, taught in secondary schools from 1957 to 1961, and was a Lecturer, later Senior Lecturer, in Sociology at the University of Aberdeen from 1965 to 1969. He was Dean of the Faculty of Education at Monash from 1977 to 1981. His main present research interests lie in the fields of the sociology of the curriculum, the changing moral values of adolescents and children's literature.

John Nisbet (Guest Editor and Chapter 1) is Professor of Education at the University of Aberdeen. He has also held appointments as visiting professor in California, Australia, New Zealand and Illinois. He was chairman of the Educational Research Board in London from 1972 to 1975, and of the Scottish Council for Research in Education in Edinburgh from 1975 to 1978. He has been editor of the *British*

Journal of Educational Psychology and of *Studies in Higher Education*. He was President of the British Educational Research Association in 1975.

Stanley Nisbet (Associate Editor) retired from the Chair of Education at the University of Glasgow in 1978. Starting his professional life as a classics teacher he was caught up in the vigorous psychometric activity at Moray House in Edinburgh under Godfrey Thomson, and his early work was in this field. After five years of war-time service in the RAF, part of the time in its Training Research Branch, and a short spell in the University of Manchester, he became professor of education in Queen's University, Belfast and was involved in some of the post-war educational developments in Northern Ireland. From 1951 to 1978 he was professor of education in the University of Glasgow, holding various administrative posts in the University (eg Dean of the Faculty of Arts, 1965-67) and serving on many bodies outside the University (eg the Scottish Council for Research in Education). His teaching was mainly on educational theory, curriculum study (in 1957 he wrote one of the earliest books in this field) and comparative education (with a special interest in Germany and the USSR). Much of his writing has consisted of contributions to official publications. Since his retirement he has participated in projects on a number of subjects, including home-school co-operation in the EEC countries and the monitoring of in-service courses for primary school teachers.

Ernesto Schiefelbein (Chapter 9) is a senior researcher in the Centro de Investigacion y Desarrollo de la Educacion (CIDE) and coordinator of the Latin American educational research exchange network (REDUC). He is a member of five editorial boards of Latin American journals of education and a frequent member in World Bank missions related to educational projects. A former Head of the Chilean Educational Planning Office during the 1965-70 period, he has taught in Latin American Universities and has been Visiting Professor of Educational Planning in Developing Countries in Harvard University. Co-author of *Development of Educational Planning Models* (Lexington Books, 1974), he subsequently has worked in a tracer study of a national sample of the Chilean students who were in eighth grade in 1970, which resulted in several reports on the determinants of school achievement and work employment patterns. He is now especially interested in the use of information as a source of power for generating improvements in the educational systems of the Third World.

Chris van Seventer (Chapter 10) is managing director of SVO (the Foundation for Educational Research in The Netherlands). This is an independent organization which was founded and sponsored by the government. It now sponsors most educational research in The Netherlands and heads a national system of specialized institutes which carry out mostly commissioned research in the educational sciences. Chris van Seventer studied classical philology at the University of Leyden in The Netherlands. In those days he was twice member of the executive committee of the National Students' Council. His concern for, and interest in, educational policy was awakened in this period. He began his career as a civil servant in the Ministry of Education. There he attained the position of director in the department of higher education. In 1976 he began his work for SVO.

Sim Wong Kooi (Chapter 14) is Director of the Institute of Education in Singapore. Until recently, he was also Director of the Research and Testing Division of the Ministry of Education. Born in Malaysia, he is a graduate of the University of Malaya and the University of Melbourne. His doctorate is from the Harvard Graduate School of Education. He has served in the University of Malaya as Dean of Education and as Professor of Pedagogical Studies. After a period in Australia, he assumed his current position in Singapore in 1981. He has also served as Consultant to many organizations, such as ASEAN, INNOTECH, RECSAM, SEAMEO, UNESCO and UNICEF.

Malcolm Skilbeck (Chapter 19) was previously the Director of the Education Centre in the New University of Ulster, Director of the Australian Curriculum Development Centre in Canberra, and Director of Studies in the Schools Council in London. He is now Professor of Education and Head of the Department of Curriculum Studies in the University of London Institute of Education.

H S Srivastava (Chapter 8) studied at the Universities of Agra, Delhi, Patna and Chicago. He is a Professor of Education and holds the post of Head of the Planning, Coordination and Evaluation Unit of the National Council of Educational Research and Training, New Delhi. His duties include participation in the evolution and review of educational policies, supervision and conduct of research, coordination and national and international programmes, evaluation of educational projects, development of technical documents and provision of consultancy. He has represented India at a number of international events. He was Visiting Professor at the Institute of Development Studies at the University of Sussex in 1977. Subsequently in 1979-80 he was a UNESCO Consultant at the International Institute of Educational Planning, Paris, and the UNESCO Institute of Education, Hamburg. Professor Srivastava has to his credit a large number of books, brochures and monographs. One of his books entitled *Examination Reforms in India* has been published by UNESCO in English, French and Spanish. Today Professor Srivastava is an international authority on pupil and project evaluation and is a pioneer in this field in India.

Robert Stake (Chapter 20) is a Professor of Education at the University of Illinois,, and is best known for his work in educational programme evaluation. Since 1976 he has been the Director of the Center for Instructional Research and Curriculum Evaluation. Once a specialist in psychometrics and instructional research, his present orientation is more to naturalistic or anthropological field study, particularly of the classroom. Among his background experiences are early years in Nebraska, graduate study at Princeton, Korean War service in the Navy and teaching at the University of Nebraska. Principal collaborators have been Terry Denny, Thomas Hastings, Jack Easley and Bernadine Stake.

William Taylor (Chapter 3) has been Principal of the University of London since 1983, having for the previous ten years been Director of the University of London Institute of Education. From 1966 to 1973 he was Professor of Education in the University of Bristol, a post he combined for five years with that of Research Adviser to the Department of Education and Science. He has been a Vice Chairman of the Educational Research Board of the Social Science Research Council, and is currently Chairman of the National Foundation for Educational Research and a Vice President of the Society for Research into Higher Education. His books include *The Secondary Modern School, Society and the Education of Teachers, Research Perspectives in Education* (ed), *Research and Reform in Teacher Education*, and *Metaphors of Education* (ed).

John Dewar Wilson (Bibliography) taught English for three years in a comprehensive school near Glasgow before lecturing, between 1964 and 1970, in the Department of Education, University of Aberdeen. Since then he has been Head of the Education Department at Moray House College of Education, Edinburgh. He has also contributed to masters' programmes at the University of Regina, Canada. His teaching interests include curriculum evaluation and development; in 1982 he undertook a consultancy to the Ministry of Education, Bangladesh, on the programme and development plan for the National Curriculum Development Centre, Dhaka. His research has been principally in the field of higher education. Publications include *Degrees of Excellence: the Academic Achievement Game* (with N J Entwistle) in 1977 and *Student Learning in Higher Education* in 1981. He is currently directing the *Criteria of Teacher Selection* (CATS) project, which is investigating selection into teaching in Scotland. He is also Chairman of the Editorial Board of *Scottish Educational Review* and Vice-Chairman of the Scottish Educational Research Association.

Index

For Product Safety Concerns and Information please contact our EU
representative GPSR@taylorandfrancis.com Taylor & Francis Verlag GmbH,
Kaufingerstraße 24, 80331 München, Germany

Printed and bound by CPI Group (UK) Ltd, Croydon, CR0 4YY
11/04/2025
01844008-0018